Software Configuration
Management

WILEY SERIES IN SOFTWARE ENGINEERING PRACTICE

Series Editors:

Patrick A.V. Hall, The Open University, UK
Martyn A. Ould, Praxis Systems plc, UK
William E. Riddle, Software Design & Analysis, Inc., USA

Software Configuration Management

H. RONALD BERLACK

John Wiley & Sons, Inc.
New York / Chichester / Brisbane / Toronto / Singapore

ISBN 0-471-53049-2

Printed in the United States of America

10 9 8 7 6 5 4 3 2 1

To those long time and current members of the
Electronic Industries Association's committees
for Date and Configuration Management and
Computer Resources who have provided the worldwide leadership for Configuration Management.

CONTENTS

7 The Planning and Organizing of Configuration Management 59

8 The Configuration Management Activities: Identification 81

9 Performing the Change Control Activity 109

This is a book on management—the management of a process within the software life cycle and of the configuration of a software system as it evolves from a bare concept to a tried-and-true product used with trust and confidence. This is also a book about communication, tailored for today's networking environment. It describes the process of communicating to all involved the identity of the software they have conceived and configured, both as prototype and as final product. It is about the status of the software system that has been established and the subsequent changes that have been made and incorporated. This, then, is a description of configuration management (CM) as a focal point for managing and communicating the configuration of software at any point in its life cycle.

Configuration management is the management of a software design as it evolves into a software product or system. It is also a means of communicating to the project's designers and developers the technical detail and events that lead to the eventual build and delivery of the final product. It is not the hard line of control or the wielding of the proverbial billy club. Those who have employed CM offer their praises. Many who did not employ CM rue the day they turned it down, never to know what caused their projects to do so poorly.

Although it is heavily used in companies serving the defense industry and other government agencies, such as the FAA and NASA, CM has not been implemented to any great extent by the commercial and academic communities. Polaroid was one of the first, as were Wang and AT&T.

It is the intent of this book to explain why all involved in the development of software products should use CM to manage the configurations of their software products. This strategy becomes more increasingly complex as software continues to expand its impact on all our daily lives.

This book is designed for those bound by contractual agreements and requirements to use software configuration management and for those who may implement it as a matter of good business practice.

CM is not an organizational entity. It is a well-defined process with well-defined activities devoted to managing a hardware or software system configuration. The process and activities described in this text can be employed by all involved or by one person designated to manage the configuration of the product as it evolves. On large projects several members may be designated to perform the CM activities and provide guidance and instruction to the other members of the team.

By incorporating an experienced CM activity, others on the project can devote their efforts to design, development, and testing—and let the CM activity take care of the details.

It is hoped that this book will make the CM process easier and more enjoyable for those responsible for implementing it.

Throughout the book the term CM is used rather than SCM (software configuration management), because many projects have hardware and software requirements and the term CM can be applied to both.

A number of people in the CM field provided the foundations for this book over a 25-year period. The immense amount of practical knowledge I gained in association with the Electronics Industries Association's Data and Configuration Management Committee and Computer Resources Committee has greatly contributed to the content of this book. My association with the EIA was also greatly enhanced by the undivided attention and support provided to these committees by the EIA's director of technical activities, Mr. Ed Nucci.

In addition, during the 1980s my association with the IEEE Computer Society and the Software Engineering Standards Committees provided a great deal of experience, especially in the opportunities to develop a seminar in software configuration management and to develop the IEEE Standard 829-1990 for software configuration management plans. This latter effort has led to a long-term commitment with the ISO/IEC on the Joint Technical Committee for Information Systems and on Subcommittee 7 for Software Engineering, through which 828 will eventually be transformed into an international standard.

Also this book would not have been possible except for the action of Earl Sparks, a founder of Sanders Associates and of a formal configuration management environment at Sanders in 1968.

Finally, special thanks to Rick Frederick for his excellent review, editorial comments, and encouragement, to Fletcher Buckly, who was most persistent in urging me to undertake this venture, and to John Cupak and Lewis Gray for their contributions to the chapter on Ada. Special thanks as well to my second reviewer, whose well-written, detailed comments were most useful in helping me stay the course.

LIST OF FIGURES

CHAPTER 1

Introduction

This book is written for people who need or wish to know about software configuration management, such as those individuals who have been given the responsibility for implementing configuration management on a project or those program or project managers who are required to use configuration management or elect to implement it on their projects.

The objective is to explain how configuration management became part of the software engineering environment and to help those responsible for implementing it plan for and perform configuration management on a software development project. The book is also intended for use as a text by persons teaching the concepts of configuration management to undergraduate college students or as a reference for those requiring this knowledge and understanding in graduate programs in computer sciences or software engineering.

Configuration management has been described as a discipline that governs the identification, control, status accounting, and auditing of a given entity, such as a software program or system, and the components that make up that entity. It has also been described as one of the many processes that occur within a developing engineering environment in which several engineering, software, and manufacturing processes are performed concurrently.

In order to understand the meaning and application of configuration management one should understand the doctrine that initiated it and has guided its evolution since its introduction in the early 1960s. One should also understand why CM is needed and how it fits into the overall development of a software product.

The early chapters of this text cover the history, environment, and definition of CM, as well as its relationship to other development processes and activities. The later chapters describe the details of CM activities.

Chapter 2 addresses the needs and concerns of corporate management, which is anxious to maintain a competitive position in the marketplace at a reasonable profit. It further discusses the project software management tasks of developing a high-quality product on time within a specified budget and the software engineering, programming, testing, and configuration management activities of working to achieve stated to objectives within a specified period of time.

The history of CM is discussed in Chapter 3. Elements of design control have always been applied by the world's foremost inventors such as Leonardo da Vinci, the Egyptian pyramid builders, Henry Ford, Thomas Edison, and others. The history discussed here begins in the early 1960s when the term *configuration management* was formalized and brings us up to the present with a description of some of the primary standards that have been developed and are in use today.

The relationship of CM to other processes, activities, and functions inherent in the software development life cycle is described in Chapter 4.

Chapter 5 defines CM as a process in terms of the CM process model and the activities that are performed. Also described are the intent and purpose of the most commonly used standards and guidance documents—their contribution and importance to the performance of CM. The new umbrella standard for CM is also described, even though it may not as yet have been published.

The performance of CM, described in Chapter 6, depends on a number of processes involved in software life cycle development and maintenance, whose outputs are the prime inputs to the CM process. These processes include the definition of the performance requirements derived from system engineering and the formulation of those performance requirements into software requirement specifications during software engineering. One should understand how system engineering and software engineering are performed so that CM can readily "capture" the documented software identification once it has been reviewed and approved. In addition, CM will be able to establish a software hierarchy of the documentation as it is placed under configuration control and communicate to those involved in the project the status of what has been defined and the specifications documenting that definition. Software engineering will provide a consistent life cycle approach to the creation of a software system [16]. Reference is also made to the contribution of information systems engineering in providing the communication links between project entities, creating the data bases used in status accounting, querying, and maintaining the software development file.

Chapter 7 describes the position of CM in a project organization, along with the other program entities such as program engineering, integrated logistics support, quality assurance, and of course the software development team. It is important that one get to know the roles of all the major entities of a project, including the hardware development side, especially if the software product is integral to the equipment. The CM plan is described and a sample outline's contents is illustrated. Other outlines are also referenced.

The description of CM activities and the discussion of their performance starts with Chapter 8. One may well find a great deal of similarity between hardware identification and software identification. In fact, the means of obtaining and controlling the approved identification may be the same, but the result will look different in form and content. The sections of this chapter deal with the software hierarchy, the selection of a software configuration item documenting the design definition, design definition relationships, numbering, identification of firmware, and the development of baselines.

Change control is addressed in Chapter 9. The topics discussed include maintaining the established baselines, processing changes within the project and within the company when applicable, and processing requests for changes to the customer when the contract or agreement has specified the conditions under which this will be done. The establishment and conduct of a configuration control board (CCB) is also described, as are CCBs with various levels of authority and control. Deviations and waivers are defined and their processing described. Also included is the handling of notices of revision, which may be prepared if the developer is not the custodian of the original documents or code. Finally, there is a brief discussion of the relationship between hardware and software changes.

How one accounts for documents planned and produced; changes made, approved, and incorporated into approved baselined documents; reports generated; and the queries provided for is discussed in Chapter 10. The data elements employed in the status accounting data base are listed, and a series of report forms are used to illustrate how easy the reports are to produce if the system is kept simple and not cluttered with unnecessary information. One may be going overboard in designing change control forms that care more about the status accounting data elements than the cause, reason, fix recommendation, and disposition of the problem—which is why we have a change form in the first place. The software development file, or the repository for everything and anything one wants to know about a software unit, module, program, and so on, is described as the primary platform for the status accounting data base, which is also defined. Finally, the provisions for reporting status and querying this information are offered.

In Chapter 11 the functional and physical configuration audit is defined as the means to determine that what was required has been developed and tested and is ready for delivery and use. This chapter emphasizes the importance of the proper documentation of the software requirements and the creation of creditable test reports, as well as the development of such documents as the product specifications and the version descriptions.

Chapter 12 is a description of interface control and its importance to the success of the software project. Interfaces such as system to system, ship to shore, police cruiser to base, and air traffic to air control all must specify what is required and provide a guidance document to instruct in their implementation. CM's role in maintaining the identified interfaces is an important part of this chapter.

Subcontractors are integral parts of any project. They are employed to assist, contribute to, and aid in the development of the software product. Chapter 13 suggests that subcontractor control should be the sixth activity (with interfacing as the fifth). The need for proper instruction, guidance, and control of the subcontractor's performance is described in this section.

Chapter 14 explains the configuration and capabilities of the software development library. The use of the software development file as the main status tool and the importance of pragmatic access control are also explained, along with the functions and contents of the working, project, master, archive, and backup libraries during the development cycle.

Software tools have become more and more important as aids to the software development process, including design, coding, testing, simulating, demonstrating/prototyping, and so on. Chapter 15 provides some insight into the study, analysis, and recommendation process; the criteria for selection; and the actual selection process. Specific tools are not listed because of the dynamic nature of the tool environment.

The Ada language is now a firm requirement for all government software projects. It is also becoming more and more prevalent in all other software development environments. Thus it is appropriate to devote a chapter to a discussion of CM as applied to the Ada environment. Chapter 16 describes the principles of CM as performed within Ada and shows how the CM process handles Ada and its associated documents.

Maintenance or support of software, once delivered to its assigned environment, is a very important activity that receives little attention as part of the software life cycle. Software support after final testing, acceptance, and delivery of the product is no different from the support provided to the buyer of a new car, appliance, or TV. From the time the buyer takes possession, a customer service support network is ready to provide periodic maintenance and repairs as necessary. Few may realize that the planning for this support must begin early in the development cycle so that the support activity is well prepared to "service" the delivered software product, enhance the product, or modify it to meet the needs of the environment in which it operates. For example, one customer may require Japanese characters to appear on a screen shipped to Japan and French text generated on a screen shipped to France. The maintenance concepts are discussed in Chapter 17, and CM's role is described.

Chapter 18 is devoted to the need to train CM personnel and those that interface with, manage, or rely on the CM process. Various training guides are discussed, and an outline for an in-house training program is provided.

CHAPTER 2

The Need and Importance of Configuration Management in Software Development

Some years ago a friend, who was a veteran configuration manager, called and asked if I knew anything about software configuration management. I replied that I did not know very much but to me the principles were the same as those applied to hardware configuration management except that the product was something one could not see or feel, much less hear. I heard nothing about how my answer was taken or applied, but some months later I read a magazine article about a near-disaster during a series of tests my friend's company was conducting. It stated that a sensor had failed to detect that the equipment being tested was overheating. The cause was determined to be an error in the software, which did not engage a safety shutoff switch when the equipment passed the cutoff point. In my mind, this incident illustrated the need for software configuration management in firms that build equipment with software that is integral to the system.

Not long after this incident, draft versions of a standard for software development appeared that made the importance of SCM become a reality, even though some excellent guidance documents had been previously published for the software community. Since that time, several such standards and guidelines have appeared at both the national and international levels. These will be discussed shortly.

CM is an important function on a software project for a number of reasons. One reason is that it facilitates the ability to communicate status of documents and coding as well as changes that have been made. Another is that corporate management, in stressing higher productivity at lower cost, looks on released software as an asset that can be used on other projects without the need to change or modify it. Figure 2.1 illustrates how the cost of software increased and the cost of hardware decreased during the 1980s. This dramatic increase also increased the demand for cost-saving software tools and associated processes, such as CM aided by the new standards, that would enable software engineers to be more productive at less cost.

A third reason for CM's importance is that it enhances the ability to provide maintenance support once the software is deployed in the field or sold in the marketplace. It does so through well-identified software elements and a history of the software's development, which enable a cost-effective fix with little impact on the user/customer.

In order to meet the requirements of a customer or the market, the project manager is charged with designing, developing, coding, testing, and delivering a high-quality, error-free software product on time within specified dollar limitations or schedule constraints to an assigned environment. Thus the manager is most concerned about how the project's time is allocated and how the allocated dollars are spent. It is a bad situation when one finds

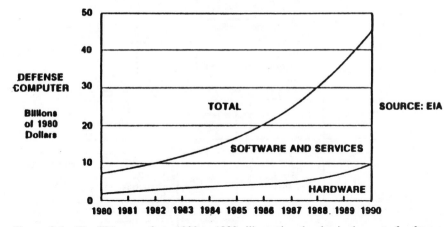

Figure 2.1   The EIA curve from 1980 to 1990, illustrating the rise in the cost of software.

that the project is severely over budget and well behind schedule. Only after all the finger pointing has ceased and the root cause is determined to be too many changes to poorly designed software does it dawn on the manager and the project staff as a whole that proper controls and good communication—which are integral to SCM—would have prevented such a situation.

The project structure portrayed in Figure 2.2 with agreement on the *what,* the *how,* the *answer,* and the *evaluation,* can provide a well understood *change* procedure that could avoid disaster. In addition, a well-constructed software hierarchy (as shown in Figure 2.3) can provide visibility to various aspects of the project such as what was to be developed and where it was located, as well as serve as a means of communication.

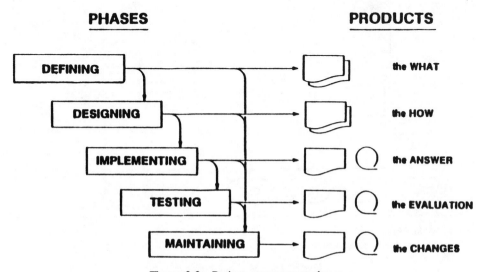

Figure 2.2   Project management phases.

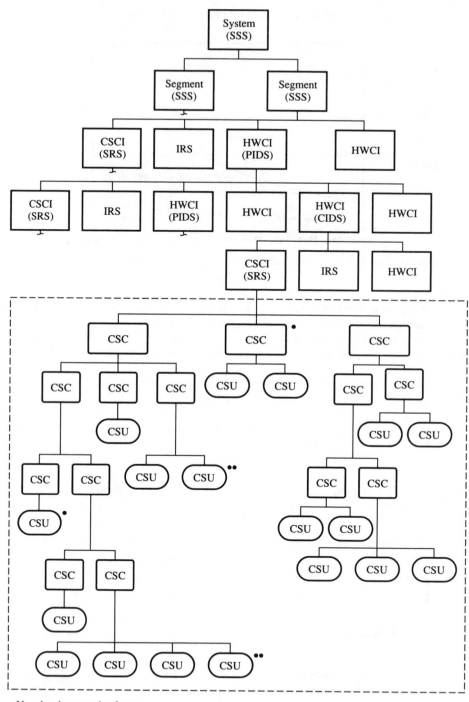

• Non-developmental software
•• Same CSU used by different CSCs

Figure 2.3 Software hierarchy.

During the software development cycle described in Chapter 4, especially during the coding/debug and initial testing segments—the programmers are constantly concerned about where their code is stored (on tape or disk) and printed. Wasted hours can occur while busy people look for code. In other words, "I can't test my code without Joe's—the code that he changed last night. Where is it? How do I know I have the module with the right changes?" SCM provides records and status to answer these questions, thus saving the programmer's time. Testing always involves questions of why an element failed: What is its development history? Were changes made and not recorded? Didn't we test this before and find it OK?

One must not forget the concerns of the customer and of the marketplace as a whole. The phrase, "quality is job one" from the Ford Motor Company can also be applied to the software development process: Are we following this credo? Can we assure our customers that our software products will not fail and are error free? Can we back this up with proper descriptive documentation and a history of the program's development? Will our technicians who go out to a customer's facility to troubleshoot have enough data to ascertain the cause of the problem and fix it? Most important, will that individual be instructed to complete a trouble report that can be analyzed so that corrective action can be taken to prevent other incidents? If not, time is being wasted and valuable company profits are being used up.

An example of this type of problem happened some time ago, but its message remains important. A technician was sent overseas to troubleshoot a very sophisticated firmware device and spent several weeks tinkering and finally making the device work as intended. On returning to the office, he was asked for his notes explaining his findings and action taken. He had none, which meant that the project staff was not able to determine the impact of the changes or modify and change the device design. SCM provides procedures that can prevent this type of occurrence and thus save those valuable corporate profits, by simplifying the development process for the engineers, reducing or eliminating many sources of irritation and conflict between project members, and instituting a logical change control process.

In today's environment the protection of intellectual property is of utmost importance. The laws governing the use of printed material, such as this book, are relatively clear. Not so with software. The jury is still out on how to determine whether a developer who markets a product that appears to use someone else's technology is violating another developer's rights. How are you going to prove it? Do you have well-controlled documents describing requirements, development, and product specifications that have been maintained under an orderly identification and control process? Can you prove in a court of law that your rights have been violated—and how? For instance, can you demonstrate a module that you developed, released, coded, tested, and integrated into your system, which did not appear in your competitor's? With a good SCM plan for implementating an identification scheme, your chances are 100 percent better than without any documented proof.

Where we once applied terms such as *design quality in, design by prototype, brainstorm,* or *do not design by committee,* we now deal with concepts such as total quality management (TQM) and concurrent engineering (CE). In the software world we hear more of environments such as the computer-aided software environment (CASE) and developer-unique environments such as software support environment (SSE) and a larger effort called manufacturing records processor II (MRP II), in which the software drives automated machinery as well as being used in test engineering.

All these newly formed disciplines and ways of planning and implementing cost-effective, error-free products in a competitive environment rely heavily on good, complete, accurate documentation that has been well identified and controlled both as hard copy and within a computer system whether on the mainframe or PC level.

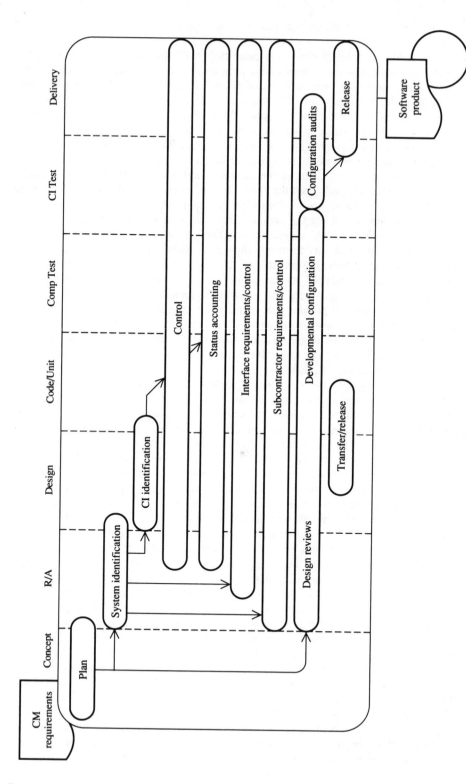

Figure 2.4 Configuration management process model.

8

Configuration management, especially software configuration management, plays an important role, but too many times has not been applied. Thus a potentially successful venture has failed because the planning document could not be found or could not be proven to reflect current activities.

CM also plays an important role in the system engineering process during conceptual development and analysis of the customer's or the market's requirements, during the design and development of the software system/product, and during the testing and acceptance of the system/product when configuration audits are performed to ensure that what was designed—to a specified requirement—is what was built.

Because the project manager and the project software leaders must attend to a great deal of planning and many problems simply to define and understand the requirements, SCM must take on the task of capturing the evolving decisions and written products and communicating the progress and status to the manager and the product team. The realistic, simple processes described in the following chapters should prove that CM can be an effective cost-containing procedure with worthwhile benefits to the project.

Figure 2.4 depicts software configuration management as a process. The inputs to this model are the requirements for CM as indicated in a contract or an agreement between buyer and seller. The initial activity is to plan how the CM process will be performed.

The subsequent activities of identification at the system and component levels during the requirements analysis and design phases initiate the change control activity. This provides the means of communicating to the project staff any changes that have been made to documentation and code placed under configuration management. The activities of interface control and subcontractor control prevail throughout the development cycle along with the design review and audit activities defined in the following chapters.

The concluding activities of the process—configuration audit and release for delivery to a customer, user, or distributor—take place in the final phases of the development cycle. They, in turn, lead in to the operational or use phase of the total life cycle (not shown in the figure).

EXERCISE

1. Think of projects you have been or are now involved with and describe how SCM could have enhanced or saved them. If SCM was employed, did it perform to everyone's satisfaction? If not, why not?
2. List the benefits you feel good documentation management and control could accomplish.
3. If you are or will be a project manager, list any reasons you have for *not* thinking SCM is necessary. Save so that you can reevaluate your argument at a later point in the text.

CHAPTER 3

A Short History of
Configuration Management

Configuration management is not a new task in the design process. Talk to any veteran engineer and you will hear how it was done in the old days. For one thing, before 1940 our designs were not as complex as they were at the end of that decade. One senior engineer used to be supported by three to five technicians. As a team, they would work to solve a problem or develop a concept. They would document each part of their strategy, discussions, decisions, and the final course of action in neat script in cloth-bound notebooks and would pore over these volumes time and time again to verify their current course of action. Thus it was when, at the beginning of World War II, the secretary of defense got together with one Joe Kelly of Lockheed Corporation and described the type of plane he felt would be needed to combat the German Messerschmitts and the Japanese Zeros. Mr. Kelly and his team went to work.

Not long after the Lockheed team started came the first prototype of the P-38, which proved so successful throughout the war. Similar tales can be told of other planes, tanks, guns, and the like. There were no voluminous specifications. The purchase orders read, "Build 300 whatever and deliver as soon as possible." And we *did*.

Wartime notwithstanding, many great inventions happened in a similar manner. Henry Ford designed the Model T, not to mention the assembly line process for it, on scraps of paper and small quarter-square notebooks. Other inventors always had at least one or two aides who, if nothing else, kept the records and maintained status reports on what had occurred and what had to be done.

At the end of World War II life in the United States changed dramatically. Thousands of veterans went to college, many coming out with engineering degrees. There was great demand for products that had been nonexistent during the war. New cars came out with more powerful engines running on more gas but getting us from here to there a lot faster. The famous DC-3 became the leading commercial carrier for several years, followed by the DC-4s and -6s plus Martin 404s, Lockheed Lodestars, and others. New to so many people were washing machines and dryers with all kinds of automatic gadgets and timers people never believed could be developed.

A great deal of electronics was involved, especially as TVs and hi-fi radios appeared, and they all sold like hotcakes. But these developments required a lot of new, freshly minted engineers to design and develop—in a hurry—and as a result, the closely knit teams of the past were no longer possible or desired. Thus what used to be a team of one senior engineer and five technicians turned into five engineers and one good technician doing the same type of work.

Configuration management got its start in the defense industry environment as a management technique and a discipline to resolve problems of poor quality, wrong parts ordered, and parts not fitting, which were leading to inordinate cost overruns. On the other hand, a number of other industries such as Polaroid and AT&T had initiated change control procedures to enable them to build "world-class" cameras and telephone systems, respectively.

It became obvious in the late 1950s and early 1960s that there had to be a better way of managing the configuration of a product than relying on individual discipline, which had heretofore proved so valuable. One had to compensate for a job's being started by one engineer and completed by another. To resolve this problem, we had to know what we were doing! A start was made by at least identifying through descriptive specifications what was required. During this same period, drawing controls were also promulgated by standard-writing organizations such as the American Society of Mechanical Engineers (ASME) to ensure that drawings were being prepared in a uniform manner.

IN THE BEGINNING...

Regardless of where the concept of configuration management was developed, the term was formally coined in the government's environment, like so many other processes and inventions that soon became familiar civilian entities. The need for a discipline to identify and control the design of complex equipment and to communicate that information was most apparent in the defense industry, where the expected high-quality workmanship appeared to be slipping. Thus corrective action was taken to provide the necessary control and communication to satisfy customer demands.

In 1962 the Air Force responded to the critical control and communication problems on the design of its jet aircraft by authoring and publishing a standard for configuration management, AFSCM 375-1 [29]. The forward, signed by General Bernard Schriver, commander of the Air Force Systems Command, stated:

> The Air Force Systems Command is faced with ever increasing management requirements in our acquisition programs. We must constantly take full advantage of new and better methods that are developed.
>
> This manual on Configuration Management contains some of the more important aspects of some of these new methods that are developed.
>
> I fully realize that the procedures, formats and requirements of this manual are different and in some cases present a radical change from some of our present and past approaches to program management. However, it is my desire that the full requirements of this manual be implemented on all new programs and be phased into all present programs whenever it is proper.

The procedures, formats, and requirements were indeed different, especially to the experienced design engineers, who had for years taken pride in their workmanship and ability to control their own destiny [1]. In other words, the days of intellectual and technical independence had gone the way of the Model T. It was no longer possible to keep one's design to oneself until the equipment was built. The rules had been changed to meet the challenges of the decade and would have to be followed. The cover for AFSCM 375-1 appeared to indicate a process of orderly design, development, build, test, and delivery (Figure 3.1). Configuration management was the key cog in the design, development, build, test, and operation of the item to be delivered because it was the communicator and controller of the design as it evolved.

Up to this time, efforts had been made to ensure that the documentation in use to develop and build the product was at least changed in an orderly manner. Thus a bulletin on requirements for control of changes to currently approved drawings and specifications was

 CONTROL

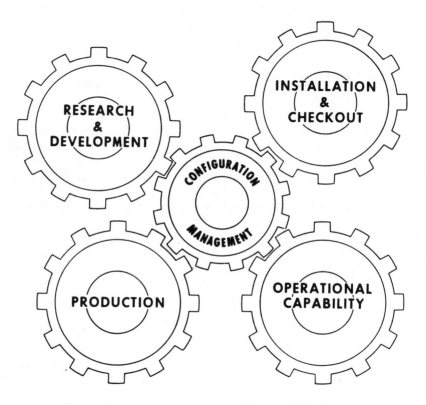

Figure 3.1   The cover of AFSCM 375-1 showing the relationships of various developmental phases.

published. This was identified as ANA Bulletin 391 and finally 391A. With the advent of 375-1, the bulletin was revised and published as ANA Bulletin 445, *Engineering Changes, Deviations, and Waivers*.

The 391A and 445 forms were simple and easy to use and except for major changes, did not require an inordinate amount of time and effort to complete. However, the complexity and sophistication of the equipment ordered by the government escalated. Technological advance was on the upswing, and many highly educated engineers were employed to meet the changes of the times. At the same time, the types of changes that were being processed to the complex designs were also very complex, and it was hoped that the issuance of Bulletin 445 would resolve the dilemma. The new bulletin, while still simple, did indeed make the submission of changes easier, but on the other hand, being just two pages long, it required an inordinate amount of supporting and explanatory data to expand on the restrictive entries on the form.

In 1964 a number of exhibits were added to 375-1 that were intended to enhance the application of the standard and meet the user demands in the areas the exhibits addressed [58]. The exhibits in question included requirements for uniform (software) specifications, configuration control, configuration identification, reviews, inspections and demonstrations, and configuration accounting.

One of the first standards to capitalize on AFSCM 375-1 was that of the National Aeronautics and Space Administration (NASA), NPC 500-1, written hurriedly for the design and development of the Saturn V spaceship program. It was admittedly a clone of 375-1 but was most instrumental in the Saturn V and Apollo development and production. In addition, the Army came out with its own version of configuration management, AMCR 11-26, and in 1965 the Navy published an instruction, NAVMATINST 4130.1, *Configuration Management Policy and Guidance Manual.*

These documents, the bibles of the times, made little or no mention of computer program control or requirements to communicate the status of a design because little software was included in the systems then being designed and developed. What computer programs were utilized were primarily on mainframe computers used for analysis of technical data or for financial computations. The requirements for these were covered by FIPS PUBs 38 and 64, which came from the National Bureau of Standards in 1964.

In spite of excellent guidance for the believers and practitioners, only Bulletin 445 could be imposed on a contract. The other documents were suggested guides, which quite frankly served the same purpose, since if one were to comply with the request for a proposal, one would certainly follow the customer's suggestion. These documents also served as the baseline for most company policies regarding CM and the implementing practices.

These documents were also primarily oriented to the preparation and control of drawings and associated lists, and thus other documents such as MIL D 1000, *Engineering Drawings,* and MIL STD 100, *Engineering Drawings and Associated Lists Practices,* were published and issued. As we shall see later on, MIL STD 100 still has application to the SCM function, along with the quality control document, MIL Q 9858A.

THE DEVELOPMENT AND ISSUANCE OF PRIMARY STANDARDS

Even with these documents, it soon became obvious that in order to invoke requirements that could implement configuration management, standards of universal application had to be developed. To be effective, the standards had to be supported by higher-level directives and instructions. Thus, in the latter part of 1965 a major writing effort was undertaken that resulted in the issuance of five major specifications and standards related to CM. These documents were also based on the exhibits contained in AFSCM 375-1. Figure 3.2 is a time line covering pre-1965 and 1965 to 1993.

The top document was Directive 5010.19, *Configuration Management,* which defined the function and set the policy for the Department of Defense (DOD) components and their contractors. The more specific Instruction 5010.21 defined and described the major components and activities of CM—identification, control, and status accounting. The development of these documents was well supported by the Electronics Industries Association and other industry groups, thus making a combined industry/government effort and reflecting a consensus among all parties involved in the writing, review, and approval prior to publication.

One of the more important standards for CM was MIL STD 480, *Engineering Changes, Deviations and Waivers,* which replaced Bulletin 445A. It reflected the complex requirements of current designs and resolved many of the problems inherent in 445. For one thing its for-

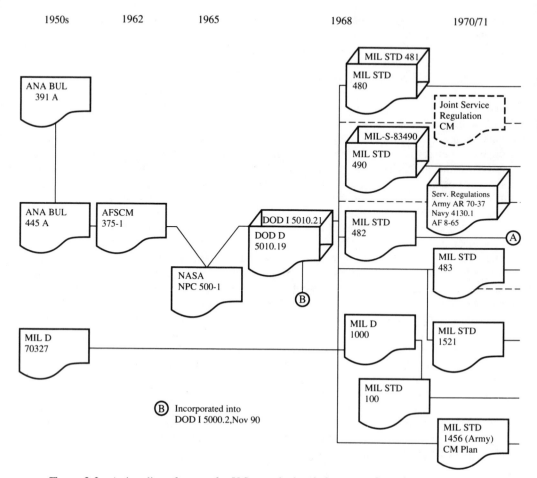

Figure 3.2   A time line of events for U.S. standards relating to configuration management.

mat, consisting of six pages, was long enough to make some sense out of all the supporting data being received with the two-page 445 form. It did not, however, provide for software changes to the extent necessary to describe the change. It referred to the use of some blocks when submitting software changes, but these references were not obvious and it was hard to make the necessary entries—thus more attachments.

Standard 480 notwithstanding, other standards such as MIL STD 83490, on types of equipment specifications, described the specifications that would be developed and followed. MIL STD 490 described the formats to be followed. These formats included a software development specification and a product specification that described how the software was developed, coded, and tested.

Another major document was the *Standard for Status Accounting* data elements, MIL STD 482, which would ensure the communication of the status of changes made to approved documents and the uniformity of such communication. Thus date was always entered as mm/dd/yy/. In addition, the collection of design status and subsequent reporting enabled the project team, the marketing and business development groups, and the customer to keep up with the development process and to plan their work accordingly.

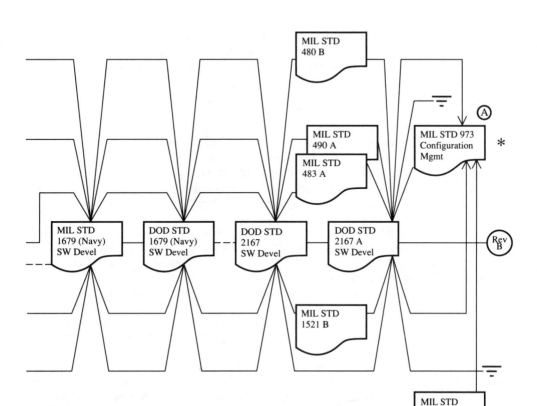

Figure 3.2   *(Continued)*

The CM process was truly enhanced by the advent of these documents in 1968. Because they now had standards that program managers would abide by, configuration managers could convince program managers and other company management that the customer meant business and that they would have to subscribe to the required document and such change control formats as a software requirements specification or problem/change request. The elements of identification in 490, control in 480, and status accounting in 482 had been solidified and were now being implemented by almost all the government's contractors as well as several commercial corporations that adapted the governments's policies and procedures to their corporate purposes.

Although all these documents were well received and instantly invoked on contracts, the Army and the Air Force felt the need for additional requirements or the refinement of present requirements. Thus from 1970 to 1971 the Army published a more detailed version of AR 70-37, *Research and Development Configuration Management,* and the Air Force issued MIL STD 483, *Configuration Management Practices for Systems, Equipment, Munitions, and Computer Programs.* This was the first standard that recognized configuration management of both hardware and software. The document also included provisions for interface control, serial number control, and field changes as well as the first outline for a configuration management plan.

In 1973 the Navy followed these documents with one of its own, Instruction 5233.1, which promulgated documentation standards that also provided for software. At this same time the DOD began to recognize a need to specify the standards for other types of software outside the military realm. Thus in December 1973 a manual for automatic data processing, DOD 4120.17M, was published. This DOD document was the first to recognize a distinction between mission-critical computer software (MCCS) and non-mission-critical software for business and statistical applications.

Because of the proliferation of computer systems for handling the massive governmental clerical work load, Congress passed the Brooks Act, which set the requirements for procurement of software and computer systems. The act was later amended to provide more specific instructions for the procurement of types of systems and a better distinction between military versus government applications. The prime example was the distinction between software embedded in a given military system and software used for automated data processing/information systems.

All the activity during the late 1960s and early 1970s made the Joint Chiefs of Staff concerned that a Tower of Babel was being developed in the definition and implementation of configuration management. To resolve this concern, the JCS published the *Joint Regulation on Configuration Management* in July 1974. It set a well-defined standard and was consistent with the primary standards 480, 490, 483, and 482. Although it could not be imposed on contracts, it was suggested as a guide and was thus adhered to and implemented on many programs. It did not, however, provide for software. Even though some insisted that it pertained to both hardware and software, it lacked the necessary lines of demarcation between the two, which MIL STD 973 Docs. Provide.

Software acquisition was growing during the mid-1970s, and the armed services were concerned with the diversity of software being ordered and the amount of unreliable software being developed and delivered by both large and small contractors. Software configuration management was not enough. The Army attempted to standardize a computer architecture that would provide for standard computers in the field known as the military computer family. The Navy, however, took the initiative to create a software development standard that it hoped would ensure lower cost of maintenance and far less down time, even though the Navy had been quite successful in controlling its standard software language, CMS-2, through its technical documentation standards.

Several accomplishments had also occurred by this time. The major development was communication through status accounting, in part, but more through scheduled design reviews and audits that brought the customer and the developer together to view the design's development and maturation. Even in the commercial environments, the emergence of world-wide communication systems built by RCA, ITT, and airline reservation systems such as SABRE were under forms of the configuration management process. Commercial salespeople began to rely on CM people to provide the necessary equipment configurations specified on the sales orders and provide the latest version of software and the hardware platforms such as the IBM 360 and Univac 1100. Of course, it was also necessary to educate the salesperson in such minor (very major, really) details as specifying cable lengths or at least the distances between peripherals.

THE ADVENT OF SOFTWARE DEVELOPMENT STANDARDS

MIL STD 1679 was developed during the latter part of the 1970s and was issued in December 1978. Although it had been closely coordinated with the industry associations and widely reviewed and commented on, many software organizations felt the final document was overly restrictive and would add to the cost of software development, especially considering the imposition of 13 software specifications and documents. (Software, no matter what its size, always seemed to require the same amount of documentation.) There was also confusion as to the amount of tailoring that could be initiated under the standard. Because this was the first real imposition of software requirements, it took a while to see some of its primary benefits, which were in keeping with the current methods of software development known as top-down analysis and programming as promulgated by Yourdan, Constantine, and DeMarco [3].

In 1979, and again in 1981, two software systems conferences were sponsored by the Joint Logistics Commanders in Monterey, California. They were known as Monterey I and II. One of their primary outputs was the decision to create a universal standard for software development. Thus in 1981 the Joint Policy Coordinating Group for Computer Resources Management initiated the development of a universal standard based on the concepts passed down from the Monterey I and II conferences. The initial project editor was Air Force Major Larry Fry, who headed a tri-service team, the Computer Software Management Subgroup (CSM), composed of representatives from the other DOD service components.

The software industry awaited the first draft with great anticipation. The industry associations, including the Electronics Industries Association (EIA), the Aerospace Industries Association (AIA), the National Security Industrial Association (NSIA), and the American Electronics Association (AEA) followed the events of development as reported to them by Major Fry but were not able to review the first draft until formally issued by the CSM.

The standard then known as MIL STD SDS and finally as DOD STD 2167 went through turbulent times and many reviews. However, the FAA, while not a direct participant in the development of the document, wanted this type of standard for the development of its Advance Aviation System (AAS) and referred to it as SDS on the request for proposal. On the other hand, the Ada language community was really just getting practical application of the language under way and did not feel it could fulfill all the SDS requirements for the structure and application of Ada. Thus there was little in the way of instruction for Ada users to follow.

When the many comments on MIL STD SDS had been reconciled, 13 major issues remained to be resolved. These were solidified at an EIA Computer Resources Workshop in fall of 1984. The standard was issued in June 1985 with a proviso that work commence on a Rev A to resolve the open issues. The CSM started work on this revision, and the industry settled down to implement 2167.

The standard was very good from a configuration management point of view. It divided CM by the phases in the life cycle. Within each phase, it described the activities to be performed, the product expected from these activities, the design reviews that were required for approvals, and, most important, the role of SCM in capturing the documented descriptions and subsequent change paper. It was the type of document a person new to CM for software could read and learn a great deal from in a short period of time.

The work on Rev A went quietly in the beginning. The industry associations had formed a task force under their Council of Defense and Space Industries Associations (CODSIA) and thus had a unified approach to the development of the A version. However, it soon became apparent that the form, fit, and function of the document had changed dramatically. There appeared to be great pressure from a variety of entities to loosen up the document to allow "total flexibility" for development. The document's requirements had been consolidated into 17—including the Software Configuration Management Plan (SCMP), which suddenly became part of the software development plan. Experience has shown that a CM plan as part of another document such as a program plan or software development plan becomes lost in a program manager's desk drawer. Another fear was that the plan could be written by a development engineer to save money and not an experienced software configuration manager.

The standard was published as Rev A in February 1988. *Military Handbook 287, Guide for Tailoring 2167A,* has also been issued. A new effort is also under way by a government/industry group, started in October 1989, to develop an application and implementation guide especially to aid the government program managers in invoking and monitoring 2167A in their contracts. This should be of great help to CM managers working with their customers to apply the CM process.

THE DEVELOPMENT OF COMMERCIAL SOFTWARE STANDARDS

The concept of an industry/government complex has worked very well in the area of standards and guidance. There is a specified protocol for review and comment by the industry before a standard is issued, and for the most part this has been followed. In 1988 Dr. Costello, assistant secretary of defense for acquisition, directed through a memorandum that more materials and services would be procured off the shelf in the commercial market and that standards written by the existing standards-writing groups such as EIA, IEEE, SAE, ANSI, and ISO would be used. The government, he stated, should get out of the standards-writing business. These remarks were made just before 1988 and the change of administration. The standards-writing groups are just beginning to put themselves in a position to become responsive to Dr. Costello's memo and in the meantime the government is still writing and revising standards.

For many years the EIA has written numerous electronics, electrical, and communications protocol standards. The Society of Automotive Engineers (SAE) is most famous for standards on grades of automobile oils and many standards relating to automotive development and production. Another society, the American Society of Mechanical Engineers (ASME), has been involved in drawing standards and other standards relating to mechanical development and fabrication.

The EIA Data and Configuration Management Committee developed several standards in the form of guides and bulletins for the software CM layperson. These included Bulletins:

4-1A – *Glossary of Software CM Terms*

4-2 – *Software CM Identification*

4-3 – *Software Libraries*

4-4 – *Software Change Control*

4-6 – *Text on Status Accounting*

5A – *Subcontractor Control*

6-1A – *Configuration and Data Management References*

6-2 – *Configuration and Data Management In-House Training Plan*

6-3 – *Configuration Identification*

6-4 – *Configuration Control*

6-5 – *Configuration Status Accounting—Textbook*

6-6 – *Configuration Audits—Textbook*

One of the primary leaders in the software development standards area has been the Computer Society of the IEEE and the Standards Department of the IEEE. They have

developed and continue to develop a number of software standards that are available to commercial and military organizations, such as:

- *Software Requirements Specifications,* IEEE STD 830-1984.
- *Software Quality Assurance,* ANSI/IEEE STD 730.1-1988.
- *IEEE Guide for Software Quality Assurance Planning,* IEEE STD 983-1986.
- *Software Configuration Management Plans,* IEEE STD 828-1990.
- *Guide to Software Configuration Management,* IEEE STD 1042-1987.
- *Software Reviews and Audits,* IEEE STD 1028-1988.
- *Software Test Documentation,* IEEE STD 829-1983, and *Software Unit Testing,* IEEE STD 1008-1987.
- *Software Project Management Plans,* IEEE STD 1058.1-1987.
- *Software Verification and Validation Plans,* IEEE STD 1012-1986.

IEEE Standards 828-1990 and 1042-1987 are slated for review by the DOD for adoption. This statement was made in the current Standardization Program Plan, Configuration Management Plan (RevI), of August 1990. Other such standards are also expected to be reviewed and adopted. Thus there appears to be a combining of standards common to government and industry requirements and methods of software development. It would also appear that the requirements of these standards will be more subject to negotiation than before. Std 1042, for instance, has several fully completed software CM plans, any one of which could be selected for a given project. In addition, Standard 830 has several options of tables of contents for the software requirements specification.

The international arena must also be considered. Many standards are now being written under the sponsorship of the International Standards Organization/International Electrochemical Commission for software engineering application as well as electronic components. The American National Standards Institute (ANSI) is the U.S. representative to the ISO/IEC. The IEEE Standards Department is the administrator for ANSI in ISO/IEC affairs. Software standards are proposed under sponsorship of a U.S. technical advisory group (TAG), which fully participates in the ISO/IEC activities as illustrated in Figure 3.2. Thus in 1990 a standard for software configuration management was proposed by the U.S. TAG and was accepted by the members of the international body as project number NWI.7.23. This author was designated project editor of that standard. In addition, the "parent standard" 7.21 on the software life cycle development process is under current review and will be of immense help to the international communities as well as support current national standards.

This short history of CM should make the reader familiar with the past, the present, and the future of CM, including the development of MIL STD 973, configuration management, to be issued in the fall of 1991 as the primary CM document for hardware and software, this will include the CM section from 2167A along with the enhancements to the communication process and control of design and development efforts. When you embark on a project for which you have responsibility for the CM process, you may well be adding to what has already been said. Your own account or postmortem of your project one or more years hence may well provide a view of the future, as in the application of CM to an Ada environment. Knowing how the software environment was developed will help you in your daily communication with your project staff.

EXERCISES

1. Recount the start of change control during the 1960s.
2. What was so important about the publication and issuance of the primary MIL STDs in late 1968?
3. Why was the *Joint Regulation for Configuration Management* developed?
4. What caused the development of MIL STD 2167? Who initiated the action? How was it received? How did it affect SCM?
5. How did 2167A affect SCM? Which would you prefer to use?

CHAPTER 4

Configuration Management Relationships

CM is a communicator: it establishes relationships with all the project activities, as shown in Figure 4.1. The importance of CM's role and its relationship to the other project activities is illustrated by the method for assessing the software engineering capability of contractors (developers) and the criteria for CM developed by the Software Engineering Institute at Carnegie Mellon University, Pittsburgh, PA, USA [64]. This method involves the following questions:

Is a mechanism used for controlling changes to the software requirements? (question 2.4.9)

Is a mechanism used for controlling changes to the software design? (question 2.4.13)

Is a mechanism used for controlling changes to the code? (question 2.4.17)

Is a mechanism used for configuration management of the software tools used in the development process? (question 2.4.18)

CM communicates by providing technical information about each specification, document, manual, code, and so forth, provided to the project team. CM first establishes relationships with system engineering, for instance, in order to help finalize the software and interface requirements. Once these requirements have been finalized, CM helps system engineering by securing the master copies, applying the appropriate identification and markings, and producing the necessary copies for distribution to the project. In turn, any subsequent changes are communicated to the project by providing copies of the change control document, reviewing the document(s) or reporting through status accounting reports.

In this manner CM forms its relationships with each of the project activities to collect their outputs/products and, in return, provide the necessary security, control, and status accounting to users of the technical data.

CM provides services to several activities and it has working relationships with some of those. One activity CM has a very close relationship to is quality assurance, which plays a major role as an independent body dedicated to ensuring the integrity of the software product from beginning to end. Quality assurance also monitors the performance of other activities, including CM. CM in turn provides status accounting to quality assurance and relies on that activity to review changes to ensure product integrity. CM is also almost intertwined with an activity that prepares and manages documents containing the requirements and design criteria as well as the testing requirements of the software system/product and documents such as the users manual to be delivered with the software product. This activity is known as data management. It is related to CM in terms of the specifications and documents that CM ensures are correctly identified, have a recorded history of changes when released or delivered to a customer, and are statused as they change or are released.

All these processes and activities are layered across a project's life cycle, as portrayed in Figure 4.1. Some of these entities may start at the initiation of the project, and some will start and end later. All are related to one another at some point in the life of the project. CM will interface with, provide data to, receive data from, and communicate with all these activities.

On the left side of the diagram in Figure 4.1 is a listing of the functions for each of the layered activities. Thus the driving force of a project—the driver—is program/project management, which has the overall responsibility for satisfying the customer's needs and requirements as contracted for or marketing's desires for a competitive product. CM represents program management for all matters relating to the CM process, such as securing identified documents, providing procedures for change processing, and reviewing and approving the changes. CM provides the plan that the project team can follow to learn its role in relation to CM. CM also interfaces with a customer's counterpart activity so that communication of changes proposed to the customer may be processed smoothly and in a timely manner. The contracts and administrative/financial/audits activities are also drivers governed by the agreements reached with the customer (or feel for the market place). For these activities CM provides guidance on technical documentation requirements and major changes that may require the renegotiation of an agreement as to the extent of the change, the reviews that must take place, and the audits that may be needed before the change can be closed out.

The overseer of the life cycle process is the quality assurance/product integrity activity, which ensures adherence to the customer requirements and standards agreed to by or imposed on the project. There are always a number of questions regarding the role of the quality assurance activity in relation to CM. One should be able to interpret this role as one of verification and validation of qualification standards.

The role of the CM process should be to perform the primary activities of identifying the evolving product, controlling the changes to that product, and communicating status.

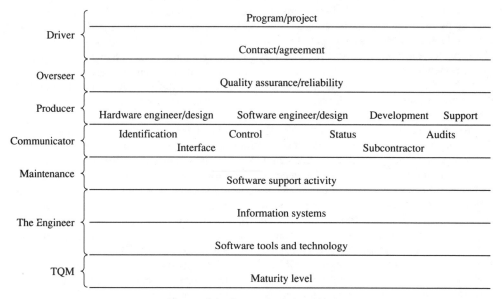

Figure 4.1 Layered relationships.

These are further defined in Chapter 5. Suffice it to say that CM has a close relationship to quality assurance in the areas of adherence to customer requirements and integrity of the developing system.

The producers of the software product are initially the system and software engineering activities. The system engineering process is devoted to interpreting customer requirements and needs and transforming them into functional requirements for the design, development, test, and delivery of a product. One of these functional requirements is the software. The software engineering process will pick up the software requirements and begin to map out the requirements for the development of the software function as a stand-alone entity until integrated with the hardware entity to form the final system product. CM serves software engineering in the same way it serves system engineering except that there are more documents to account for, identify, and control.

The communicator, of course, is the CM activity, which should be in place at the start of the project to communicate to the project team such activities as the identification and approval of documents, changes that have occurred or are pending, and releases, deliveries, returns, and so on.

The maintainer function is the support of the software once it has been sold on the market or delivered to a customer. CM works closely with this activity to provide information about the software product and process changes, and initiating releases of revised software.

The engines are the information systems CM will use for statusing, baselining, and storing. In addition, the software tools used for development and test are all identified and controlled in the same manner as the deliverable/marketable software.

Other activities include reliability, which is involved in maintaining the integrity of the product as it evolves, and product support/logistics support, which is the publisher of the user manuals and the eventual maintainer of the software once sold or delivered to the ultimate users. These activities rely on the CM function to provide documentation and code at the latest revision with proper traceability to the hardware platform(s), other software systems, or associated user systems.

If one's objective is to deliver a reliable product, the documentation that goes with it must accurately represent its functions and allow quick maintenance in the field or at the user sites. Without close CM relationships this can become a problem and a cause of higher cost, missed schedules, and possibly a product of marginal quality.

The latest methods of total quality management (TQM), concurrent engineering (CE), and computer-aided/acquisition logistics support (CALS) are most apparent in the activity of CM and its relationships with the project entities. If recognized as such, these methods will help the manager perform the CM activity in an economical and timely fashion.

Figure 4.2 illustrates a standard program organization and the positions most supporting functions have in the project. This will be discussed further when we talk about organizing for a given project. Figure 4.3 illustrates the many functions CM deals with in each particular phase. In the beginning phases, as everyone is gathering the facts, there is a good deal of interfacing, but during the development and testing phases everyone is concentrating on completing the coding and getting the testing under way. It isn't until the end, at acceptance test and point of delivery, that CM communicates with a number of others who are involved in the final validation and verification process.

CM is the communicator. By maintaining close working and processing relationships with all the project entities, CM keeps everyone informed of the product's status as it evolves from a requirement into a physical entity. CM captures and stores approved documentation defining the product and makes it available to all that require it. CM convenes the review bodies or configuration control boards for the review of design definition for either release

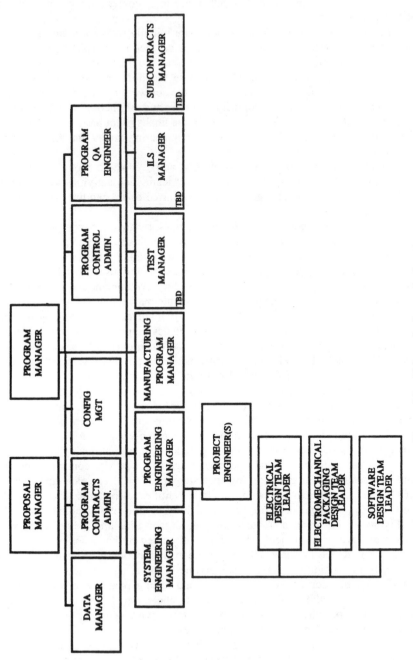

Figure 4.2 CM standard organization chart.

Conceptual	R&A	Design	Code · U/TST	Integr/Test	Syst/Test. Accpt
Marketing/Sales	Marketing/Sales	System Engr	Quality Assur	Quality Assur	Quality Assur
Contracts	System Engr	Design Engr	SSS	SSS	SSS
Accounting	Design Engr	Quality Assur	Test	Test	Test
System Engr	Quality Assur	SSS	SW Supt	SW Supt	SW Supt
Design Engr	Data Mgmt	Data Mgmt		Accounting	SSF
• • • •	ILS	ILS			Marketing Sales
Cust. CM	Accounting	Accounting			Accounting
Sub Contr CM	SSE	Test			

Figure 4.3   Functional Interface.

or approval of changes. Thus the CM activity should be involved to the appropriate degree for the good of the project.

EXERCISES

1. Describe the CM activity or other controlling activity in your company or firm and compare with others to determine the similarities and/or differences.

CHAPTER 5

Configuration Management Defined

This chapter provides the formal definitions of CM in a software development environment, then goes on to list and describe the government and industry standards and guidelines that are in effect or planned nationally and internationally. It also describes some of the government and industry activities and the organizations that address, monitor and apply SCM. Chapter 3 has given some of the history leading up to the current world of configuration management for software. We shall now expand on that history and describe what guides us in our conduct of CM today.

The formal definitions of configuration management are in MIL STD 973. Many of the definitions are also found in the IEEE dictionary of computer terminology, IEEE STD 973 [10], and are equivalent to the DOD versions. The terms in the Glossary, Appendix 1, are based on MIL STD 973 except where noted.

The primary activities of configuration management are *identification, change control, status accounting, and configuration audit*. Also added is *interface control and subcontractor CM control*. Experience has shown that these are most essential to the successful conduct of the CM process when interface and subcontractors are part of a project.

FORMAL DEFINITIONS OF THE CM ACTIVITIES

The term *configuration* is defined as

> The functional and/or physical characteristics of hardware/software as set forth in technical documentation and archive in a product. [7]

The term *configuration item* is defined as

> An aggregation of hardware or software or any of its discrete portions that satisfies an end use function and is designated for configuration management. Configuration items may vary widely in complexity, size, and type. . . . [7].

In practice a CI is a stand-alone, test-alone, use-alone element. It does not rely on any means of support or input, being less like a light bulb, which needs an electric current to light up, than a flashlight, which is self-sufficient because of its batteries.

The term *management* is described as

> The act or art of overseeing and making decisions about the configuration of the hardware/software product as it evolves from conceptual form to a deliverable physical element.

Configuration management may then be described as

The Engineering Management Procedure that includes the following:

A. *Configuration identification*—The selection of documents that identify and define the configuration baseline characteristics of an item.

B. *Configuration control*—The controlling of changes to the configuration and its identification documents.

C. *Configuration status accounting*—The recording and reporting of the implementation of changes to the configuration and its identification documents.

D. *Configuration audit*—The checking of an item for compliance with the configuration identification.

E. *Interface control*—The process of identifying . . . all characteristics relevant to the interfacing of two or more [CIs] provided by one or more organizations and . . . the control of these characteristics.

F. *Subcontractor control*—The management of subcontractors' or vendors' adherence to the provisions of their respective contracts as related to the conduct of configuration management. [MIL STD 973]

In detail, the six activities identified here are defined as follows

Configuration identification is the current approved or conditionally approved technical documentation for a configuration item as set forth in requirement and design documents such as specifications, drawings, or associated lists and other documents referenced therein. [7]

Configuration control is the systematic evaluation, coordination, approval or disapproval, and implementation of all approved changes in the configuration of a configuration item after formal establishment of its identification[7].

Configuration status accounting is the recording and reporting of the information that is needed to change a configuration effectively, including a listing of the approved configuration identification, the status of proposed changes to the configuration, and the implementation status of approved changes. [7,10]

Configuration audit is the process of verifying that all required configuration items have been produced, that the current version agrees with the specified requirements, that the technical documentation completely and accurately describes the configuration items, and that all change requests have been resolved[7].

Interface control is the evaluation, coordination, and approval or disapproval of all proposed changes to established functional and physical interfaces as defined in specifications, documents, and drawings.

Subcontractor control is the evaluation, coordination, and approval or disapproval of all changes submitted by the subcontractor to approved configuration documentation and the monitoring of the subcontractor's performance of the CM function.

These descriptions have been universally applied by those working in a variety of commercial and defense configuration management environments and describe very well the actual activities that take place during the course of a project. One may find some variations on these definitions, but they will be minor. As a case in point, international definitions are identical, and thus one can say that they are truly compatible worldwide.

To clarify the nature of these activities, Figure 5.1 illustrates the phases within the software development cycle. The identification activity is performed during the software requirements, preliminary, and detailed design phases. For example, during the requirements phase one defines the performance requirements of the software system in a software requirements document. This definition is subsequently broken down into greater detail dur-

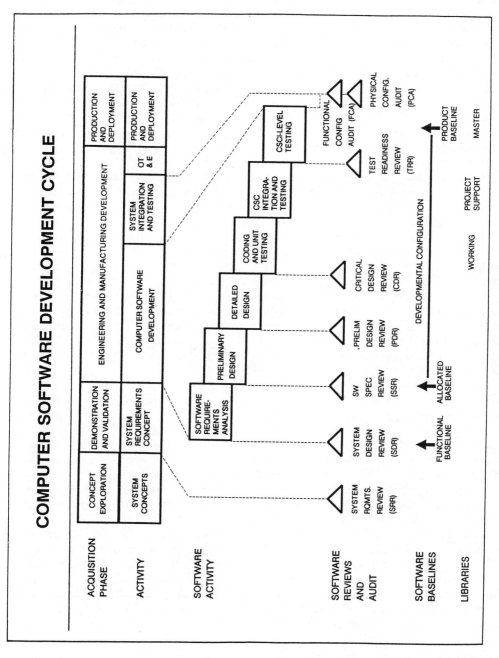

Figure 5.1 Computer software development cycle.

ing preliminary design and then into the instructions for the coding of the software during detail design in a preliminary version of the design document and the details written into the final draft of the design document. Also included during these phases are the interface requirements specifications and test plans and associated test case descriptions.

The configuration control activity is in effect during all of these phases for control of changes to the approved and released documents, but during the coding and unit testing phase few changes will be processed because the coding is being produced and one will not know what state that coding is in until it goes into the testing phase and is approved and placed under configuration control. During test many changes normally occur. Most may be minor, but one also is on the lookout for the major ones that may affect many different software elements (code and documents) that will, in turn, cause additional changes to be processed and communicated to the project software team.

Status accounting is the reporting system that spans the entire development cycle. Its major function is required during the heavy volume of changes in reporting the advent of a change, its status during processing and review, its final approval, and the date of its incorporation into the system.

The same holds true for interface and subcontractor control. Interface is concerned with the connection between computer systems. Subcontractor control is concerned with the monitoring of those who are also contracted to develop software for the system in some specialized area that the principal firm does not process.

Configuration management for software is inherent in most systems within the government and to a lesser extent in the commercial community, which has used it to control its documentation and is now beginning to apply it to areas employing programmable read-only devices such as those used in automobiles and automated machinery. This is becoming evident through the interest shown in the IEEE standards listed in Chapter 3 and the attendance at the IEEE software engineering seminars.

Commercial software developers face a different competitive situation today. Their survival depends on fast delivery at the marketplace of high-quality software products at a competitive price. Commercial software is also becoming more influenced by regulatory bodies such as the Federal Communications Commission (FCC) and the Nuclear Regulatory Commission (NRC) because the software procured is being used more and more in devices that were mechanical before. For example, a speaker at a recent software conference proclaimed that today's jet aircraft are some 60,000 parts held together by software! Furthermore, the speaker claimed that the number of safety features built into these aircraft and those on the ground were all software-driven, leading one to the conclusion that software saves lives and bad software may be hazardous to one's health!

Thus, in its need for CM, the commercial environment is now at the point the defense establishment was in the middle and late 1960s. One can, however, bridge the experience and learning gap by studying the defense establishment's experiences and applying them to the development and support of software sold on the open market. More and more one begins to realize that a company that implements CM to control the software it sells gains a competitive advantage over those who still produce helter-skelter without regard to the quality and reliability of their products.

STANDARDS RELATING TO CONFIGURATION MANAGEMENT

What follows is a listing of the major documents and references relating to software configuration management [11]. Figure 5-2 depicts the document tree associated with this list and includes those IEEE standards listed in Chapter 3.

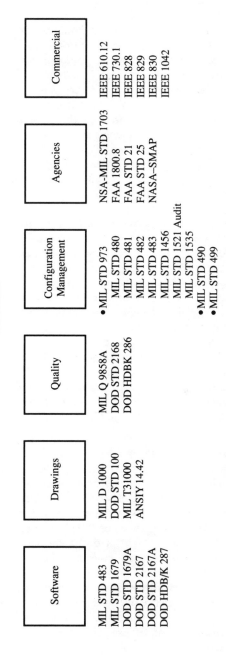

Figure 5.2 Document tree for standards applicable to CM.

Policy
5000.2 Part 9A
Configuration
Management

Software

MIL STD 483
MIL STD 1679
DOD STD 1679A
DOD STD 2167
DOD STD 2167A
DOD HDB/K 287

Drawings

MIL D 1000
DOD STD 100
MIL T31000
ANSIY 14.42

Quality

MIL Q 9858A
DOD STD 2168
DOD HDBK 286

Configuration
Management

●MIL STD 973
MIL STD 480
MIL STD 481
MIL STD 482
MIL STD 483
MIL STD 1456
MIL STD 1521 Audit
MIL STD 1535
●MIL STD 490
●MIL STD 499

Agencies

NSA-MIL STD 1703
FAA 1800.8
FAA STD 21
FAA STD 25
NASA–SMAP

Commercial

IEEE 610.12
IEEE 730.1
IEEE 828
IEEE 829
IEEE 830
IEEE 1042

MIL STD 973	*Configuration Management*
DOD STD 100	*Engineering Drawing Practices*
MIL STD 480	*Engineering Changes, Deviations, and Waivers*
MIL STD 483	*Configuration Management Practices for Systems, Equipment, Munitions, and Computer Programs*
MIL STD 1679	*Weapon System Software Development*
DOD STD 1679A	*Weapon System Software Development*
DOD STD 2167	*Defense System Software Development*
DOD STD 2167A	*Defense System Software Development*
DOD STD 2168	*Defense System Software Quality Program*
MIL STD 7435	*ADP Software Development*
MIL STD 490	*Specification Practices*
MIL STD 499	*Engineering [System] Management*
MIL STD 1456	*Contractor Configuration Management Plans*
MIL STD 1521	*Technical Reviews and Audits for Systems, Equipments, and Computer Programs*
MIL STD 1535	*Supplier Quality Assurance Program Requirements*
MIL STD 1703	*[NSAM 80-1] Documentation Standards*
MIL STD 52779	*Software Quality Assurance Requirements*
MIL Q 9858A	*Quality Program Requirements*
MIL HDBK 287	*Defense System Software Development*
FAA ORD 1800.8	*NAS Configuration Management*
FAA STD 21	*NAS Software Configuration Management*
FAA STD 25	*Preparation of Interface Control Documentation and Interface Requirements Documentation*
IEEE STD 610.12	*Glossary of Software Engineering Terminology*
IEEE STD 730.1	*Software Quality Assurance*
IEEE STD 828	*Software Configuration Management Plans*
IEEE STD 1042	*Guide to Software Configuration Management*
NASA—SMAP	*Information System Life Cycle and Documentation Standards, Release 4.3*

These documents represent a well-rounded reference library for those implementing or responsible for the CM process. Although most are of military origin, one should not look at them in terms of requirements unless one's contract happens to state that one will perform "in accordance with." In the commercial world, with documents authored by IEEE and other professional societies or the EIA, requirements will most likely say "may perform in accordance with" or "*may* use as a guide." This wording indicates that the customer would prefer the use of a given standard or document but will recognize the right of the performing contractor to use what he or she considers best to meet the specified requirements and negotiate an appropriate agreement.

You should therefore consider all the listed documents as references and in many cases tutorials or guides for the performance of configuration management that can be tailored and adapted as necessary. Also please keep in mind that all these documents were coordinated with industry, both defense and nondefense, and in many cases written in concert with the primary authors and users.

HOW THE STANDARDS ARE USED

One may wonder why a document entitled *Engineering Drawing Practices* is included. The reason is that DOD STD 100 is the only standard to address the reidentification of a

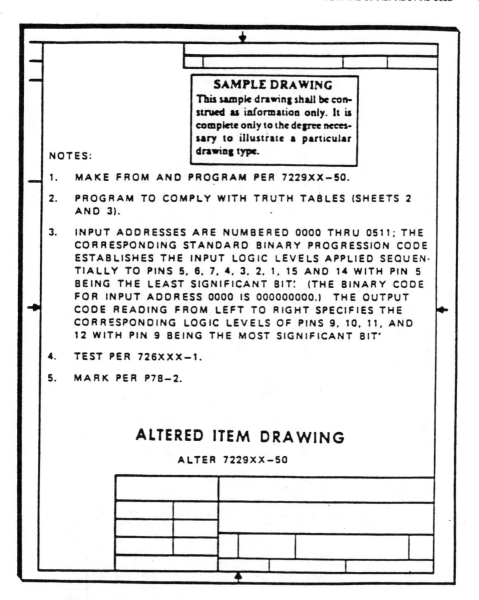

NOTES:

1. MAKE FROM AND PROGRAM PER 7229XX–50.

2. PROGRAM TO COMPLY WITH TRUTH TABLES (SHEETS 2 AND 3).

3. INPUT ADDRESSES ARE NUMBERED 0000 THRU 0511; THE CORRESPONDING STANDARD BINARY PROGRESSION CODE ESTABLISHES THE INPUT LOGIC LEVELS APPLIED SEQUENTIALLY TO PINS 5, 6, 7, 4, 3, 2, 1, 15 AND 14 WITH PIN 5 BEING THE LEAST SIGNIFICANT BIT: (THE BINARY CODE FOR INPUT ADDRESS 0000 IS 000000000.) THE OUTPUT CODE READING FROM LEFT TO RIGHT SPECIFIES THE CORRESPONDING LOGIC LEVELS OF PINS 9, 10, 11, AND 12 WITH PIN 9 BEING THE MOST SIGNIFICANT BIT'

4. TEST PER 726XXX–1.

5. MARK PER P78–2.

ALTERED ITEM DRAWING

ALTER 7229XX–50

* Procurement drawing for programmable microcircuit device, includes instructions for electrical alteration.

(A) Sheet 1

Figure 5.3 Document tree for standards applicable to CM.

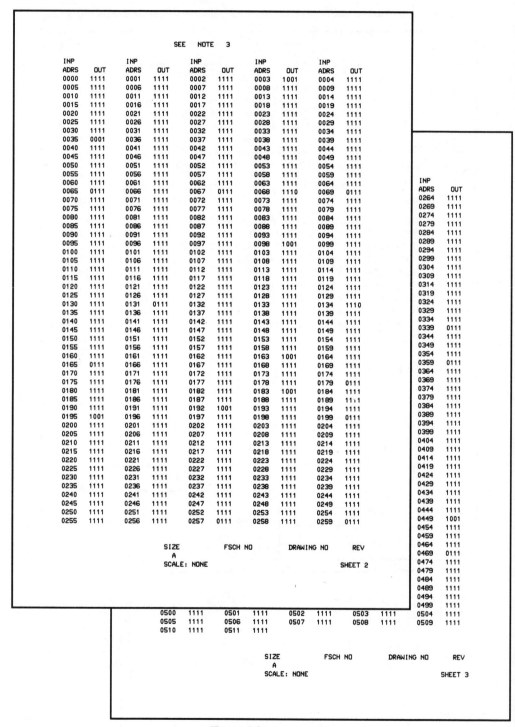

Figure 5.3 *(continued)*

software element when its function may have been changed and a new identification number is required. When this happens, the next-higher software elements containing the particular element may also require new identification numbers. DOD STD 100 also contains the format and the rules for programmable read-only memory (PROM) software identification as illustrated in Figure 5.3. This is the altered item drawing. Because we have altered a physical device, an integrated circuit (IC), by burning in a truth table or other type of software, we have altered the device's identification. DOD STD 100 is also used when it is necessary to prepare a *software drawing*. This occurs when one may be delivering a magnetic tape with many programs that have to be listed and are under configuration control. There are also times when a customer will want to know the type, size, composition, dimensions, and so on, of the tape, disk or device being delivered, either for installation or maintenance purposes or for the procurement of spares for defective read-only memory devices or the circuit boards they reside on.

There are always a number of instances when the developer must ask customers or even ultimate users if they will approve a change in the requirements as set forth in a contract or sales agreement. In order to standardize the manner in which such changes could be processed and still contain all the information for the customer to assess the impact on costs, schedules, and other systems, a standard was established known as MIL STD 480. It is commonly used throughout the world to submit software changes to the customer, especially if the change affects previously delivered software or software documentation or if the change causes changes in the contract terms, cost, fee, or schedule. The latest version in 973 delineates those blocks of the seven-page form for software entries in its Appendix B. The common term for this form is ECP—*Engineering Change Proposal*. NASA and other bodies also call their change forms ECP, but their format may differ significantly. For instance, the NASA form is only one page long, and the FAA is only two pages long. Also remember that this standard describes preparation requirements only. It does not prescribe the processing of the form. Such information is usually found in software development standards or in a contract statement of work. If not found, it is up to the developer to establish a workable process described in a software configuration management plan and found to be acceptable by the customer.

As noted earlier, the first document to address configuration management as well as computer software was Mil STD 483 (USAF). The standard's Appendix I outlined a configuration management plan that was used for hardware, software, or both. The standard was also the only document to describe the interface control function. Several of this document's other appendixes provided good information on various aspects of CM, such as document identification numbering and marking; engineering release records, which, while hardware oriented, can be adapted to the software development process; engineering changes for software; and most important, the criteria for the selection of configuration items.

The first standards to address the software development process and to be compatible with the then-popular top-down structured analysis methods were 1679 and 1679A. As noted in Chapter 3, this development methodology was introduced by Constantine, DeMarco, and Yourdon [3,12,13]. The top-down structured programming approach that was consistent with the overall approach to delving into a problem from the top down rather than the bottom up. Standard 1679 also partitioned the specification for the prime-item computer program development (B5) and the prime-item computer program product (C5), which are part of MIL STD 490.

The initial standards for software development specifications addressed the design, development, interface, and database requirements. Also required was a second specification describing how the software was developed, the final size of the data base, and the number of interfaces and their connections. This requirement was later reduced somewhat to a two-part specification for, first, design and, second, product—all in one volume which for many large systems was also very large.

In order to avoid the need to change a large document in total if one of its sections were changed, MIL STD 1679 introduced separate documents for design, development, interface, data base, and product. This allowed each document to be tailored to specified requirements and changed without impact on other documents or their schedule of preparation, reviews, approvals, and implementation at the most realistic times in the given life cycle.

During the 1980s many new concepts were introduced to software developers. Foremost was the software life cycle diagram (Figure 5.1), which showed the major segments of the development cycle embedded within the acquisition phases: conceptual, requirements (advanced development), full-scale development, and production/operational. The segments were portrayed within the full-scale development phase. This concept also formally established the term *mission-critical computer resource (MCCR)*—that is, software involved in the command, control, or communication of equipment or applications whose integrity and reliability would achieve the intended mission in a safe and successful manner. It was also tailorable to the unique characteristics of each software acquisition.

Although the term MCCR sounds strictly like defense jargon, consider a police radar detection device used to snare speeders. Likewise, consider the radar detection devices that many install in their cars to warn of radar surveillance. Both devices are software-driven. Both contain software embedded in microelectronic devices, and both are mission critical to the task of either catching a speeding vehicle or learning of radar detection in the immediate area.

The approach taken by MIL STD 1679 was expanded by DOD STD 2167, which delineated the primary software segments of the development life cycle phases, which were requirements analysis, preliminary design, detailed design, coding and unit testing, component (CSC) integration and testing, and CI testing. Each segment was divided into activities, products, controls/reviews and configuration management.

Also introduced by DOD STD 2167 was the concept of *developmental configuration*. Although this was originally thought of as a developer's internal baseline and control function, developers felt that the term *baseline* implied customer approval, which was not the intended meaning. On the contrary, developmental configuration is involved in the entire process, from the approval of the requirements analysis phase to the approval of the product for delivery. During this time the developer is solely responsible for the control of the documentation and code developed and produced. In other words, the developer places software documents and code under configuration control as these elements are approved throughout this period.

Other new concepts contained in DOD STD 2167 were specific provisions for software configuration management and software quality evaluation. There was also emphasis on planning and control and, most important, the treatment of risk, which up to this point had not been very well addressed for software. This provision required developers to establish and implement risk management procedures for any risk identified in their software development plans.

It was also noted in Chapter 3 that DOD STD 2167 increased the number of documents that could be delivered to a customer from 13 to 25. Some of the additions included the *System/Segment Specification, Software Standards and Procedures Manual, Version Description Document, Computer System Diagnostic Manual, Firmware Support Manual,*

Operational Concept Document, and *Computer Resources Integrated Support Document (CRISD).*

Because of the tailoring provisions in MIL STD 2167, not all 25 documents were required for each CI; however, documents such as the software requirements specification; preliminary design and detailed design document; product specifications; and test plans, procedures, and reports were required. In any case, with either of the standards one had to be most careful in how many CIs were selected in order to avoid too many documents as opposed to too few. Also introduced were the requirement to determine the benefits of commercially available (off-the-shelf) software and the requirement to control a developer's nondeliverable software. The latter, in particular, come as a shock to everyone. The requirement implied that any software procured or developed with customer funds was owned by the customer and subject to delivery at any point in time. Up to this point most developers took it for granted that any routines used during development but not delivered belonged to the creators. Now each routine had to be identified, controlled, and made subject to disposition by the customer. The former also caused consternation because many developers do not trust someone else's software and thus are most reluctant to procure it for one of their own projects. This was evidenced with the award of the software engineering environment for the Space Shuttle. Almost 90 percent of the software for this project was to be procured off the shelf. The primary concern was maintenance by the primary seller, many times a third party, who may be out of business at the time maintenance is required.

The introduction of a new standard naturally affected existing concepts and standards dealing with software and software documentation. The affected standards were changed to delete the performance and product specification formats in 490, which were replaced by a software requirements specification and product specification format. Revisions were also made to the criteria for selecting a configuration item, and the two-part specification mentioned previously was eliminated from 483. In addition, two new design reviews were added in 1521. These were the software design review and the test readiness review. The checklists for several other reviews were modified in 1521 to conform to the current concepts.

It was learned three months after these new concepts appeared that revisions were in the making to improve them. When one considers that it takes a good six months to a year for new concepts to appear as requirements, there was not enough learning time for developers to feel at home with the initial concepts. More important, however, was the lack of adequate time to find and enumerate all the perceived and real flaws in the concepts. Some had been detected immediately, especially in the Ada environment, as was to be expected, but also in the C and C++ languages, which were fast emerging as a competitors to Ada. From a CM point of view, the software engineers required a lot of education to convert from the concepts of the 1960s and 1970s to those of the 1980s—and to fit the developer's "clocks" into the design review and baseline schedules. It also became a problem to ensure that most of the key project people had the revised copies of the essential requirement standards. In one instance I received a call from a system engineer saying that what he was writing about for design reviews was not in agreement with what the statement of work was saying. This was remedied quickly with a copy of the latest standard—a fortunate instance before the fact.

Revision A of the original development concepts reduced the number of documents required from 25 to 17. The software CM plan, however, was relegated to a chapter in the software development plan. CM had some valid concerns here (as noted in Chapter 3) regarding the developer's inability to maintain custody and control of the CM plan as a chapter in the SW development plan.

The revised standard contained concepts that were quite different from the original ones. The chapter outlines diverged as follows:

Original	Revised
Activities	Software Development Management
Products	Software Engineering
Formal Reviews	Formal Quality Testing
Baseline/Development CM	Software Product Evaluation
xxxxxxxxxxxxxxx	Configuration Management

The revised standard emphasized the role of CM and by no means diminished its importance. But, on the other hand, it added some requirements for CM and the project. It stated that all draft documents submitted for review and evaluation would be "placed under configuration control" prior to delivery to the customer for review. The degree of control expected, however, is not stated but is left to the developer to determine. The key to successful implementation of the new requirements is the development of a good software development plan. If the plan is well prepared in a concise, accurate manner, and adhered to, the project will be in good hands.

Standard 490, issued in 1986, prevailed for many years as the primary authority for preparation of specifications for hardware and software. Other government agencies, however, developed their own requirements, which were certainly equal to, if not sometimes better than the 490 formats. The National Security Agency produced the noteworthy NSAM 80-2 and 80-3 for documentation standards. The FAA and NASA both had good guideline documents and what was then the National Bureau of Standards—now the National Institute of Science and Technology (NIST), developed some excellent guidance for the ADP community in FIP Pubs 38 and 64. Standard 490 is now primarily a hardware-oriented document except for the system/segment specification, which precedes the development of the software requirements and design specifications.

Standard 499 specifies the requirements for system engineering and the management of the system engineering process. It is still the basis for most documents defining the requirements for system engineering. It also requires that CM "shall be maintained."

The System Engineering Committee of the EIA also has successfully published an *EIA Guidance Bulletin on the System Engineering Process SYSB-1 [15]*. The IEEE Computer Society has established a working group to develop a *System Engineering Standard (Working Group P1202)*. The Air Force is actively pursuing a means to create a new revision at this time.

For years the Army has had a standard on configuration management (1456), but few in U.S. Industry have written in accordance with it. Sanders can claim such an achievement on the Patriot trainer program in the late 1970s. This author called throughout the United States looking for a contractor who had written to 1456 but could find no one. Thus the program CM and the author wrote to it, and it was approved and lauded as a magnificent effort. The standard, however, lay dormant for some years but has suddenly appeared over a good deal of industry objections as a universal DOD standard for configuration management plans. There is no mention of software in this document, and a user attempting to apply it to software will be confused.

The current standard for design reviews and configuration audits is a very good document for anyone in the software development business. If nothing else, this standard has checklists for the several design reviews to which all good developers of hardware or software products should adhere. The criteria and checklist data can be readily tailored to meet the needs of any project with little expense of time or dollars. The document also covers the vital final configuration audits for ensuring that the product has met its requirement specifications and been produced as designed—prior to delivery to the customer or the market.

IEEE STD 828-1990 was developed for the commercial, academic, and scientific communities. Its content, however, follows the same logic as current defense standards. It may be invoked in an agreement, contract, purchase order, or the like, or simply followed by the developer as good business practice. It has been well accepted by the defense community and may well be adopted by the government.

IEEE STD 1042-1986 is the guide for IEEE STD 828-1990 and provides a good explanation of the requirements for a successful CM plan. It also contains five fully written CM plans covering large, medium, small, and laboratory environments.

The *NASA Information System Life-Cycle and Documentation Standards, Release 4.3, 2 Feb 1989,* is a very comprehensive, easy-to-use set of documents divided into five volumes. These relate to documentation standards, management plan documentation standards, product specification documentation standards, management control and status reports documentation standards, and assurance specification documentation standards.

The material covered so far has been an introduction to the documentation that governs the conduct of software configuration management. It has been found, among a goodly number of us, that to understand what these standards represent and what they say will help and has helped us all in performing CM functions on a variety of programs throughout the past 20-plus years.

INDUSTRY/GOVERNMENT WORKING GROUPS

A number of interested parties throughout the United States and Europe have banded together to work with the developers of hardware and software requirements to ensure a form of requirement that both buyer and seller can work to and deliver by. Entities such as the IEEE and the ACM have provided valuable guidance, support, and standards documents that individuals or companies may use internally or impose on their suppliers. All this has been a voluntary effort, while the governments of the world have imposed similar requirements on their contractors. The difference is that the governments are using public funding for the procurement of a hardware/software product, whereas the private world must answer only to its owners or stockholders, which may be many or very few.

Some primary organizations devoted to software development and software configuration management include the following (15):

DOD—Defense Quality Standards Office

JLC—Computer Resources Management Committee

NASA—Software Management Assurance Program

IEEE—Computer Society and IEEE Standards Office

EIA—Computer Resources Committee (G-34)

EIA—Data and Configuration Management Committee, (G-33)

NSIA—Software Quality Committee

AIA—Technical Management Committee—Software Subcommittee

ADPA—Technical Documentation Committee

SUMMARY

The definition of CM is identification, control, status accounting, and audit. Interface control and subcontractor control may also be included depending on the scope and magnitude of the project. The support for these activities is evidenced by the standards and specifications related to the CM process, some of which are wholly directed to software while others contain provisions to accommodate software requirements.

EXERCISES

1. Define the primary elements of CM.
2. List the primary documents that provide the guidance and direction necessary for performing CM.
3. Describe the differences between commercial and military standards. State which is best for your environment.

CHAPTER 6

Configuration Management in the Software Engineering Environment

Successful software development requires a well-defined software engineering process plus a great deal of planning, analysis, description, and procedural guidance to produce a high-quality product that meets complex requirements in any environment—military, government, commercial, industrial, scientific, academic. Configuration management is a key contributor to successful software development.

This chapter describes the role of configuration management in the software engineering process. It also describes the life cycle of software engineering and the development phases within this cycle.

Because of the coexistence that should obviously prevail between CM and software engineering, both should be able to communicate through plans and the education of the software engineer to CM concerns and vice versa. If one can achieve this through good organizational logic, in which one function must interact with the other throughout the software life cycle, the CM activity can then capture the software documentation and apply an agreed-on amount of control to ensure that the documentation is protected.

THE SOFTWARE ENGINEERING PROCESS

In 1967 a NATO Science Committee described software engineering as "promoting the establishment of theoretical foundations and practical disciplines for software, similar to those found in the established branches of engineering." What then are the key differences between a hardware product and a software product? The following list shows how software is both like and unlike hardware:

Like Hardware	Unlike Hardware
Can be broken down into managable parts	Lacks physical appearance
Has personal accountability by task	Has few measurable elements
Has reportable progress events	Has greater logical complexity
Is traceable to requirements	Is easier to change
	Is explosive
	Tends to propagate change effects
	Is data as well as logic

More formally, software engineering can be defined as the branch of science and technology that deals with the design, development, implementation, test, evaluation, verification, operational use, and maintenance of computer software throughout its life cycle.

In his text on software engineering with Ada [16] Grady Booch states that, "Simply put, the purpose of software engineering is to provide a consistent, life cycle approach to the creation of software systems." In addition, Booch recognizes that "a paramount goal of software engineering is . . . that execution of solutions meet stated requirements."

Software engineering is an extension of the system engineering process for software design and development. CM might look at it as the second-level breakout of system engineering, the first being hardware along with other disciplines such as quality, reliability/maintainability, CM, and so forth.

Along with software engineering, CM relies a great deal on the methodology, analysis, and trades carried out by system engineering in determining the first, second, third, and fourth levels of functional performance required to design, develop, build, and test the software product. Once CM, in particular, has knowledge of the software hierarchy, its role is to begin planning for the number of documents and changes that will occur. Once software engineering has determined the number of source lines of code, CM will then be able to estimate, based on previous history, the number of changes that will occur, the number of software development files (SDFs), and the number of units and modules that will be transferred or released during the development cycle and incorporate this information into the CM plan for a given project.

Software engineering can also be characterized as an environment that surrounds the user/developer with tools needed to program [17]. When viewed as an entity within this environment, CM can be associated with a number of guidelines, methodologies, and tools such as the software life cycle, the overall development process, programming framing, integration, human factors, and the like [17]. If CM can indeed be considered a tool for the promotion and betterment of the development process, then the CM process is very much a part of the software engineering environment.

The software engineering process uses the *System/Segment Specification* or a similar requirements document, which it produces, to develop a top-down structured analysis of the software requirements. This is also known as decomposing the system's software requirements into manageable functional entities. This task consists of determining

- The size and complexity of the system's software.
- The number of readily identifiable functions, and modules within each function; whether each identifiable function is a manageable entity or should be broken down into smaller tasks.
- The complexities of call-ins and call-outs—from and to modules/units; whether a complex module should be declared a function.
- Whether module sizes have an equal number of lines of code to be programmed. By definition, this could be a large number of lines or a very few depending on the complexity of one's environment.
- The efficiency of data flow and data file; how "easy" the flow is between modules and units. Figure 6.1 is an example of a flow used to determine this (further discussed in Chapter 8).
- Data input/output requirements.
- System-to-system interfaces.

Decomposition creates the software system–level breakdown (Figure 6.2) and the document tree (Figure 6.3). With these two documents, CM determines what software elements will be identified in the software system and thus begins the identification activity discussed in Chapter 8. These breakdowns will also provide a roadmap for CM to trace the creation,

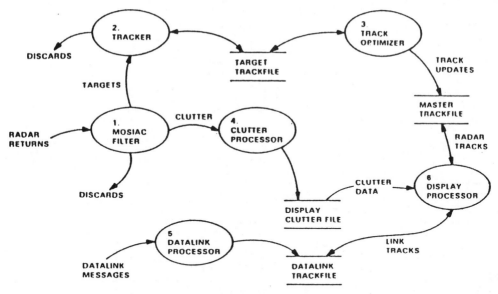

Figure 6.1 Data flow diagram.

existence, change, and release of the documents and code produced in accordance with the breakdowns. This information is communicated through status accounting reports or, in many instances, placed on walls with color dot status notations for all in the project to view and be aware of.

In a commercial environment, when the requirement is developed from analysis of or demand from the marketplace, a requirements team approach is used. By means of problem-solving/brainstorming techniques, a consensus is reached on the "system engineering" analysis, trades, and recommendations for functional criteria. This approach many times leads directly to rapid prototyping and subsequent development without formal documentation or, as a minimum, with data flows or products of software development tools such as a product specification. CM may be absent in name, but for the most part there is a sufficient element of control to minimize losses due to lack of formal documentation.

Software engineering thus provides guidance and direction to the CM as well as the other supporting functions to ensure a cost-effective, well-run project in present or even future time frames.

THE SOFTWARE LIFE CYCLE

The life cycle phases of software engineering, as illustrated in Figure 6.4, has been almost universally accepted. There are variations, but mostly in descriptions of what occurs within the accepted phases and segments of the cycle. The overall cycle has three major phases. The conceptual or front end is for the most part implemented within the customer's or acquiring agency's environment. There may, however, be times when the ultimate developer also conceives the concept and requirements document or system specification. Software development is the primary phase during which the design, development, and test of the software product occurs. This, in turn, is divided into several segments or subphases. The

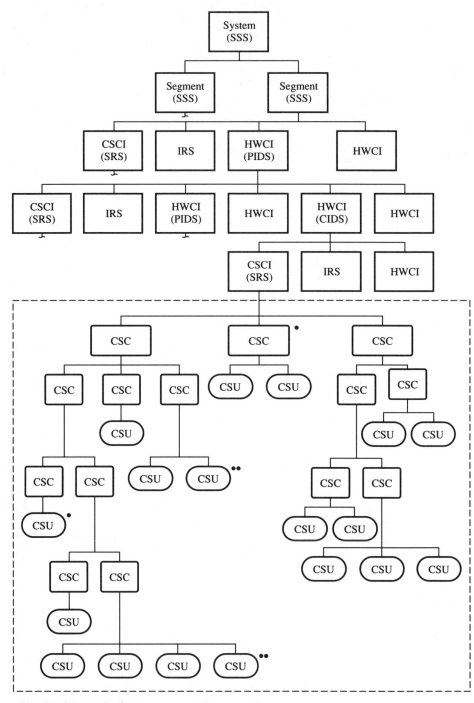

• Non-developmental software
•• Same CSU used by different CSCs

Figure 6.2   Software-level breakdown.

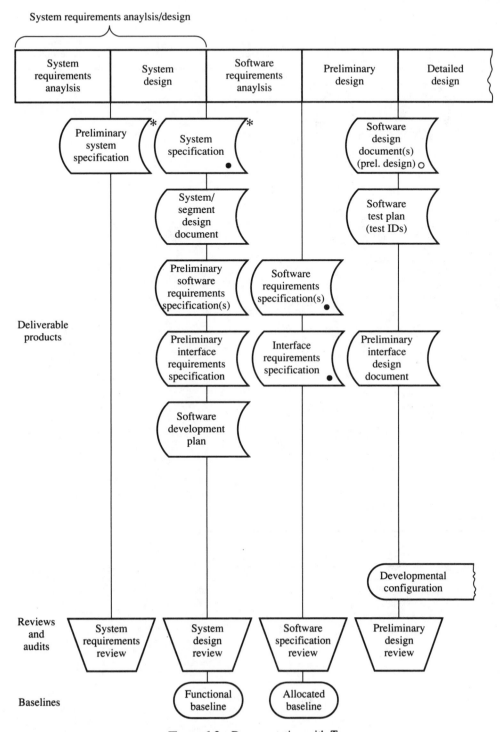

Figure 6.3 Documentation with Tree.

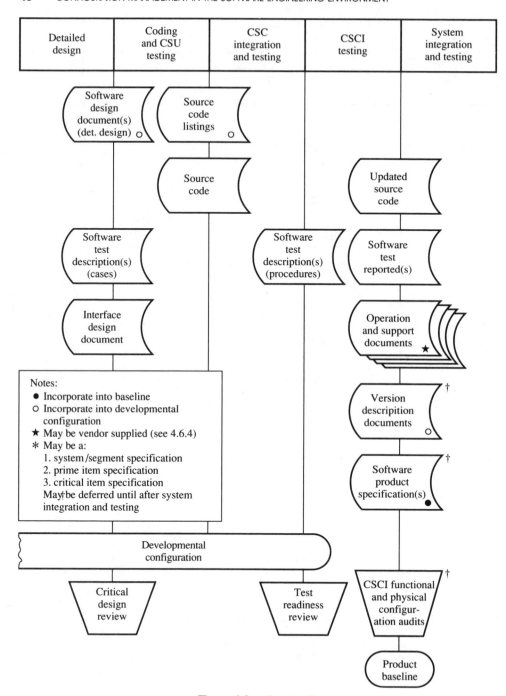

Figure 6.3 (*Continued*)

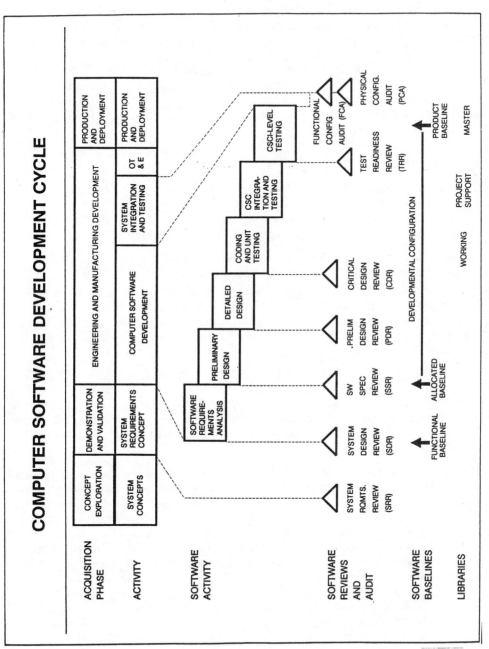

Figure 6.4 Computer software development cycle.

third phase, which is most important but receives far too little emphasis, is the operational and maintenance phase. This phase is also known as the postdeployment (of the software system) phase or as the software support phase. While concentration is on the software development phases, the product and many of the activities of the development phase are carried into the operational and maintenance phase described in Chapter 17. The activities performed during the software development life cycle portion are matrixed in Figure 6.5.

The role of CM in the software engineering life cycle starts with a response to a request for a bid, estimate, or proposal and ends by initiating action to turn over products of the development phase to the customer, ultimate user, or support facility that can remain in existence for several years.

THE PROPOSAL/ESTIMATE OR BID

CM responds to a request for proposal, bid, or estimate with a written description of how it will perform during the proposed project.

The plan may be a stand-alone document or a section of the software development plan. However, in order to be completely responsive, CM must know the following:

- How software engineering has decomposed the requirements and how many documents will be developed and placed under configuration control.

- How the configuration items are selected and how many there are. This allows CM to determine how many documents it will be responsible for controlling and statusing.

- What and how much software will be developed by subcontractors and where they are located. This will allow CM to monitor the subcontractors' activities, as described in Chapter 13.

- What specifications and documents will be written early in the project and what product specification, version description documents will be produced prior to shipment of the software.

- An estimation of the number of lines of code or other metric, to determine the size of the project, and the number of changes that will occur based on the ratio of number of changes per 100 lines of code.

Because the principles of CM are the same for almost all projects, a certain amount of tailoring for specific implementation is usually required to fit the needs of a given program. Thus a plan written for proposal A can most of the time be adapted or modified for proposal B, and so on. Normally, within a company software organization, consistent implementation of CM is very important. Once the engineers and the CM staff are familiar with the details of using CM, its application on future projects is that much easier. It is therefore suggested that the efforts of each proposal by the CM function be stored and be retrievable by those assigned the task of developing the CM plan and the related cost estimation and scheduling.

Some requests for bids do not require a CM plan but ask bidders to discuss their plans to conduct CM or may simply include the CM plan requirement on a list of documents to be prepared and purchased by the customer. CM responds accordingly. If there is no requirement, then CM should review the proposal to ensure that the CM process can be performed. This review would involve checking for sections relating to the preparation of documents, reviews, establishment of a software development library, and final audits prior to delivery. In addition, an estimate for performing the CM process should be reflected in the budget.

ACTIVITIES	PRODUCTS	REVIEWS	BASELINES
PRE-SOFTWARE DEVELOPMENT SYSTEM REQUIREMENTS ANALYSIS	• SOFTWARE DEVELOPMENT PLAN*	SYSTEM ROMTS REVIEW (SRR)	FUNCTIONAL
• AUTHOR SOFTWARE DEVELOPMENT PLAN INCLUDING: CONFIGURATION MANAGEMENT PLAN, (OR SYSTEM CMP) QUALITY PROGRAM PLAN STANDARDS, PROCEDURES METHODS AND TOOL PROVISIONS	• OPERATIONAL CONCEPT DOCUMENT	SYSTEM DESIGN REVIEW SDR	
• CONDUCT SYSTEM TRADE-OFF ANALYSIS-IDENTIFY CSCIs	• PRLM INTERFACE REQUIREMENTS SPEC		
• DEVELOP OPERATIONAL CONCEPT DOCUMENT	• PRLM SOFTWARE REQUIREMENTS SPEC		
• DEVELOP PRELIMINARY INTERFACE REQUIREMENTS SPECIFICATION(S)	• SYSTEM CONFIGURATION MGMT PLAN		
• DEVELOP PRELIMINARY SOFTWARE REQUIREMENTS SPECIFICATION(S)	*INCLUDES SCMP, SOPP, AND S&P DOC.		
• DEVELOP PRELIMINARY QUALIFICATION REQUIREMENTS			

Figure 6.5   Software development.

49

ACTIVITIES	PRODUCTS	REVIEWS	BASELINES
SOFTWARE REQUIREMENTS ANALYSIS • COMPLETION OF REQUIREMENTS FROM SYSTEM ENGINEERING PHASE • INTERNAL REVIEW OF REQUIREMENTS	• SOFTWARE REQUIREMENTS SPECIFICATIONS • INTERFACE REQUIREMENTS SPECIFICATIONS, IF APPLICABLE	SOFTWARE SPECIFICATIONS REVIEW (SSR)	ALLOCATED
SOFTWARE PRELIMINARY DESIGN • ALLOCATE REQUIREMENTS TO TOP LEVEL COMPONENTS • DEFINE ALGORITHMS AND DATA/CONTROL FLOW • IDENTIFY TESTS • REVIEW DESIGN INTERNALLY	• SOFTWARE TOP-LEVEL DESIGN DOCUMENT • SOFTWARE TEST PLAN • (SW DEVELOPMENT FILE)	PDR	DEVELOPMENTAL CONFIGURATION
SOFTWARE DETAILED DESIGN • DESIGN TO UNIT LEVEL • DEFINE UNIT TESTS • DESIGN TEST CASES FOR UNIT INTEGRATION (INFORMAL) AND FORMAL TEST • INTERNAL REVIEWS OF DESIGN AND TEST PLANS/CASES	• SOFTWARE DETAILED DESIGN DOCUMENT • INTERFACE DESIGN DOCUMENT, IF APPLICABLE • DATA BASE DESIGN DOCUMENT, IF APPLICABLE • SOFTWARE TEST DESCRIPTIONS • (SW DEVELOPMENT FILE)	CDR	DEVELOPMENTAL CONFIGURATION

Figure 6.5 (continued)

ACTIVITIES	PRODUCTS	REVIEWS	BASELINES
CODING AND UNIT TESTING • CODE UNITS • DEVELOP UNIT TEST PROCEDURES • TEST UNITS • DEVELOP TEST PROCEDURES FOR INFORMAL INTEGRATION AND FORMAL TESTS	• SOURCE AND OBJECT PROGRAMS • (SW DEVELOPMENT FILE) • (SOFTWARE TEST PROCEDURES–INFORMAL)	(INFORMAL)	DEVELOPMENTAL CONFIGURATION
SOFTWARE INTEGRATION AND TESTING • INTEGRATE UNITS AND INFORMALLY TEST • CAPTURE AND ANALYZE TEST RESULTS • MAKE CORRECTIONS	• (SW DEVELOPMENT FILE) • SOFTWARE TEST PROCEDURES–FORMAL • (INFORMAL INTEGRATION TEST RESULTS)	TEST READINESS REVIEW (TRR)	DEVELOPMENTAL CONFIGURATION
SOFTWARE PERFORMANCE TESTING • CONDUCT FORMAL TESTS • CAPTURE AND ANALYZE THE RESULTS • MAKE CORRECTIONS	• SOFTWARE TEST REPORTS • SOFTWARE PRODUCT SPECIFICATION • VERSION DESCRIPTION DOCUMENT	FCA PCA	PRODUCT

Figure 6.5 (*continued*)

SYSTEM REQUIREMENTS ANALYSIS

Many development contracts start with a system requirements analysis. During this phase, the contractor writes the system/segment specification while CM writes or updates the CM plan, preparing detailed procedures and automated tools. The preliminary versions of these documents are reviewed at the system requirements review. The final versions are completed during the latter half of the phase along with the software development plan, the preliminary software requirements specification, and the preliminary interface requirements specification. These documents are reviewed at the system design review and once accepted are placed under configuration control by CM, which enters them in a master library file under "formal change control procedures." Also during this phase, CM develops the plans, schedules, and organization needed to perform the activities within the CM process. Any changes to the CM plan, such as changes in the schedules, will require an approved change order and upgrade of the plan's revision level.

During system requirements analysis, CM may have to prepare a system-level CM plan when several multicontractor systems will be developed and integrated under a joint venture or multinational consortium as well as the individual contractor's CM plans for each system. A good example is a joint venture between two or more companies or a multinational consortium such as the Airbus Aeroplane. In this case three or more plans may be prepared: one for the joint venture/consortium and one each for the two or more companies involved in the venture.

SYSTEM REQUIREMENTS AND SYSTEM DESIGN REVIEWS: THE FUNCTIONAL BASELINE

During the system requirements analysis phase, there are two significant design reviews, the system requirements review (SRR) and the system design review (SDR). The SRR is really a handshake between customer and developer to signify that

- Each side knows what the other plans to do and is in agreement.
- Important questions or issues have been raised and resolved.
- Schedule requirements are realistic.
- Documentation requirements are understood and fully budgeted and control procedures have been prepared by CM; that is, there is a mechanism for control of design, code, and so forth.

The SDR occurs when the contractual or customer specification, such as the *System/Segment Specification,* has been modified to meet current contract requirements and customer desires brought out during SRR have been accommodated. This review and the acceptance of the system requirements establishes the *functional baseline,* the point of departure that both parties have agreed represents the requirements for the software product to be built during the development process. The system specification and related documentation are "captured" by CM and placed under configuration control. The details of this action will be discussed in Chapter 9.

The establishment of a functional baseline also indicates entry into the phases for development of the software and the full-scale development phase (a working prototype) of the software life cycle.

SOFTWARE REQUIREMENTS ANALYSIS

The software requirements analysis phase carries forward the software requirements established during system requirements analysis. This activity finalizes the software requirements specification for each configuration item (CI) selected as well as the interface requirements specifications necessary to tie the items and other identified interfacing systems together. Also included during this segment is the initial test plan for each CI (not noted in Figure 6.5). The products will be the final drafts to be reviewed by the developer's review boards and the customer or a customer-designated representative, such as a plant representative or a marketing group executive, at scheduled software specifications reviews (SSRs) and placed under control by CM. It is important to both acquirer and developer that there be uniform agreement as to the content and purpose of each system component with traceability to the upper-level requirements document depicted on the software hierarchy and documentation tree maintained by CM.

SOFTWARE SPECIFICATION REVIEW: THE ALLOCATED BASELINE

The SSRs, when completed, establish the system's *allocated baseline*. In other words, all the systems functions have been allocated to one or more configuration items of software, the requirements for each function have been described, and their accuracy and trustworthiness have been agreed on. Once placed under configuration control, the documents for these systems become the precursors of the design and detail design descriptions that will follow.

CM places these documents under formal configuration control so that if such documents are delivered to the customer, and changes occur, a formal change proposal may be prepared and submitted to the customer's review authority for approval before the change can be incorporated. For the most part, the need for formal change control by the developer is waived by both parties due to the dynamic aspects of software and the software development process. The formal acceptance of the documents may well not occur until the product baseline is established. However, these documents should be protected within the developer's confines, and the changes that do occur should be controlled and communicated by CM to the rest of the project. Thus internal configuration control within the development process should be implemented to preserve the integrity of the design definition.

PRELIMINARY DESIGN, PRELIMINARY DESIGN REVIEW, AND DEVELOPMENTAL CONFIGURATION

The allocated baseline for the final software system will not be established until all the configuration item documents have been reviewed and accepted/authenticated. If this turns out to be a lengthy process, work can still progress for those documents that have been accepted, and the preliminary design segment, also known as the system-level design, can begin. The activities in this segment entail describing how the developer will design the software to satisfy the requirements of a specified SRS and interface requirements specification (IRS). It also initiates a phase of activity called the *developmental configuration*. This activity enables CM to maintain configuration control of the approved documentation and code produced between the allocated baseline point and the product baseline. The customer/buyer is not involved in the change review and approval activity during developmental configuration but should have the right to review the status and integrity of the elements under the developer's control.

The process up to this point has been dealing with *what* is required and not *how* to do it. One can now become most inventive and innovative in describing how the top-level components of the system will be designed. At this time the algorithms associated with the design criteria will be developed, and data flows and design constraints will be identified and dealt with. One will also identify the major qualification requirements in the form of specified tests that will be performed during the testing phases, which must correlate upward to the SRS and IRS requirements.

The products of this segment will be the preliminary draft of the design specification and the final test plan for each configuration item. The design review is called the preliminary design review, at which time the reviewers compare the preliminary system-level design to the SRS requirements to ensure upward and downward traceability. One may well wonder why the allocated baseline is not established at this point, as it is for hardware items. One could conceivably be holding two PDRs—one for hardware and one for software—but the former will establish the allocated baseline while the latter is simply being placed in the developmental configuration environment. The reason for this, as one may see in Figure 6.6, is that the requirement specification for the software has come earlier than that for the hardware's prime-item requirement specification.

CM will place the preliminary design specifications and their related test plans into the developmental configuration under configuration control. This control should be protective to ensure that one has not made changes to these documents without coordinating and communicating them to the rest of the project members. This will be described further in later chapters.

DETAIL DESIGN, CRITICAL DESIGN REVIEW, AND DEVELOPMENTAL CONFIGURATION

Software progress is to the detail design segment, using a copy of the preliminary design specification. This will avoid the need to repeat a large amount of system-level detail contained in the PDS. There may also be a number of volumes related to this document because of the way the software was decomposed or broken down into its component parts. If there are not volumes, then chapters will provide the detail instructions to the programmer coding the software regarding what is to be coded, what conventions and standards as spelled out in the software development plan are to be used, and what unit tests are to be performed prior to acceptance by one's peers in a code walkthrough.

Since there can be many units, CM must be careful to have an approved breakdown at hand and well-defined data flows to ensure continuity in the programming environment. CM can get totally out of sync if, when trying to determine the impact of subsequent changes, it breaks or loses the continuity and traceability string.

During this segment, software engineering will begin to define the interfaces described in the interface requirements specification to a greater level of detail and author the interface design document, which will provide the necessary design criteria for the external interfaces that will occur or that have been prescribed. These data are placed under configuration control and may be subject to change impact when other requirements or design documents are changed.

The database design document will also be developed, if applicable. This document will remain dynamic right up to the time of delivery. It is placed under configuration control in the developmental configuration and may well be in constant revision even during deployment.

The formal design review for this phase is the critical design review (CDR). There has been an axiom for a number of years that stated that one could not commence coding until a successful CDR. In today's world this is not always possible, and in most instances a peer

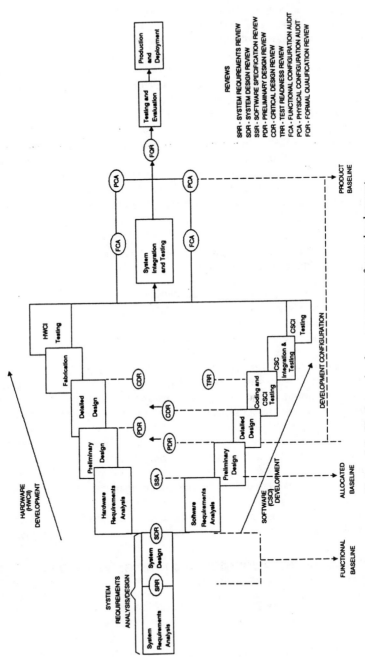

Figure 6.6 Hardware development versus software development.

REVIEWS

SRR - SYSTEM REQUIREMENTS REVIEW
SDR - SYSTEM DESIGN REVIEW
SSR - SOFTWARE SPECIFICATION REVIEW
PDR - PRELIMINARY DESIGN REVIEW
CDR - CRITICAL DESIGN REVIEW
TRR - TEST READINESS REVIEW
FCA - FUNCTIONAL CONFIGURATION AUDIT
PCA - PHYSICAL CONFIGURATION AUDIT
FQR - FORMAL QUALIFICATION REVIEW

review concept has been developed which has been quite successful. Known as the design walkthrough, the session will consist of two programming teams reviewing each other's detail design prior to coding. Suggestions and issues are resolved and the event recorded. CM ensures that the records of action taken are maintained for each walkthrough. This process complements the SDR and enables coding to begin earlier with minimal risk.

The CDR, however, is still conducted to review and pass on each configuration item's detail design specification. CM will place each document in the developmental configuration mode as change cannot be made without specified approvals.

During the preliminary and design phases, CM and the project librarian have established software development files (SDFs) for each configuration item, configuration component, and configuration unit. The SDF, which may be kept in a standard file folder or as part of an SDF database segment, is the repository for the history of each identified configuration element from the time of conception to final completion. Thus the events of the review and approval of the various documents previously described will be entered into their respective files and will be available for members of the project, supporting function, and auditors at any time. The SDF, as described in Chapter 10, is the primary source for status accounting reports.

CODING AND UNIT TEST, DESIGN AND CODE WALKTHROUGHS, AND DEVELOPMENTAL CONFIGURATION

The coding and unit test phase is the "production phase" in which code is produced in accordance with the instructions contained in the design documents passed at the CDR and the design walkthroughs.

When coding and test tasks have been completed, the code and the unit test reports will be reviewed at a code walkthrough to ensure that the coding and the tests complied with the design document instructions and that there are no known serious problems or glitches in the software. A successful walkthrough will enable the CSU code, test data, design document, and test case description to be placed in a software development file and transferred into the project support library for component software testing. Once transferred, the software and associated documentation should be under the contractor's developmental configuration control procedures. When this event is over and considered successful, CM will ensure that the SDF is updated by approved changes only. Project members who need to review a particular unit can do so on a read-only basis at any time. The master, however, can be updated only by personnel authorized by the project manager, which is usually the project librarian or chief programmer, and performed by CM.

In addition to the code and unit test activity, additional test descriptions and test cases are prepared by software engineering for the following test and integration phases described.

SOFTWARE COMPONENT INTEGRATION AND TESTING, TEST READINESS REVIEW, AND DEVELOPMENTAL CONFIGURATION

The software component (SC) integration and testing segment takes units, combines them to form components, and records the test results as the process is carried out in accordance with test procedures developed during the coding phase. These records will be entered into the SDF for the component being tested and the test results made known to the project members for their reference. Changes made for correction purposes will be processed by CM and entered into the SDF. As the software components are tested and accepted, they will be assigned to the next-higher elements at the computer software configuration item level. As this occurs, test readiness reviews (TRR) will be held to ensure that all the components of a configuration item have been tested properly and are ready for testing. CM will provide the accepted test reports and latest versions of the design documents plus the code lists for these reviews. MIL STD 1521 has a checklist for the TRR that may be referred to or used as a guide to achieve successful reviews.

Components accepted at the TRR are in turn released to the master library (ML) file by CM and are under full review board control for any changes requested.

SOFTWARE CONFIGURATION ITEM PERFORMANCE TESTING, FUNCTIONAL AND PHYSICAL CONFIGURATION AUDIT, AND THE PRODUCT BASELINE

The final segment of the development cycle is the configuration item system-level tests. This is considered the formal test. CIs passing this point are considered deliverable and are entered into the project master file if they were not entered after the TRRs. These CIs are now subject to formal controls both internal to the project and external to the developer's domain.

Also during this phase one will be preparing the final form of the product specifications for each CI as well as the version description documents. In addition, the final test report will be edited and made ready for the last of the formal reviews, the configuration audits.

The configuration audits, managed by CM and chaired by the developer's and customer's project managers, are designed to ensure that the coded and documented software, as described in the formal test reports, verify that the requirements stated in the software requirements specifications have been met. This is known as the functional configuration audit. Subsequently, when this audit has been authenticated by the customer, the physical configuration audit will verify and validate that the coded software has been described adequately in the documentation that will be delivered with it. Thus the product specification, which must also provide traceability up to the SRS, and the version description documents must reflect the code to be delivered.

The product specification and the version description documents plus the manuals that will be delivered with the software product are placed under formal CM controls so that almost all changes will require the customer's review and approval prior to their incorporation.

SOFTWARE MAINTENANCE AND SUPPORT

With the conclusion of the FCA and the PCA, the product baseline will have been established and the operational phase, also known as the software support phase, will begin. This third phase of the software life cycle, as noted in Chapter 16, requires detail planning that should start early in the software development cycle.

The CM process continues into the operational environment. The procedures and the records established during development are carried forward by the designated software support activity to ensure the integrity of such software until phased out of its assigned environment.

COTS—COMMERCIAL OFF-THE-SHELF SOFTWARE ENVIRONMENT

The previous sections described the internal development of software. Commercial off-the-shelf software products are those bought directly from the developers or through distributors and retail establishments for use in specific applications such as accounts payable, tax preparation, word processing, and graphics presentations. There is a shared relationship of trust between buyer and seller in the purchase and use of this type of software.

In the commercial off-the-shelf (COTS) software environment the need to develop error-free software is very high because the software development firms are selling their products to a faceless public, through distributors, value-added retailers, and dealers. Such products must work the first time. Indeed, success is built on error-free products that are user friendly to the level of user procuring them. Thus those who develop and sell to the open market have developed methods that, although not addressed as configuration management, come very close to the intent, purpose, and concepts that we are discussing here and may be embodied within a quality assurance or product integrity activity.

Most of the open-market developers copyright and treat their products as corporate assets. They thus rely on the ability to reuse and modify these products to meet the market's demands. This requires good CM techniques of controlled documentation, good traceability, and good maintenance/customer service.

The buyer of COTS is obligated by law to protect the copyrights of procured software. The buyer's CM activity has a responsibility to "log in" the procured software, maintain a written functional description, test and demonstration results, correspondence pertaining to licenses, permission to change or modify the software, and so on, in a controlled file for the use of and reference by the buyer's software personnel. In other words, CM treats COTS in almost the same manner as developed software for identification, control, and status accounting.

EXERCISE

1. Describe how you would perform the software engineering process for a moderate-size project (10,000 lines), how you would interface with the system engineering process, and how the CM process would be employed.

CHAPTER 7

The Planning and Organization of Configuration Management

The planning and organization of the CM activity within a firm, a division, a line of business, or a program involves many considerations. The most important consideration is the scope and magnitude of the environment in which the activity will be performed. The ultimate responsibility for CM rests with the highest level of management within the organizational structure. This may be the president, the division general manager, or the program manager. The activity may be relegated to everyone, a group such as product support, or an individual or individuals within projects.

The CM activity, no matter how well structured, cannot exist without written and agreed-on procedures. The CM plan may well outline the procedures for the project only, the line of business, the division, or the firm or corporation. At whatever level, it should be the guiding document for all those involved in the project, including the customer—some of whom like to know how the software they ordered is being developed.

THE POSITION OF CM IN THE PROJECT ORGANIZATION

The recognition of the CM activity in the organizational structure of a project is important. The higher the level of this recognition, the better able is the project to perform the activity in a cost-effective mode and maintain the focal point for communication of the developing software product.

The configuration management activity for software is responsible for all matters relating to CM. Therefore, to attain the greatest degree of visibility and receive guidance and advice from CM as the configuration of the software product evolves, configuration management should be recognized by the program/project manager.

The program organization chart illustrated in Figure 7.1 is typical for a hardware-oriented project. It does, however, provide for software development. Most hardware products today have some software, ranging from a small read-only memory to many thousands of source lines of code. In the latter case, the software may well be driving the hardware and thus must be a prominent entity in the project organization.

The functional interface illustrated in Figure 7.4 (discussed later) demonstrates the importance of CM as a point of communication during the evolution of the item's configuration.

Is there a need for company-level performance of CM? This writer has been involved in this level of CM for over 25 years, and it has proven to be a worthwhile focal point for the dissemination of information regarding CM throughout the corporate entities. As mentioned later, the company-level function can be an important contributor during proposal/estimate or bidding phases, negotiations, and the start-up of large or small projects.

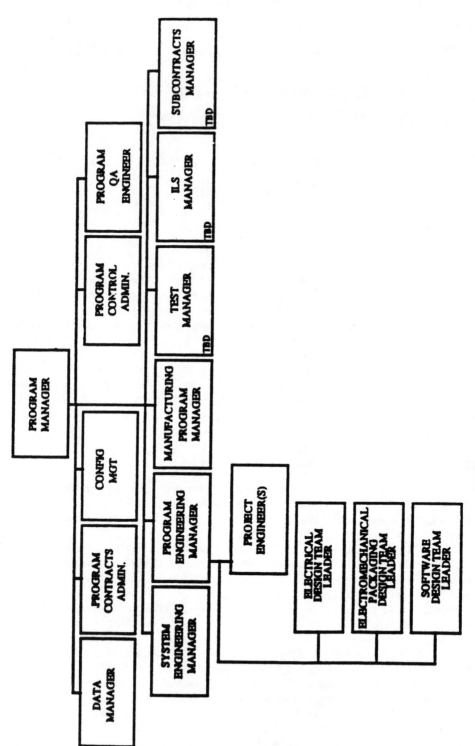

Figure 7.1 Program organization chart.

On the other hand, to be truly beneficial to the company's well-being, the CM process must be performed at a level that bears the authority to produce and implement directives and practices that will allow cost-effective compliance to customer requirements. If the process is being performed at a second or third level within the company organization, this will readily be accomplished. At lower levels, the infusion of intermediaries, no matter how well intentioned they are to communicate the needs of the CM process to the top, will make the process less effective. Fortunately, CM can be performed at any level and will be effective.

The proposal, prepared in estimating or bidding to requirements set forth by a customer, is where the CM process is first described for the project. The person assigned the CM task for a proposal should be able to ensure that the CM process is recognized by the program manager and prepare the CM plan, describing how CM will be conducted for the project. The responsible CM person should ensure that the text describes the hardware and software tasks that will be integrated, identified, and controlled. The cost estimate for performance should be based on previous projects of like size and character in support of the bid. The CM person should also advise the proposal manager—who well may become program manager—on problems and risks that may appear during the proposal stages, such as the impact of changes on a certain unit of equipment (for example, "You mean if we have a change request to enlarge the communications antenna, we will have to enlarge the hole size in the aircraft, too?" or "How are we going to add another million bites of software when there is no more room in the equipment to add another disk?").

Thus, if the position of the CM process on the organization chart is close to the program manager's level, it will most likely draw little or no comment from a buyer's source selection team. If it is several levels below the program manager, then in most cases it will draw questions as to why it appears more like a clerical process than an authoritative entity.

CM INTERFACE AND COMMUNICATION

The organization chart in Figure 7.1 shows the CM process along with other functions that CM will interface with at various times throughout a project's life at the program management level. These include contacts administration, program administration, and quality assurance.

A heavy interface will exist between CM and system engineering in the early phases of the life cycle, especially up to the point that the system has been decomposed for the hardware and the software elements and a handoff has been made by system engineering to program engineering.

For configuration management, interfacing and communicating with the program engineering function is most important. This function is charged with the communication of requirements for engineering documentation including that for software. In addition, the program engineering function must provide for the review board process and the scheduling of formal reviews and audits in accordance with the desires of the customer when specified to do so.

CM supplies the "road map" for the documented identification of software hierarchy to the test manager and reports the status of documentation and subsequent code relative to completeness, release for test, and changes pending or incorporated. In addition, CM and the test activity should have a procedure for the preparation of change requests, establishing their priorities and forwarding them for processing. This is especially important if testing is a 24-hour activity and immediate action must be taken to satisfy a problem such as a priority one—the system is down and there is no known way to circumvent the problem at 2:00

A.M. Or one could encounter requests from a 24-hour testing activity located in some remote part of the world. How will the changes be processed and communicated in a priority-one situation?

Integrated logistics support [(ILS)] provides service and maintenance to the customer for hardware and software. CM, again, provides the software hierarchy and reports the status of documents such as the product specification and version description for each CI as well as the status of change activity during development. This will enable the logistics people to plan for software support after delivery of the software product.

CM has a primary role in the application of computer-aided/acquisition logistics support (CALS), which includes the electronic transmission of digital data, text, and graphics to any designated point. This element of information systems engineering also includes data input and output, security of the data transmitted, and the ability to confidently utilize the data or software received. CM procedures provide for ensuring transmission of approved/released data, changes and change instructions for previously submitted data, identification and protection of data received, subsequent incorporation of changes received, and finally status maintenance of all data received and transmitted. This may well be a joint effort among several activities, but it cannot be ignored.

CM provides the subcontracts administrator with the CM portion of the statement of work or instructions to a subcontractor for the conduct of CM. This will include submission of required documents for review, approval and release to a given baseline, submission of change requests requiring buyer review and approval, establishment of a change review board, and a plan that will indicate how the subcontractor is to perform the CM process. If this information is not provided, little or no CM instruction will be forwarded.

Project engineers, as illustrated in Figure 7.1, develop assigned tasks. Software engineers are included in this group. CM maintains a constant dialogue with these people, who also include coders, librarians, and testing technicians, to promulgate the CM procedures applicable to the project, the status of documents and changes, the receipt and processing of change requests, notification of change review board meetings, and notification of design reviews and audits and their results.

A project organization should be considered from a functional point of view and be tailorable to fit the size of a given program. Many functions can be combined or even enlarged depending on the type of contract or agreement the program is working under. Figure 7.2 depicts a very tailored project for a simple hardware/software product.

What kind of organizational structure is needed for an all-software project? Figure 7.3 illustrates a normal structure—not full size but not small. The functions of proposal/program manager remain, as do those of data, configuration management, program control, and software QA. At the engineering level, the system engineer is integral as leader of the sys-

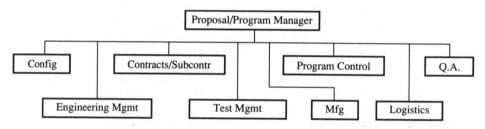

Figure 7.2　Tailored program for hardware and software.

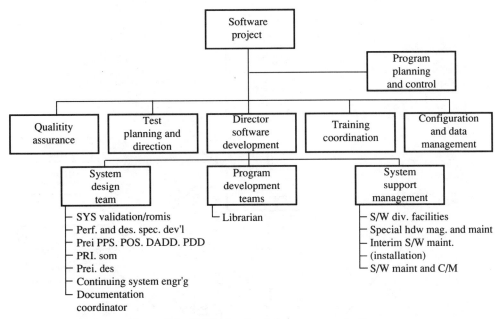

Figure 7.3   Tailored software program organization.

tem design team. The program engineering manager block now becomes the director, software development function. Test management is of course most necessary. ILS management may well become system support management depending on the objectives or customer requirements for support of the software product once delivered.

The interrelationships of CM to other company functions exist within the project, as noted in Figure 7.4. If there is a company CM function, then the heads of contracts, QA, engineering, manufacturing, test, and ILS will interact at the policy and procedure levels and must agree on what the functions will and can contribute to the success of the projects in house. Figure 7.5 is a model of the interfaces CM has during a given project. Note that some interfaces in effect in the beginning phases disappear in the middle and reappear at the end. It is thus important for purposes of communication that CM understands what the other functions are responsible for and what their authority is.

THE CONFIGURATION MANAGEMENT PLAN

The key to a successful CM endeavor is the plan written during the earliest stages of program preparation (or, for government projects, during the proposal or shortly thereafter) detailing how CM will be performed. There are a number of CM and CM plan outlines from a variety of sources, including the U.S. Department of Defense, the U.S. Federal Aviation Agency (FAA), National Aeronautics and Space Administration (NASA), and other government agencies. In addition, the IEEE has a *Standard for Software Configuration Management Plans*, IEEE STD 828-1990 [19], as well as a guidebook, IEEE STD 1042-1986, *Guide to Software Configuration Management* [20], which includes four fully written CMPs for various functions. The British government also has a standard for software CM, as does the British Electronic Engineering Association.

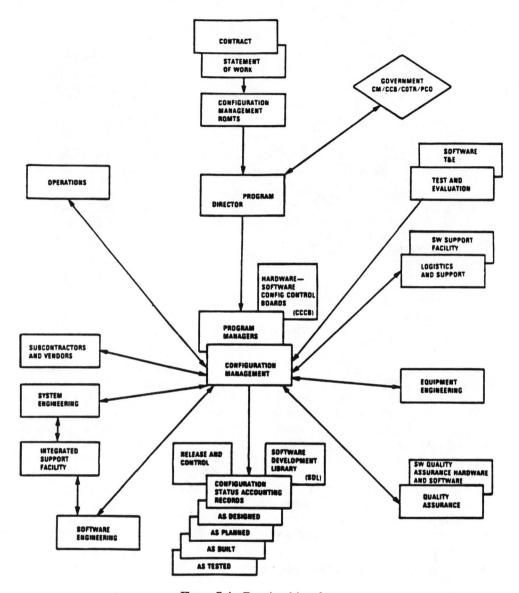

Figure 7.4 Functional interface.

The basic plans follow the same outline:

- Scope and purpose
- Organization and resources
- CM activities for
    Identification
    Control

Conceptual	R&A	Design	Code · U/TST	Integr/Test	Syst/Test · Accpt
Marketing/Sales	Marketing/Sales	System Engr	Quality Assur	Quality Assur	Quality Assur
Contracts	System Engr	Design Engr	SSS	SSS	SSS
Accounting	Design Engr	Quality Assur	Test	Test	Test
System Engr	Quality Assur	SSS	SW Supt	SW Supt	SW Supt
Design Engr	Data Mgmt	Data Mgmt		Accounting	SSF
• • • • •	ILS	ILS			Marketing Sales
Cust. CM					
Sub Contr CM	Accounting	Accounting			Accounting
	SSE	Test			

Figure 7.5 Functional interface by phase.

>   Status accounting
>   Configuration audits
- Subcontractor control
- CM milestones/schedules
- Notes and appendixes

Some variations include:

- Configuration traceability [21]—STD 1456
- Interface management [21]—STD 1456
- Support environment and tools [22]—NASA SMAP DID M920
- Controlled storage and release management [22]
- Implementation schedule [23]—STD 483
- Plan maintenance [19]—IEEE STD 828-1990

The preparation of a plan may seem simple enough when one reads the requirement and receives the assignment to write. But simplicity goes away very quickly when the "pen touches the paper." One's first inclination in this situation is to find a plan that has already been written and preferably approved or accepted by a customer. One will then begin to "doctor" the words to fit the latest proposal effort or contract requirement by changing names and faces. The result of this, too many times, is that the plan is rejected because it does not address the current program or does not appear to have been written for the program toward which it was intended to be implemented. Figure 7.6 lists 10 common errors found in writing plans.

These are risks one must be aware of when using past plans. On the other hand, it can be done and there is no law against it, especially if one wrote the previous plan.

The principal purpose in preparing a CM plan is to design and document the CM process early in the software life cycle so that the process is identified and accepted by the project team prior to the start of development. In writing the plan, one must keep in mind that it is not only aimed at assuring the customer that one knows what one is doing but it is also intended to guide the writer and those who are assigned to the CM task and those on the

1   **ERROR**
>   Plagiarized plan from another projects plan.
>   **RESULT**
>   Plan many times does not address all of the requirements of the
>   current project and may not be tailored to that project.

2   **ERROR**
>   Plan written for proposal, but not updated at contract award.
>   **RESULT**
>   Does not reflect new/modified requirements negotiated with the
>   customer. Also has been written more to sell SCM rather than
>   provide the necessary direction to the project in implementing SCM.

3   **ERROR**
>   SCM milestones/schedule not kept up to date with current project
>   changes.
>   **RESULT**
>   Provides misleading information to project in preparing for and
>   responding to scheduled reviews, audits and submission dates.

4   **ERROR**
>   Incorrect spec/doc tree and or software hierarchy.
>   **RESULT**
>   Can cause more or less documents to be prepared. Causes
>   uncertainty as to next higher level document or software element
>   thus incorrect status reporting, scheduling, manloading etc.

5   **ERROR**
>   Software change process procedure/data flow not complete, vague, or
>   too restrictive.
>   **RESULT**
>   Poor and costly change process, slow turn around or avoidance of
>   the process because it's too restrictive. Causes loss of time, and
>   ill will within the project

6   **ERROR**
>   Applicable Company/Project procedures for SCM are not referenced,
>   summarized or included.
>   **RESULT**
>   Violates SCMP requirement [Std 828, Mil Std 2167]. Leaves customer
>   project personnel and responsible SCM Mgr in the dark in adhering
>   to stated or desired internal requirements.

7   **ERROR**
>   Requirement for Status Accounting records, maintenance and
>   reporting are vague or inconclusive.
>   **RESULT**
>   The GIGO syndrome is in effect. Record data elements will vary and
>   report formats not consistent. The records may or may not be
>   maintained in a way to insure accurate query information to the
>   project.

Figure 7.6   Ten most common errors in software configuration management plans.

8   ERROR
       No provisions for Sub Contractor/Supplier requirements or control
       when there are known or anticipated Sub Contractors/Suppliers.
     RESULT
       The Sub Contractor/Supplier is left to their own methods which may
       not be compatible with the project SCMP. Software documentation
       and code will be received as uncontrolled and cause vast
       integration problems. Provisions for rights in data can also be
       affected and vital data not supplied to the prime/principle
       contractor.

9   ERROR
       No provisions for archiving or storage at close out of the project.
     RESULT
       Lost or misplaced documents and code. Reuse is grossly affected.
       Inability to reconstruct for reuse or even demonstration.

10   ERROR
       No provisions for maintenance or support of delivered documents and
       code.
     RESULT
       May result in lack of a baseline for changes. Unnecessary time
       spent in correcting or modifying documents and code. No history
       retained for other maintainers for refer to. Could require a total
       rewrite of critical software - at great expense to developer
       especially if delivered with a warranty.

Figure 7.6   *(Continued)*

project that have a constant interface with CM. Thus some explanation of a typical plan's contents follows.

Scope and Purpose

This is the introduction to the plan and explains to the reader what the project is, the objectives of the project, the interfacing entities that will be involved, the reason the plan is being written—in accordance with what standard—and the specified outline. This section may also include an overview of the CM function. In some outlines it may be a separate section, but in any case it is a good opportunity to expand on the philosophy and methodology that is usually employed in implementing CM on any given software project—especially the one being written about.

Organization and Resources

This section describes the organization chart of the program/project in graphic and narrative form and indicates where CM is positioned at the program level and at the company level—to to identify who in the company has overall responsibility for CM. The resources segment of this section describes the number and skill levels of the people who will conduct configuration management during a specified software development life cycle. It also includes responsibilities and authority of CM as well as the other interfacing and supporting organizations, such as CM authority versus that of software quality. In addition, the qualifications of the CM personnel are stated: that is, number of years in CM or related fields such as drafting release and control or minimum qualifications cited in the company's position description documents for the job of, say, librarian. One would also specify any unique requirements for the position such as long-term on-site support—away from the home base—security levels above the normal ones required, or special knowledge or skills required (e.g., knowledge of Ada or C++ programming languages).

CM Activities—Identification

In this activity the process of identifying the configuration items and their components in a documented manner is described (see Figures 7.7 and 7.8) [24]. This includes the capturing of the software documents and specifications as they are presented to a duly constituted review board and accepted for further activity in the software development process. The standards required to produce the documentation are described, along with any special processing techniques such as desktop publishing or documentation as a by-product of the programming process.

This section also describes the manner in which the document numbers will be obtained, applied, and controlled; how titles will be constructed; and how the documents will be marked, including the format of the cover page and page numbering both during development and at time of shipment.

Requirements traceability is of great concern at this point because of its importance to the concurrent engineering or integrated product development process, total quality management, and statistical process controls prevalent in today's quality assurance programs.

Requirements traceability refers to the ability to trace a documented path from the lowest-level unit up to the system/segment specification or customer requirements document/statement and also the ability to do this in reverse—a downward trace. The methodology is based on a parent-child relationship otherwise known as "used one" or "next-higher

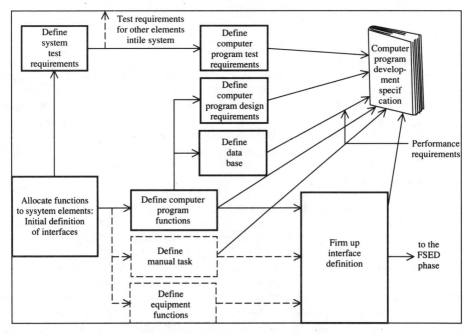

Figure 7.7 Development specification.

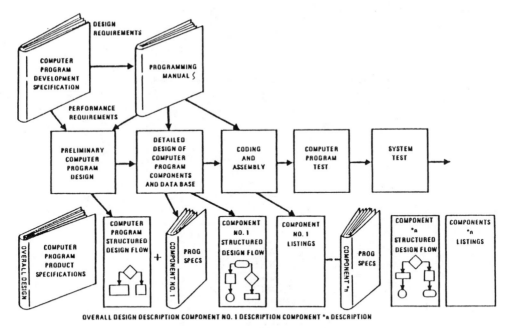

Figure 7.8   Document development flow.

software element." Thus an element always reports to a higher element unless a code indicates that this is the top element and always breaks down to a lower level of element(s) until a code indicates that there is no lower level. The system gets more complicated when interfacing elements are introduced and changes start to occur. Thus the whole operation, while very necessary and an invaluable aid, is also quite expensive. Quite a bit of tradeoff analysis will therefore be necessary in determining whether the function is worthwhile (it is) and thus should be promoted.

CM Activities—Control

This is an important activity. One may be called on to describe many different functions related to software change control or simply to provide a flow chart of the control process. It is at this point, however, that the levels of control are identified and approval authority is described.

A principal requirement is to describe how the software documents and subsequent code are released to the next-higher level of effort or into the formal test environment. In other words, when is control initiated on a document, specification, or plan, and by what means is it placed under configuration control? Once this has been described, a narrative description of the control process, illustrated by a flow chart such as the one in Figure 7.9 [27] will be prepared.

In support of the flow chart, the forms to be used and the intent and purpose of each form are also described. A montage of the forms used is effective and saves pages, especially when one is faced with a page count restriction. Figure 7.10 provides examples of the several forms that may be used in a change control process.

If one is using electronic media, then the description will include the screen format and final product format. As we shall see later, they can be different. Figure 7.11 illustrates

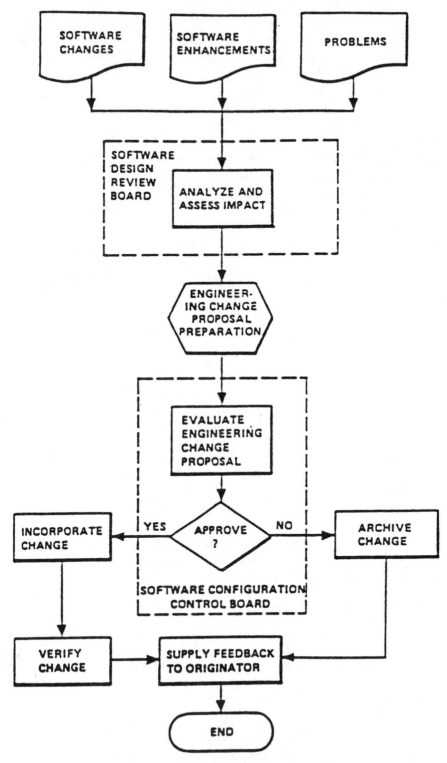

Figure 7.9 Sample software change formats.

PROGRAM TROUBLE REPORT

PTR NO._____

PTR

TITLE/DESCRIPTION			PROJECT IDENTIFIER	CONTRACT NO.
PROBLEM DATE/TIME	SITE	COMPUTER/TERMINAL	OPERATING SYSTEM	
TEST NAME	FAILED OR SUSPECTED ELEMENT (NAME)		ELEMENT ID NO.	VER/REV
RELATED S/W DOCUMENT TITLE			S/W DOC. NO.	CURR REV

PROBLEM DESCRIPTION:

ACTION REQUESTED/RECOMMENDED

SUBMITTED BY/DATE	ASSIGNED TO/DATE	PRIORITY H M L	SCHED. COMPL. DATE

SOFTWARE REVIEW BOARD DISPOSITION ☐ APPROVE ☐ DISAPPROVE ☐ DEFER   DATE: CODE:

SRB CHAIRPERSON	DATE	SRB MEMBER	DATE	SRB MEMBER	DATE	SRB MEMBER	DATE

DISPOSITION:

S/W DOC(S) REQ CHANGE ☐ Y ☐ N	DCR OR SCN NO.(S)	ATTACH TO SCO NO.(S)	RELATED ECO NO.(S)

Figure 7.10(a)   Problem/trouble report.

SOFTWARE CHANGE ORDER   **SCO NO.**_____

PAGE _____   OF _____

SOFTWARE ELEMENT NAME	VER/REV	IDENTIFICATION NO.	NEXT HIGHER LEVEL ID NO.	NEW VER/REV

SCO

REQUESTED BY	DATE	PROJECT IDENTIFIER	ECP/SCP/SEP NO.	CLASS ☐ I ☐ II	CONTRACT NO.

TOP LEVEL S/W PROGRAM NAME	TOP LEVEL ID NO.	OTHER USING PROJECTS

PTR(S) ATTACHED:

1. SUMMARY OF CHANGE AND REASON PER ATTACHED PTRs: (ATTACH ADDITIONAL PAGES AS NECESSARY)

2. ACTION REQUIRED: (ATTACH DCR(S) IF AFFECTED)

    A. SOFTWARE ELEMENTS: _____

    B. DOCUMENTATION: (ATTACH DCR(S) IF AFFECTED)_____

    C. TESTS: _____

3. COST ESTIMATE OF CHANGE	☐ INCREASE ☐ DECREASE ☐ N/A	4. RELATIONSHIP TO OTHER CHANGES: (REF. RELATED H/W ECO)
HRS $		

5. SCHEDULE:	6. EFFECTIVITY

7. IMPACT ON:

	Y	N		Y	N		Y	N		Y	N
			SCHEDULE			TEST SOFTWARE			DELIVERABLE HDW			HOST/TARGET COMPUTER
			CUSTOMER SPEC			SOFTWARE TOOLS			FACILITY/SITE			SW DOCUMENTATION
			SUBCONTRACT			FIRMWARE			TRAINING			DATA ITEM
			SUPPORT SOFTWARE			TEST EQUIP HDW			SW MANUALS			OTHER:

SOFTWARE REVIEW BOARD DISPOSITION ☐ APPROVE ☐ DISAPPROVE ☐ DEFER DATE: CODE:

SRB CHAIRPERSON	DATE	SRB MEMBER	DATE	SRB MEMBER	DATE	SRB MEMBER	DATE

SOFTWARE CHANGE CONTROL BOARD DISPOSITION ☐ APPROVE ☐ DISAPPROVE ☐ DEFER DATE: CODE:

SOFTWARE ENGR.	DATE	CONFIGURATION MGMT.	DATE	SOFTWARE TEST	DATE		DATE
S/W TEAM LEADER	DATE	PROGRAM MGMT.	DATE	SYSTEMS ENGR.	DATE		DATE
PROJECT S/W MGMT.	DATE	QUALITY ASSURANCE	DATE	PRODUCT SUPPORT	DATE		DATE

Figure 7.10(b)   Software change order.

SOFTWARE CHANGE ORDER   SCO NO._____
CONTINUATION SHEET

PAGE   OF

SOFTWARE ELEMENT NAME	VER · REV	IDENTIFICATION NO	NEXT HIGHER LEVEL ID NO	NEW VER/REV

SCO

Figure 7.10   *(Continued)*

PROBLEM/CHANGE REPORT

PCR NO.__________

SYSTEM/PROJ ________________ PAGE _____ OF _____

PCR

TITLE/DESCRIPTION			SITE		CONTRACT NO.
PROBLEM DATE/TIME	FAILED OR SUSPECTED ELEMENT (NAME)		ELEMENT ID NO.	VER/REV	NEXT HIGHER LEVEL ID NO.
TEST NAME	RELATED DOCUMENT (TITLE)		DOCUMENT NO.		REV
SUBMITTED BY DATE	ECP NO.	CLASS ☐ I ☐ II	CUSTOMER CONCURRENCE IN CLASSIFICATION DATE		EFFECTIVITY

PROBLEM DESCRIPTION:

SUMMARY OF CHANGE AND REASON:

—SOFTWARE ELEMENTS AND DOCUMENTS CHANGED

SOFTWARE ELEMENT NAME OR DOCUMENT TITLE	IDENTIFICATION NO.	NEXT HIGHER LEVEL ID NO	NEW VER/REV

ACTION REQUIRED TO CLOSE:

IMPACT ON: ☐ PSL ☐ ML	Y	N		Y	N		Y	N		Y	N	
			SCHEDULE			TEST EQUIPMENT/SW			DELIVERABLE HDW			SW DOCUMENTATION
			SUBCONTRACT			FIRMWARE			TRAINING			SUPPORT SW/SW TOOLS
			DATA ITEM			FACILITY/SITE			SW MANUALS			OTHER:

SRB DISPOSITION ☐ **APPROVE** ☐ **DISAPPROVE** ☐ **DEFER UNTIL:**

SRB CHAIRPERSON DATE	SYSTEMS ENGR DATE	SRB MEMBER DATE	SRB MEMBER DATE
PROBLEM/CHANGE TYPE	ASSIGNED TO DATE	PRIORITY SCHED DATE	ANALYSIS TIME DATE COMPLETE (HRS)

SCCB DISPOSITION ☐ **APPROVE** ☐ **DISAPPROVE** ☐ **DEFER UNTIL:**

SCCB CHAIRPERSON DATE	SW PROJECT LEADER DATE	SYSTEMS ENGR DATE	PROGRAM MGMT DATE
CONFIGURATION MGMT DATE	QUALITY ASSURANCE DATE	SOFTWARE TEST DATE	ILS MGMT DATE

CLOSURE ACTION

INCORPORATED BY DATE	VERIFIED BY DATE	INCORP. TIME (HRS) VERIF. TIME (HRS)	CLOSED BY DATE

Figure 7.11 Problem/change report.

PROBLEM/CHANGE REPORT

PCR No. VWW-0009
Page   1

Title/Description: SADDS PDL EXTRACTOR ENHANCEMENT
Problem Date: 02/28/91   Submitted By: L. L" _____   Site: _____   Library ML

Problem Description
An increasing number of users are complaining about the PDL extraction system. It is
currently not flexible enough to handle
the type of Ada PDL being written. Possibly need to increase
the number of files held in memory to speed up the extraction process.

Recommendations
Need to save 4 rather than 3 files when extracting PDL. Algorithm for the unit
extractions needs to handle some of the more obscure instances. Update the SADDS User
Guide as needed.

CSUs Affected	CC #	Nxt Higher CC #	Versions Old	New
FILE_MANAGER (ADA BODY)	1980018	1980016	0005	
LINE_MANAGER (ADA SPEC)	1980026	1980025	0005	
LINE_MANAGER (ADA BODY)	1980027	1980025	0005	
KEYWORD_SECTION_MGR (ADA SPEC)	1980023	1980022	0005	
KEYWORD_SECTION_MGR (ADA BODY)	1980024	1980022	0005	
UNIT_MANAGER (ADA SPEC)	1980020	1980019	0005	
UNIT_MANAGER (ADA BODY)	1980021	1980019	0006	
SADDS USER GUIDE (DOC)	1980003	1980000	A	

Assigned To: Date:
Priority: Scheduled Completion Date:

RELATED DOCUMENTS
SRS: T   SDD: T   System Test Plan: F   Software Test Plan: F   CSOM: F   SDP: F

Classification Category: Software

PROBLEM TYPE
S/W Requirements: T   Interface Detail: F   Data: F   Logic Error: F
Conventions/Standards: F   Environment: F   Math: F   Other: T

SRB Dispostion: (N = Analysis, A = Approve, D = Disapprove,
SCCB Disposition: F = Defer, C = Cancelled)

SRB Chairperson   SRB Member   SRB Member   SRB Member

CCB Chairperson   SDTL   System Eng Mgr   Program Eng Mgr

Software Test   Quality Assurance   Configuration Mgmt.

Verified — See Database   Closed   See Database

Figure 7.11   *(Continued)*

CCB Memberships - Typical

Development Level CCB Members

SOFTWARE	HARDWARE
• PROJECT SOFTWARE MANAGER*	• PROGRAM MANAGER*
• CONFIGURATION MANAGER	• CONFIGURATION MANAGER
• QUALITY ASSURANCE	• QUALITY ASSURANCE
• SOFTWARE SYSTEMS ENGR.	• RELIABILITY/MAINTAINABILITY
• PROGRAMMER(S) (A/R)	• MANUFACTURING (ALL)
• TEST MANAGER	• E&M ENGINEERING
• O/M (WHEN APPLICABLE)	• CHIEF ENGINEER/ SYSTEMS ENGINEER
	• PRODUCT SUPPORT

*PSM OR PM ARE OFFICIALLY CHAIRMEN OF A CCB. HOWEVER, IN MANY INSTANCES THIS RESPONSIBILITY IS DELEGATED TO THE CONFIGURATION MANAGER.

Figure 7.12   CCB membership list.

this difference and the conversion from a screen format to a printed document. The data elements associated with each form are also described, including their contribution to query and status accounting reports.

Finally a description of the review process conducted by the configuration control board is described, including the membership of the board and the function of each member. The role of the CCB chairperson is also important, as is the authority invested in the board by the company and the project manager. Providing the names and titles of prospective CCB members, as illustrated in Figure 7.12, is also a good strategy because it demonstrates that one is thinking and planning ahead. It should also give credence to the high integrity of the proposed board, whose members will make the monumental decisions.

CM Activities—Status Accounting

One's plan for the development or use of the current status accounting system must not be understimated. Status accounting is fast becoming an important element in determining the status of the latest revisions and changes. More important, however, is the reporting of document activity (number of document numbers assigned, number of documents approved or released, number of changes processed, number approved, number incorporated). Also important is the history of each document from the time it received a number to the current state of the last revision. Figure 7.13 illustrates a compendium of screen formats that can be queried or printed.

ALL STRs
SOFTWARE TRANSFER NOTICES

STR	MODULE NAME	MODULE CC NQ	PROCEDURE NAME	GEN	R E S P RC	T L D R RC	CLOSE DATE
							3/22/85

ALL PTRS

SCO ID PTR DCR NAME	MODULE NAME	MODULE CC NO	PROCEDURE NAME	GEN	PTR ISSUE DATE	SCO ISSUE DATE	DCR ISSUE DATE	T L D R BP	P R T H	DELAYED INCORP DATE	APPROVAL DATE	CLOSE DATE	CLOSE GEN	S T A T	RELATED CHGS

DOCUMENT HISTORY REPORT FORMAT -

[] QUERY ONLY   [X] REPORT ONLY   [] BOTH

D O C U M E N T   H I S T O R Y

REPORT DATE: 890613   PROGRAM NUMBER: 528   PROGRAM NAME: AN/ALZ-13X, COMMAND MODULE

REPORT DEFINITION FOR TIME PERIOD: INCEPTION TO DATE

DOCUMENT NO.	REV DOC/APP		EVENT	EVENT NUMBER	EVENT STATUS	ASSIGN DATE	APPVL DATE	BASIC EFFECT	RETROFIT FROM	THRU	DOCUMENT TITLE
1234564											SIGNAL PROCESSOR MAIN MODULE CODE
	D	D	SCO	123477	PENDING	890601					
	C		SCO	123456	APPROVED	890601	890608	0001	0001	0025	
			PSO	AAA0002	RESUME	890601	890605				
	B	B	SCO	123777	APPROVED	890317	890404	0001	0001	0010	
	A	A	SCO	122333	APPROVED	890226	890303	0001	0001	0010	
	-		REL	AAA1234	APPROVED	890109	890121	0001			
	-				ENG-USE	881228					
	-				ASSIGNED	881221					

Figure 7.13 Sample status accounting reports.

Query capability is becoming vital to instant information needs of the project. "When in doubt, query it" is a good way to provide service to the project because this strategy portrays the current status, even if an event occurred seconds before the query was made. Software tools such as SQL make all this possible. Also vital is the ability to prescribe the format in which the data are to be printed. Known as query by form (QBF), this technique can generate a format that may satisfy a customer requirement or a requirement within the project.

The plan must therefore be explicit in what will be available and how the data will be collected, processed, and reported in accordance with the customer's requirements and those of project and company management.

Above all, the plan should demonstrate the user friendliness of the status accounting system. It must be evident that it is available to everyone who has a terminal and access to the system, from the president of the company or firm to the newest clerk.

CM Activity—Configuration Audit

The plan should show how the product of the development process will be examined to ensure that the testing activity records verify that the requirements for the product's performance have been met and that the documentation that will accompany the software product represents the software being delivered, sold, and distributed. The plan should also describe how the audit will be conducted, the authority of those conducting the audit, and the people who will determine that the product baseline has been established. The checklists or guidance provided by the government or IEEE standards can be most valuable in planning the audit activity.

CM Activity—Interface Control

The fact that interface design specifications and interface design documents are placed under configuration control requires that changes made to these documents be processed in the same manner as the other software documentation. The focal point for this activity is the interface control working group (ICWG), which is composed of representatives and experts from other interfacing systems, associate contractors, subcontractors, and the customer. CM supports the ICWG activity for the establishment of interface control document baselines and processing and incorporation of the approved changes. Figure 7.14 [25] illustrates a typical flow of the interface control process. The only standard in which it is fully addressed as a requirement is MIL STD 483A. The plan should address this activity even if not specifically mentioned in the statement of work or other instructions document. It is also fundamental to the open-system architecture of many of today's commercial software systems. There is always an interface to be contended with during development.

CM Activity—Subcontractor Control

The plan describes how the provisions of the prime contract or requirements of the buyer are passed to the seller or subcontractor(s). If there are several subcontractors, each must be addressed as to the magnitude of requirements that will be imposed. It is a good idea to present as an appendix the terms and conditions and statement of work for each subcontract.

The role of CM and other supporting functions is spelled out in the subcontractor section of the plan, including the schedules for receipt of data, design reviews, and audits.

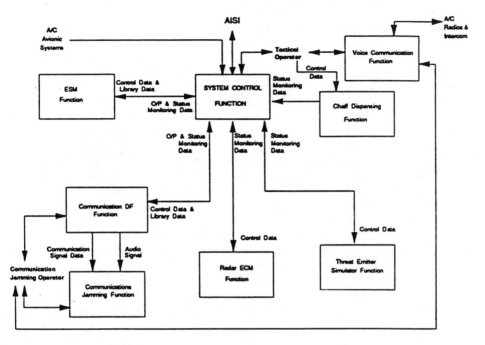

Figure 7.14   Sample top level functional block diagram.

The review process for the subcontractor's CM plan, in addition to other procedures, is also spelled out. (Data management provides the procedures for the review and approval of all data items, including subcontractors' specifications.)

Other sections of a CM plan may include the significant milestones to be met by CM, such as the formal design reviews, SSR, PDR, CDR, and the like, plus other events such as submission of the CMP, release dates for specifications, establishment of the status accounting system, the CCB, and change control processing.

In almost all plans one will be asked to describe the planning for the functional and physical configuration audits usually conducted in accordance with MIL STD 1521, if for no other reason than to use the checklists provided in this document. Normally, the CM manager is the manager of the audits and supports them by providing all the necessary and required documents and assistance, plus follow-up to ensure that action items from the audit are carried out and completed so that the audits will be accepted and the product baseline established.

Appendix 2 contains several examples of CM plan outlines that will meet the needs of a given project. Reference to the source documents are also listed. Most should be available as of now.

Review and approval of a CM plan can go quickly or be very lengthy depending on the customer and the experience of the customer's reviewers. The more experienced the reviewers are in CM, the easier, it appears, for approval to be given even with minor questions of clarification. The less experienced the reviewers, the more questions are asked, especially in the area of procedure and definition. Of course, if one has not written a good document, the experienced reviewer will kill it immediately while the inexperienced may be more polite and ask a few far-reaching questions before rejecting it.

In some instances there may be no specific requirement for a plan, but as in so many other processes to be performed a plan can provide the necessary steps for success. Many times this writer has suggested that seminar attendees write a plan for their current project to get the experience and practice in following the adage of "Write your plan and then work your plan." In these instances a review, even approval, could come during initial program reviews or an early design review that provides evidence of a plan.

Where joint ventures or consortiums are involved, there is usually a round robin of reviews to approve all participants' plans or evidence of such plans. One must also be prepared for multinational reviews in which translation into a reviewing country's language could provide different connotations from those the originating nation intended. If this happens, one must be ready to patiently pursue lengthy negotiation and prepare schedules accordingly.

The bottom line, however, is not to take anything for granted and write for approval or recognition. A checklist is also an aid in writing a good plan. To prepare a list, simply turn the topics contained in the outline you are using into questions and then hand them to a friend or peer to use in reviewing your work. It works!

Sometimes a combined hardware and software CM plan will be needed. There are a couple of ways to write such a plan. One way is to write one part for hardware and a second part for software. The second part will be about one third the length of the first part because of the redundancy of activities. Most plans today tend to combine when necessary and separate when one or the other function is not an issue.

For example, combined writing might be used to describe the change processing to be employed, stating:

> For hardware, the approved engineering change order will be the action document for incorporating a change. For software, the approved software change order is the action document.

A combined plan outline from MIL STD 1456 is included in Appendix 2. One must note, however, that if involved in a predominantly firmware project, one writes only to the software requirements and not to the hardware. This is because the "hardware" device is a part in which the software resides and not an assembly.

Finally, the CM plan is a living document, and CM should have the custody and control of the document to maintain it as noted in IEEE STD 828-1990. It should reflect changes to the project, for example, scheduled reviews, baselines and audits, additions of SCIs or deletions of SCIs or additional documents such as an interface control or database document that had not been forecast in the beginning.

EXERCISES

1. Draw an organization chart for a hardware/software project.
2. Explain how you would project the CM activity at the corporate level in relation to that at the project level.
3. Write a CM plan for a software project. Submit to the class for review and comment.
4. Review several CM plans and rank them. Explain your ranking relative to the content and presentation of the plan.

CHAPTER 8

The Configuration Management Activities: Identification

As noted in Chapter 1, there are four if not six primary configuration management activities that not only define configuration management but also guide the functions performed during a software project's life cycle. To reiterate, the primary activities are *identification, control, status accounting,* and *audit.* Two others have been added because this author feels that they are critical to the success of good configuration management. They are *interface control* and *subcontractor control.*

This chapter is devoted to identification. The following chapters cover configuration control [Chapter 9], status accounting [Chapter 10], configuration audit [Chapter 11], interface control [Chapter 12], and subcontractor control [Chapter 13].

THE IDENTIFICATION ACTIVITY

Several tasks are associated with the identification activity, including the development of the proposed software hierarchy as produced by the system and software engineer, the selection of the configuration items to be developed and described in various levels of documentation such as the system specification, the software requirements specification, and others. Once the CIs have been selected, a number of additional tasks are carried out by the system and software engineering and CM activities and later by the project engineering activity and CM. These include developing and releasing the final version of the software hierarchy, establishing a numbering scheme, authoring the required software specifications and documents for the appropriate baseline definition, and transferring or releasing the approved documentation and subsequent code. These tasks are explained in the following section.

CREATING THE SOFTWARE HIERARCHY

The task of creating the software hierarchy is important to CM because it provides the first structural overview of the software system and its elements. Too many times, in the rush to get started, the hierarchy is not developed until the project is well under way, and then it may well be the CM that, in self-defense, constructs one for its own purpose. A hierarchy similar to the one in Figure 8.1 enables CM to preassign document numbers, identify the preparer, keep track of the progress of each block as it matures, and finally estimate the manpower and resources that will be required for the project. It is also from the initial structure that the candidate configuration items are selected.

SELECTING SOFTWARE'S CONFIGURATION ITEMS

The selection of the software's configuration items (CIs) is most important to the decision-making process of the project management and, in many cases, the company or firm. This is especially true if this is the only project of the firm at this point in time. E. R. Buley at Mitre Corporation notes in a draft paper that the selection of CIs "can have a major impact

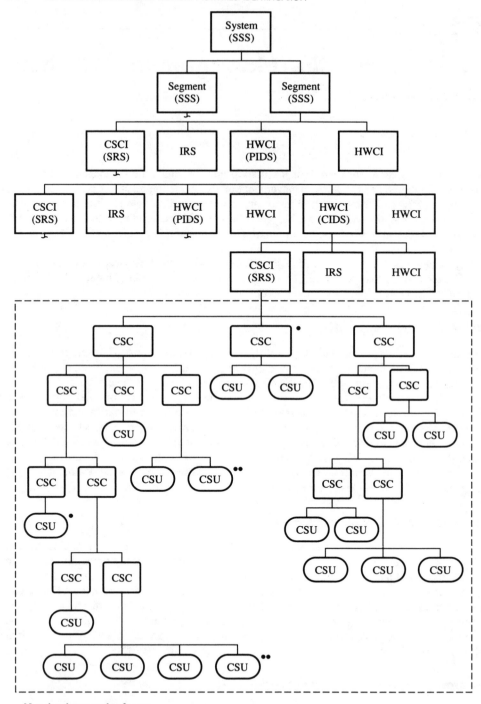

• Non-developmental software
•• Same CSU used by different CSCs

Figure 8.1 Software hierarchy.

on the system life cycle in terms of development, cost and schedule" [28]. Beyond this, the selection of too many CIs creates an inordinate number of specifications and documents. On the other hand too few selections will not provide sufficient visibility to the overall design and development requirements.

The proper selection of CIs is critical to the maintenance activity that follows the development process. The grouping of functions into several dissimilar CIs can cause excessive rework in rebuilding and releasing new versions of the selected CI. Proper selection can simplify the efforts of software engineering, quality assurance, and configuration management during the maintenance and support phase by concentrating related functionality within a CI and thus increasing the chances that change activity will be isolated to software units within the CI. The obvious advantage will be in reduced testing time and reissue of documentation as well as better baseline management and version description preparation.

According to DOD D 5010.19, configuration item [CI] is an aggregation of . . . computer software or any of [its] discrete portions, which satisfies an end-use function . . . It is an item whose performance parameters and physical characteristics must be separately defined and controlled to provide management insight needed to achieve the overall end-use function and performance [9]. This definition has many connotations that must be applied during the selection process.

Simply stated, a CI is a stand-alone, test-alone, use-alone element of software that requires control during development and subsequent use in the field. A good example is a command, control, and communications system used for air traffic control, police dispatching (as in the 911 system), nuclear control, and sensor systems. Additional examples include a compiler, a word processing utility, or an operating system. Depending on size, complexity, and management needs, these items may require several CIs to properly identify and define them. The system usually has the three major components of command, control, and communication. Each is independent in that it can work without another item, but when all items are joined, they form the C3 system. Each component's software is considered a CI, and the connected system is also a CI.

A number of criteria—rules—can be applied to the selection of a CI. They include factors such as the following:

- Multiple use—Is the item/element to be used in several equal or higher-level elements?
- Criticality—Would the failure of this assembly adversely affect security or safety? Would it have a significant financial impact?
- Presence of existing or modified design elements—Have software elements been reused or "borrowed"? This is especially important if an element has already been designated a CI in the current or past environment.
- Interface—Is the element a collection of highly data- or control-independent functions or separate functions that exhibit highly disparate input and output data rates?
- Maintenance—Will the element be maintained by diverse groups at many different locations?
- Function—Is the element one of a kind in that its application is different from that of the primary elements of test software and training/simulation?
- Use of computer off-the-shelf (COTS) or subcontractor—Can the element be procured off the shelf or must it be developed by a subcontractor?
- Generality—Does the element have a general purpose use for many other people/functions (such as arithmetical tools)?
- Schedule/delivery—Can several copies be delivered at different times (i.e., one copy with each equipment unit delivered)?

Some additional criteria or variations on those above include:

- Is the element critical, high risk, and/or a safety item?
- Is the element relative to existing CI?
- Does the element incorporate new technologies not found in existing CI or candidates for CI?
- Does the element interface with other CIs whose configuration is controlled by another organization?
- Will it be reused or designed for reuse?

If all of the answers to the questions are Yes, then the element is designated a CI. Naturally if all answers are No, then no CI. But if the vote is half and half or close to that, the selection committee must make an intelligent management decision. Because of the expense involved in maintaining a CI, it is an important decision, especially if the decision not to designate must be reversed downstream.

Once a software element is designated a CI, it may require

- Discrete/separate specifications/documents, test plans, user/maintenance manuals.
- Customer's review and approval of major changes.
- Detailed Status Accounting and reporting by each CI.
- Traceability from top to bottom of the software hierarchy.
- Individual design reviews.
- Individual qualification testing.
- Individual functional and physical configuration audit.
- Separate numbers, nomenclature, and marking.

These requirements are of course tailored to the type of software being developed, but on the whole they make a lot of sense if one is going to track a critical element whose failure could affect the safety of persons and property, such as the automated aircraft landing system prevalent on all wide-bodied commercial aircraft such as the Boeing 747 and AIRBUS 300.

Thus a CI is identifiable, controllable, traceable, functional and modular, necessary and homogeneous. To be identifiable the primary CI must remain whole and cannot be divided even though it may contain other lower-level CIs. In other words:

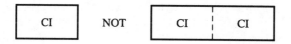

The only way such division can be legal, as will be explained under Control, is if the right block contains two unique identification numbers and is described in two unique requirement specifications and detail design documents, and so on. If the CI is to be optimally traceable and functional, it should be loosely coupled; that is, it should not contain so many interfaces that it will fail if one of the many other connecting interfaces fail.

Once the CI have been selected, the entire project will revolve around them. Most reporting is to the CI level, which is really level 2. Unless one has segment specs as illustrated in Figure 8.1, all changes made to components and units are in respect to their parent CI, not to a CI that is child to another CI. Thus, from this point on in this text, the reader will be constantly referred to the ever-present CI.

Identifying a CI is not just giving it a number, the way one is assigned a social security number. The CI is described by a definition of its attributes and its contribution to the overall structure, including assigning name/nomenclature and subsequent text relating to what the CI does, how it does it, where it is done, how fast, what supports it, what the product of the function is, and how big it is. A complete and concise description will leave no doubt in anyone's mind as to the identification of this particular CI.

For example, when one's car breaks down and one is calling an auto club or service station, a number of questions will be asked to identify the exact location of the breakdown, the description of the car, its license plate number, a cross street if known, and finally the caller's personal club number. When this occurs, we are really establishing the functional and physical characteristics of a CI—the stalled car.

DOCUMENTING THE DESIGN DEFINITION

The task of documenting a typical software CI starts with the software requirements specification (Figure 8.2) [31]. There are currently several versions of this specification, the DOD, the IEEE, NASA, and NSA (National Security Agency). In addition, FIPS PUB 38, an NIST publication provides for a requirements document. The NASA document's outline consists of the following sections:

Introduction
Related documentation
Requirements approach and tradeoffs

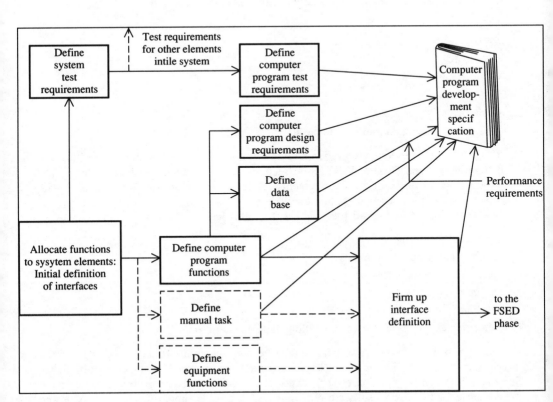

Figure 8.2 Development specification flow.

External interface requirement
Requirements specification
Process and data requirements
Performance and quality engineering requirements
Safety requirements
Security and privacy requirements
Implementation constraints
Site adaption
Design goals
Traceability to parent's design
Partitioning for phased delivery

This outline, as well as the IEEE one that follows, describes the the system engineer's requirements as stated in the system/segment specification. At this point, the software engineer is developing the software requirements specification from which the design specifications will be written.

IEEE STD 830-1984, *IEEE Guide to Software Requirements Specifications* [30] states that "this guide does not specify industry-wide SRS standards nor state mandatory requirements. It describes the necessary content and qualities of a good SRS and presents a prototype outline."

The guide also describes the characteristics of a good SRS, which is

• Unambiguous
• Complete
• Verifiable
• Consistent
• Modifiable
• Traceable
• Usable (in operation and maintenance)

The guide provides four prototype or sample outlines for a requirements specification. The Introduction and General Description sections are common to the four outlines. The differences are in the Specific Requirements sections, which are structured to deal with different situations, environments, and applications.

In one fashion or another all four address the following:

Functional requirements
External interface requirements
Performance requirements
Design constraints
Attributes
Other (for example, data base, operations, site adaptation)

This type of menu provides software engineers with the ability to tailor and adapt to the needs of their projects. In one instance one of the options was used most successfully for an information system application (ADP), and a short time later another option was selected for an embedded computer software requirement. This guide should therefore be reviewed when there is the option to select a format.

The MIL STD 2167A, *Defense System Software Development,* by no means has to be used on defense contracts only. Its software requirements specification data item description, MCCR 80025, is as versatile as the NASA and IEEE versions and most tailorable to the project requirements. Its primary section is Engineering Requirements, which breaks down into the following subsections:

External interface Requirements (Figure 8.3)

Capability Requirements

Internal Interfaces

Data Elements

Adaptation Requirements

Sizing and timing Requirements

Safety Requirements

Design Constraints

Software Quality Factors

Human Performance Requirements

Requirements Traceability

The last section addresses qualification requirements.

In this outline Requirements Traceability cross references the requirements of this CI's SRS to the higher-level system specification (upward) and the system spec requirements to this specification (downward). This then can give QA, software engineering, and CM the visibility needed to ensure the proper flow of the documented identification and a road map to those documents placed under CM control.

The importance of Requirement Traceability to the CM activity is threefold. It provides the necessary information on how the system will be developed, and in the change control activity it shows CM where to go, where to look, and how to find if any documents have been affected by a given change. Lastly, it enables CM to ensure unique identification, traceability upward and downward, and maintenance of document status at all times. Thus the more one knows about the requirement, the better one can fulfill the CM requirement.

The approval or conditional approval, a recognition that the contents are dynamic and subject to change, comes at the software specification review (SSR). Once successfully conducted, this review allows the developer to establish the design criteria to meet the software requirements. The design document may be a single document or two. If there is only one document, as required by 2167A, it begins as a system-level, preliminary design description and evolves into a detail design description when reviewed at the critical design review. If there are two documents, one represents the system level and the other the detail

IDENTIFIER	DESCRIPTION	SOURCE CSCI	DESTINATION CSCI(s)	UNIT OF MEASURE	LIMIT/ RANGE	ACCURACY	PRECISION/ RESOLUTION
IFA001	VELOCITY	CSCI-A	CSCI-B CSCI-C	ft/sec	20-1000	+20	10^{-3}
IFA002	AZIMUTH	CSCI-A	CSCI-D	RADIANS	$0 - \pi/2$	+0.05	10^{-3}
IFA003	ALTITUDE	CSCI-C	CSCI-A CSCI-B CSCI-D	ft	0-1500	+10	10^{-2}

Figure 8.3 Interface data element definition table.

level. Which form is better is a matter of conjecture. The rationale for the single-document form was to minimize data item descriptions. The two-document form was intended to progressively develop a preliminary design at the system level and review it at the preliminary design review (PDR), before progressing on the detail level, which is for programmer guidance and instruction. If the document is too voluminous, it could be at a disadvantage compared to a document that does only one thing—provide the detail design requirements necessary for a successful walkthrough and reliable coding.

The following is the NASA version of the preliminary version of the design document, titled *Software Architectural Design Document*. (The IEEE does not have a similar standard published at this time.) Its Purpose section states:

> The purpose . . . is to record the logical/functional design information for the software component. This includes design rationale and trades, the selected architecture of the component including at least one level of decomposition in the software sub-components or software design element, the relationships and interface description between the sub-components or design elements, the allocation of the software component requirements to the sub-components or design elements . . .

This is the system level/preliminary design approach to describe the rationale, tradeoffs, and other design considerations, including any use of prototyping, that influence the major decisions affecting the design of the software. The outline includes the following sections:

Design Approach and Tradeoffs

Architectural Design Description

External Interface Design

Requirements Allocation and Traceability

Partitioning for Incremental Development

Each of these sections further amplifies the identification of the CI described in the SRS. In other words, what is our design approach and the trades to meet the specified requirements? What type of platform/environment/device will this software operate in (as illustrated by the data flow in Figure 8.4)? What will be the interface design to other elements, components, and so on? How is this CI decomposed to the lower components or elements/units? If ordered, how can segments of this software be partitioned and delivered for concurrent testing or outright application?

NSA's document, NSAM 81-3/DOD STD 1703[NS], provides the requirements and outline descriptions for that agency's software documentation. The contents are derived from a number of different sources, taking the best of each, including DOD STD 2167A and DOD STD 7935, for automated data systems documentation. It may be considered more generic than DOD STD 2167A and more on par with NASA and IEEE. NSA's subsystem specification is a preliminary design format whose content is derived from the SRS and is the bridge to the detail specification. The design detail section looks at

- General operating procedures
- System logical flow
- System data, including I/O
- Program descriptions for N programs
- Data base, defining the content of the data elements

There may be one or more of these documents depending on how the CI was broken down into the lower levels as illustrated on the software hierarchy chart. The CM will know if there is to be one or many and can prepare for this through scheduling and preassignments

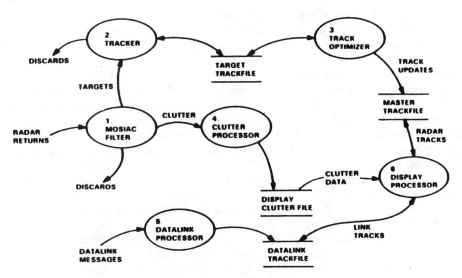

Figure 8.4   Data flow diagram.

of document numbers. This document is reviewed at the preliminary design review (PDR) and is placed under configuration control in a final or "preliminary final" form. The latter recognizes that the document is dynamic and subject to change. Thus, while under control, the form does not have to be as rigorous as it would in final form.

Detailed design documents are critical to the success of the coding and unit test phase. In addition, most changes will be made to these documents and thus will require close inspection by the coder, the quality control function, and CM in order to understand their format and content. The NSA outline includes these sections:

- Detailed Design Approach and Tradeoffs
- Detailed Design Description
- Compilation Unit Design and Traceability to Architectural Design
- Detailed Design of Compilation Units
- External Interface Detailed Design
- Coding and Implementation Notes
- Firmware Support Manual (A pointer to a DID (data item description) if required)

The NSA outline for its program specification is an extension of its preliminary design specification for the design detail necessary "to permit program production by the programmer/coder." (NSAM 81-3, DOD STD 1703) Thus, detail design section covers

- Operating procedures
- System logical flow
- System data—I/O
- Program description and logic (for each of N programs)
- Data base characteristics and data environment

These documents are prepared for each software component that breaks into units. The recorded information is detailed to the level necessary to code the individual compilation of units and all lower-level coded units/routines. The documents are normally reviewed at design walkthroughs, which are also known as design peer reviews. In these reviews one programmer team meets with another, with someone from, say, quality assurance acting as the facilitator, to review the detail design of each other's component or unit. This ensures that upward and downward requirements traceability has been achieved and the next-higher level of preliminary or architectural design has been attained. A subsequent review of the code will be compared with these detailed documents. Any changes that may occur during the coding of the particular unit must be processed in a timely manner and incorporated into the document to facilitate the code walkthrough. Changes not incorporated will also be referred to but are more cumbersome to handle. In this day of the word processor, incorporation should not be a problem.

We have now described the three primary identification documents: requirement, system (architectural) design, and detailed design. Each document is uniquely described in a given CI or series of interfacing CIs so as to leave no doubt of the identity and ownership of the CI and its "children."

The culmination of these specifications/documents is the product specification or the description of how the developer met the requirements to produce the specified product.

The product specification can take several different forms. For the most part the DOD, NASA, and others compile the basic identification documents previously described into the product specification document along with a version description of what was done and a description of final allocations, assignments, data base schema, interface input and output, safety features, communication links, and so on. Thus the NASA outline contains the following sections:

- Concept Document
- Requirements Specification
- Design Document(s)
    Architectural
    Detail
- Version Description Document (how it was done)
- User's Manual (how to use it)
- Maintenance Manual (how to support it)

What appears above is the history of the "XYZ" CI in full or abstracted form. For those who have small projects these documents can be incorporated into a software engineering notebook or a software development file, folder, or book. This can be general or most specific, hardcopy or computer file. The primary thing to remember is that these documents represent the software product and are used to maintain the software in its assigned environment—whether a unique item or equipment off the shelf of your local computer store. Those who initially scoff at having to do all these documents generally regret they did not when it comes time to upgrade their software to meet the competition or satisfy their best customer—and the person who developed the golden fleece has left the company! The CM activity's mission will have been satisfied if there is documented evidence of the software product updated to the version sold, shipped, or delivered.

Some related documents are most important during the identification cycle. First, as mentioned earlier, one must deal with interfaces in order to describe them and provide the necessary guidance to construct them during the coding phase. Thus there are two primary documents: the interface requirements specification, which describes what interfaces are required, and the interface design document, which, like a detail design document, describes how the interfaces are to be constructed and tied to the system. The NASA specification is the *Software External Interface Requirements DID, SMAP P210*. The outline is very simple and has one main section, Interfaces, which covers the following:

- Purpose of the interface
- Requirements for the interface, such as process, performance, safety, and security
- Implementation constraints on the interface
- Traceability to next-higher element

The interface requirement also describes each interface with each class of user including human users and other information systems. Each such interface should represent a bidirectional flow of information, and graphic representations are of paramount importance. The document also specifies the requirements governing each interface and explains such requirements to avoid misunderstanding.

The NASA *Software External Interface Design Document, SMAP P321SW* stresses interface allocation design and physical interface design. The Allocation section describes the mapping (or traceability) of the external interface design of the software component into its specific compilation units and lower-level units.

The Physical Interface section describes the specified interfaces in great detail and covers:

- Type and purpose of the interface
- Data transmission—details of the data records and elements transmitted across the interface
- Message descriptions
- Interface priority
- Communication protocols and description of the technical details

With this type of detail, CM will be able to plan for the interface control process, the convening of a review board such as an interface control working group or interface CCB, and the incorporation of the approved interface changes.

One may be wondering, at this time, about the internal interfaces that occur between processes and files and I/O devices. These interfaces are described in the SRS for each CI and the software design document (SDD). They become important if a change affects a given interface or series of interfaces. Although internal interfaces are researched and resolved by the assigned software analyst, the CM may have to trace them in the SRS or SDD to ensure that change to code is covered in the relevant documentation.

With the generation of these documents we are faced with a classification, cataloging, and numbering requirement that can be enormous if not planned for and described in procedural format in the CMP or project directives. The documentation or specification tree illustrated in Figure 8.1 at least starts our classification process by placing the system/segment specs at levels one and two, the preliminary design at level three, and the detail design at levels four and five if necessary when critical routines are documented.

DESIGN DEFINITION RELATIONSHIPS

The task of cataloging involves defining how the CI and subsidiary documentation relate to each other. Five relationships are important. The first involves *equivalence*. As noted in Figure 8.5 a CI can be stored as a master in the master disk and as copy in a magnetic tape file or the programmer's floppy. One must thus know which is which and why it is there.

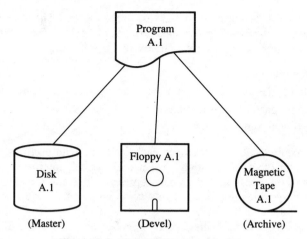

Figure 8.5 Relationships—equivalence.

In other words, if the CI is not in the master file, it has not been approved and must be in the floppy or working file.

Another relationship involves *dependence*. One must define the parent-child relationship, as a minimum always referring a lower-level document to its parent (Figure 8.6). If this is not done, it is assumed that the document is the top parent. This relationship is most important for requirements traceability and the creation of indented units, components, or CI Christmas tree lists. Any automated system will always produce a listing of missing upper elements as part of its edit routine so that the parent may be identified.

In defining a *derivation* relationship, one describes where the code came from (Figure 8.7). The most obvious derivation is object from source, but some code may well be an abstract or package from larger bodies of code and thus must be understood and cataloged accordingly.

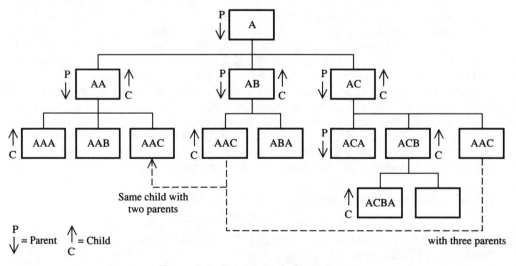

Figure 8.6 Relationships—dependence.

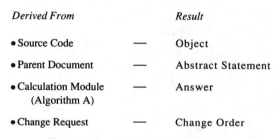

Derived From		Result
• Source Code	—	Object
• Parent Document	—	Abstract Statement
• Calculation Module (Algorithm A)	—	Answer
• Change Request	—	Change Order

Figure 8.7 Relationships—derivation.

Finally, we have the successor and variant relationships. One defines the *successor* relationship by tracing an element's change history from revision A to revision B, and so on as shown in Figure 8.8. (A revision may also be a reidentification of the element with a new number or dash number.) The *variant* relationship is similar to a variation on a theme. It has no effect on the form, fit, or function of the element except that variant A may be faster than B. Both are interchangeable with other elements.

The relationships described here tell where the software elements come from and how they relate to the project. This is important for those who support of the project, including the software librarians, quality assurance, and of course the CM team. Because these support people are really on the outside (of the developer's mind and methodology) looking in, they need a road map, such as a dependency flow, to understand where an element affected by a change is positioned in relation to all the other elements.

NUMBERING SOFTWARE ELEMENTS

Whether one identifies elements by descriptions, color coding, indexing, or indentation, a unique identifier in the form of specified characters must be applied. The national unique number for all U.S. citizens today is the social security number. A similar type of identifier is used in all countries. Other unique numbers include automobile license numbers—no two cars within a given state can have the same number, and between states the color of the license plate and state name maintain the uniqueness. A serial number provides uniqueness for a given piece of equipment, such as an automobile motor or camera.

Uniqueness has its bounds. Each of the numbering systems described above is bounded by country, state, or manufacturer, so there can be duplication. Each identifier can be unique within its own domain, but few identifiers if any could be guaranteed unique worldwide.

Within the U.S. government the bounding identifier is the commercial and government equipment code (CAGE) that precedes all design definition documentation, including specifications, drawings, and documents such as preliminary design documents and test plans, but not necessarily CM plans. The CAGE provides an identification for the design activity; if the manufacturer or producer is different, that organization's CAGE number will also appear. In software development, one organization could have designed the software product from SRS through test through DDD, and a separate producer organization could have supplied the programmers and computer equipment to code, test, and integrate the software product. This is a frequent occurrence in the design and development of hardware items where the designer does not have the capacity and resources to produce all of its own design and thus goes to a separate manufacturing source. A better example is the design that is now done in the United States and then farmed out for manufacture in low-cost labor countries. These items normally do not have a CAGE code, but the notation "MADE IN XYZZA."

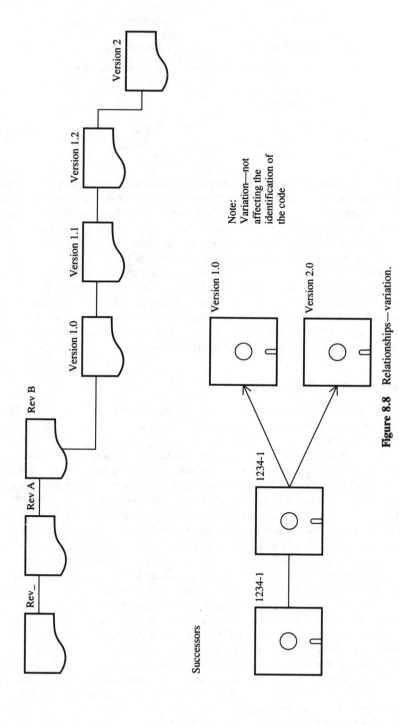

Figure 8.8 Relationships—variation.

Why assign a number in the first place, especially if one is working a small project with few lines of code? Why go to the trouble of getting a number assigned to a very thin design documentation? Who cares? The answer is that a requester must have a way of retrieving a lot of small projects captured and stored in the firm's library master file quickly and confidently—especially since the original design organization might have had two versions different enough to have two different identifiers even though title of both was the same.

There are two types of numbering systems: the nonsignificant and the significant. Each is noteworthy, but which is better depends on the complexity of the number's purpose.

A nonsignificant numbering system is a simple "one up" assignment, for example, from 0001 to 1999. This system requires the establishment and maintenance of a number assignment log book, which should contain the following information for each number pulled or assigned in a manual or automated mode:

NUMBER	S/W TITLE	PROJ NAME	AUTHOR	LOCATION	PO/CNTR #
00032	SIGNL PROC	ARJAY	STONE	DEPT 345	90-1234
00033	CLUTTER	ARJAY	ALLEN	DEPT 345	90-1234

Normally a "corporate" block of numbers is established such as 0 to 1,000,000. This block is then allocated to the one or more entities producing document and code at the second level of the management's organizational structure. For instance, 0 to 99,999 is assigned to the corporate level; 100,000 to 299,999 is assigned to the communications division; 300,000 to 499,999 is assigned to the controls division; and so on. Within those entities, a responsible function would assign a series to a product line or significant program. Thus one might well assign 100,000 to 150,000 to the Cellular I product line, whose authority may then allocate to the Red, White, and Blue program numbers 140,000 to 142,999. Beyond this, there is no implied significance the number assignment. These assigned series can be entered in a book or journal or in a computer file that will automatically assign the next available number once the pertinent information described is provided.

00034	ESM JAM	EXTASY	POTTS	DEPT 498	88-7890
00035	(SRS)BULL	BULLDOG	JONES	DEPT 089	89-0098

The advantage is that one simply deals with the next number. The disadvantages are that one must have a central point of control and, more important to the critics, one does not know by reading the number whether it is code, document, test report/data, or what and must look the number up find out what it identifies.

The significant number system can be quite simple or very complex, as illustrated in Figure 8.9. A significant system tells about the element it is identifying. It could simply use numbers as in the following:

YEAR	DAY NUMBER	NUMBER
90	135	012345
90	138	012345
90	140	012347
90	140	012347-1

EXAMPLE

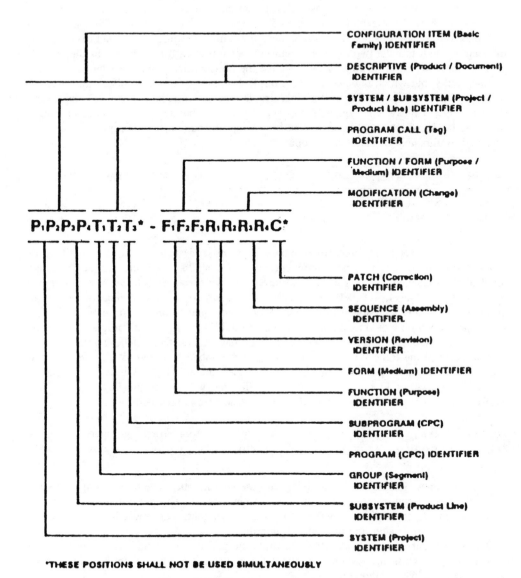

Figure 8.9 Significant numbering schemes.

You may have noticed that the number 012345 is duplicated. This is because the day numbers 135 and 138 were adequate to make both number sets unique and therefore correct. The dash one number is also correct, although it would appear much farther down the log than immediately after the prime family number.

Alternatively, the system can use a complex quasi-significant number set, which one might argue could be significant or nonsignificant depending on one's viewpoint. This could include a project code such as AA, BG, or a number such as 34 or 98. Thus the numberous system might appear as

AA   12345
AA   A123456
AA   B123456
AA   B123457

In this illustration AA-12345 is the top program number/software element number. AA is the program code. The prefix A or B indicates whether the item belongs to the control program or the communications program.

These are simple examples. The example in Figure 8.9 is much more complicated, requiring much work to remember all the numbers and what their contents stand for.

The advantage of the significant number system, to its proponents, is that one does not have to look at a log, have a description or document title dictionary at hand, or provide or support a central point for the distribution of numbers. The instructions for the construction and application of the number are written one time in an approved company or firm procedure. The person using a document numbered in this way simply has to remember what each set of numbers stands for to know what he or she is reading. The chances of duplicate numbers is almost nil because of the way the numbers are constructed, but one should have an audit procedure that will determine whether duplicates are in evidence.

The EIA's Data and Configuration Management Committee took a poll some years ago and published the results in their Bulletin CMB 4-2, *Identification,* which states:

> It has been the experience of industry in general that users of numbers containing built-in significant bits of intelligence rarely use or remember the meanings of the various number characterizations. They are, more often than not, quite unaware of the information conveyed by coded number characters. Those most likely to use significant numbers would be library personnel and they do not necessarily need this since they rely on other records. [31]

The bottom line is that one should use a numbering scheme that the people involved feel most comfortable with and that provides the easiest means of retrieval and the most accessibility.

FIRMWARE IDENTIFICATION

The term *firmware* has been applied to software, normally written in what is called a truth table form, that is, 1 or 0 burned or blown into a microelectronic device known as programmable read-only memory, (PROM), read-only memory (ROM), or erasable programmable read-only memory (EPROM). Today, cars and many household appliances have some devices with computer programs that measure fuel consumption, temperature, and water volume; act as thermal switches; and the like. These are examples of firmware.

Many people forget that PROMs and ROMs contain some software. Should this software be controlled? In most cases, yes. Some can get very large and should be documented. There was one instance where an engineer had developed a 375-line truth table and could not decompose it, much less describe it, so that someone else could maintain it. If it broke, he fixed it. If he left the project, the code went with him.

Some requirements can go overboard in requiring firmware to be documented the same as application software. This may be overkill, for which one must be on the lookout so as to negotiate some sensible tailoring.

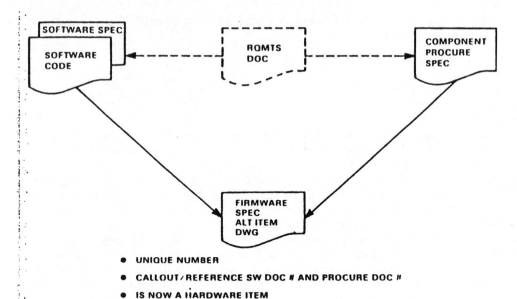

- UNIQUE NUMBER
- CALLOUT/REFERENCE SW DOC # AND PROCURE DOC #
- IS NOW A HARDWARE ITEM

Figure 8.10 Firmware identification.

- **HARDWARE PROM**
  - ▲ **PROMS CONTAINING DATA THAT IS NOT EXECUTABLE BY A COMPUTER PROGRAM**
- **SOFTWARE PROM**
  - ▲ **PROMS CONTAINING INSTRUCTIONS EXECUTABLE BY A COMPUTER PROGRAM AND CODED AT THE DEVICE LEVEL**

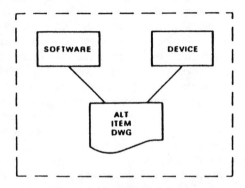

Figure 8.11 PROM definition.

- **HARDWARE PROMS**
  - ▲ **DOCUMENTED ON ALTERED ITEM DRAWING WHICH INCLUDES:**
    - **PART NUMBER OF UNCODED DEVICE**
    - **TRUTH TABLE FOR CODED DEVICE**
- **SOFTWARE PROMS**
  - ▲ **DOCUMENTED ON ALTERED ITEM DRAWING WHICH INCLUDES:**
    - **PART NUMBER OF UNPROGRAMMED DEVICE**
    - **TRUTH TABLE OF CODED DEVICE**
    - **REFERENCE TO:**
      - **SOURCE PROGRAM**
      - **OBJECT PROGRAM**
      - **PROGRAM DESIGN SPECIFICATION**

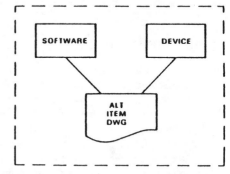

Figure 8.12   PROM documentation.

DOCUMENTATION
FOR
ASSEMBLIES CONTAINING EAROMS/EEROMS

- **IDENTIFICATION OF SOFTWARE AT THE ASSEMBLY LEVEL**
  - ▲ **ASSEMBLY DRAWING WILL INCLUDE:**
    - **— MARKING THE SOFTWARE IDENTIFICATION NUMBER ON THE ASSEMBLY THAT HAS BEEN PROGRAMMED**
    - **— REFERENCE TO:**
    - **PROGRAM DESIGN SPECIFICATION**

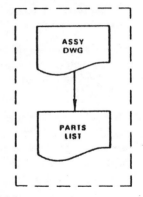

Figure 8.13   EEPROM/EAPROM documentation.

Some very sensible firmware documentation schemes can identify the software and the hardware device it resides in. Figure 8.10 illustrates the overall scheme and the use of the altered item drawing contained in MIL STD 100. Figure 8.11 defines a PROM, and Figure 8.12 illustrates firmware documentation requirements. When one is using EPROMS, it is almost the same as if one were simply loading software onto a disk or mag tape (Figure 8.13). Thus, rather than use an altered item drawing, one would treat the EPROM as an assembly and the software as a part of the assembly along with its documentation. Thus the software identification can change but the EPROM device cannot, unless physically altered, as when more connector leads are added to the device. The EPROM is really a common carrier, which can carry one type of software today and another tomorrow.

BASELINE DEVELOPMENT

Most simply expressed, a baseline is an agreed-on point of departure, after which any change must be communicated to all parties involved. Thus, if one agrees that all parties will meet under the dome at 12:00 noon and that time changed, someone must notify the others. A meeting might even be required to determine a better time.

With product definition, a baseline is a CI or a collection of CIs formally reviewed, agreed on, or designated at a given point in time during a project's life cycle. What may be designated for project A may not be the same for project B. The baseline can mark the end of one phase or segment of a phase as well as the beginning of a new phase. This line of demarcation is the result of formal review and agreement either among those on a project or between those on the project and their primary customer.

In a generic sense there are five principal baseline points one always works with. These generic points (Figure 8.14) include the following:

The *definition* baseline is the culmination of the software requirements definition, the decomposition, the final solution to how one will design the software product to meet the requirement.

The *design* baseline is the point at which one has determined how to build or, more properly, code to meet the system requirements.

The *Code/unit test* baseline is the point at which one proves that the program language entered in the computer and tested to defined test requirements meets the design requirement, which in turn meets the requirements baseline documentation.

The *testing* baseline is the point at which formal tests have been written to prove that the software product meets the requirements and is now ready for delivery to the customer or user.

The *maintenance* baseline is the point at which the form, fit, and function of the delivered product can be modified, corrected for latent errors, or enhanced.

Figure 8.15 shows the three formal baseline points that form the basis for the generic: functional, allocated, and product. An evolving (cumulative) baseline occurs between the allocated and the product, which is known as the developmental configuration. These are defined as follows:

The *functional* baseline is the initially approved documentation describing a CI's functional characteristics and qualification criteria required to demonstrate the achievement of specified functional characteristics: the interfaces, data base requirements, and satisfaction of design constraints.

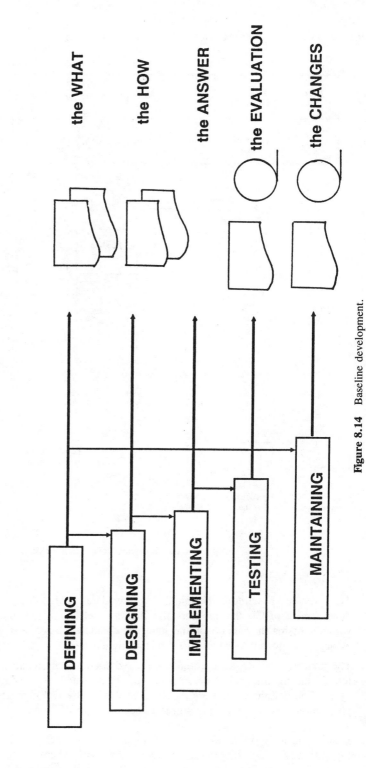

POINTS OF DEPARTURE FOR CONTINUED DEVELOPMENT

PHASES

BASELINES

DEFINING — the WHAT

DESIGNING — the HOW

IMPLEMENTING — the ANSWER

TESTING — the EVALUATION

MAINTAINING — the CHANGES

Figure 8.14 Baseline development.

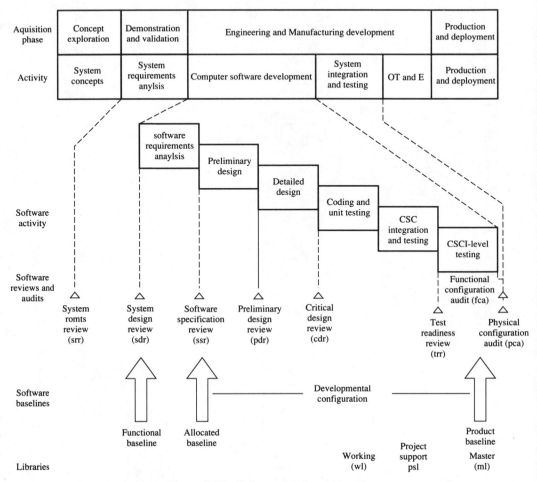

Figure 8.15 Software development cycle.

The *allocated* baseline is the initially approved/designated documentation governing the development of CIs that are part of a higher-level CI, that is, the system specification, which contains the functional and interface characteristics and qualification criteria necessary to demonstrate achievement of the higher-level CI's requirements.

The *product* baseline is the initially approved documentation and source code that defines the CI during the production, operation, maintenance, and support phases of its life cycle. The definition includes the functional and physical characteristics designated for production acceptance testing and tests necessary to the support the CI.

In addition, the term *developmental configuration* has been applied to define the evolving configuration of a CI during its development—that period between the allocated and product baselines. The agreed-on definition is under the control of the developer.

The generic and formal baselines can be integrated as follows:

Generic	Formal
Definition	Functional and allocated
Design	Allocated and Developmental Configuration
Code/unit test	Developmental Configuration
Testing	Developmental Configuration
Maintenance	Product

DESIGN REVIEWS AND AUDIT CONSIDERATIONS

As noted in Figure 8.16, each of the baselines discussed in the previous section is the result of a formal review of specific documentation normally scheduled, by agreement, at the end of a phase of development, such as the conceptual definition, or on completion of a defined segment of a phase such as during full-scale development. The functional baseline, (see Figure 8.15) is established at the end of the concept exploration. The system design review (SDR), with the formal review of the system specification and agreement on its functional and physical characteristics for subsequent design and development, can enable the baseline to be declared by the customer or by agreement between buyer and seller.

The allocated baseline received its name from the fact that, once system engineering has decomposed the system specification, the elements of the system that have been identified are allocated to specified functions. This baseline is established upon completion of the validation and demonstration phase when the software requirements specification for each CI at the software specification review (SSR) has been reviewed and accepted. Note that the allocated baseline for hardware is normally declared after review of the hardware development specifications at the preliminary design review and is one of the features that distinguishes the hardware from the software life cycle.

Several segments of the software development life cycle occur between the establishment of the allocated baseline and the subsequent product baseline, which is the point of departure for the delivery of the software product. During this period the preliminary design and detail design segments are performed as well as the coding/unit test, integration and testing, and performance/system test. In order to capture the documentation and test data resulting in these phases, the developmental configuration environment was established to place approved documentation and code under configuration control and protect the integrity of the software product that matured during the requirements definition phases.

As noted in Figure 8.16, the top-level or preliminary draft of the design document is developed for each CI and software component (SC) and reviewed at the preliminary design reviews (PDR). Once accepted, the documents are placed under configuration control—protected in a safe haven. In some cases this must be done before submission to the customer, but depending on one's contract, it may be sufficient to have the documents entered into a controlled data base and available for review by the customer when requested. Entry at this point should ensure the ability to trace design requirements to higher-level and lower-level specifications. Change control provides historical records from this point forward while ensuring the identification and integrity of the element for all users.

During the detail design segment the preliminary document incorporates the detail design criteria to become the software design document. This medium provides the instructions to

ACTIVITIES	PRODUCTS	REVIEWS	BASELINES
PRE-SOFTWARE DEVELOPMENT SYSTEM REQUIREMENTS ANALYSIS	• SOFTWARE DEVELOPMENT PLAN*	SYSTEM RQMTS REVIEW (SRR)	
• AUTHOR SOFTWARE DEVELOPMENT PLAN INCLUDING: CONFIGURATION MANAGEMENT PLAN, (OR SYSTEM CMP) QUALITY PROGRAM PLAN STANDARDS, PROCEDURES METHODS AND TOOL PROVISIONS	• OPERATIONAL CONCEPT DOCUMENT	SYSTEM DESIGN REVIEW SDR	FUNCTIONAL
	• PRLM INTERFACE REQUIREMENTS SPEC.		
• CONDUCT SYSTEM TRADE-OFF ANALYSIS–IDENTIFY CSCIs	• PRLM SOFTWARE REQUIREMENTS SPEC.		
• DEVELOP OPERATIONAL CONCEPT DOCUMENT	• SYSTEM CONFIGURATION MGMT PLAN DOCUMENT		
• DEVELOP PRELIMINARY INTERFACE REQUIREMENTS SPECIFICATION(S)			
• DEVELOP PRELIMINARY SOFTWARE REQUIREMENTS SPECIFICATION(S)			
• DEVELOP PRELIMINARY QUALIFICATION REQUIREMENTS	*INCLUDES SCMP, SQPP, AND S&P DOC.		

Figure 8.16 Software life cycle activities.

ACTIVITIES	PRODUCTS	REVIEWS	BASELINES
SOFTWARE REQUIREMENTS ANALYSIS • COMPLETION OF REQUIREMENTS FROM SYSTEM ENGINEERING PHASE • INTERNAL REVIEW OF REQUIREMENTS	• SOFTWARE REQUIREMENTS SPECIFICATIONS (F) • INTERFACE REQUIREMENTS SPECIFICATIONS, IIF APPLICABLE (F)	SOFTWARE SPECIFICATIONS REVIEW (SSR)	ALLOCATED
SOFTWARE PRELIMINARY DESIGN • ALLOCATE REQUIREMENTS TO TOP LEVEL COMPONENTS • DEFINE ALGORITHMS AND DATA/CONTROL FLOW • IDENTIFY TESTS • REVIEW DESIGN INTERNALLY	• SOFTWARE TOP-LEVEL DESIGN DOCUMENT • SOFTWARE TEST PLAN • (SW DEVELOPMENT FILE)	PDR	DEVELOPMENTAL CONFIGURATION
SOFTWARE DETAILED DESIGN • DESIGN TO UNIT LEVEL • DEFINE UNIT TESTS • DESIGN TEST CASES FOR UNIT INTEGRATION (INFORMAL) AND FORMAL TEST • INTERNAL REVIEWS OF DESIGN AND TEST PLANS/CASES	• SOFTWARE DETAILED DESIGN DOCUMENTS • INTERFACE DESIGN DOCUMENT, IF APPLICABLE • DATA BASE DESIGN DOCUMENT, IF APPLICABLE • SOFTWARE TEST DESCRIPTIONS • (SW DEVELOPMENT FILE)	CDR	DEVELOPMENTAL CONFIGURATION

Figure 8.16 (Continued)

ACTIVITIES	PRODUCTS	REVIEWS	BASELINES
CODING AND UNIT TESTING • CODE UNITS • DEVELOP UNIT TEST PROCEDURES • TEST UNITS • DEVELOP TEST PROCEDURES FOR INFORMAL INTEGRATION AND FORMAL TESTS	• SOURCE AND OBJECT PROGRAMS • (SW DEVELOPMENT FILE) • (SOFTWARE TEST PROCEDURES—INFORMAL)	(INFORMAL)	DEVELOPMENTAL CONFIGURATION
CSC INTEGRATION AND TESTING • INTEGRATE UNITS AND INFORMALLY TEST • CAPTURE AND ANALYZE TEST RESULTS • MAKE CORRECTIONS	• (SW DEVELOPMENT FILE) • SOFTWARE TEST PROCEDURES—FORMAL • (INFORMAL INTEGRATION TEST RESULTS)	TEST READINESS REVIEW (TRR)	DEVELOPMENTAL CONFIGURATION
CSCI TESTING • CONDUCT FORMAL TESTS • CAPTURE AND ANALYZE THE RESULTS • MAKE CORRECTIONS	• SOFTWARE TEST REPORTS • SOFTWARE PRODUCT SPECIFICATION • VERSION DESCRIPTION DOCUMENT	FCA PCA	PRODUCT

Figure 8.16 (*Continued*)

the coders for the production of the operational software. The document outlines portrayed for NASA, NSA, DOD, and IEEE all fall into this phase of activity and are reviewed at the critical design reviews (CDR) for each CI, SC, and software unit (SU). All the documents reviewed and accepted at CDR are also placed in the evolving developmental configuration and are under configuration control.

What does configuration control really mean? As discussed in Chapter 9, it is a means of ensuring that any changes are consistently communicated to the project as well as incorporated into the documentation and its ultimate code. To achieve consistency, it may not be deemed necessary to hold a formal meeting of a review board, but by agreement or developer's practice three to four people from that board may convene a smaller meeting, sometimes known as the software review board (SRB), to review and make decisions concerning the requested changes. If this is done, procedures for the SRB should be described in the CM plan. The advantage of the SRB is that it can be convened at a moment's notice, a change request reviewed and disposed of with minimum time away from assigned tasks.

DEVELOPMENTAL CONFIGURATION

The developmental configuration segment can also be broken down into subsegments. The first marks the point in the development phase when the software performance, design, and other related specifications/documents are in a preliminary state—that is, approved by the project but awaiting formal customer approval/authentication subsequent to PDR/CDR—and have been placed in the Master File under internal configuration control.

The second subsegment marks the point in the development phase when software elements and supporting data have been coded and tested and are transferred from the programmer/development file to the program support library for change control under the cognizance of the software review board.

The third subsegment is the point in the development phase when software elements/builds are released to the master file for change control under the cognizance of the CCB. This control point normally concludes with the establishment of the product baseline and delivery of the software product to the customer. However, when the product is delivered either with waivers or to a transitional operation phase, this developmental configuration is extended until prescribed actions are completed.

The software configuration management plan and the company or firm's directives should spell out how the developers will satisfy the requirements of this phase.

At the culmination of the software integration and testing activity, a test readiness review is conducted to ensure that the testing just performed will justify the final system integration and test activity. In order to conduct this review, one must evaluate the history and trends in the number and types of changes due to defects that have been found and fixed. This evaluation supports the need for internal change control. At this time the final system test procedures are reviewed and, once accepted, are placed in the developmental configuration and subject to control.

The developmental configuration ends with the completion of software performance testing, system test and hardware/software integration. During this period, the product specification (or how-we-did-it) document is finalized, as well as the version description (or what's-in-it, what-does-it-do) document. These volumes, for each CI and the formal test reports, are some of the items reviewed at the functional and physical audits. Once accepted by the combined customer developer audit teams the Product Baseline is established from the developmental configuration. This point of departure is the one which all subsequent software support activity will key off of.

SUMMARY

Without a baseline it is hard to set up the controls necessary to ensure adequate protection of agreements reached for document identification and code. One should be able to acquire any accepted/designated/authenticated document or code with confidence that it is accurate and up to date. The important thing to remember is that one can establish a baseline at any time and call it anything one wants as long as one thinks of it as a point of departure in the software life cycle.

It may be that one will "call time out" if everything seems out of control. This allows the project to regroup and start out fresh with a new agreed-on point of departure. On the other hand, one may want to mark the success of an important breakthrough and start a new phase of activity from that point in time. There is no set of points where a baseline must be placed unless it is spelled in an agreement, purchase order, or contract. The exception is at the end of the development phase when a product baseline is essential to fielding and/or marketing the software product.

Identification, as the preceding sections may attest to, is not simply a matter of applying a number or name to a document or floppy disk. The written description of what is required, what will be designed, and what will be coded is most important when the baselines are established and the control of those approved documents is initiated. The more integrity the baseline content has, the fewer unavoidable errors will occur.

EXERCISES

1. Describe what you think the most important tasks of the Identification activity are and why. What tasks could you do without if limited to just two?
2. Describe how you would plan to prepare a software hierarchy for your customer.
3. Discuss the most important tasks in selecting CIs. What makes them important? Propose a tailored method for the selection process.
4. Describe the purpose and scope of the principal identification documents. Are there others that should be included? What are they and why?
5. Describe how you would establish a baseline on your project as in the CMP or SDP (Software Development Plan).

CHAPTER 9

Performing the Change Control Activity

This chapter describes CM's performance of the change control activity. As long as a project maintains communication among the software development organization and the customer or buyer, there will always be a form or format for proposing changes and procedures for the preparation and submission of these changes. In addition formal agreements may request a description of how the developing team intends to process changes and what type of form or content of the request will be provided. Once CM has established one or more baselines, changes begin to occur and should be expected and planned for, because no one is perfect and even decisions made in good conscience may not come out as expected and thus must be changed.

Changes should, however, be processed, communicated, and incorporated in an orderly manner, a manner that is described here along with the overall process and responsibility for maintaining the established baselines, the procedures for changes, the review process, and the changes that may be proposed to the customer when necessary. In addition the use and processing of deviations and waivers will be described. Finally the relationship between hardware and software changes and the effects on change processing will be discussed.

MAINTAINING THE BASELINES

Good business practice in the use of the configuration management process dictates that software be baselined and under control when provided to a customer or user within the project or other inside organizational entity.

As noted in Chapter 8, baselines consist of approved documents and subsequently the related code. In order to maintain the integrity of these elements CM must provide for proper protection of the master media, normally on a computer data base or in file cabinets. At all times CM must ensure controlled access to the master copy files for the purpose of adding, deleting, or changing a software element. The project team must have confidence that copies obtained from master files, whether hardcopy or database, represent the latest revision or requested version and are accurate.

To maintain the established integrity of the baseline, one can incorporate changes into these masters only from approved change documents and replace them only by an approved updated version. A verification of the incorporation is also necessary to guarantee that the document is correct and that no other elements within or any other documents or code have been affected. Maintaining the baselines is a CM control activity. The assurance of this baseline maintenance is a responsibility of CM for processing and software quality for verification.

Baseline maintenance procedures should also account for the increased employment of software prototyping during the early phases of the software life cycle. Prototyping is a means of trying out the product by generating code from documents not yet approved in order to prove the design integrity of a given theory or design description. To maintain adequate data in support of the prototyping effort, changes and change incorporation are the responsibilities of the software engineers. Provisions must be made, however, for change control activity to take effect when it is determined that baselined documents or code is affected by the prototyping process. For example, this would be necessary if a designed and approved interface were found to be inefficient and a better way prescribed. This in turn would affect several approved documents and code, which would require changes to the approved elements.

Prototyping can also be used to prove the validity of a proposed change. This effort could be lengthy, but the changes that occur during this period are made by the software engineers and the final changes are submitted to the change control activity when the engineers are satisfied that they have arrived at the proper solution to the problem.

One must naturally be concerned about cost due to the increasing emphasis on cost of maintaining quality placed on developers by the customers. The developer thus must keep careful records of the number of changes to approved documentation and code placed under configuration control and their relative cost for preparation, processing, review and incorporation. If the changes are found early enough, they are unlikely to have as great an impact as if detected in the integration and test phase.

Too many changes early in the cycle, however, may well indicate that the documentation being prepared is inadequate and the review process is failing to catch the errors in the documents under review.

CM must be constantly alert for the two types of changes that act as primary cost drivers. The first is the change that is avoidable, and the second is the change that must be made or because of errors create new changes. Avoidable changes are caused by flaws in the design's development, lack of good checking of the design documents or subsequent code during the design walkthrough and the code walkthrough, and lack of a good peer review of the SRS, PDD and DDD. Although CM may have little control over the review and checking process, it should be able to detect avoidable changes and bring them to the attention of the project managers.

The need for revision or error correction is the result of poor preparation of change documents, inaccurate entries, or lack of entry in the blocks provided on the change form. In addition, although a form's data blocks may be filled out, the entry may not be correct or sufficient. For example, the justification block is rarely completed correctly for a variety of reasons, including shame on the part of the preparer for admitting an error. More important, however, are the explanations for cause of the problem or incident that made the change necessary and the accurate description of the root cause. Erroneous data could lead the correcting analyst to make a change that has far greater impact than the original problem. CM should be able to verify the content before others have to take the time to review the change.

Use of a software change review board of two to three experts has proven most worthwhile in detecting possibly erroneous data that, when corrected early, can eliminate the need for costly revisions in a change document or a new change.

PROCESSING INTERNAL CHANGES

There is no standard for processing internal or project-only changes; no procedures have been prescribed. There are, however, a number of guidelines that have been published. One is the IEEE 1074, *Software Life Cycle Process*, and IEEE STD 1042, *A Guide to Software*

Configuration Management, as well as the EIA Bulletin 6-4, *Software Change Control* [61]. A number of company descriptions of change processing are also available, and most companies will share such information, or even discuss it, with anyone who enquires.

The following generic descriptions offer a baseline from which to enhance current procedures followed by one's own company or project.

To begin with, CM should make provision within a procedure for changes to documents, as opposed to code, and subsequently changes from the field. The basic procedural issues are the form, the processing of the form, the review, the level of authority to approve a change, the incorporation, and the closeout and recording of time, cost, and lessons learned. This recording is necessary whether for documents or code—in any form, on any media, in any system.

Form and format are important. The data elements of the form/format must be sufficient to explain why the change is needed, what is to be changed, who is requesting it, and in what environment it resides. Next, one must provide the information needed to describe the problem, incident, or cause in sufficient detail and to recommend corrective action. Also important is information for other documents/code that may be affected or changes that are related to the one being prepared. The review and signature blocks, as well as other statistical information, must also be accommodated. Finally a block must be set aside for describing how the problem was solved, corrected, enhanced, and so on. Figure 9.1 is a sample form. Figure 9.2 illustrates the automated layout containing the same data elements.

The most famous form in the U.S. government is the *Engineering Change Proposal*, prepared in accordance with MIL STD 480 (Figure 9.3). Figure 9.4 contains the Canadian equivalent, the *Aerospace Engineering Change Proposal*. Appendix 3 provides a written description of what should be contained in the NATO form as agreed on by the buyer and the seller.

One important thing to remember about the construction of a form is that it must be kept simple. Further, it must be accepted by all persons on a project or within a company or organization (or as noted in the NATO document, by a country). It is preferable if an organizational entity has agreed to use a common form. With reuse becoming more and more prevalent, it is important that if the using group feels a change is necessary, the other users can review the change request in a familiar format rather than have to search around for the data elements most important to them. If the format is not acceptable, people will find ways to get around the form, which in many instances can result in no form at all. The bottom line here is that the form is the communicator and control is communication.

The procedure process is not complicated, but it does spawn a number of questions that will arise in any number of different situations. First and foremost is what constitutes the need for a change. Many times a programmer will argue about the need for the change, unless the system is down and there is no way known to bypass the cause of the problem. In essence, the programmer is asking if there is really a problem or if other events will eliminate the perceived need. The need for the change will be questioned a number of times during processing and review. Many would prefer not to go through this change, and thus the best strategy is to create an environment in which any perceived need is welcomed and those changes that are not needed are filtered out.

Sometimes the need for change is obvious—the system will not work as advertised. Often the system works inconsistently and it is not known if a problem really exists or even where the problem may be located. Many times, as the system is used, new features become evident. The change process should provide for and encourage the documentation of

PROBLEM/CHANGE REPORT PCR NO._____

SYSTEM/PROJ _____ PAGE _____ OF _____

TITLE/DESCRIPTION				SITE		CONTRACT NO.

PCR

PROBLEM DATE/TIME	FAILED OR SUSPECTED ELEMENT (NAME)	ELEMENT ID NO.	VER/REV	NEXT HIGHER LEVEL ID NO.

TEST NAME	RELATED DOCUMENT (TITLE)	DOCUMENT NO.	REV

SUBMITTED BY	DATE	ECP NO.	CLASS □ I □ II	CUSTOMER CONCURRENCE IN CLASSIFICATION DATE	EFFECTIVITY

PROBLEM DESCRIPTION:

SUMMARY OF CHANGE AND REASON:

—SOFTWARE ELEMENTS AND DOCUMENTS CHANGED

SOFTWARE ELEMENT NAME OR DOCUMENT TITLE	IDENTIFICATION NO.	NEXT HIGHER LEVEL ID NO.	NEW VER/REV

ACTION REQUIRED TO CLOSE:

IMPACT ON:	Y	N		Y	N		Y	N		Y	N	
□ PSL □ ML			SCHEDULE SUBCONTRACT DATA ITEM			TEST EQUIPMENT/SW FIRMWARE FACILITY/SITE			DELIVERABLE HDW TRAINING SW MANUALS			SW DOCUMENTATION SUPPORT SW/SW TOOLS OTHER:

SRB DISPOSITION	□ APPROVE	□ DISAPPROVE	□ DEFER UNTIL:

SRB CHAIRPERSON	DATE	SYSTEMS ENGR	DATE	SRB MEMBER	DATE	SRB MEMBER	DATE
PROBLEM/CHANGE TYPE		ASSIGNED TO	DATE	PRIORITY	SCHED DATE	ANALYSIS TIME DATE COMPLETE (HRS)	

SCCB DISPOSITION	□ APPROVE	□ DISAPPROVE	□ DEFER UNTIL:

SCCB CHAIRPERSON	DATE	SW PROJECT LEADER	DATE	SYSTEMS ENGR	DATE	PROGRAM MGMT	DATE
CONFIGURATION MGMT	DATE	QUALITY ASSURANCE	DATE	SOFTWARE TEST	DATE	ILS MGMT	DATE

CLOSURE ACTION

INCORPORATED BY	DATE	VERIFIED BY	DATE	INCORP. TIME (HRS)	VERIF. TIME (HRS)	CLOSED BY	DATE

Figure 9.1 Problem/change report.

PROBLEM/CHANGE REPORT

PCR No. VWW-0009
Page   1

Title/Description: SADDS PDL EXTRACTOR ENHANCEMENT
Problem Date: 02/28/91   Submitted By: L. L" _____   Site: _____   Library ML

Problem Description
    An increasing number of users are complaining about the PDL extraction system. It is
    currently not flexible enough to handle
    the type of Ada PDL being written. Possibly need to increase
    the number of files held in memory to speed up the extraction process.

Recommendations
    Need to save 4 rather than 3 files when extracting PDL. Algorithm for the unit
    extractions needs to handle some of the more obscure instances. Update the SADDS User
    Guide as needed.

CSUs Affected	CC #	Nxt Higher CC #	Versions Old	New
FILE_MANAGER (ADA BODY)	1980018	1980016	0005	
LINE_MANAGER (ADA SPEC)	1980026	1980025	0005	
LINE_MANAGER (ADA BODY)	1980027	1980025	0005	
KEYWORD_SECTION_MGR (ADA SPEC)	1980023	1980022	0005	
KEYWORD_SECTION_MGR (ADA BODY)	1980024	1980022	0005	
UNIT_MANAGER (ADA SPEC)	1980020	1980019	0005	
UNIT_MANAGER (ADA BODY)	1980021	1980019	0006	
SADDS USER GUIDE (DOC)	1980003	1980000	A	

Assigned To: Date:
Priority: Scheduled Completion Date:

RELATED DOCUMENTS
    SRS: T   SDD: T   System Test Plan: F   Software Test Plan: F   CSOM: F   SDP: F

Classification Category: Software

PROBLEM TYPE
    S/W Requirements: T   Interface Detail: F   Data: F   Logic Error: F
    Conventions/Standards: F   Environment: F   Math: F   Other: T

SRB Dispostion: (N = Analysis, A = Approve, D = Disapprove,
SCCB Dispostion: F = Defer, C = Cancelled)

SRB Chairperson	SRB Member	SRB Member	SRB Member
CCB Chairperson	SDTL	System Eng Mgr	Program Eng Mgr
Software Test	Quality Assurance	Configuration Mgmt.	

Verified — See Database   Closed   See Database

Figure 9.2 P/CR form, computer printout.

all these cases. Every change request should receive serious consideration and the submitter
should be treated with respect.

Another major issue is whether a change is a correction of a bug, fault, or defect in the
product or an enhancement. Engineers will continually lobby for changes to be classified
as enhancements because defects normally reflect badly on the engineers and programmers.
Customers will lobby for the change to be classified as the correction of a defect because they

ENGINEERING CHANGE PROPOSAL, PAGE 1	DATE *(YYMMDD)*	Form Approved OMB No. 0704-0188

Public reporting burden for this collection of information is estimated to average 2 hours per response, including the time for reviewing instructions, searching existing data sources, gathering and maintaining the data needed, and completing and reviewing the collection of information. Send comments regarding this burden estimate or any other aspect of this collection of information, including suggestions for reducing this burden, to Washington Headquarters Services, Directorate for Information Operations and Reports, 1215 Jefferson Davis Highway, Suite 1204, Arlington, VA 22202-4302. and to the Office of Information and Regulatory Affairs, Office of Management and Budget, Washington, DC 20503.

PROCURING ACTIVITY NO.

1. ORIGINATOR NAME AND ADDRESS

2. CLASS OF ECP

3. JUST. CODE

4. PRIORITY

5. ECP DESIGNATION

a. MODEL/TYPE	b. CAGE CODE	c. SYSTEM DESIGNATION

6. BASELINE AFFECTED
☐ Functional ☐ Product ☐ Allocated

d. ECP NO.	e. TYPE	f. REV

7. OTHER SYS/CONFIG. ITEMS AFFECTED
☐ YES ☐ NO

8. SPECIFICATIONS AFFECTED - TEST PLAN

9. DRAWINGS AFFECTED

	CAGE CODE	SPECIFICATION/DOCUMENT NO.	REV	SCN	CAGE CODE	NUMBER	REV	NOR
a. SYSTEM								
b. ITEM								
c. TEST PLAN								

10. TITLE OF CHANGE

11. CONTRACT NO. AND LINE ITEM

12. PROCURING CONTRACTING OFFICER
CODE | TEL

13. CONFIGURATION ITEM NOMENCLATURE

14. IN PRODUCTION
☐ YES ☐ NO

15. LOWEST ASSEMBLY AFFECTED

NOMENCLATURE	PART NO.	NSN

16. DESCRIPTION OF CHANGE

17. NEED FOR CHANGE

18. PRODUCTION EFFECTIVITY BY SERIAL NUMBER

19. EFFECT ON PRODUCTION DELIVERY SCHEDULE

20. RETROFIT

a. RECOMMENDED ITEM EFFECTIVITY	c. SHIP/VEHICLE CLASS AFFECTED
b. ESTIMATED KIT DELIVERY SCHEDULE	d. LOCATIONS OR SHIP/VEHICLE NUMBER AFFECTED

21. ESTIMATED COSTS/SAVINGS UNDER CONTRACT

22. ESTIMATED NET TOTAL COSTS/SAVINGS

23. SUBMITTING ACTIVITY AUTHORIZED SIGNATURE

23.a. TITLE

24. APPROVAL/DISAPPROVAL

a. CLASS I	b. CLASS II	c. CLASS II
☐ APPROVAL RECOMMENDED ☐ DISAPPROVAL RECOMMENDED	☐ APPROVED ☐ DISAPPROVED	☐ CONCUR IN CLASSIFICATION OF CHANGE ☐ DO NOT CONCUR IN CLASSIFICATION OF CHANGE

d. GOVERNMENT ACTIVITY	SIGNATURE	DATE *(YYMMDD)*

e. APPROVAL ☐ APPROVED ☐ DISAPPROVED	f. GOVERNMENT ACTIVITY	SIGNATURE	DATE *(YYMMDD)*

Figure 9.3 Engineering change proposal, pages 1–6.

ENGINEERING CHANGE PROPOSAL, PAGE 2	Form Approved OMB No. 0704-0188

Public reporting burden for this collection of information is estimated to average 2 hours per response, including the time for reviewing instructions, searching existing data sources, gathering and maintaining the data needed, and completing and reviewing the collection of information. Send comments regarding this burden estimate or any other aspect of this collection of information, including suggestions for reducing this burden, to Washington Headquarters Services, Directorate for Information Operations and Reports, 1215 Jefferson Davis Highway, Suite 1204, Arlington, VA 22202-4302, and to the Office of Information and Regulatory Affairs, Office of Management and Budget, Washington, DC 20503.

ORIGINATOR NAME AND ADDRESS	PROCURING ACTIVITY NUMBER
	ECP NUMBER

EFFECTS ON FUNCTIONAL/ALLOCATED CONFIGURATION IDENTIFICATION

25. OTHER SYSTEMS AFFECTED	26. OTHER CONTRACTORS/ACTIVITIES AFFECTED

27. CONFIGURATION ITEMS AFFECTED

28. EFFECTS ON PERFORMANCE ALLOCATIONS AND INTERFACES IN SYSTEM SPECIFICATION

29. EFFECTS ON EMPLOYMENT, INTEGRATED LOGISTICS SUPPORT, TRAINING, OPERATIONAL EFFECTIVENESS OR SOFTWARE

30. EFFECTS ON CONFIGURATION ITEM SPECIFICATIONS

31. DEVELOPMENTAL REQUIREMENTS AND STATUS

32 TRADE-OFFS AND ALTERNATIVE SOLUTIONS

33. DATE BY WHICH CONTRACTUAL AUTHORITY IS NEEDED

Figure 9.3 *(Continued)*

ENGINEERING CHANGE PROPOSAL, PAGE 3							*Form Approved* *OMB No. 0704-0188*

Public reporting burden for this collection of information is estimated to average 2 hours per response, including the time for reviewing instructions, searching existing data sources, gathering and maintaining the data needed, and completing and reviewing the collection of information. Send comments regarding this burden estimate or any other aspect of this collection of information, including suggestions for reducing this burden, to Washington Headquarters Services, Directorate for Information Operations and Reports, 1215 Jefferson Davis Highway, Suite 1204, Arlington, VA 22202-4302, and to the Office of Information and Regulatory Affairs, Office of Management and Budget, Washington, DC 20503.

ORIGINATOR NAME AND ADDRESS

PROCURING ACTIVITY NUMBER

ECP NUMBER

EFFECTS ON PRODUCT CONFIGURATION IDENTIFICATION, LOGISTICS, AND OPERATIONS

(X)	FACTOR	ENCL	PAR	(X)	FACTOR	ENCL	PAR
	34. EFFECT ON PRODUCT CONFIGURATION IDENTIFICATION OR CONTRACT				36. EFFECT ON OPERATIONAL EMPLOYMENT		
	a. PERFORMANCE				a. SAFETY		
	b. WEIGHT-BALANCE-STABILITY (Aircraft)	•			b. SURVIVABILITY		
	c. WEIGHT-MOMENT (Other equipment)				c. RELIABILITY		
	d. CDRL TECHNICAL DATA				d. MAINTAINABILITY		
	e. NOMENCLATURE				e. SERVICE LIFE		
					f. OPERATING PROCEDURES		
	35. EFFECT ON INTEGRATED LOGISTICS SUPPORT (ILS) ELEMENTS				g. ELECTROMAGNETIC INTERFERENCE		
					h. ACTIVATION SCHEDULE		
	a. ILS PLANS				i. CRITICAL SINGLE POINT FAILURE ITEMS		
	b. MAINTENANCE CONCEPT PLANS AND PROCEDURES				j. INTEROPERABILITY		
	c. LOGISTICS SUPPORT ANALYSES						
	d. INTERIM SUPPORT PROGRAMS						
	e. SPARES AND REPAIR PARTS				37. OTHER CONSIDERATIONS		
	f. TECH MANUALS/PROGRAMMING TAPES				a. INTERFACE		
	g. FACILITIES				b. OTHER AFFECTED EQUIPMENT/GFE/GFP		
	h. SUPPORT EQUIPMENT				c. PHYSICAL CONSTRAINTS		
	i. OPERATOR TRAINING				d. COMPUTER PROGRAMS AND RESOURCES		
	j. OPERATOR TRAINING EQUIPMENT				e. REWORK OF OTHER EQUIPMENT		
	k. MAINTENANCE TRAINING				f. SYSTEM TEST PROCEDURES		
	l. MAINTENANCE TRAINING EQUIPMENT				g. WARRANTY/GUARANTEE		
	m. CONTRACT MAINTENANCE				h. PARTS CONTROL		
	n. PACKAGING, HANDLING, STORAGE, TRANSPORTABILITY						

38. ALTERNATE SOLUTIONS

39. DEVELOPMENTAL STATUS

40. RECOMMENDATIONS FOR RETROFIT

41. WORK-HOURS PER UNIT TO INSTALL RETROFIT KITS
a. ORGANIZATION   b. INTERMEDIATE   c. DEPOT   d. OTHER

42. WORK-HOURS TO CONDUCT SYSTEM TESTS AFTER RETROFIT

43. THIS CHANGE MUST BE ACCOMPLISHED
☐ BEFORE   ☐ WITH   ☐ AFTER THE FOLLOWING CHANGES

44. IS CONTRACTOR FIELD SERVICE ENGINEERING REQUIRED?
☐ YES   ☐ NO

45. OUT OF SERVICE TIME

46. EFFECT OF THIS ECP AND PREVIOUSLY APPROVED ECPS ON ITEM

47. DATE CONTRACTUAL AUTHORITY NEEDED FOR

PRODUCTION _____

RETROFIT _____

Figure 9.3 *(Continued)*

ENGINEERING CHANGE PROPOSAL, PAGE 4		*Form Approved* *OMB No. 0704-0188*

Public reporting burden for this collection of information is estimated to average 2 hours per response, including the time for reviewing instructions, searching existing data sources, gathering and maintaining the data needed, and completing and reviewing the collection of information. Send comments regarding this burden estimate or any other aspect of this collection of information, including suggestions for reducing this burden, to Washington Headquarters Services, Directorate for Information Operations and Reports, 1215 Jefferson Davis Highway, Suite 1204, Arlington, VA 22202-4302, and to the Office of Information and Regulatory Affairs, Office of Management and Budget, Washington, DC 20503.

ORIGINATOR NAME AND ADDRESS	PROCURING ACTIVITY NUMBER
	ECP NUMBER

48. ESTIMATED NET TOTAL COST IMPACT *(USE PARENTHESES FOR SAVINGS)*

FACTOR	COST / SAVINGS UNDER CONTRACT					OTHER COSTS/ SAVINGS TO THE GOVERNMENT
	NON- RECURRING	RECURRING			TOTAL	
		UNIT	QUANTITY	TOTAL (Recurring)		
	(1)	(2)	(3)	(4)	(5)	(6)
a. PRODUCTION COST / SAVINGS						
CONFIGURATION ITEM / SOFTWARE CI						
FACTORY TEST EQUIPMENT						
SPECIAL FACTORY TOOLING						
SCRAP						
ENGINEERING, ENGINEERING DATA REVISION						
REVISION OF TEST PROCEDURES						
QUALIFICATION OF NEW ITEMS						
SUBTOTAL OF PROD COSTS / SAVINGS						
b. RETROFIT COSTS						
ENGINEERING DATA REVISION						
PROTOTYPE TESTING						
KIT PROOF TESTING						
RETROFIT KITS FOR OPERATIONAL SYSTEMS						
PREP OF MWO / 1CTO / SC/ ALT / TD						
SPECIAL TOOLING FOR RETROFIT						
CONTRACTOR FIELD SERVICE ENGINEERING						
GOV'T PERSONNEL INSTALLATION						
TESTING AFTER RETROFIT						
MODIFICATION OF GFE / GFP						
QUALIFICATION OF GFE / GFP						
SUBTOTAL OF RETROFIT COSTS / SAVINGS						
c. INTEGRATED LOGISTICS SUPPORT COSTS/ SAVINGS						
SPARES / REPAIR PARTS REWORK						
NEW SPARES AND REPAIR PARTS						
SUPPLY / PROVISIONING DATA						
SUPPORT EQUIPMENT						
RETROFIT KITS FOR SPARES						
OPERATOR TRAINING COURSES						
MAINTENANCE TRAINING COURSES						
REV. OF TECH MAN / PROGRAMMING TAPES						
NEW TECH MAN / PROGRAMMING TAPES						
TRAINING / TRAINERS						
INTERIM SUPPORT						
MAINTENANCE MANPOWER						
COMPUTER PROGRAMS / DOCUMENTATION						
SUBTOTAL OF ILS COSTS / SAVINGS						
d. OTHER COSTS / SAVINGS						
e. SUBTOTAL COSTS / SAVINGS						
SUBTOTAL UNDER CONTRACT						
f. COORDINATION OF CHANGES WITH OTHER CONTRACTORS						
g. COORDINATION CHANGES BY GOVERNMENT						
ESTIMATED NET TOTAL COSTS / SAVINGS						

Figure 9.3 *(Continued)*

ENGINEERING CHANGE PROPOSAL, PAGE 5					Form Approved OMB No. 0704-0188

Public reporting burden for this collection of information is estimated to average 2 hours per response, including the time for reviewing instructions, searching existing data sources, gathering and maintaining the data needed, and completing and reviewing the collection of information. Send comments regarding this burden estimate or any other aspect of this collection of information, including suggestions for reducing this burden, to Washington Headquarters Services, Directorate for Information Operations and Reports, 1215 Jefferson Davis Highway, Suite 1204, Arlington, VA 22202-4302, and to the Office of Information and Regulatory Affairs, Office of Management and Budget, Washington, DC 20503

ORIGINATOR NAME AND ADDRESS				PROCURING ACTIVITY NUMBER
				ECP NUMBER

49. ESTIMATED COST / SAVINGS SUMMARY RELATED ECP'S (USE PARENTHESES FOR SAVINGS)		CAGE CODE (1)	ECP NUMBER (2)	COSTS / SAVINGS UNDER CONTRACTS (3)	OTHER COSTS / SAVINGS TO GOVERNMENT (4)
a. PRODUCTION COST / SAVINGS (Subtotal of Costs / Savings Elements from block 48a applicable to aircraft, ship, tank, vehicle, missile or its subsystem)					
SUBTOTAL PRODUCTION COST / SAVINGS					
b. RETROFIT COSTS (Applicable to aircraft ship, tank, vehicle, missile or its subsystem)					
SUBTOTAL RETROFIT COSTS					
c. INTEGRATED LOGISTICS SUPPORT COSTS / SAVINGS					
REVISED REQUIREMENTS					
1. ITEM RETROFIT (if not covered under "b") (Applicable to aircraft, ship, tank, vehicle, missile or its subsystem)					
2. ILS SUBTOTAL (Applicable to aircraft, ship, tank, vehicle missile or its subsystem)					
3. OPERATOR TRAINER (Net total cost / saving from each ECP covering operator trainer)					
4. MAINTENANCE TRAINER (Net total cost / saving from each ECP covering maintenance trainer)					
5. OTHER TRAINING EQUIPMENT					
6. SUPPORT EQUIPMENT (Net total cost / saving from each ECP on support equipment)					
7. ILS PLANS					
8. MAINTENANCE CONCEPT, PLANS, SYSTEM DOCUMENTS					
9. INTERIM SUPPORT PLAN					

NEW REQUIREMENTS	PROCURING ACTIVITY CODE	NON-RECURRING COSTS	RECURRING COSTS				
			UNIT	QTY	TOTAL		
10. PROVISIONING DOCUMENTATION							
11. OPER TRNR / TRNG DEVICES / EQUIP							
12. MANUALS / PROGRAMMING TAPES, SPARES, REPAIR PARTS (For 11)							
13. MAINTENANCE TRNR / TRNG DEVICES / EQUIPMENT							
14. MANUALS / PROGRAMMING TAPES, SPARES REPAIR PARTS (FOR 13)							
15. SUPPORT EQUIPMENT							
16. MANUALS / PROGRAMMING TAPES (For 15)							
17. PROVISIONING DOCUMENTATION (For 15)							
18. REPAIR PARTS (For 15)							
SUBTOTAL ILS COSTS / SAVINGS (SUM OF c.1 THROUGH c.18)							

d. OTHER COSTS/SAVINGS (Total from block 48d or related ECP'S)	CAGE CODE	ECP NUMBER		
TOTAL OTHER COSTS / SAVINGS				
SUBTOTALS OF COLUMNS				
SUBTOTAL UNDER CONTRACT				
e. ESTIMATED NET TOTAL COSTS / SAVINGS (a + b + c + d)				

Figure 9.3 *(Continued)*

ENGINEERING CHANGE PROPOSAL, PAGE 6
HARDWARE

DATE (YYMMDD)

ORIGINATOR NAME AND ADDRESS

PROCURING ACTIVITY NUMBER

CAGE CODE   ECP NUMBER

CONFIGURATION ITEM NOMENCLATURE   TITLE OF CHANGE

DATE AUTHORIZED TO PROCEED ——▶
RECEIVED BY CONTRACTOR ▼

⟨S⟩ START DELIVERY   ⟨C⟩ COMPLETE DELIVERY   ▼ PROGRESS POINT

NO. OF MONTHS	1	2	3	4	5	6	7	8	9	10	11	12	13	14	15	16	17	18	19	20	21	22	23	24	25	26	27	28	29	30	31	32	33	34	35	36
CONFIGURATION ITEM																																				
PRODUCTION																																				
TECH MANUALS																																				
RETROFIT																																				
MWO / TCTO / SC / ALT / TD																																				
SPARES / REPAIR PARTS																																				
SOFTWARE																																				
SUPPORT EQUIPMENT																																				
PRODUCTION																																				
TECH MANUALS / PROG TAPES																																				
RETROFIT																																				
MWO / TCTO / SC / ALT / TD																																				
REPAIR PARTS																																				
TRAINING																																				
OPERATOR																																				
MAINTENANCE																																				
NO. OF MONTHS	1	2	3	4	5	6	7	8	9	10	11	12	13	14	15	16	17	18	19	20	21	22	23	24	25	26	27	28	29	30	31	32	33	34	35	36

Figure 9.3 (*Continued*)

ORIGINATOR – AUTEUR

FILE NUMBER   NUMÉRO DE DOSSIER

PMRB NUMBER – NUMÉRO CPEM

CFTO – ITFC

(for CF use only)
(Réservé aux FC)

AEROSPACE
ENGINEERING CHANGE PROPOSAL

PROJET DE MODIFICATION
DE MATÉRIEL AÉROSPATIAL

SECTION I

1. CONTRACTOR
   AECP NUMBER   Numéro PMMA du constructeur ou réparateur

| REVISION
Révision | DATE | CATEGORY
Catégorie | CONTRACT CD NUMBER (if applicable)
Numéro du contrat ou de la demande de contrat (s'il y a lieu) |
|---|---|---|---|
| | | | |

2. NAME OF COMPLETE ASSEMBLY (aircraft, engine, etc)
   Nom de l'ensemble (aéronef, moteur, etc.)

MODEL/TYPE DESIGNATION
Appellation du modèle ou du type

AECP TITLE – Titre du PMMA

3. PART OR SUB ASSEMBLY AFFECTED
   Pièce ou sous-ensemble touché

NATO STOCK NUMBER
Numéro nomenclature OTAN

PART NUMBER
Numéro de pièce

MODEL TYPE
Modèle ou type

4. NATURE OF CHANGE – Nature de la modification

Figure 9.4   Aerospace engineering change proposal, pages 1–7.

can get the fix under warranty or a support agreement if one exists. Otherwise, the customer will most likely have to pay unless the buyer and seller agree that there was an obvious defect not meeting specified requirements. In either case, complete and well-maintained requirements specifications, documents, and agreements can solve the dilemma. This is why CM should maintain these requirements and be able to trace them to the defective unit and, in turn, trace a defective unit to the requirement. In some instances, the requirement can

5. CHECK ITEMS THAT ARE AFFECTED BY THE CHANGE AND EXPLAIN IN BLOCK 6 OR BY ATTACHMENT
Cocher les articles touchés par la modification et donner des explications à la case 6 ou sur feuillet annexé.

AIRWORTHINESS
Navigabilité □

COMBAT EFFECTIVENESS
Efficacité au combat □

PERFORMANCE
Rendement □

OPERATING PROCEDURES
Méthodes d'exploitation □

INTERCHANGEABILITY
Interchangeabilité □

OVERHAUL METHODS
Méthodes de révision □

ELECTRO MAGNETIC COMPATIBILITY & ELECTRICAL LOADING
Compatibilité électro-magnétique et charge électrique □

WEIGHT & BALANCE
Masse et centrage □

TOOLS & TEST EQUIPMENT
Outils et matériel d'essai □

MAINTENANCE PROCEDURES
Méthodes d'entretien □

SPARES
Pièces de rechange □

SIMULATORS & TRAINERS
Simulateurs et maquettes d'instructions □

AMSE
Matériel aéronautique de servitude □

OTHER
Divers □

6. REASON FOR CHANGE — Raison de la modification

7. CHANGE INITIATED BY CONTRACTOR FOR — Modification proposée par le constructeur ou le réparateur pour:

COMPLIANCE WITH NEW OR REVISED SPEC
Se conformer à une nouvelle norme ou à une norme révisée

(quote Spec number and CF authority — Citer le numéro de la norme et l'autorité FC)
FIX FOR UCR NUMBER
Donner suite au RENS Nº

(quote UCR number and CF authority — Citer le numéro du RENS et l'autorité FC)
COMPLIANCE WITH CF INSTRUCTION NUMBER
Se conformer à l'Instruction des FC nº

(quote CF Instruction Number and CF authority — Citer le numéro de l'Instruction des FC et l'autorité FC)
OTHER
Autre raison

8. EFFECT ON WEIGHT AND BALANCE — Influence sur masse et centrage

| WEIGHT CHANGE | LBS | AT STATION |
| Changement de masse | lb | à la référence |

| VERIFIED AIRCRAFT PROJECT OFFICER — Vérifié Officier de projets (aérons ts) | | |
| SIGNATURE | DESIGNATION — Fonction | DATE |

Figure 9.4 *(Continued)*

9. ELECTRO MAGNETIC COMPATIBILITY AND ELECTRICAL LOADING ASSESSMENT
   Evaluation de la compatibilité électro-magnétique et de la charge électrique

SPECIAL OFFICER — Officier spécialiste

SIGNATURE	DESIGNATION — Fonction	DATE

10. NON RECURRING COSTS — Frais non répétés

	MAN HOURS Heures-hommes	COST MH Coût/ heures-hommes	TOTAL
ENGINEERING Technologie			
TOOLING Outillage			
PUBLICATIONS			
TRAINING Formation			
PROTOTYPE			
OTHER Divers			

11. COST OF KITS/REWORK ITEMS — Coût des lots de modifications ou des articles réusinés

	MAN HOURS heures-hommes	COST MH Coût/ heures-hommes	TOTAL
MATERIAL PER KIT — Matériel par lot			
FABRICATION/REWORK (per item or kit) Fabrication ou réusinage (par articles ou par lot)			
ASSEMBLY PER ITEM KIT Assemblage par article ou par lot			
OTHER Divers			

TOTAL COST PER KIT REWORK
COÛT TOTAL PAR LOT OU PAR ARTICLE RÉUSINÉ   a) _____

INSTALLATION COST (per kit)
FRAIS D'INSTALLATION (par lot)   b) _____

TOTAL KIT REWORK PLUS INSTALLATION PER KIT
TOTAL LOT OU RÉUSINAGE PLUS INSTALLATION PAR LOT = a + b = _____

12. NUMBER OF KITS (include spares training and trainers)
    Nombre de lots (y compris rechange, formation et maquettes)   (c) _____

NUMBER OF INSTALLATIONS
Nombre d'installations   (d) _____

TOTAL KIT COST (a x c)
Coût total des lots (a x c)   (e) _____

TOTAL INSTALLATION COST (b x d)
Coût total des installations (b x d)   (f) _____

TOTAL COST KITS PLUS INSTALLATION (e + f)
Coût total: lots plus installations (e — f)   (g) _____

DUTY AND TAXES (if applicable)
Douane et taxes (s'il y a lieu)   (h) _____

GRAND TOTAL
   (non recurring + total kits + installations cost + duty and taxes)
      (para 10 total + g + h)
   (Frais non répétés + coût des lots + coût des installations + douanes et taxes)
      (total du par. 10 + g + h)   _____

Figure 9.4   *(Continued)*

13 CHECK ITEMS THAT ARE AFFECTED AND LIST CFTO OR PUBLICATION (Attach list if necessary)
Cocher les publications touchées et en indiquer le numéro (annexer un feuillet au besoin)

AIRCRAFT OPERATING INSTRUCTIONS
Instructions d'exploitation de matériel aérien
☐ CFTO/PUB
ITFC/Public.

DESCRIPTION AND MAINTENANCE
Description et instructions d'entretien
☐ CFTO/PUB
ITFC/Public.

REPAIR AND OVERHAUL/REPAIR SCHEMES
Instructions de réparation et de révision
☐ CFTO/PUB
ITFC/Public.

PARTS LIST
Nomenclature des pièces
☐ CFTO/PUB
ITFC/Public.

SIMULATORS AND TRAINERS
Simulateurs et maquettes d'instruction
☐ CFTO/PUB
ITFC/Public.

OTHER
Divers
☐ CFTO/PUB
ITFC/Public.

14. LIST DRAWINGS AFFECTED — Dessins touchés

---

15. ASSEMBLY IN PRODUCTION?
Incorporation lors de la fabrication?

YES ☐ NO ☐
Oui   Non

IF YES — ESTIMATE EFFECTIVE DATE
OR SERIAL NUMBERS
Le cas échéant, date approximative de prise d'effet
ou premier numéro de série modifié

IF YES – IS GOVERNMENT SUPPLIED MATERIAL
AFFECTED?
Le cas échéant, est-ce que le matériel fourni par l'État est
touché?

YES ☐ NO ☐
Oui   Non

DATE REQUIRED AT PLANT
Les lots doivent arriver à l'usine le

16. DOES CONTRACTOR RECOMMEND THAT CHANGES BE MADE RETROACTIVE ON ITEMS ALREADY DELIVERED TO CF?
Est-ce que le constructeur ou le réparateur recommande que les modifications soient incorporées aux articles déjà livrés?

YES ☐ NO ☐   IF YES COMPLETE BLOCKS 17, 18, 19, 20 AND SECTION 2.
Oui   Non   Le cas échéant, remplir les cases 17, 18, 19 et 20, ainsi que la section 2.

REASONS FOR RECOMMENDATION — Raisons de la recommandation

---

17. SERIAL NUMBERS AFFECTED (aircraft, engine, components)
Numéros de série touchés (aéronefs, moteur, organes)

WHEN MODIFICATION SHOULD BE EMBODIED?
(ie next periodic, on overhaul)
Quand la modification devrait-elle être incorporée?
(ex prochaine inspection périodique, révision)

18. BY WHOM WORK SHOULD BE PERFORMED   (ie mobile repair party contractor)
Par qui la modification devrait-elle être incorporée? (ex: équipe mobile de réparation, réparateur)

SOURCE OF KITS OR PARTS
Source des lots ou des pièces

DATE AVAILABLE
Disponibles le

Figure 9.4   *(Continued)*

19. ASSOCIATED MODIFICATIONS (CFTO Number and Title if known)
Modifications connexes (Citer le n⁰ et le nom de l'ITFC, autant que possible)

20. SPECIAL INSTRUCTIONS RE SPARES IN STOCK
Instructions spéciales sur les pièces de rechange en stock

21. CONTRACTORS CERTIFICATION — Attestation du constructeur ou du réparateur
REMARKS — Remarques

SIGNATURE
DESIGNATION/POSITION Fonction
DATE

22. AREA CANADIAN FORCES REPRESENTATIVE — REMARKS
Remarques du représentant régional des CF

SIGNATURE
RANK — Grade
DESIGNATION — Fonction
DATE

Figure 9.4   *(Continued)*

SECTION 2

MODIFICATION DATA — LISTE DES PIECES

PARTS REQUIRED NATO STOCK NUMBER Pièces nécessaires Numéro nomenclature OTAN	PART NUMBER Numéro de pièces	DESCRIPTION	QUANTITY Quantité

24. CERTIFIED THAT — Je certifie que:

  (a) NATO stock numbers are correct
     les numéros de nomenclature OTAN sont exacts,

  (b) Items without NSN are accounted for by part number
     les articles sans NNO sont comptabilisés par numéro de pièce,

  (c) Cataloguing action initiated on items listed at para (b) above
     des mesures ont été prises pour cataloguer les articles énumérés en (b) et

  (d) Modification kit alloted NSN
     qu'on a donné au lot de modification le NNO

TECHNICAL AUTHORITY/EQUIPMENT SPECIALIST — Responsable technique/spécialiste du matériel
REMARKS — Remarques

SIGNATURE
RANK — Grade
DESIGNATION — Fonction
DATE

Figure 9.4 *(Continued)*

25. MODIFICATION DATA – LISTE DES PIÈCES

PARTS REMOVED NATO STOCK NUMBER Pièces déposés Numéro nomenclature OTAN	PART NUMBER Numéro de pièce	DESCRIPTION	QUANTITY Quantité	DISPOSAL CLASS Catégorie d'affecta. (SEE PARA 26) (Voir par. 26)

26. STANDARD DISPOSAL CLASSES – CATÉGORIES RÉGULIÈRES D'AFFECTATION

(a) Items removed as a result of this modification, plus total stocks of these items, are of no further use to the CFSS.
   Les articles déposés à la suite de la présente modification ainsi que tous les stocks de ces articles ne sont plus d'aucune utilité au SAFC.

(b) Items removed as a result of this modification, are of no further use to the CFSS. Serviceable items in stock are required.
   Les articles déposés à la suite de la présente modification ne sont plus d'aucune utilité au SAFC. Les articles en stock et en état de service doivent être retenus.

(c) Items removed as a result of this modification, if serviceable, are to be returned to stock.
   Les articles qui sont déposés à la suite de la présente modification et qui sont en état de service, doivent être remis en stock.

(d) Repairable items removed are to be actioned in accordance with CFP 189.
   Les articles déposés et réparables doivent être traités conformément à la PFC 189.

(e) Items not listed in CFP 189 are to be reported to NDHQ/DPSUPS5 requesting allotment of repair authority.
   Les articles qui ne figurent pas à la PFC 189 doivent être signalés au QGDN/DOMSA5 pour qu'il en autorise la réparation.

(f) Items removed as a result of this modification plus total stocks are to be retained for instructional purposes.
   Les articles déposés à la suite de la présente modification ainsi que tous les stocks de ces articles doivent être retenus comme matériel didactique.

(g) Items removed as a result of this modification, plus total stock, are to be reworked and reused.
   Les articles déposés à la suite de la présente modification ainsi que tous les stocks de ces articles doivent être réusinés et réutilisés.

27. APPROPRIATE DISPOSAL ACTION TAKEN FOR ITEMS LISTED AT PARA 25
Les mesures appropriées ont été prises pour l'élimination des articles énumérés au par. 25.

TECHNICAL AUTHORITY/EQUIPMENT SPECIALIST – Responsable technique/spécialiste du matériel
REMARKS – Remarques

	SIGNATURE
	RANK – Grade
	DESIGNATION – Fonction
	DATE

Figure 9.4 *(Continued)*

be defective; for example, it might say "The sensor shall record temperature in centigrade" when it should have been Fahrenheit.

A small set of changes will always fall into the "unable to duplicate" category. The software engineer will say that the user is in error, and the user will say that the product is defective. Who is right? According to Rick Frederick, a configuration management consultant at Compass Corporation, Shrewsbury, NJ, 80 percent of the support engineer time is spent on engineering analysis and investigation of a small number of the reported changes. Good test cases allow the engineer and the user to work more closely together to resolve this type of change more quickly, according to Frederick. He goes on to say that such disputed changes become CM issues due to the level of involvement needed to review the completeness of the proposed changes, to support the review and approval of the changes, and to perform the status accounting activity. He concludes that accurate and complete processing and tracking of changes is paramount in any software quality metrics program and that change statistics form the basis of many of today's accepted criteria for successful software development.

Primary sources for change are varied, as noted in Figure 9.5. In instances when the system will not work, there is no argument about need or the cause. The need for some changes detected during test will be questioned if some feel that the test results did not validate a software requirement. Other errors detected may have been caused by the several categories noted in Figure 9.6, in addition to design review decisions, customer desire, added environmental requirements such as increased traffic volume in the air traffic control environment, suggested enhancements, or the root causes noted in Figure 9.7.

From whatever source, CM information and reports communicate the need or request for change in a lucid format to the primary processing body, such as a change review board. Figure 9.8 and Figure 9.9 illustrate the general flow of events for documentation and the subsequent handling of software code.

A must-fix situation requires little thought other than to ensure that the facts on the form/format are correct and that further change will be avoided. Other types of changes require more thought before valuable dollars are expended on an unnecessary change. One must consider the value of the change to the project/organization, the return on investment if the product is a marketable item, the impact on others working on interfacing modules and systems, and the likely overall cost of the change. The format should be able to accommodate these types of questions or at least provide continuation sheets to amplify the argument or discussion. This is the last chance before others expend time and dollars processing the change. When money is tight, discretion is the better part of valor—do not make the change unless there is no other way around the problem.

Once committed, the change is logged into a status accounting system to ensure traceability, thus avoiding the "what do you mean you did not get my change" remark. The log-in also sets up "flags" or warnings that a change is pending against a document, component, or unit. If a software review board is convened, the log-in will alert the leader of the board that a change is in the pipeline. Finally when one queries status accounting or gets a report, the change and affected documents and code will be shown.

If a review board is convened, it should quickly review a requested change, and assign a software engineer to evaluate it, recommend a corrective action, make the recommended change, and test the changed unit. An alternative is for the review board to request the evaluator to provide the factual information on the change form and forward it to the designated approval authority via the CM. In this case the approval authority will determine if the change has merit, approve the change request, and authorize an evaluator to make the change, test it, and incorporate it accordingly.

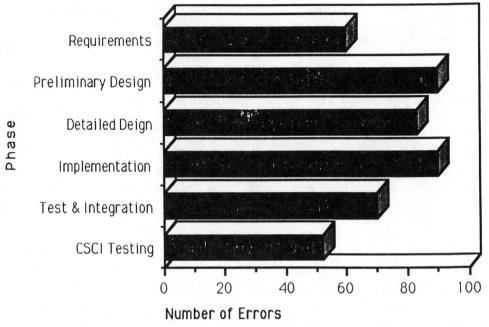

Figure 9.5 Error distribution by phase.

If the change under review is determined to affect the form, fit, or function of a software element or falls within some stipulated categories of criticality, then an engineering change proposal to the buyer may be required and processed as described below.

Much of what has already been discussed above can be done electronically and communicated to the reviewer/approver if the project is connected to a computer network. The automated version of the P/CR in Figure 9.2 is a good example.

All members of a project team and its support personnel are responsible for performing change control. At the management level, the software design team leader assures that the provisions of the project's or firm's procedures for performing change control are adhered to and that these procedures are included by description or reference in the software development plan. The team leader will also review proposed changes for their impact on other software elements, as well as cost and schedule, and report the status of changes and performance of the procedure to the program engineering manager who has overall responsibility for hardware and software change performance.

Additional responsibility rests with the system engineer, who reviews the proposed changes for their impact on system-level documentation, established baselines, interface, and test requirements.

Configuration management implements and performs the control process in accordance with the configuration management plan or, if this has not been written, with internal procedures. The software librarian provides the appropriate technical support to configuration management as well as quality assurance and software engineering during the processing and incorporation of the changes into the code or related documentation.

Overall, everyone on a given project is responsible for communicating that changes have occurred, have been processed, and have been incorporated. They must also ensure that

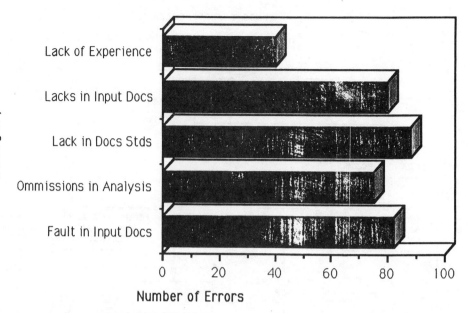

Figure 9.6   Error distribution by cause category.

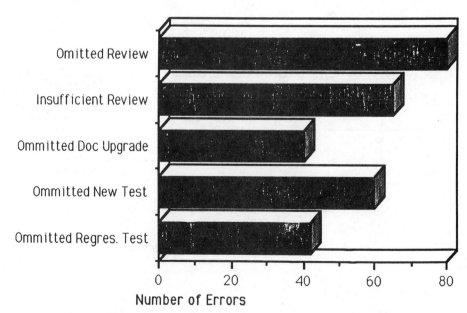

Figure 9.7   Error distribution by root causes.

CLASS I ECP PROCESSING

(AFTER BASELINE IS ESTABLISHED)

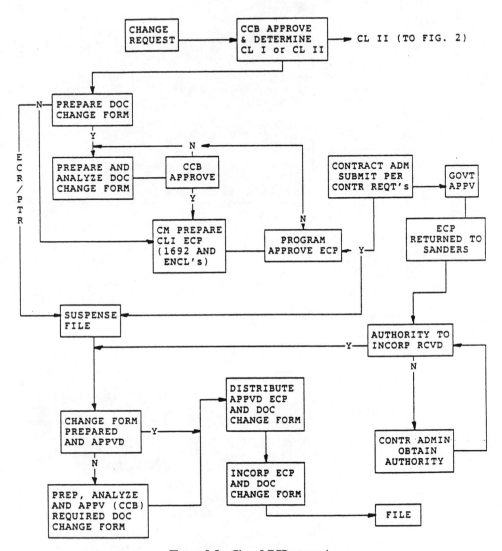

Figure 9.8 Class I ECP processing.

CLASS II ECP PROCESSING

(AFTER BASELINE IS ESTABLISHED)

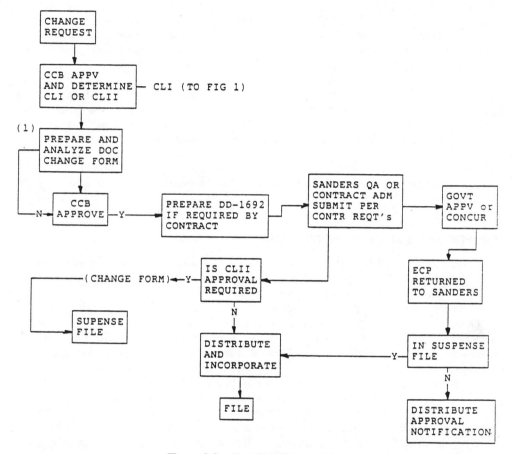

Figure 9.9 Class II ECP processing.

records are updated and that everyone can work with the system's documentation and code with confidence in its accuracy.

Some of the general requirements for control include describing the change procedure to be followed in the software development plan and the CM plan. In addition program directives may also be written and issued to those on the project, but it is important that they be in accordance with any customer requirements, company directives and practices, and company procedure for CM.

A very important requirement is that control must also apply to nondeliverable software (NDS) such as software support tools, editors, debuggers, and simulation routines. Specific details are described in DOD STD 2167. This requirement ensures that software developed in-house is not changed without proper communication to the users or that acquired third-party software (COTS) is not modified without being duly processed by the change control activity.

Normally code is transferred to the project support library from the working file/development library on acceptance of the code and its units test by a code walkthrough review committee. For affected code to be changed, a copy of the code must be transferred by the librarian from the protected project support library file to the corrector's working file. This means that the master remains protected throughout the change process and may be used in its current state until updated by the approved change.

The control process also requires the establishment of a configuration control board to review and dispose of the proposed changes and a software review board (SRB) to take a quick look at requested software changes before proceeding with sometimes lengthy processing. In addition, once a change has been approved and is incorporated, the updating of the software protective files and the software development file must be provided for and carried out.

One final requirement is that a proposed change, although approved internally, cannot be incorporated until approved by the customer or until other arrangements have been agreed to by both parties.

PROPOSING CHANGES TO THE CUSTOMER

When custom software is being procured, some provision must be made and agreed on by a buyer and a seller/developer to allow the submission of proposed changes affecting the form, fit, function, cost, schedule or terms of the original agreement.

Normally, when one orders a custom-built item such as a house, a boat, or even a suit or dress, one has the right to inspect the progress being made, make changes, consult about possible changes, and even reject the final product if not satisfied—as in the old song "Sam, You Made the Pants Too Long!" This same process occurs when a software product is developed for the marketplace, outside customers, or inside groups such as other corporate companies or one's own division. In fact, the customer could be you!

In order to ensure that the customer is satisfied, the project team needs to establish a process for effectively and efficiently communicating with the customer about changes. In many cases the agreement will be that the customer will pay for changes above and beyond what was estimated in the original contract. Thus the general rule: if a change affects the form, fit, or function of the affected item, it must be approved by the customer before incorporation.

There are also changes that do not affect the form, fit, or function of an item, but are more akin to clerical errors. These include programming errors, transpositions, missing call-ins or call-outs, and missing flag. These changes normally require concurrence but not formal approval by the customer and may be incorporated as soon as approved by the developer's review board.

There are also times when the customer requires that all changes be approved. This often occurs when the project has not been going well, there have been too many changes, the quality and reliability are poor, and so on. Changes may, in some instances, be incorporated before approval, but at far greater risk to the developer.

A number of different forms are in use for proposing changes today. Possibly the most famous is the *Engineering Change Proposal* (ECP) described in MIL STD 480 [7]. Others have variations on the ECP form (See Appendix 3). This form is all-inclusive. As noted in Chapter 3 on the history of CM, earlier ECP formats were not sufficient for the information required on complex change proposals, and thus the form grew from two pages to six. One must be careful to note that the standard simply describes how to prepare the form, not how to process it.

In addition to the full ECP, there is also a short form described in a separate standard, MIL STD 480 [62], for small businesses and the less complex hardware changes. This form is the first two pages of the full ECP form but may still carry the same classification and approval requirements. In the early stages of software development, many contracts called for use of the short form as the vehicle to propose software changes. It was found, however, that it could not cover complex descriptions of a software change containing many algorithms and interfaces.

The reason for dwelling on the ECP is that it is a formal communication to the customer that one is changing what was agreed on during the establishment of the baselines and as such is a change in the provisions of one's contract. The approved ECP is thus an amendment to the contract. Likewise, the internal software change such as the sample P/CR is an amendment to the agreed-on documentation and/or code that forms part of the affected baseline. This is no different from refinancing a house mortgage or in renegotiating a contract with the architect designing one's new home.

Although the ECP format may seem overwhelming, not all of its parts must be used all the time. As a minimum, pages 1 and 2 are used for every condition, but even then there may be some relief. Figure 9.10 describes when and how much detail is desirable. Even this may be tailored to fit the scope and magnitude of the project and in many instances the tailoring will be greater with software than hardware.

Figure 9.11, is page 1 of the ECP. The first 14 blocks are pretty much housekeeping data, although blocks 8 and 9 may require significant research and analysis of the change request before the data are entered. For software, block 9 would not be filled in unless one had software drawings describing software media and its contents. In blocks that refer to assembly or production, one should substitute software element and coding, respectively. In block 18 one should substitute the term "cut in point" and, in block 19, software for production. In block 20, *retrofit* refers to software systems already delivered and in operation where changes to that software must be made.

Figure 9.12 is page 2 of the ECP. The data required are straightforward and should not present any great problems. Appendix 3 contains the additional pages with notes pertaining to their completion.

For the most part, CM will not have to contend with this form at all. If any other organization requires it, one will find it very simple and clear. It may, however, require a great deal of backup information. These data were accounted for under the 480B standard.

The processing of ECPs requires proper precautions for detail and accuracy of the information provided. One's customer may be many miles away, and even though the means of transmission and communication are very quick and reliable, it is hard to describe or depict a complex change without some type of face-to-face discussion.

The flow in Figure 9.13 [63] is a good but simplistic description. It does, however, show the source of the primary changes for corrective action, enhancement, and planned modifications. The most important activity is analyzing and assessing impact. This must be done several times during the processing cycle from the time the internal change was initiated to the time the ECP is processed to the time the customer must review the proposed change. Don't forget—contract dollars are at stake here and sometimes this could be in the millions.

DD FORM		LIFE CYCLE PHASES			
NO. AND PAGE	USAGE	Program Initiation (Conceptual)	Demonstration and Validation	Engineering and Manufacturing Development	Production/ Deployment and Operational
1692 Page 1	Cover Sheet	REQUIRED Only when functional characteristics are to be controlled	REQUIRED Cover sheet summarizes the ECP	REQUIRED Cover sheet summarizes the ECP	REQUIRED Cover sheet summarizes the ECP
1692-1 Page 2	Effects on Functional Allocated Configuration Identification	NOT REQUIRED	REQUIRED USED to: Describe proposed changes in functional configuration identification	REQUIRED USED to: Describe proposed changes in functional or allocated configuration identification as defined by system and appropriate item specification	REQUIRED if: (a) System specification change is associated with design change (b) Two part specification method used & part I specification needs to be changed (c) Development & product fabrication specifications used and development specification needs to be changed (d) Other Systems or Configuration items are affected
1692-2 Page 3	Effects on Product Configuration Identification Operations and Logistics	NOT REQUIRED	NOT REQUIRED	REQUIRED when: Prototypes are undergoing operational or service testing USED to: Provide an index to impacts of the change	REQUIRED USED to: Describe effects of change in product configuration identification & changes in parts or assemblies
1692-3 Page 4	Estimated Net Total Cost Impact (one item)	NOT REQUIRED	NOT REQUIRED	REQUIRED when: (a) ECP requires change to contract cost (b) Future production cost is a consideration in evaluating desireability of effecting the proposed change	REQUIRED USED to: Tabulate cost impact
1692-4 Page 5	Estimated Cost/Savings Summary Related ECPs	NOT REQUIRED	NOT REQUIRED	REQUIRED if: (a) There are related ECPs applying to two or more items (b) New trainers or items of support equipment are required USED to: Summarize cost impact of all related ECPs	REQUIRED if: (a) There are related ECPs applying to two or more items (b) New trainers or items of support equipment are required USED to: Summarize cost impact of all related ECPs
1692-5 Page 6	Milestone Chart	NOT REQUIRED	NOT REQUIRED	REQUIRED if: There is a schedule change in more than delivery date for item USED to: Show-inter-relationships in schedules	REQUIRED if: There is a schedule change in more than delivery date for item USED to: Show-inter-relationships in schedules

Figure 9.10 Changes by life cycle changes (MIL STD 973).

ENGINEERING CHANGE PROPOSAL, PAGE 1 (See MIL-STD-480 for instructions)	DATE (YYMMDD)	Form Approved OMB No. 0704-0188

Public reporting burden for this collection of information is estimated to average 2 hours per response, including the time for reviewing instructions, searching existing data sources, gathering and maintaining the data needed, and completing and reviewing the collection of information. Send comments regarding this burden estimate or any other aspect of this collection of information, including suggestions for reducing this burden, to Washington Headquarters Services, Directorate for Information Operations and Reports, 1215 Jefferson Davis Highway, Suite 1204, Arlington, VA 22202-4302, and to the Office of Information and Regulatory Affairs, Office of Management and Budget, Washington, DC 20503

PROCURING ACTIVITY NO.

1. ORIGINATOR NAME AND ADDRESS

2. CLASS OF ECP

3. JUST. CODE

4. PRIORITY

5. ECP DESIGNATION

a. MODEL / TYPE	b. CAGE CODE	c SYSTEM DESIGNATION

6. BASELINE AFFECTED
- ☐ FUNCTIONAL
- ☐ ALLOCATED
- ☐ PRODUCT

d. ECP NO.		e. TYPE	f. REV	g. AMEND

7. OTHER SYS./ CONFIG. ITEMS AFFECTED
☐ YES ☐ NO

8. SPECIFICATIONS AFFECTED - TEST PLAN

9. DRAWINGS AFFECTED

	CAGE CODE	SPEC./DOC NO	REV	SCN	CAGE CODE	NUMBER	REV	NOR
a. SYSTEM								
b. ITEM								
c. TEST PLAN								

10. TITLE OF CHANGE	10.a WEAPON SYSTEM CODE OR DESIGNATION

11. CONTRACT NO. AND LINE ITEM	12. PROCURING CONTRACTING OFFICER
	CODE	TEL.

13. CONFIGURATION ITEM NOMENCLATURE	14. IN PRODUCTION ☐ YES ☐ NO

15. LOWEST ASSEMBLY AFFECTED

NOMENCLATURE	PART NO.	NSN

16. DESCRIPTION OF CHANGE

17. NEED FOR CHANGE

18. PRODUCTION EFFECTIVITY BY SERIAL NUMBER	19. EFFECT ON PRODUCTION DELIVERY SCHEDULE

20. RETROFIT

a. RECOMMENDED ITEM EFFECTIVITY	c. SHIP / VEHICLE CLASS AFFECTED
b. ESTIMATED KIT DELIVERY SCHEDULE	d. LOCATIONS OR SHIP / VEHICLE NUMBERS AFFECTED

21. ESTIMATED COSTS / SAVINGS UNDER CONTRACT	22. ESTIMATED NET TOTAL COSTS / SAVINGS

23. SUBMITTING ACTIVITY AUTHORIZED SIGNATURE	23.a. TITLE

24. APPROVAL / DISAPPROVAL

a. CLASS I	b. CLASS II	c. CLASS II
☐ APPROVAL RECOMMENDED ☐ DISAPPROVAL RECOMMENDED	☐ APPROVED ☐ DISAPPROVED	☐ CONCUR IN CLASSIFICATION OF CHANGE ☐ DO NOT CONCUR IN CLASSIFICATION OF CHANGE

d. GOVERNMENT ACTIVITY	SIGNATURE	DATE (YYMMDD)

e. APPROVAL ☐ APPROVED ☐ DISAPPROVED	f GOVERNMENT ACTIVITY	SIGNATURE	DATE (YYMMDD)

Figure 9.11 ECP, page 1.

ENGINEERING CHANGE PROPOSAL, PAGE 2 *(See MIL-STD-480 for instructions)*	Form Approved OMB No. 0704-0188

Public reporting burden for this collection of information is estimated to average 1 hour per response, including the time for reviewing instructions, searching existing data sources, gathering and maintaining the data needed, and completing and reviewing the collection of information. Send comments regarding this burden estimate or any other aspect of this collection of information, including suggestions for reducing this burden, to Washington Headquarters Services, Directorate for Information Operations and Reports, 1215 Jefferson Davis Highway, Suite 1204, Arlington, VA 22202-4302, and to the Office of Information and Regulatory Affairs, Office of Management and Budget, Washington, DC 20503.

ORIGINATOR NAME AND ADDRESS	PROCURING ACTIVITY NUMBER
	ECP NUMBER

EFFECTS ON FUNCTIONAL/ALLOCATED CONFIGURATION IDENTIFICATION

25. OTHER SYSTEMS AFFECTED	26. OTHER CONTRACTORS/ACTIVITIES AFFECTED

27. CONFIGURATION ITEMS AFFECTED

28. EFFECTS ON PERFORMANCE ALLOCATIONS AND INTERFACES IN SYSTEM SPECIFICATION

29. EFFECTS ON EMPLOYMENT, INTEGRATED LOGISTICS SUPPORT, TRAINING, OPERATIONAL EFFECTIVENESS OR SOFTWARE

30. EFFECTS ON CONFIGURATION ITEM SPECIFICATIONS

31. DEVELOPMENTAL REQUIREMENTS AND STATUS

32. TRADE-OFFS AND ALTERNATIVE SOLUTIONS

33. DATE BY WHICH CONTRACTUAL AUTHORITY IS NEEDED

Figure 9.12 ECP, page 2.

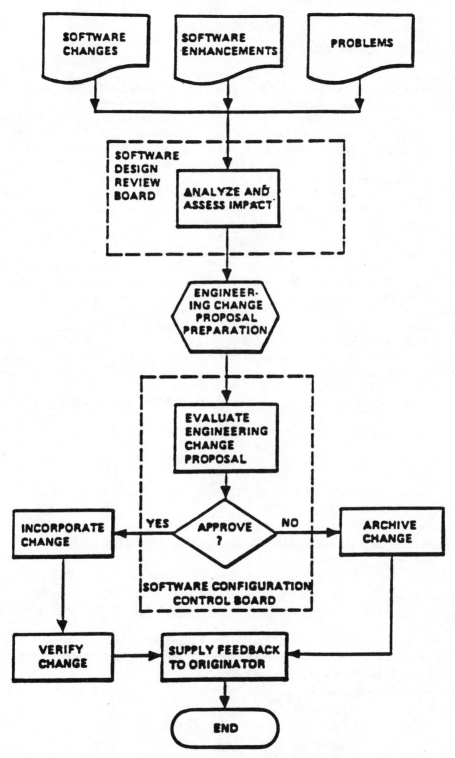

Figure 9.13 Change control flow.

RESPONSIBILITY FOR PREPARATION

The responsibility for preparation of an ECP rests with program management and contracts administration. Remember, this is a change to the project contract and carries proposed additional funding requirements. In addition, it is important that the system engineering group closely review the approved internal change to ensure that the system-level document—the system specification—and the CI level—the SRS—are covered by the impact analysis. If there is impact, then system engineering has important input to the final preparation of the ECP. In most cases a specification change notice (SCN) describing the document correction necessary is a part of the ECP.

Configuration management is responsible for gathering the data necessary for the ECP as well as the supporting data from the internally approved change, such as red-lined source listings and document changes. Changes that require customer approval will most likely require more detailed information than those that do not. The latter may only require concurrence, but should nonetheless be well written and unambiguous.

Figures 9.8 and 9.9 provide a more detailed illustration of the ECP change process. Note that Figure 9.8 also describes the approval of the internal change prior to preparation of a change requiring customer approval and Figure 9.9 does the same for the other type of change. Figure 9.8 also indicates that the approved internal change is left pending until the authority to incorporate is received. Changes that will obviously require customer approval can be prepared as the internal change is being processed. Thus the internal change and the ECP are often reviewed by a review board at the same time. If corrections are necessary to one or both documents, the corrective action instructions are made on the spot, saving one or more additional meetings.

Candidate data elements [63] are listed below for inclusion in an internal change control form.

Candidate Data Elements for Internal Change Control

a. System or project name—The name of the system or development project to which this P/CR applies.

b. Originator—Name of person(s) preparing the P/CR, with phone number, etc.

c. P/CR log (identification) number.

d. Problem name/title—Brief description of the problem/modification/enhancement.

e. Software element (code/unit) or document affected, including identification number and/or version number.

f. Date of report, date of problem detection, submission date.

g. Category Priority—Category of the problem is software, design, or documentation. Priority ranges from 1—system is down—to 5—enhancement or scheduled modification.

h. Description of problem, modification, or enhancement, including detailed data to permit recreation of problem, simulation of modification/enhancement.

i. Name of analyst assigned to investigate.

j. Date assigned to analyst.

k. Date analysis completed.

l. Elapsed time for analysis.

m. Recommended solution, including alternative, if any, with supporting rationale, test results if tried first, etc.

n. Impact of cost, schedule, interface if approved or not approved, as well as effect on other systems, developers, physical resources, employment, training requirements, human resource availability, product support, and software support.

o. Problem status as designated by configuration control procedure.

p. Approval of the P/CR and date.

q. Follow-up action required, if any, including date to correct or incorporate.

r. Name of person assigned to correct problem or incorporate change.

s. Incorporation/correction date.

t. New version number.

u. Elapsed time for correction/incorporation.

v. Description of analysis, investigation, resolution, and incorporation of solution into the system—a postmortem of the change.

Any or all of these suggested data elements may be tailored to meet the needs of the project. However, one should be aware that enough good, concise data will make analysis and correction easier and faster.

Other agencies and organizations such as NATO and NASA have lists or forms similar to those of the Canadian AECP. The IEEE STD 1042 provides several different options in its sample CMPs. The developer may design a universal for internal and external use. If for any reason the required format or content is not adaptable to the project contracted for, then further contractual negotiation may be required.

In some instances the customer may notify the developer that a change is required and direct the developer to prepare a proposed change based on the customer's change request. The preparation and processing are the same as for the developer's internally produced changes. The customer, in turn, will review the change in the same manner as an unsolicited one, and thus CM should ensure that all requirements for submission have been addressed

Finally, it is important to remember that change data are entered into one's status accounting system. Such data are necessary and important to communicating information that can be trusted to the project team and therefore must be entered accurately. Incorrect query data can cause all kinds of problems, some immediate and some later, such as an indication that a given change had been approved when it had not been or an incorrect revision or version-level indication that caused the wrong software to be changed. Status accounting data should be treated in the same manner as financial accounting data, and are discussed in detail in Chapter 10.

PROCEDURES FOR CHANGE CONTROL BOARDS

Once the ECP preparation instructions described in the previous section have been carried out, the next step is the evaluation of the change by the one or more review boards, commonly known as change control boards (CCBs). These boards must interpret what has been entered and evaluate it accordingly. As noted, program-oriented CCBs tend to have prior knowledge of the cause and correction of a change and thus will approve it quickly. The same change given to an independent board might be rejected or deferred due to interpretation of what is entered on the form. Therefore one must try to think how others will react to the data and information provided.

A CCB is a unique body within a product development group that is itself group oriented. Even though there may be upper-level CCBs, made up of the group's higher-level managers and supervisors, the board is charged with reviewing change requests from its peers—in some cases those sitting on the board—and recommending disposition to the board's chairperson, who is normally the group's manager, but many times may be the configuration manager.

The chairperson is the approval authority. Others on the board make recommendations regarding approval, disapproval, or deferment as representatives of their respective functional activities, such as quality assurance, system engineering, and test engineering. If the chairperson does not agree with the board members' recommendation, he or she can determine how to dispose the change independently.

The CCB is established at the start of the project. Although it may not meet for a long time in the beginning, it is available to be called together in the event that a change requiring customer approval has to be considered to correct a problem found in one of the early design reviews. As change activity becomes more pronounced, the board will meet more frequently until the project is completed. It is not uncommon for boards to meet twice a day. Most likely, once a day is more common with a time span of one to one and a half hours. The frequency of the CCB meetings depends on the criticality of the schedule and severity of the requested changes. The board's responsibility will continue into the maintenance phase, if the group has maintenance responsibility, which is is certainly the case in most commercial establishments.

During high test activity, the CCB will normally delegate approval defects found during test to the SRB, which can respond quickly to requests and provide for an immediate fix so that testing can proceed or be concluded on schedule. Testing to baseline items, however, will require full CCB review and approval. This could mean an emergency session if necessary to resolve a critical problem.

The board is made up of senior development and support people who are expert in their field and most knowledgeable of the current software system or project. This group is really the human element of the project and must assess the merits of change requests. It must make recommendations on the disposition of changes that may cost many thousands of dollars to incorporate. In some cases it is a life-or-death situation. A change is made to meet the competition or to woo back or mollify unhappy customers. Many times the firm may not have the resources and the funds to undertake such monumental changes. It is therefore most important that the CCB be taken seriously and that the best of the project team are its members. Alternates are also important, and they must be selected with care. Naturally if the entire project/company is small (say, five people), a CCB is more like a board of directors, but agreements must be reached and communicated to ensure that all are in agreement.

The functional composition of the board is listed in Figure 9.14. Each function is represented by a person. Note that there are primary functional representatives, other functional representatives on call for given types of changes, and still others who may have to make important decisions when contract terms or the firm's market area may be affected by the requested change. The list is also divided for hardware and software. Some changes will affect both hardware and software, and thus both the hardware CCB and software CCBs will have to meet to evaluate this change. However, these types of sessions usually do not occur until system integration where both products are involved. Cross-functional membership is important to ensure that all aspects of a change request are addressed prior to expending customer and or company resources.

The primary functional representatives are important. The Software group leader/manager is the chairperson unless the leadership of the CCB has been delegated to another function. Many times this is a representative of configuration management. On the other hand it

CCB MEMBERSHIP

Hardware	Software

PRIMARY FUNCTIONS

Hardware	Software
• Program Management	• Program Management
• System Engineering	• System Engineering
• Program Engineering	• Program Engineering
• Configuration Management	• Software Design Team Leader
• Quality Assurance	• Software Configuration Management
• Integrated Logistics Support	• Software Quality Assurance
• Manufacturing Engineering	• Integrated Logistics Support

Hardware	Software

OTHER FUNCTIONS
(As required)

Hardware	Software
• Project (Mechanical/Electrical) Engineering	• Project Software Engineering
• Reliability/Maintainability/ Safety	• Data Management
• Manufacturing Program Management	• Technical Writing
• Manufacturing Configuration Control	• Software Testing
• Production Control	• Software Support Facility
• Program Test	• Software Support Specialist
• Data Management	
• Technical Writing	
• Component Engineering	
• Release and Control	
• Designer	

SPECIAL INTEREST FUNCTIONS
(Consultants)

- Contract
- Marketing
- Legal/Patents
- Other Using Programs
- Subcontractor/Joint Venture
- Customer
- Financial/Administration
- Specialty Performing Areas

Figure 9.14 CCB detailed member list.

can also be the software team leader/manager. The representative from CM is normally the clerk/secretary of the board, if not delegated as chairperson. For each session, the clerk is responsible for notifying the board members of meetings, taking minutes of the meetings, and distributing action items with appropriate follow-on. If the software team is small, there may not be the requisite number of functions discussed here. Usually one function will then assume the role of two or more functions. The minimum number of functions in a CCB has to be two. If there is only one function involved, such as software engineering, that function should get a peer function to consult on any changes that would affect other functions working on the software.

Assuming that the program manager is chairperson, the other functions represented, including CM, are quality assurance, software team leader/management, software system engineering, test team leader/management, programmer requesting change—if necessary—and maintenance or software support leader/management when necessary. In addition to software engineering, it is advisable to have program system engineering to represent hardware as well as software. In addition, customer service or software support activity has become most important in terms of integration, communication, and good will with the customers by providing immediate and expert support to any user's software at any location. The customer support activity also has the best understanding of the problem in the eyes of the customer.

It is up to the chairperson to notify other functions with special interests in a given change. This could involve marketing/business development if the product is for sale and could also involve manufacturing, if the change could affect the equipment the software resides in, as in a larger disk requirement. One might need purchasing if the medium is an electronic device such as an integrated circuit that has to be changed and a new one ordered. Document control may well be involved if the change is affecting documents that are ready to deliver or have been delivered. This in turn may affect proprietary data, which would require legal opinion. Finally, in some instances, the customer is invited. This may be standard if the customer has a "plant representative." The procedure has proved most beneficial for both sides in communicating concerns, issues, and problems between buyer and seller. It makes understanding what is happening at a remote location that much easier.

The CCB is a serious undertaking. It involves money. Granted one is primarily concerned about getting a change reviewed, approved, and incorporated, but the bottom line is that changes cost money, many times in addition to that which was budgeted. Resources are also important. Is there anyone available to make this change? If it is massive, the whole project might have to be suspended while everyone works on it. Thus, what about schedule, customer dissatisfaction, possible withholding of payment because of schedule slippage? Funds are often critical to determining the disposition of a change.

Determining disposition requires complete information. CM is responsible for providing all the information needed to make an intelligent decision on a change. Too many times, members have prior knowledge of a problem that has to be fixed because they may have been involved in the test or demonstration at the time the defect was discovered and had some input to the solution. This can obscure their decision making and a bad disposition could cause additional changes because the board did not take the time or have all the pertinent facts available.

Some of the areas of evaluation for software include the following:

- Operational Impact—What effect will this change have on the ultimate product as known at this moment?

- Classification—Will this change require customer approval and reidentification? Will an engineering change proposal or problem/change report form be required?
- What must be changed/modified/enhanced? What is the impact of other interfaces or segments of the software unit/module?
- What is the affectivity? When can one make this change? Critical changes must go in right away, but modification and enhancement could be scheduled for incorporation at the most appropriate time.
- Cost impact—How long will it take to incorporate? How many people are involved? Are resources available? Can they be utilized? If a major change—to meet competition—how is it to be funded without affecting profits?
- Schedule impact—Will the change cause the schedule to slip? What happens if a public announcement of introduction has been made? Can one meet the date or must the market be notified of a slippage? How can this be avoided?
- Feasibility—Can this change be made in a reasonably economical manner? Is it a case of "start all over again," or can it be made with the current resources available and with minimum impacts?
- Interface—Will this change affect other systems that this software communicates with? Who has to be notified, warned, consulted? What is the nature of the impact?
- Impact on quality and reliability—Will this change dilute the integrity of the product? Will it cause loss of sales or fail to meet stipulated quality and reliability criteria?

Clearly, there are many things to be considered. One might wish to stop for a moment and think of other criteria as well. For instance, what is the effect on hardware, test equipment, test beds, training and simulation programs, and, most important, software documentation and manuals? A list of 21 criteria is contained in Appendix 3.

Based on the decisions reached, the board will recommend to the chairperson to approve, defer, or reject. To approve means to set in motion the change and incorporation process. To defer means to wait for other events or additional data before making a decision. To reject means that the change is not needed or not feasible, there are other ways to get around the problem, or possibly the change request has errors or omissions that, when returned to the requester, can be resolved and returned to the CCB for a second look.

As mentioned earlier, the use of a software review board with a recommended minimum of four functions from the CCB can be very effective in getting a first look at a requested change and making on-the-spot decisions as to how to proceed.

The SRB will normally consist of the CCB chairperson, the software team leader/manager, test team leader/management and software quality assurance. The board should be available to gather quickly and take little time in considering how to proceed.

The SRB reviews all requests, usually in consultation with the requester, for:

- Criticality of the change
- Estimated number of lines of code or documentation affected.
- Complexity of the problem.
- Estimated time to analyze.
- Estimated time to fix, test, and incorporate.
- Assessment of available resources and related cost.
- Gross impact on schedule and other units.

Based on a quick appraisal, the SRB chairperson may assign an available programmer to analyze, fix, and test the change prior to submission to the full CCB. Or the chairperson may direct that the request be formalized for CCB review and disposition with analysis only being conducted and results entered on the PCR. The chairperson may also reject the change or request additional data prior to making a disposition.

The review by the SRB may seem lengthy, but it will save many hours of CCB time in sorting out the requests and enabling the CCB to concentrate on complete and workable changes. It eliminates that shadow of a doubt that would defer a change until it was tried and tested. Savings of eight to ten manhours of labor per CCB meeting by utilizing an SRB is not uncommon. It will also improve the response time for minor defects change requests.

In summary, CCBs and, where established, SRBs are the focal point for product communication. The CCBs and SRBs are and must be independent from the rest of the project while in session, but still provide guidance and assistance to peers in the process of dispositioning a requested change. There can be no recriminations by unhappy requesters.

PROCEDURES FOR DEVIATIONS AND WAIVERS

A deviation or a waiver is a means of obtaining relief from a provision of a specification or contract in order to be able to continue to produce and/or deliver a software product within the time required. CM processes deviations and waivers in the same manner as the ECP (Figures 9.15 and 9.16). As a simple example, if one were not able to code a specified software unit in time to make delivery, a waiver would be requested to allow the use of a substitute software unit until the required one is available and can be installed on all units delivered.

Deviations are temporary departures from the requirements of the approved configuration identification prior to the coding of a given software element, component, or system if the developer considers it necessary in order to proceed into the coding phase. These deviations may be minor, major, or critical. They may also be made in place of an ECP if the requested departure is superior to the approved design. This would make the deviation permanent. On the other hand, a requested deviation might be turned into an ECP if the customer wished the deviation to be made permanent.

A minor deviation usually consists of a departure from a characteristic in a governing document that is, by definition between parties, considered minor and does not affect health, safety, reliability, interchangeability, effective use, or operation.

A major deviation is a departure from certain characteristics in a governing document that does affect health, safety, durability, reliability, maintainability, use, or operation. These are the normally accepted definitions of classifications of deviations. However, one may wish to elaborate or expand these definitions as long as they are clearly stated in the CM plan.

Critical deviations affect safety.

Deviations are not used to deviate from code listings but may be used for software documentation such as a programmer's user's manual or a maintenance manual.

Additional detail is spelled out in paragraph 5.3 of MIL STD 480B. When this standard is not used, then agreement between buyer and seller should spell out the rules for requests for deviations.

Waivers, such as inclusion of a specified software element until a later period in development, are requested during or after the coding of the software product.

Waivers can be minor, major, and critical. The primary distinction is the degree to which safety, reliability, use, or operation is affected by not conforming to a certain requirement. A critical waiver always involves safety.

REQUEST FOR DEVIATION/WAIVER		DATE *(YYMMDD)*	Form Approved OMB No. 0704-0188

Public reporting burden for this collection of information is estimated to average 2 hours per response, including the time for reviewing instructions, searching existing data sources, gathering and maintaining the data needed, and completing and reviewing the collection of information. Send comments regarding this burden estimate or any other aspect of this collection of information, including suggestions for reducing this burden, to Washington Headquarters Services, Directorate for Information Operations and Reports, 1215 Jefferson Davis Highway, Suite 1204, Arlington, VA 22202-4302, and to the Office of Information and Regulatory Affairs, Office of Management and Budget, Washington, DC 20503.

PROCURING ACTIVITY NUMBER

1. ORIGINATOR NAME AND ADDRESS

2. ☐ DEVIATION ☐ WAIVER

3. ☐ MINOR ☐ MAJOR ☐ CRITICAL

4. DESIGNATION FOR DEVIATION/WAIVER				5. BASELINE AFFECTED	6. OTHER SYSTEM/CONFIGU- RATION ITEMS AFFECTED
a. MODEL/TYPE	b. CAGE CODE	c. SYS DESIG	d. DEV/WAIVER NO.	☐ FUNC-TIONAL ☐ ALLO-CATED ☐ PRODUCT	☐ YES ☐ NO

7. TITLE OF DEVIATION/WAIVER

8. CONTRACT NO. AND LINE ITEM	9. PROCURING CONTRACTING OFFICER
	CODE TEL

10. CONFIGURATION ITEM NOMENCLATURE	11. CLASSIFICATION OF DEFECT
	a. CD No. b. Defect No. c. Defect Classification ☐ Minor ☐ Major ☐ Critical

12. NAME OF LOWEST PART/ASSEMBLY AFFECTED	13. PART NO. OR TYPE DESIGNATION

14. LOT NO.	15. QTY	16. RECURRING DEVIATION/WAIVER ☐ YES ☐ NO

17. EFFECT ON COST/PRICE	18. EFFECT ON DELIVERY SCHEDULE

19. EFFECT ON INTEGRATED LOGISTICS SUPPORT, INTERFACE, OR SOFTWARE

20. DESCRIPTION OF DEVIATION/WAIVER

21. NEED FOR DEVIATION/WAIVER

22. CORRECTIVE ACTION TAKEN

23. SERIAL NUMBER(S) AFFECTED

24. SUBMITTING ACTIVITY AUTHORIZED SIGNATURE	24a. TITLE

25. APPROVAL/DISAPPROVAL   a. RECOMMEND ☐ APPROVAL ☐ DISAPPROVAL

b. APPROVAL ☐ APPROVED ☐ DISAPPROVED	c. GOVERNMENT ACTIVITY	SIGNATURE	DATE *(YYMMDD)*
d. APPROVAL ☐ APPROVED ☐ DISAPPROVED	e. GOVERNMENT ACTIVITY	SIGNATURE	DATE *(YYMMDD)*

Figure 9.15 Request for deviation/waiver, list.

Defence nationale

DESIGN CHANGE/DEVIATION
MODIFICATION DU MODÈLE OU ÉCART AUTORISÉ

Change ☐ Modification   Deviation ☐ Écart

CONTRACTOR'S SERIAL NO N° D'ORDRE DE L'ENTREPRENEUR	
CONTRACT DEMAND NO N° DE LA DEMANDE DE CONTRAT	
DSS CONTRACT SERIAL NO N° D'ORDRE DU CONTRAT DU MAS	
DSS FILE NO N° DU DOSSIER DU MAS	
DESIGN AUTHORITY SERIAL NO N° D'ORDRE DU BUREAU TECHNIQUE RESPONSABLE	

PART – PARTIE – I

1 ITEM AFFECTED – ARTICLE TOUCHÉ

2 MAIN EQUIPMENT(S) AFFECTED – MATÉRIEL TOUCHÉ.

3 DESCRIPTION OF DEPARTURE FROM ORIGINAL TECHNICAL DATA
DESCRIPTION DES POINTS QUI DIFFÈRENT DES DONNÉES TECHNIQUES

4. REASON FOR REQUEST – NOTIF DE LA DEMANDE

5. WILL INTERCHANGEABILITY BE AFFECTED? –
L'INTERCHANGEABILITÉ EST-ELLE RÉDUITE?
Component Parts – Yes ☐ No ☐   Organes: Oui   Non
Assemblies – Yes ☐ No ☐   Ensembles – Oui   Non

6 WILL SPARE PARTS SCHEDULE BE AFFECTED?
LE TABLEAU EN PIÈCES DE RECHANGE EST-IL MODIFIÉ?
Yes ☐ No ☐ Oui   Non
(If "YES" state details)
(Le cas échéant, donner des détails)

7 PRODUCTION DATA – RENSEIGNEMENTS SUR LA PRODUCTION
7 1 COST AND DELIVERY
COÛT ET LIVRAISON

7 1 1 Estimated Effect on Delivery
Effet prévu sur la livraison _____

7 1 2 Estimated Added Tooling Cost $
Coût supplémentaire prévu de l'usinage $ _____

7 1 3 Estimated Surplus Material Value $
Valeur prévue des matériaux supplémentaires $ _____

7 1 4 Estimated Change in Contract Cost
Including Sales Tax and 7 1 2 and
7 1 3 above (indicate + or –) $
Variation prévue du coût stipulé dans le contrat
(y compris la taxe de vente et les montants
prévus en 7 1 2 et 7 1 3) Indiquer + ou –) $ _____

7 2 PRODUCTION CHANGE POINT
INTRODUCTION DE LA MODIFICATION

7 2 1 Estimated Starting Date and Serial No
Date d'introduction et
N° de série prévue _____

7 2 2 Total Number of Units Involved
Nombre total d'unités touchées _____

7.3 RECOMMENDATIONS FOR PRIOR BUILT UNITS IN SERVICE
RECOMMANDATIONS QUANT AUX UNITÉS DÉJÀ EN SERVICE

7.3.1 Should Prior-Built Units be modified?
Les unités déjà en service devraient-elles
être modifiées?
Yes ☐ No ☐ Oui   Non

7.3.2 Estimated Cost Per Unit – Coût prévu par unité

Cost of Kit
Coût du lot $ _____

Cost of Rework
Coût de réusinage $ _____

7.3.3 Government held Spare Parts –
Pièces de rechange appartenant à l'État

Use ☐   Rework ☐   Scrap ☐   Utilisez   Réusinage   Mise au rebut

Estimated Cost Each to Rework or Replace $
Coût unitaire prévu du réusinage ou du remplacement $ _____

8 ORIGINATOR – AUTEUR DE LA DEMANDE

DATE   SIGNATURE (If other than Prime Contractor
autre que l'entrepreneur principal)

DATE   SIGNATURE (Prime Contractor
entrepreneur principal)

ND 672 (8-84) 7530-21-896-8621

Figure 9.16 Design change/deviation, Canada.

PART – PARTIE II

9. RECOMMENDATIONS OR QUALITY ASSURANCE REPRESENTATIVE – RECOMMENDATIONS DU REPRÉSENTANT DE L'ASSURANCE DE LA QUALITÉ

DATE	DESIGNATION – DÉSIGNATION	SIGNATURE

10. RECOMMENDATIONS OF DESIGN AUTHORITY – RECOMMENDATIONS DU BUREAU TECHNIQUE RESPONSABLE

Approved: Approuvé:	Change Modification ☐	Deviation Écart ☐	Per Part I Voir partie I ☐	or ou	See remarks Voir observations ☐	Not approved Rejetée

DATE	DESIGNATION – DÉSIGNATION	SIGNATURE

11. APPROVAL OF PROCUREMENT AUTHORITY – APPROBATION DE L'INSTANCE D'ACQUISITION

DATE	DESIGNATION – DÉSIGNATION	SIGNATURE

12. REFERENCES – DOCUMENTS DE RÉFÉRENCE (Departmental file numbers etc. – numéros de dossier ministère etc.)

13. AUTHORIZED PRODUCTION ACTION ON THIS CONTRACT – MESURE DE PRODUCTION AUTORISÉE POUR LE PRÉSENT CONTRAT

		Existing Stock Stock actuel	Complete Units Unités entières	Assemblies Ensembles	Component Parts Organes
a. Change Modification ☐		Use Utilisez	☐	☐	☐
When to take effect: Prise d'effet: _____		Rework Réusinage	☐	☐	☐
		Scrape Mise au rebut	☐	☐	☐
b. Deviation ☐ Écart	TOTAL NUMBER OF UNITS INVOLVED NOMBRE D'UNITÉS TOUCHÉES _____	SERIAL NO. S N° (S) DE SÉRIE _____			

14. FORM DND 678 REQUIRED FROM MANUFACTURER
DND 678 EXIGÉE DU FABRICANT MESURE À PRENDRE À L'ÉGARD DU MATÉRIEL EN STOCK ET EN SERVICE   Yes Oui ☐   No Non ☐

15. ACTION ON EQUIPMENT IN STOCK AND USE – MESURE À PRENDRE À L'ÉGARD DU MATÉRIEL EN STOCK ET EN SERVICE:

16. ACTION ON SPARES IN STOCK – MESURE À PRENDRE À L'ÉGARD DES PIÈCES DE RECHARGE EN STOCK:

17. DATE	SIGNATURE (for Department of National Defence pour le ministère de la Défense Nationale)	18. DATE	SIGNATURE (for Department of Supply and Services pour le ministère des Approvisionnements et Services)

19. DISTRIBUTION LIST – LISTE DE DIFFUSION	Copies Exemplaires	DISTRIBUTION LIST – LISTE DE DIFFUSION	Copies Exemplaires

Figure 9.16 *(Continued)*

Here again, if MIL STD 480B is not used, the buyer and seller should agree on the definitions of waivers and the procedure for processing and submission. Both deviations and waivers, when used properly, can be a great benefit in properly documenting the characteristics of a product and in keeping on schedule, maintaining budgets, and meeting delivery points with a quality product. If overused, they become costly and time consuming and add a great deal to status accounting input and output.

NOTICE OF REVISION

The notice of revision (NOR) is a means of notifying the custodian of master documents of changes made by other organizations or developers (Figure 9.17). CM processes the NOR in the same manner as an ECP. An NOR would be required, for example when one is contracted to develop and produce software and is provided with copies of the necessary software specifications and documents. In the event a change is necessary or recommended and is in turn approved by the customer, the developer making the change will notify the owner of the master copies/files of such approved changes so that they can be incorporated into the document and updated copies distributed.

The great benefit to using NORs is that CM has the ability to make sure the master copies or files are updated and reflect the latest revision. Another benefit is the ability to make licensed changes to third-party software and to notify the developer of such a change in a formal manner. This then gives the developer a chance to decide whether to make a universal change or consider it limited to the customer who sent in the notification. When submitting the NOR to the designated custodians CM should, however, request verification that the changes have been incorporated into the master software copy in order to avoid having subsequent changes not work because the previous change was not incorporated.

Provisions for NORs should be spelled out in the CMP and should also reflect any agreement made with a document control activity and the orginating development organization.

RELATIONSHIP OF HARDWARE AND SOFTWARE CHANGES

A change is a change, but hardware changes differ from those for software. Because hardware is a physical object, one can scan drawings to look for the cause and effect of a change. Because software is intangible, one must not only scan many pages of a specification or many sheets of code listing, but also simulate (or make happen) the cause and effect to verify the root cause indicated in a document or code listing.

Too many times software code has not been documented sufficiently or identified beyond some unmarked disks with some notation that this is indeed the software that is not working. With hardware, at least one may have a physical item to look at and work with, and if the hardware is not documented on a drawing or specification it can be identified by relatively simple means.

Problems involving hardware and software can appear at any time. They usually occur, however, during system integration, when the software is loaded into hardware. At that point it may be found that certain routines do not work or requirements have not been met. In looking for the cause, one must examine both hardware and software. The finding may indicate that both require change—for instance, there may be a programmer error for software and a missing sensor in the hardware.

On the other hand, an error in the hardware may have been caused by the software, for example, when the amount of code written overflows the hard disk, which must be replaced by a larger disk, and room found to accommodate it. This situation sometimes leads one

NOTICE OF REVISION (NOR) This revision described below has been authorized for the document listed.	DATE (YYMMDD)	Form Approved OMB No. 0704-0188

Public reporting burden for this collection of information is estimated to average 2 hours per response, including the time for reviewing instructions, searching existing data sources, gathering and maintaining the data needed, and completing and reviewing the collection of information. Send comments regarding this burden estimate or any other aspect of this collection of information, including suggestions for reducing this burden, to Washington Headquarters Services, Directorate for Information Operations and Reports, 1215 Jefferson Davis Highway, Suite 1204, Arlington, VA 22202-4302, and to the Office of Information and Regulatory Affairs, Office of Management and Budget, Washington, DC 20503.

1. ORIGINATOR NAME AND ADDRESS	2. CAGE CODE	3. NOR NO.
	4. CAGE CODE	5. DOCUMENT NO.

6. TITLE OF DOCUMENT	7. REVISION LETTER	
	(Current)	(New)
	8. ECP NO.	

9. CONFIGURATION ITEM (OR SYSTEM) TO WHICH ECP APPLIES

10. DESCRIPTION OF REVISION

11. THIS SECTION FOR GOVERNMENT USE ONLY

a. CHECK ONE	☐ EXISTING DOCUMENT SUPPLEMENTED BY THIS NOR MAY BE USED IN MANUFACTURE	☐ REVISED DOCUMENT MUST BE RECEIVED BEFORE MANUFACTURER MAY INCORPORATE THIS CHANGE	☐ CUSTODIAN OF MASTER DOCUMENT SHALL MAKE ABOVE REVISION AND FURNISH REVISED DOCUMENT

b. ACTIVITY AUTHORIZED TO APPROVE CHANGE FOR GOVERNMENT	SIGNATURE AND TITLE	DATE (YYMMDD)

12. ACTIVITY ACCOMPLISHING REVISION	REVISION COMPLETED (Signature)	DATE (YYMMDD)

Figure 9.17 Notice of revision.

ENGINEERING CHANGE ORDER

ECO NO.

DOCUMENT DRAWING NUMBER	NEW REV	DOCUMENT DRAWING TITLE		
			PAGE	OF

PROGRAM NOMENCLATURE	CONTRACT NUMBER	NEXT HIGHER ASSEMBLY

REQUESTED BY	ECR NO.	OTHER USING PROGRAMS	ECP NO.

ECO

DESCRIPTION OF CHANGE

JUSTIFICATION FOR CHANGE

MAKE BUY CODE CHG	RETROFIT EFFECT	CMICS APPENDIX APPLICABLE	BY
Y N ☐	RETRO INSTRUCTION	Y N ☐	

PARTS STATUS AND DISPOSITION

PART NUMBER	QTY ON ORD	QTY IN STK	QTY IN PROD

AREAS AFFECTED

AREA	Y/N	BY	AREA	Y/N	BY	AREA	Y/N	BY
CAD			SPARE PARTS			TOOLS		
TEST EQUIP			TECH MAN					
SOFTWARE			PROCESS SHEETS					
INTER-FACE			CAM					

SEE REVERSE FOR DISPOSITION CODE DEFINITIONS

DISPOSITION CODES ➤	U USE AS IS	T TRANSFER	C CANCEL
	R REWORK	O OBSOLETE	

APPROVALS

					ACTION	
EFFECTIVITY SER NO		CUT-IN	REWORK	N A SEE JUSTIFICATION

PREPARER	DATE	MANUFACTURING ENGR	DATE
ENGR	DATE	R M S	DATE
ENGR	DATE	PRODUCT SUPPORT	DATE
QUALITY ASSURANCE	DATE	CONFIGURATION MGMT	DATE
PRODUCTION CTRL	DATE	PROGRAM MGMT	DATE

GOV CLASS PER DOD-STD-480	INTERCHANGEABLE
I ☐ II ☐	YES ☐ NO ☐

CUSTOMER CONCURRENCE IN CLASSIFICATION

Figure 9.18 Engineering change order (ECO).

PROBLEM/CHANGE REPORT   PCR NO._____

SYSTEM/PROJ _____   PAGE _____ OF _____

PCR

TITLE DESCRIPTION		SITE		CONTRACT NO.	
PROBLEM DATE TIME	FAILED OR SUSPECTED ELEMENT (NAME)	ELEMENT ID NO.	VER/REV	NEXT HIGHER LEVEL ID NO	
TEST NAME	RELATED DOCUMENT (TITLE)		DOCUMENT NO.		REV
SUBMITTED BY DATE	ECP NO. CLASS □I □II	CUSTOMER CONCURRENCE IN CLASSIFICATION DATE		EFFECTIVITY	

PROBLEM DESCRIPTION:

SUMMARY OF CHANGE AND REASON:

—SOFTWARE ELEMENTS AND DOCUMENTS CHANGED

SOFTWARE ELEMENT NAME OR DOCUMENT TITLE	IDENTIFICATION NO.	NEXT HIGHER LEVEL ID NO	NEW VER/REV

ACTION REQUIRED TO CLOSE:

IMPACT ON:	Y	N		Y	N		Y	N		Y	N	
□ PSL			SCHEDULE			TEST EQUIPMENT SW			DELIVERABLE HDW			SW DOCUMENTATION
□ ML			SUBCONTRACT			FIRMWARE			TRAINING			SUPPORT SW SW TOOLS
			DATA ITEM			FACILITY SITE			SW MANUALS			OTHER:

SRB DISPOSITION	□ APPROVE	□ DISAPPROVE	□ DEFER UNTIL:
SRB CHAIRPERSON DATE	SYSTEMS ENGR DATE	SRB MEMBER DATE	SRB MEMBER DATE
PROBLEM CHANGE TYPE	ASSIGNED TO DATE	PRIORITY SCHED DATE	ANALYSIS TIME DATE COMPLETE (HRS)

SCCB DISPOSITION	□ APPROVE	□ DISAPPROVE	□ DEFER UNTIL:
SCCB CHAIRPERSON DATE	SW PROJECT LEADER DATE	SYSTEMS ENGR DATE	PROGRAM MGMT DATE
CONFIGURATION MGMT DATE	QUALITY ASSURANCE DATE	SOFTWARE TEST DATE	ILS MGMT DATE

CLOSURE ACTION

INCORPORATED BY DATE	VERIFIED BY DATE	INCORP. TIME (HRS) VERIF. TIME (HRS)	CLOSED BY DATE

Figure 9.19   Problem/change report (P/CR).

to ask why the size of the software can't be reduced to fit the original disk. In fact, many times the CCB feels that it is cheaper to change the software than to change the hardware. This may be true, but when the delay caused by excessive changes to the software becomes evident, it will turn out that it would have been better to fix the hardware.

One should be able to write a change for either hardware or software on the same form, but in most cases semantics and terminology require two types of forms. The forms for hardware, the engineering change order (ECO) and software, PCR, are shown in Figures 9.18 and 9.19. A combined form, developed for MIL STD 480B, ECP, shown in Figures 9.11 and 9.12 enables one to write software ECPs. If hardware is also involved, it may take two forms or references to hardware drawings or software documents on one form. Attempts at designing combination forms for internal use have not been very successful, but if one is limited on the hardware side — software is the driver or vice versa — one should attempt to use one form for both and thus save time of design, printing, and storage.

SUMMARY

A number of subjects have been discussed relating to control, starting with maintaining the baseline subsequent to its formal establishment. Once this is accomplished, provisions for the internal control of the changes to these baselines have been set up and lines of communication established so that everyone on the project will know what is going on. In some cases proposing changes, and thus the processing to changes, to a government agency as well as nongovernment groups is really a matter of proposing changes to the developer's contract.

Configuration control boards and software review boards were also described and their functions and responsibilities discussed. The use of deviations and waivers as well as notices of revisions were included, and finally the distinction between hardware and software changes and change form requirements was provided.

EXERCISES

1. Describe how you would establish a change control procedure in your organization. Include responsibility, format or content, processing, and review of the change request.
2. Flow chart or create a data flow of the change control process in your organization. Review, with others if you wish.
3. Create a recommended data flow for changes based on review of the one you developed in exercise 2.
4. Describe the function of a CCB and compare this to the present practice of your organization. Is there much difference? Discuss with others and make recommendations for improvement, if necessary.

CHAPTER 10

Performing the Status Accounting Activity

Status accounting is the recording activity and follows up on the results of the configuration management activities that have been described to this point. It keeps track of the current configuration identification documents, the current configuration of the delivered software, the status of changes being reviewed, and the status of the implementation of approved changes [67].

Why is it part of CM? Basically, status accounting refers to the record-keeping functions inherent in the other CM activities and to the specialized management information system that must exist to provide all the technical information about the configuration of software. Thus, for each document authored, reviewed, approved, and distributed, one records all the current data for a document/specification or change in order to communicate this information to the project/users/support activities as fast as it becomes available. The data must be in a form to allow traceability from top to bottom and bottom to top for software in development, in the field, or sold on the open market. To understand this, note how often each piece of software one procures has a return card—mostly for marketing purposes—but also for notifying all the software's owners of the latest status of the software at a given version level.

Status accounting is information. It is also a part of the software project decision-making process that determines how the project is doing, what the major problems are, and where they are emanating from. From the reports and queries of status accounting information, the project manager should be able to determine how the project is going in relation to documentation required, baselines established, changes, and the rate of changes—how many per day, week, and so on. One can also look at the types of changes, causes of change, cost and schedule of changes scheduled or in progress. The one thing the system is not designed to do is provide the budget, cost incurred, and variance data that normally come from accounting system reports and queries.

A major reason status accounting records and reports are needed is for maintenance of the software. It is important to recognize that maintenance begins when the first change has to be made. This usually occurs during the early testing phases and will continue for the life of the software product. In order to make corrections, enhancements, or modifications to the existing software, one refers to the history of the unit, component, and so on, for information that will tell what changes occurred in the past, what problems were encountered during development—in meeting the SRS or detailed specification requirement—as well as what occurred during test and integration. Although it is most desirable to have this information, too many times the software that requires maintenance has not been well documented, few if any records have been kept, and evidence of the latest version was left in the originating programmer's head rather than imprinted on the disk or the software code's header section.

The history records in a status accounting system are also used to analyze and improve the software development process. The number of changes processed, the time taken to analyze, and the time to correct can tell a lot about how efficient the project was and how well it met (or did not meet) cost and schedule requirements. In addition, the statistics derived provide a good basis for future bidding and cost estimates. Most important, one can derive process improvements that can provide reduction in software costs and increase competitive position in the marketplace.

Another equally important reason for status accounting is keeping the project's personnel informed on a day-to-day basis of the current versions of the developing software, the software under test, and software awaiting final acceptance. One of the first evidences of status one will see is the creation of the software hierarchy as the functions are defined from the system/segment specification down to the second and third levels of detail. Figure 8.1 (Chapter 8) depicts the interaction of the software breakdown along with the hardware of which it may be part. As noted in Chapter 7, this is the beginning of the identification process but will now be on continual display, physically or in a computer file, showing the unit blocks as they emerge, the identification numbers assigned, and, from that, the progress of the software as it evolves. Thus, at any time, one can call for a listing of the software hierarchy and learn about the project's progress in meeting schedules and budgets and other targets management and software engineering are interested in.

There are a number of ways one can accomplish good, workable status accounting, manually and electronically. The latter now has many options. Some are built in to the development tools and generated as part of the development process, while others may at this time require independent input but provide a great deal more information to a wider audience. These software tools are discussed in Chapter 15. The basic methods to be discussed in this chapter are computer data base oriented in terms of the platform for status accounting, the selection of the primary data elements required in defining and using a status accounting data base, and the mechanisms for reporting and querying the data bases.

In order to ensure a standard set of data elements that would provide a common mode of communication, MIL STD 482 was developed in 1968 so that status accounting information could be expressed in terms of standard data elements and related features. The standard allowed no substitutes, but did provide for additional elements and data chains as required. The standard data elements are listed in two appendixes, and sample status accounting records are listed in a third appendix for either manual or electronic generation of the required data.

Appendix I (Figure 10.1) of MIL STD 482 is an index of the data elements and data use identifiers arranged in alphabetical sequence and also configuration management numbers in numerical sequence. Appendix II (Figure 10.2) of the standard is a compilation of the data elements, data use identifiers, and related features in the format of the current arrangement used for publication of individual standard data elements. An illustration of a sample format is shown in Figure 10.3.

THE STATUS ACCOUNTING PLATFORM

The status accounting platform has become known as the software development file (SDF). When first conceived, it was known as the unit development folder (UDF) because it was based on the use of the common manila file folder. The intent of the UDF was to gather and retain everything and anything one ever wanted to know about a given unit of software from the time it was conceived to the time it was accepted, integrated, and delivered.

APPENDIX I. *Index of configuration status accounting data elements and data use identifiers*

TITLE	TYPE	DOD 5000.12M REF NO.	CM	PAGE NO.
Action Priority	Element	AC-TJ	21	II-38
Action Sequence	DUI-Element	CH-SA-AB	3	II-2
Admendment Numbers for Solicitation Document	DUI-Element		58	II-86
Air Force Time Compliance Technical Order Number	DUI-Chain	MO-BR-AE	55	II-81
Air Alteration Number (Navy)	DUI-Chain	MO-BR-AD	55	II-81
Call/Order Modification Serial Number	Element	CA-FB	2	II-1
Call/Order Numbers Under Contract	DUI-Element		58	II-86
Chronological Sequence	Element	CH-SA	3	II-2
Component/Function Index	DUI-Element		64	II-93
Computer Program Identification	DUI-Element	CO-LE-AB	4	II-3
Configuration Audit Actual Date – Functional	DUI-Chain	DA-FA-AE	10	II-7
Configuration Audit Actual Date – Physical	DUI-Chain	DA-FA-AD	10	II-7
Configuration Audit Schedule Date – Functional	DUI-Chain	DA-FA-AC	10	II-7
Configuration Audit Schedule Date – Physical	DUI-Chain	DA-FA-AB	10	II-7
Configuration Identification	Chain	CO-LC	62	II-91
Configuration Item Identification	Element	CO-LE	4	II-3
Configuration Item Variant	Element	CO-LI	5	II-4
Configuration Resource Affected	Element	CO-LK	45	II-62
Contract Basic Line Item Serial Number	Element	CO-OG	6	II-5
Contract Modification Serial Number	Element	CO-QS	8	II-6
Contract Number	DUI-Element		40	II-55
Countries of the World	Element	CO-XV	54	II-73
Date	Chain	DA-FA	10	II-7
Date of Document	DUI-Chain	DA-FA-AF	10	II-7
Day	Element	DA-NA	11	II-8
Day of Year	Element	DA-OB	57	II-85
Design Proofing Requirement	DUI-Element	PR-SB-AB	43	II-60

Figure 10.1   Index of CM status accounting data elements.

APPENDIX II. *Standard data chain and related features (cont'd)*

EFFECTIVE DATE 68-09-27   ARA NAVY   REFERENCE NUMBER CO-LC

DATA CHAIN Configuration Identification   ABBREVIATION CONFIG-IDENT

DEFINITION   A data chain consisting of Configuration Item Identifier and Configuration Item Variant.

DATA USE IDENTIFIER NAME	ABBREVIATION	EXPLANATION
AA Configuration Identification	CONFIG-IDENT	See definition.

DATA CODE CHARACTERISTICS   LENGTH 10   STRUCTURE AN

REFERENCE NO	DATA ELEMENT NAME	STRUCTURE
CO-LE	Configuration Item Identification	7AN
CO-LI	Configuration Item Variant	3AN

EFFECTIVE DATE 68-09-27   ARA NAVY   REFERENCE NUMBER CO-LE

DATA ELEMENT Configuration Item Identification   ABBREVIATION CII

DEFINITION   Designation of an item, discrete assembly, or part for the application of the management disciplines of configuration identification, control, and status accounting.

DATA USE IDENTIFIER NAME	ABBREVIATION	EXPLANATION
AA Configuration Item Identification	CII	See definition.
AB Computer Program Identification	CPI	The unique identifier of a computer program.
AC Tactical Computer Program Identification	TCPI	The unique identifier of a tactical computer program.

RELATED DATA CHAINS
CO-GV Complete Configuration Identification
CO-LC Configuration Identification

DATA CODE CHARACTERISTICS   LENGTH 07   STRUCTURE AN

DATA ITEM NAME	ABBREVIATION	CODE	EXPLANATION
Literal	None		The items to be managed are designated by the procuring activity. The identifying number is assigned by the design organization. This number is non-structured and will establish a base for serializing individual units of an item. When changes to a design are of such a nature or magnitude to preclude the modification of existing units to the current design, a new configuration item identifier shall be assigned and become a base for new serial number assignment.

Figure 10.2 Standard data chain and related configuration identification.

APPENDIX III

CONFIGURATION STATUS ACCOUNTING REPORT (U)
⑥③   ⑰   ㊻

BASE LINE INDEX
⑮

AS OF 69 11 20
⑩

A-7B
㊳

CONFIGURATION ITEM IDENTIFICATION ④	NOMENCLATURE ⑥③	MILITARY SPECIFICATION NUMBER ⑰ ⑯	DATE ⑩	MFG CODE ㊲
7051110	AIR VEHICLE	A-2729891444	670215	80378
7051111	AIRCRAFT COMMANDER TRAINER	A-1910314947511	650710	97928
7051112	POWER PLANT	PP-294992104-82	671112	00624
7051113	FIRE CONTROL	F-531642574772	670312	70709
7051114	NAVIGATION/GUIDANCE	N-1225968311	661230	73030

Figure 10.3   Configuration status accounting report.

A file folder should be set up for every unit or module containing N units or a component containing N modules. If one were to have 1,000 units, then one could have 1,000 files at 1 unit per file or 100 files at 10 units per file. In most instances, one would choose 100 instead. However, as the developers gained experience with the use of these files, they found that having 1,000 was a good idea, especially if there were a number of multiuse units. Then they could make a change to the unit and only one entry into the UDF rather than 100 if the unit were used in all modules.

The primary contents of the file include the following:

- The initial SRS requirement.
- The resulting design requirement.
- The subsequent code listing or reference to previous position.
- The test plan/description and procedure for the unit/module.
- Other data such as interface, data base information.
- Copies of the changes from the time they are logged in by the software librarian to the time they are incorporated.
- All test data and reports, along with records of the design and code walkthrough and other review and audit data such as an action item and follow-up from an internal or formal design review.
- Reference/copy of the product specification and version description document plus user, maintenance manual references or copy pertaining to the element.

Figure 10.4 depicts a typical structure of an SDF. The format of an SDF contains the following sections:

General—Includes the software hierarchy or segment pertaining to the element, access information, name of developer, location of bulky data not in the library, and subcontactor information—who, where located, point of contact, and so on.

Cover or status sheet—Contains necessary identification data and status of the element's development (Figure 10.5).

Requirements—Contains the description of the requirement or functional capability or references to appropriate sections of a requirements documents describing this element.

Design—Includes data describing the system-level and detail design criteria of the element.

Test plan—Describes or references the tests to be conducted on the element or with other software elements during development.

Code listings or reference—If there are a few lines of souce/object code, they may be listed in this section, otherwise a reference to location of the listing is necessary. In some cases hard copy of marked-up listings from previous changes may be located elsewhere and may be important to the person analyzing a requested change.

Test cases and test results—Describes or references documents containing the procedures for testing and the copies of the test results. This is important at the time of functional configuration audit.

Change control/reports and data—Contains the reference to locations of changes both in process or approved/incorporated. Since these data are normally bulky with attached data and marked-up source/object listings, they may not be on line. When on-line problem/

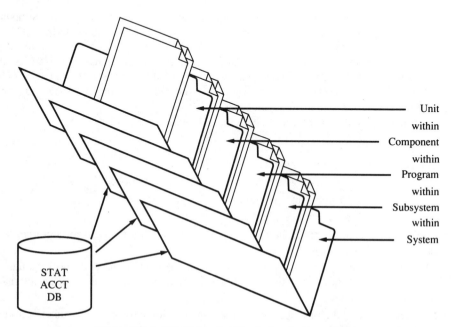

Figure 10.4 Example of software development folder.

CSCI/CSC/CSU/INTEGRATION NAME:_____

SECTION NO.	DESCRIPTION	DUE DATE	COMPLETION DATE	ORIGINATOR	REVIEWER AND DATE
1	REQUIREMENTS				
2	PRELIMINARY DESIGN				
3	DETAIL DESIGN				
4	TEST REQUIREMENTS				
5	CODE				
6	TEST CASES				
7	TEST RESULTS				
8	PROBLEM/CHANGE REPORTS				
9	DESIGN & CODE WALK-THROUGH SUMMARIES				
10	NOTES, MISC.				

RELEASE APPROVAL:

_____   _____

                                                          DATE

Figure 10.5 Configuration management (DB) areas.

change reports are completed, the completed form may be available, but reference will then be made to where the back-up is stored.

Notes and appendix—Data in this section can include problems and solutions for correction, change requests for enhancements received but not processed or rejected by the CCB, and additional interface control data that may be of interest. If the section is a marketed item, it may contain user/customer comments, complaints, recommendations for enhancements, descriptions of competitive systems or software elements, and marketing plans to meet that competition.

Each unit normally requires three to five pages, including the cover. Each component and CI of course require many more. If on-line, the data can be readily available to anyone at any time. If access control is necessary, this can also be accomplished and only those with a need to know can view the data. Entry of data by others may be permissible with use of software tools that will record the what, who, and when of the entry. Otherwise, entry should be restricted to the librarian activity.

There are many benefits in establishing and maintaining a file. The foremost is that a software engineer can review the file when analyzing a change request to determine what went on before. Is this a recurring problem, a pattern failure? What other units/modules are affected? In addition, the file serves as the primary reference for the postmortem, or history and lessons learned about a project.

In an automated environment, the concept and content of the SDF is the same and the ability to reference necessary identification data, change data and test data is done quickly on line without requiring a search through the infamous thousand files that one may have started out with. Figure 10.4 is a good example of an automated concept overview (see SDF). It illustrates that each segment of the system from unit up is represented in the data base with all the required data elements for recording and reporting status.

The automated environment also provides for the import of data as it is created by the user, the holding of the data until a prescribed activity such as test, the export of the data to test, and the subsequent import of the tested and accepted data, which will support a continuing baseline of accepted data. At this point the data are ready for export to an activity such as system integration and delivery to the product baseline process which, in turn, forms the product baseline.

ESTABLISHING THE PRIMARY DATA ELEMENTS

Manually or electronically, primary data elements must be selected, defined, and prescribed on hardcopy-formatted forms or in status accounting or SDF data base. Some of the primary elements are obvious, as listed here:

Specification number
Specification revision letter
Software identification number
Software revision letter
Software code number
Software code version number
Item/equipment number (firmware)
Item/equipment revision letter (firmware)
Contract number/customer ID number
As-built revision/version number/letter

Maintenance indicator
Retrofit/modification indicator
Internal change:
    Date logged
    Change number
    Description
    Requester name/code
    Identification of other elements affected
    Date reviewed by the SRB
    Disposition and date
    Change analyst name
    Date reviewed at CCB
    Disposition and date
    New revision/version number/letter
    Date incorporated
Proposed change to customer:
    Number
    Internal change number reference
    Date logged
    Date reviewed by CCB
    Disposition and date
    Date submitted to customer
    Disposition return date
    Rework date
    Resubmission date
    Disposition date
    Incorporation date
    Closeout date
Technical manual identification and revision
Procured software identification and revision:
    Vendor/supplier identification
    Date procured, test/demo, accepted
    Software elements used
    Data rights provisions/restrictions
    License expiration dates, if applicable
    Support tools identification and revision.

These are just a few of the types of data elements one will want to select and identify.

For automated configuration status accounting, each data element must have its configuration spelled out in a data element dictionary, including such information as number of characters (alpha or numeric) in the element, the function of the element, and mnemonic elements such as software change order = SOCHOR, which is the code the computer will understand and will always be cross-referenced to the software change order.

Because of the varied users of the status accounting information, all parties should review the data elements list and be able to contribute to it in order to receive desired information. For instance, marketing may have a series of customer categories it wants available, such as who would be affected by a given change. In another instance, the security department will insist on a data element to show the classification of the software and related documentation, such as *secret* or *company private* or *competition sensitive*. Each request for additional data elements must be reviewed, assessed, and tested before a decision is made to include them. A data element for a very few appears to be quite counterproductive and should therefore not be included unless determined to highlight a critical situation. There can be anywhere from 100 to 200 data elements so it is wise to prepare for a maximum number rather than a minimum when determining the size of the data base to be used. It is very wise to plan ahead for expansion. As the users of the configuration status accounting information become more familiar and dependent, the need for more information becomes apparent. The configuration status accounting information, utilized properly, will become the central source for all technical data for the project.

DEFINING THE STATUS ACCOUNTING DATA BASE

The data base can be a stand-alone entity or integral to the development data base depending on the project's number of source lines of code. In either case, the status data base must interface with the SDF, the software library, the developer's working files, and the project support and master libraries. It should also be a "livelink" to other data such as that maintained for hardware, other related software projects, the customer and software support facilities, and software maintenance activities. Much depends on what information will be required. As noted, there were some 22 categories of information. A relational data base may provide a superior choice data base tool due to the interrelated nature of CM information. Relational data bases simplify the linking process of data elements. Each category becomes a segment of the status data base, and as reports are generated by query or direct command, may pull data from other data bases and vice versa.

Some examples of this would be

- Traceability of a model number to a serial number in a group of units.
- Traceability of a software part number to a detailed specification or test description/report.
- Traceability of a software program's current version to a group of linked modules or units and to a specific customer. In this example, more than one data base will be tapped, even to foreign data bases, for the information.

In addition to these examples, one will also have to consider the scope and magnitude needed to satisfy internal company requirements. For example:

- Number of projects within the company and how they relate to one another and to the current project
- Number of CI, components, modules, and units to be accounted for.
- Number of versions to be retained at each level: All copies of each version/revision or maybe just three?
- Number of changes anticipated from within the project and from subcontractors or the customer.
- Number of customers receiving custom versions of this software and number requiring access to the data base, such as the DOD.

To be able to satisfy customer and internal requirements, one must also provide the following capabilities:

- Generation of an indented listing of all the software units, modules, components, programs, SCI and top level. This is known as the "goes into" chart, christmas tree, or top-down breakdown of the software. The indent capability is based on each software unit having a parent or indication of the next-higher software element it is used on. Each lower-level unit must have a parent. A parent does not necessarily have to have a child.
- The capability to produce the software hierarchy charts, which is the graphic version of the indented list shown in Figure 10.6 and the list it came from in Figure 10.7.
- Specification revision levels and history of all revisions subsequent to release, Figure 10.8 depicts the history of the item and also indicates the identification number of the change that initiated a new version.

Mobile Interpretation System Components

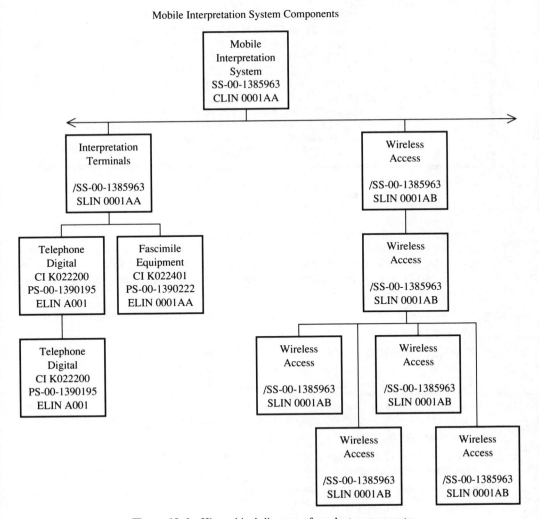

Figure 10.6 Hierarchical diagram of product components.

```
MOBILE INTERPRETATION SYSTEM  (SS-00-1385963)
    INTERPRETATION TERMINALS  (SS-00-1385963)
        TELEPHONE DIGITAL  (PS-00-1390195)
            HANDSET, H-350  (MIL-H-59078)
        FACSIMILE  (PS-00-1390222)
    WIRELESS ACCESS  (SS-00-1385963)
        TERMINAL, RAD-TELEPHONE  (PS-00-1390228)
            RECEIVER-TRANSMITTER  (PS-00-1390235)
                DATA ENCRYPT DEVICE  (PS-00-1390235)
            ANTENNA  (PS-00-1390209)
            VOICE TERMINAL  (TT-CI-7205-0102)
            POWER DISTRIBUTION CENTER
    HARD-LINE ACCESS  (SS-00-1385963)
        RADIO INTERF UNIT  (TT-CI-5205-0127)
        REMOTE NODE  (SS-00-1385963)
            REMOTE NODE SWITCHES  (PS-00-1385966)
                SWITCH ASSEMBLAGE 1  (PS-00-1385966)
                SWITCH ASSEMBLAGE 2  (PS-00-1385966)
            RADIO TERMINAL ASSEMBLAGE A (PS-00-1385914)
    CONTROL CENTER NODE  (SS-00-1385963)
        MGT FACILITY ASSEMBLAGE  (PS-00-1390230)
        RADIO TERMINAL ASSEMBLAGE D  (PS-00-1385914)
        CONTROL CENTER NODE  (PS-00-1390190)
            SWITCH GROUP ASSEMBLAGE  (PS-00-1390190)
            OPS GROUP ASSEMBLAGE  (PS-00-1390190)
            MULTIPLEXER/COMBINER, TD-1234  (MIL-M-49239)
```

Figure 10.7 Indented list.

- Software element (unit, module, program, SCI) revision levels and history of all their revisions subsequent to transfer to the project support library and release to the master library. Figure 10.9 illustrates a software element history retrieved from the respective software development files and also indicates what library it was part of at the time the change was made.

- Provide statistics for number of changes, causes by category, justifications, cost for analyzing, processing, and incorporating.

- Provide for reporting changes received, in process, in review, how disposed, date of incorporation.

- Provide the same information for proposed changes to the customer (ECP).

- Provide for status of elements created and their control number, elements transferred, date, transfer notice number, code walkthrough, and the design walkthrough that enabled the element to be code.

- Provide for the release date of the software elements, the release notice number, and the master library it resides in.

- Provide for date delivered, to whom, where, with what documentation, and who and where the support facility is.

```
┌────────────────────────────────────────────────────────────────────────┐
│                    CONFIGURATION ITEM SUMMARY                            │
│                        (AS OF 1 APR 93)                                  │
│                                                                          │
│  PROGRAM NUMBER:   950                                                   │
│  CI/SWCI NOMEN:    REMOTE COMMAND UNIT (RCU)                             │
│  CUSTOMER P/N:     AS216-00000                                           │
│  FSC PART NUMBER:  9501-00-000-0000                                      │
└────────────────────────────────────────────────────────────────────────┘
```

SUBJECT/ITEM	DOCUMENT NO.	REV	ECN	RELEASE
RCU ATE SYS SDO SPEC	950-SDO1000	-	-	920919
		A	0047	921211
		B	0048	930113
		C	0049	930327
RCU ATE S/W MEDIA DESC	950-SMD1000	-	-	911203
		A	0453	911211
		B	0458	920102
		C	0009	920326
		D	0016	920513
		E	0019	920516
		F	0028	920711
		G	0035	920812
		H	0038	920905
		J	0045	920926
		K	0046	921030
		L	0048	930113
		M	0049	930327
RCU ATE OPER'L S/W CODE	950-SM01000-01	-	-	911203
	950-SM01000-01	02	0453	911211
	950-SM01000-02	03	0458	920102
	950-SM01000-03	04	0009	920331
	950-SM01000-04	05	0016	920513
	950-SM01000-05	06	0019	920516
	950-SM01000-06	07	0028	920711
	950-SM01000-07	08	0035	920812
	950-SM01000-08	09	0038	920905
	950-SM01000-09	10	0045	920926
	950-SM01000-10	11	0046	921030
	950-SM01000-11	12	0048	930113
	950-SM01000-12	13	0049	930327

Figure 10.8 Where used list.

The data base may also be designed to issue identification numbers for specifications and documents as they are created as well as transfer notice numbers, release notice numbers, software change numbers, and ECP numbers from designated blocks of numbers. It should also be capable of interfacing with the hardware data bases, especially if this software is integral to the hardware, rather than one of several applications loaded when needed, such as test processing sets.

Overall, the data base should reflect the software development plan for which it is maintaining the status as the plan is implemented and the software documentation and code are developed, tested, and delivered.

SOFTWARE REVISION STATUS (AS OF 1 APRIL 1992)

CONFIGURATION ITEM NUMBER: SWD1000
SPECIFICATION NUMBER: 950-SWD100-1B

CHANGE NUMBER	CHANGE TYPE	VERSION/ INT VERS	PREP'N DATE	SUBMIT TO BUYING ORGZN	BUYING ACTIV APRVL	REDSGN AND TSTING COMPL	SW DOCS PREP'D	LIBR'Y RELEAS	VDD PREP'D	REPRO ON MEDIA	FINAL VERIF COMPL	ACCEPT BY BUYING ORGZN
				SUSPENSE DATE/ACTUAL ACCOMPLISHMENT DATE								
R00259	SCR	2-14	920126	920128 920128	920210 920212	920205 920204	920208 920207	920210 920212	920215 920218	920222 920228	920224 920302	920229 920307
R00261	SCR	2-15	920127	920129 920130	920211 920209	920206 920208	920209 920210	920211 920210	920216 920216	920223 920223	920225 920225	920301 920302
R00278	SCR	2-16	920211	920213 920213	920227 920227	920221 920221	920224 920224	920227 920227	920302 920301	920309 920308	920311 920311	920316 920315
S00282	ECP	2-17	920215	920217 920219	920517	920701	920715	920720	920720	920727	920811	920815
R00291	SCR	2-18	920304	920306 920307	920318 920317	920314 920315	920317 920317	920317 920327	920321	920328	920330	920404
S00299	ECP	2-19	920320	920323 920323	920623	920808	920822	920828	920828	920905	920920	920926

Figure 10.9 Software revision status.

SOFTWARE CHANGE REQUEST STATUS (AS OF 1 APRIL 1992)

CONFIGURATION ITEM NUMBER 27S0012

SPR NO.	DATE RCVD	EMERG MGT ACTION	ASGN TO	PRELIM AN'SIS COMPL	SCR NUMBER	UNITS AFFECT	SUSPENSE DATE/ACTUAL ACCOMP DATE				
							SCR DATE	SCB APRVL	SOURCE CODE UPDATE	SW DOCS UPDATE	SCR CLOSED
12S-0101	920115	ACCEPT	1F8S	920120	27S0410	A500	920121 920121	920130 920202	920202 920205	920205 920207	920205 920207
12S-0102	920130	REJECT									
12S-0103	920130	ACCEPT	2X40	920210	27S0414	F402 F430	920211 920211	920301 920302	920310 920310	920315 920315	920315 920315
12S-0104	920202	ACCEPT									
12S-0105	920210	ACCEPT	7A10	920215	27S0422	T202	920217 920226	920229	920306	920309	920309
12S-0106	920215	ACCEPT	4M5S	920220	27S0434	A304	920222 920222	920303 920309	920305 920311	920309	920309

Figure 10.10 Software element history.

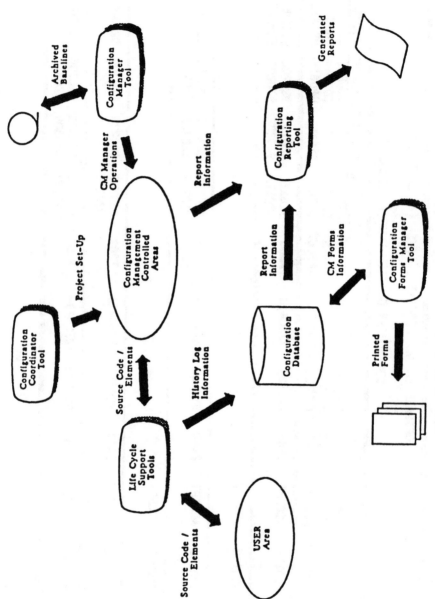

Figure 10.11 Database architectural flow example.

The architecture flow of the data base may look like that illustrated in Figure 10.11. Note that it is designed to handle the immediate demands of the project, which take first priority; then interfacing data bases directly related to the project, such as hardware; and finally other data bases outside of the project, which could include financial, marketing (customer identification), software support data, and the like.

PROVIDING FOR REPORTING AND QUERY

The output from a status accounting system is the only means to determine the merits of the system. Does the output in the form of hard copy or on-line query provide the information one was told to expect? Can one readily query a software identification number for its history and see this on the screen and subsequently on a printout of the query if desired? Is the information requested easy to read and interpret, and, most important, is it current and useful for the purposes it was requested?

As noted in the previous section, an important requirement for a status accounting package is the ability to produce the software hierarchy or level breakdown for the project by element as well as by specification and document—also known as the document tree or specification tree. A good breakdown is the essence of good requirements traceability for tracing continuity of the documentation and code from unit level to the top or detailed design document to the top or tracing the SRS down to the lowest entity.

Although display of graphics is limited on normal monitors, more can be displayed on the workstation monitors—Sun, DEC, Apollo, IBM—which should be available to most software engineers using advanced programming techniques. In any case, the hierarchy can be plotted or printed with ease and one audit might be to go to all the developing engineers and look for the breakdown on their walls!

One is also encouraged to design a few good reports that contain the essential information rather than many reports that will go unread and pile up in the corner of an office. The objective then is to design a universal format that can portray the data in as many as 12 to 13 sorted states (Figure 10.12). Many columns can be sorted to provide given information. In this picture, they are sorted by program trouble report (PTR), but can easily be sorted by software change order (SCO) or if desired by team leader (TLDR). This format can provide 18 reports by simply designating the sort and can be viewed on the screen in a 132-character format.

A more simple format is illustrated in Figure 10.13 for software transfer notices. Although it can be sorted several different ways, it is focused on STNs, unlike the previous illustration, which had several different options.

While these represent multiple listings of units and so on, one is also going to want individual records of specified software elements, as illustrated the document history provided in Figure 10.14. This is also screen size and can be queried and or printed. Some of the other examples in Figures 10.15, 10.16, 10.17, provide different configurations of the same data shown on the history form and are designed to answer almost any question one might have regarding the status of a given software element. In addition, the information provided for status can be compiled into statistics of performance and quantity. If one had estimated 300 software changes, one would want to know how that estimate was holding up—over or under? A project manager will always want to know how many changes are in process, how many approved, how many incorporated. The manager may also want to know how long it took to implement the average change. All these statistics are possible and will help during the project and at a later time as justification for costing and scheduling future projects.

ALL STNS
SOFTWARE TRANSFER NOTICES

STN	MODULE NAME	MODULE CC NO	PROCEDURE NAME	GEN	R E S P	T L D R	CLOSE DATE
0044	ACVRDO	19344122	ACVRSN		RC	RC	3/22/85
0045	AMVRDO	1934105	AMVRDO.FTN	3	JS	JS	3/29/85
0045	AMVRDO	1934105	AMVRDO.HDR	5	JS	JS	3/29/85
0045	AMVRDO	1934105	AMVRDO.TST	4	JS	JS	3/29/85
0045	AMVRDO	1934105	AMVRNM		JS	JS	3/29/85
0046	AGTSLO	1934115	AGTSLO.FTN	7	RD	TG	4/02/85
0046	AGTSLO	1934115	AGTSLO.HDR	9	RD	TG	4/02/85
0046	AGTSLO	1934115	AGTSLO.TST	6	RD	TG	4/02/85
0046	AGTSLO	1934115	AGTSLD		RD	TG	4/02/85
0046	AGTSLO	1934115	AGTSLM		RD	TG	4/02/85
0047	AUZAMO	1919570	AUZAMO.DSN	2	JS	JS	4/03/85
0047	AUZAMO	1919570	AUZAMO.DSN	3	JS	JS	4/03/85
0047	AUZAMN	1919570	AUZAMN.MAC	2	JS	JS	4/03/85
0048	AUCPRO	1934127	AUCPRO.FTN	4	JS	JS	4/05/85
0048	AUCPRO	1934127	AUCPRO.HDR	7	JS	JS	4/05/85
0048	AUCPRO	1934127	AUCPRO.TST	4	JS	JS	4/05/85
0048	AUCPRO	1934127	AUCPRS		JS	JS	4/05/85
0049	AMVRNM	1934109	AMVRNM.INC	1	JS	JS	4/09/85
0050	ADVRDO	1934123	ADVRDO.FTN	3	RG	RG	4/10/85
0050	ADVRDO	1934123	ADVRDO.TST	2	RG	RG	4/10/85
0050	ADVRDO	1934123	ADVRSN		RG	RG	4/10/85
0050	ADVRDO	1934123	ADVRSN.HDR	4	RG	RG	4/10/85
0051	AULRBO	1934126	AULRBO.DSN	4	KS	JS	4/25/85
0051	AULRBO	1934126	AULRBO.TST	4	KS	JS	4/25/85
0051	AULRBO	1934126	AULRBC.DSN	3	KS	JS	4/25/85
0051	AULRBO	1934126	AULRBC.FTN	4	KS	JS	4/25/85
0051	AULRBO	1934126	AULRBY.DSN	3	KS	JS	4/25/85
0051	AULRBO	1934126	AULRBY.FTN	4	KS	JS	4/25/85
0052	AGUPRO	1934128	AGUPRO.FTN	3	GL	TG	4/29/85
0052	AGUPRO	1934128	AGUPRO.HDR	6	GL	TG	4/29/85
0052	AGUPRO	1934128	AGUPRO.TST	2	GL	TG	4/29/85
0053	GLOSAL	1934129	ADRSLT.INC	1	RG	RG	5/08/85

18-14

Figure 10.12 Status accounting report by STM.

ALL PIRS

SCO	SCO ID	PTR	DCR	MODULE NAME	MODULE CC NO	PROCEDURE NAME	GEN	PTR ISSUE DATE	SCO ISSUE DATE	DCR ISSUE DATE	T L D R	P R T	DELAYED INCORP DATE	APPROVAL DATE	CLOSE DATE	CLOSE GEN	S T A T	RELATED CHGS
-		0018	-	CTT000	1911632	CTT0AC.FTM	13	12/12/84	-	-	BP	H				0	I	
0015	X	0019	-	MDTVER	1919617	MDTVER.INC	0	12/12/84	12/12/84	-	JS	H		12/14/84	12/19/84	0	C	
0031		0020	-	AXCN00	1911336	AXCNSC.DSN	7	12/12/84	12/20/84	-	JS	H		12/27/84	12/27/84	8	C	
0031		0020	-	AXCN00	1911336	AXCNSC.FTN	24	12/12/84	12/20/84	-	JS	H		12/27/84	12/27/84	25	C	
0031		0020	-	AXRP00	1911786	AXRPRC.DSN	25	12/12/84	12/20/84	-	JS	H		12/27/84	12/27/84	26	C	
0031		0020	-	AXRP00	1911786	AXRPRC.FTN	24	12/12/84	12/20/84	-	JS	H		12/27/84	12/27/84	25	C	
0031		0021	-	AXFP00	1911339	AXFPDS.DSN	5	12/13/84	12/20/84	-	JS	H		12/27/84	12/27/84	6	C	
0031		0021	-	AXFP00	1911339	AXFPDS.FTN	7	12/13/84	12/20/84	-	JS	H		12/27/84	12/27/84	8	C	
0018		0022	0011	CMID00	1911650	CTML00.TST	4	12/13/84	12/14/84	12/14/84	BP	M		12/13/84	12/28/84	5	C	
0018		0022	0011	CTML00	1911650	CTMLTG.DSN	6	12/13/84	12/14/84	12/14/84	BP	M		12/13/84	12/28/84	7	C	
0018		0022	0011	CTML00	1911650	CTMLTG.FTN	4	12/13/84	12/14/84	12/14/84	BP	M		12/13/84	12/28/85	6	C	
0025		0023	0013	CTAT00	1911640	CTAT00.TST	5	12/13/84	12/14/84	12/17/84	BP	H		12/18/84	1/17/85	7	C	
0025		0023	0013	CTAT00	1911640	CTATHR.DSN	14	12/13/84	12/14/84	12/17/84	BP	H		12/18/84	1/17/85	16	C	
0025		0023	0013	CTAT00	1911640	CTATHR.FTN	11	12/13/84	12/14/84	12/17/84	BP	H		12/18/84	1/17/85	13	C	
0024		0024	-	AGLDFN	1919623	AGLDFN.INC	4	12/13/84	12/27/84	-	TE	M		12/14/84	4/23/85	5	C	
0024	X	0024	-	AGLVER	1919623	AGLVER.INC	33	12/13/84	12/27/84	-	TE	M		12/14/84	4/23/85	33	C	
0024	X	0024	-	AGRVER	1919621	AGRVER.INC	4	12/13/84	12/27/84	-	TE	M		12/14/84	4/23/85	4	C	
0024	X	0024	-	BFECOM	1919626	BFECOM.INC	25	12/13/84	12/27/84	-	TE	M		12/14/84	4/23/85	25	C	
0024	X	0024	-	BFEVER	1919626	BFEVER.INC	9	12/13/84	12/27/84	-	TE	M		12/14/84	4/23/85	9	C	
0024	X	0024	-	BMCVER	1919624	BMCVER.INC	34	12/13/84	12/27/84	-	TE	M		12/14/84	4/23/85	34	C	
0016		0025	0009	CMID00	1919454	CMIDST.DSN	19	12/13/84	12/13/84	12/14/84	BP	H		12/17/84	12/28/84	20	C	
0016		0025	0009	CMID00	1919454	CMIDST.FTN	14	12/13/84	12/13/84	12/14/84	BP	H		12/17/84	12/28/84	15	C	
0017		0026	-	AUIGP0	1911514	AUIGPA.MAC	6	12/13/84	12/13/84	-	LS	M		12/14/84	12/19/84	7	C	
0019		0027	-	AGUMS0	1911439	AGUMSP.FTN	13	12/13/84	12/14/84	-	PM	H		12/14/84	2/6/85	16	C	
0020		0028	0008	CTI000	1911631	CTIDBS.DSN	13	12/14/84	12/14/84	1/14/85	BP	H		12/17/84	1/17/85	14	C	
0020		0028	0008	CTI000	1911631	CTIDBS.FTN	15	12/14/84	12/14/84	1/14/85	BP	H		12/17/84	1/17/85	17	C	
0021		0029	-	AIMPCM	1928468	AIMPCM.INC	0	12/14/84	12/13/84	-	CG	M		12/17/84	12/19/84	0	C	

18-15

Figure 10.13 Screen query printed document history.

DOCUMENT HISTORY REPORT FORMAT - PRELIMINARY

[] QUERY ONLY   [X] REPORT ONLY   [] BOTH

D O C U M E N T   H I S T O R Y

REPORT DATE: 890613   PROGRAM NUMBER: 528   PROGRAM NAME: AN/ALZ-13X, COMMAND MODULE

REPORT DEFINITION FOR TIME PERIOD: INCEPTION TO DATE

DOCUMENT NO.	REV DOC	/APP	EVENT	EVENT NUMBER	EVENT STATUS	ASSIGN DATE	APPVL DATE	BASIC EFFECT	RETROFIT FROM	THRU	DOCUMENT TITLE
1234564	D		SCO	123477	PENDING	890601					SIGNAL PROCESSOR MAIN MODULE CODE
	D	D	SCO	123456	APPROVED	890601	890608	0001	0001	0025	
			PSO	AAA0002	RESUME	890601	890605				
	B	B	SCO	123777	APPROVED	890317	890404	0001	0001	0010	
	A	A	SCO	122333	APPROVED	890226	890303	0001	0001	0010	
	-		REL	AAA1234	APPROVED	890109	890121	0001			
	-				ENG-USE	881228					
					ASSIGNED	881221					
1234567	B	C	SCO	123456	APPROVED	890601	890608	0001	0001	0025	PROTOTYPE OUTPUT GENERATION MODUL
			PSO	AAA0002	RESUME	890601	890605				
	A	A	SCO	122333	APPROVED	890226	890303	0001	0001	0010	
	-		REL	AAA1234	APPROVED	890109	890121	0001			
	-				ASSIGNED	881221					
1234568	A	B	SCO	123490	PENDING	890601					TRACKER/ANALYSER MODULE ALGORITHM
	A		SCO	123450	CANCEL	890314					
	A		REL	AAA1245	RELEASE	890301	890305				
	A		SYS	AAA0009	CHG-SYS	890213	890215				
	-		SYS	AAA0001	REL-SYS	890122	890122				
	-				PRELIM	890121					
					ASSIGNED	890601					

END

Figure 10.14 Screen query print—SCO pending.

SCO PENDING CHANGES BY PROGRAM REPORT FORMAT - PRELIMINAR'

[] QUERY ONLY   [] REPORT ONLY   [X] BOTH

S C O - P E N D I N G

REPORT DATE: 890608

PROGRAM NUMBER: 322   PROGRAM NAME: TIGERSHARK

REPORT DEFINITION FOR TIME PERIOD FROM: 890301 TO: 890605
* *

SCO NUMBER	DATE ASSIGNED	CCB APP DATE	ON HOLD BY	DOCUMENT(S) AFFECTED	
123456	890107	890204		1234556	SEARCH ALGORITHM - GLOBAL
				1234567	REPORT GENERATOR
				TS1234567	TEST SPECIFICATION - OUTPUT
				1234568	ERROR CHECKING PROCEDURE
				1234569	ERROR HANDLER & HELP MODULE
123488	890609	890609	J. ENGINEER	2468111	MAIN PROCESSING MODULE
				1246811	GLOBAL PARAMETER LIST

* * * * * * * * * * * * * * * * END *

Figure 10.15   Screen query print—baseline description.

A status accounting system is only as good as the information in it. The design of a system requires much care, thought, and planning to ensure that the data are available and can be updated with available project resources.

Thus the closing paragraph of the EIA bulletin, *Text Book for Configuration Status Accounting:*

> Status accounting is the capstone to the other CM activities in assuring that your organization will be able to service what it sells to the satisfaction of its customers. Having spent a considerable amount of time, money and effort to set up a system of documentation and change control, status accounting provides a monitoring system to keep the system up to date and to assure the supportability of the products being sold to your customers. EIA Bulletin, 6-5 Electronic Industry Association, Washington DC, March 1988.

One can only say amen to this statement.

BASELINE DESCRIPTION REPORT - PRELIMINARY   13-SEP-89

    [ ] QUERY ONLY   [X] REPORT ONLY   [ ] BOTH   FREQUENCY: MONTHLY

BASELINE DESCRIPTION

REPORT DATE: 890701   CONTRACT NUMBER: N00039-C-89-01234

BASELINE TYPE: PRODUCT   NOMENCLATURE: RECEIVER-MODULE

TYPE DESIGNATION: AN/ALQ-999   BASELINE DATE: 890101

* *

REVISION		CAGE	DOCUMENT	CODE	TITLE
CURRENT	BASELINE	CODE	NUMBER	NUMBER	
-------	--------	----	-----------	-----------	----------------------
B	A		1234567	1234567P1	ANALYZER PROCESS
A	A		1234568		MAIN PROCESS MODULE
-	-		1234569		SYSTEM MODULE DRIVER
A	-		TS1234577		TEST SPEC. DRIVER
					- 80 character field

* * * * * * * * * * * * * * * * END *

- 130 character output per line

Figure 10.16   Screen query print—released documents.

RELEASE DOCUMENTS BY PROGRAM REPORT FORMAT - PRELIMINARY   13-SEP-89

[] QUERY ONLY   [] REPORT ONLY   [X] BOTH

R E L E A S E D - D O C U M E N T S

REPORT DATE: 890609

PROGRAM NUMBER: 266   PROGRAM NAME: TIGER TAIL

REPORT DEFINITION FOR TIME PERIOD FROM: 890401 TO: 890601
* *

DOCUMENT NUMBER	REL REV	RELEASE DATE	NOTICE NUMBER	TITLE
1234557	-	890203	AAA1234	SIGNAL PROCESSOR - ALGORITHM
1234567	-	890203	AAA1234	SIGNAL PROCESSOR - EXECUTABLE ADA CODE
1234568	A	890531	AAA1245	OUTPUT REQUIREMENTS - REPORTS
1234569	A	890422	AAA1239	PARAMETER SPECIFICATIONS - GLOBAL
TS1234555	-	890502	AAA1247	TEST SPECIFICATION, SPECTRUM ANALYZER
1239999	A	890404	AAA1269	MAIN PROCESSING MODULE - EXECUTABLE ADA
TS1239999	-	890404	AAA1269	TEST SPECIFICATION - MAIN MODULE

* * * * * * * * * * * * * * * * END *

Figure 10.17   Screen query print—released documents.

EXERCISES

1. Develop a proposal to your management for a status accounting system, its need, its benefits, drawback, cost savings, and importance to the success of the project. Assume that the customer has not requested any status accounting reports.

2. Draw up a status accounting history report to cover the requirements needed to indicate the status of a given software element at any time.

3. Write a procedure or policy for performing status accounting.

CHAPTER 11

Performing Configuration Audits

The performance of the CM activities during the development phase of the software life cycle is almost complete. The identification requirements have been carried out, the primary functional and allocated baselines have been established and are being maintained. The developmental configuration, design, coding invoked during test, and integration has accounted for all of the control activities and status accounting of the evolving product maintained.

Now it is time to establish that the software product has been "built" in accordance with these requirements and that the software is truly represented in the related documentation that will accompany the software into the operational phase. This is the critical phase for a software product—only if it works as advertised and promoted will it be considered a "winner." Therefore, it is important that formal review and accounting be performed on the software and associated documentation before the operational phase.

Configuration audits provide such an analysis. They are not the same as quality audits, nor are they meant to be part of a design verification audit. Instead, a *configuration audit* of the developed software product provides assurance that what was required has been "built" as evidenced by the software test reports, documentation, and media.

There are two types of configuration audits—functional and physical. Both are a prerequisite to establishing the product baseline once the documentation (product specification and version description document) has been authenticated by the customer. Quality and product assurance activities have other performance criteria to determine product integrity and reliability.

THE FUNCTIONAL CONFIGURATION AUDIT

The objective of the functional configuration audit (FCA) is to verify that a CI's actual performance agrees with its software requirements as stated in its SRS and IRS.

The procedure for determining compliance is to review the test report data and to compare the statements in the test report or other qualification data to the requirement in the SRS and IRS, if applicable. Determining whether the requirement was met may be difficult, and the audit team may have to reach a consensus as to compliance. The agreement may also be deferred until further requirement audits have been performed or an acceptable demonstration of the requirement has been conducted for the audit team. For complex software requirements, such as those in the nuclear, space, and air traffic control environments, one cannot take anything for granted in making the determination of compliance.

In addition to agreement on compliance, the documentation (such as user manual, diagnostic manual, or operator's manual) that will accompany the software may have to be reviewed to verify that a given requirement in the SRS or IRS has been included. This may involve the testing of certain interfaces between computer systems (such as air-to-ground communication checks for signal strength, etc.).

For complex systems, the FCA process may be an incremental one, with the FCA procedure being conducted as each segment of the CI is completed. A summary FCA will then ensure that all segments have been verified, all interfaces have been checked out, and all open action items have been completed. Valuable resources can be saved by the use of such incremental audits; they move at a quicker pace since the needed information is fresh and less research effort is needed to perform the audit.

Prior to conducting the FCA, the functional and allocated baselines must be established and all open action items must be resolved. That includes all deferred or pending decisions regarding the documentation making up the allocated baselines. The final draft of the software product specification also must be reviewed by the customer or designated review authority to ensure that the content and format requirements of software product specification descriptions have been met and are complete (for example, has the compiler and applicable assembler used for this software been adequately specified?).

To prepare and conduct the FCA, the developer must accomplish the following tasks:

- Select the personnel who will participate in the FCA, including the person who has been responsible for the software testing and the generation of the test reports.
- Identify and describe the CI or CIs to be audited at a given session as well as the status of any test software tool that may be used to demonstrate compliance.
- Identify deviation and waivers requested but not approved, and compile a list of any outstanding change requests submitted but not yet approved.
- Prepare an agenda, and distribute it to developer and customer personnel for agreement.
- Compile a notebook for each participant containing a copy of the agenda, the SRS and IRS to be audited, the SPS, and the source code list (if it is too large, include a reference to where the list is located). In addition, all forms, checklists, and other administrative information (especially for visitors) should be included. This ensures that all participants utilize the correct material and record their findings on a common format; it also simplifies compiling the audit results. Minutes of the audit are important and should include the corrective action items, if any, that may result from the audit. The minutes become a prerequisite for the physical audit. The resolution of the corrective actions should be included in the minutes as well.

The audit is performed as a joint endeavor for the benefit of the customer and the developer. The preceding tasks are normally performed by the developer's CM activity who is really managing the audit while the developer and customer project managers co-chair the audit. If everything is in place prior an audit and all the necessary documentation is available, the session can go very quickly. For instance, if the quality assurance person can guarantee that the test reports have been verified against the SRS and IRS the audit can be completed in possibly one day.

Normally, the audit begins with the developer describing: (1) the methods employed for testing, (2) how the tests were conducted and how the test reports were prepared, and (3) who witnessed the tests—that is, who verified the test's conduct in accordance with the descriptions and who signed to verify that the report was creditable.

The developer will also describe those tests that did not meet the specified requirements, the reason or possible reasons for not meeting them, and the suggested solutions. If there is action pending, the developer will report on its status and on when the results will be available to the audit committee. This normally is a corrective action item and will be recorded in the FCA minutes.

If there are still ECPs outstanding, these must be addressed at this time. It may well be that a given ECP is still being considered by the customer and was not returned in time for this audit. If some approved ECPs have been incorporated, but the CI has not been tested for the new change, the committee should be informed and necessary corrective action should be directed by the co-chairs. Any other problems or issues involving the CI should also be examined at this time so that the committee can take appropriate action.

Subsequent to the briefing, the committee will review the software test plan, the SRS and IRS, the SPS, the test descriptions, the procedures, and the test reports. At the discretion of the co-chairs, each requirement may be reviewed against its corresponding test report or the committee may review the list of successfully completed tests and examine only those noted to be unsuccessful or marginal.

In some cases, there may not be formal test reports (for instance, if the testing was conducted by field demonstration or laboratory simulation). In such cases, the developer will furnish a list of the successful tests from which the committee could request a demonstration of a given test to satisfy that requirements have been met.

In other cases, certain tests may not have been performed at the time of the audit (for instance, if a test bed or computer resource or tool was not available prior to the audit). If it was to be a simple test, the co-chairs might waive the testing requirement; however, they might opt to adjourn the audit until the test is performed or to complete the audit with the stipulation that a corrective action item be added requiring that the test be conducted before acceptance of the audit is certified by the customer.

Finally, in those instances where simulations or demonstrations are the test for certain elements of the CI, the committee will witness these events to ensure, in their view, that performance requirements have been met.

Although such steps may seem excessive, in critical environments, such as NASA or the nuclear industry, this audit is a crucial milestone that assures everyone that the credibility of the CI can be certified and that the software is error-free and meets its intended purpose.

The checklist useful for ensuring a successful FCA is illustrated in Figure 11.1, and the specification and test reports sheet is illustrated in Figure 11.2. A sample of the FCA certification checklist for each CI is illustrated in Figure 11.3. If corrective action is required, a sheet similar to Figure 11.4 must be completed and used by CM to follow up on the Figures 11.1 to 11.4 completion of the action item.

THE PHYSICAL CONFIGURATION AUDIT

The objective of a physical configuration audit (PCA) for software is to determine if the design and product specifications and referenced documents represent the software that was coded and tested for a specified CI or CIs.

When the PCA is successfully completed and authenticated, the product baseline is established. All future change activity will involve formal proposals to the customer, and there will be a change in approval authority. The developing function no longer has ownership of the software product; instead, the customer service, marketing activity, or other designated software support activity controls the product. In many cases, the customer has the capability and resources to control the product and tailor it to its assigned environment.

The audit procedure entails examining the design documentation with the CI's source listings and the software manuals that will be sent with the software. In addition, the software product specification and version description document's final draft must be reviewed and approved by the customer/buyer prior to the audit.

The PCA usually follows the successful completion of the FCA and will be conducted as soon as it is known that all the software for the CI has gone through the FCA. If the software is integral to the hardware, however, the software PCA may be held in conjunction with the hardware PCA. In any case the rules for audit of the software will be the same as those used during the hardware PCA.

SAMPLE FCA CHECK SHEET

NOMENCLATURE _____

CONFIGURATION ITEM NO _____ DATE _____

CONTRACTOR REQUIREMENTS	YES	NO
1. Waiver/Deviation List Prepared	——	——
2. Qualification Test Procedures Submitted	——	——
3. Qualification Testing Completed	——	——
4. Qualification Test Results Compiled & Available	——	——
5. Facilities for Conducting FCA Available	——	——
6. Qualification Test Procedures Reviewed and Approved	——	——
7. Qualification Testing Witnessed	——	——
8. Qualification Test Data and Results Reviewed and Approved	——	——

COMMENTS _____

_____

_____

_____

_____

DEFINITIONS:

COMMENT: A note explaining, illustrating, or criticizing the meaning of a writing. Items of this nature should be explored by the contractor and/or the Government, but corrective action is NOT necessary to successfully accomplish a FCA.

DEFICIENCY: Deficiencies consist of two types: (1) conditions or characteristics in any hardware/software which are not in compliance with specified configuration, or (2) inadequate (or erroneous) configuration, identification which has resulted, or may result in configuration items that do not fulfill approved operational requirements.

Figure 11.1   Sample certification attachment pre-FCA checklist.

At the start of the project, the FCA/PCA dates are usually designated to coincide with the required delivery of the software or introduction into the market. The requirements for the audit include making available the source code listings for the CI, the final draft of the SPS and VDD that had been submitted prior to the audit, and evidence of acceptance or approval if available.

The developer will list the audit's participants (including the test director), the CIs that are to be audited, the software being developed, and any deviations and/or waivers that have been requested, any that have been approved, and any outstanding formal change requests to the customer that have not been approved or incorporated into the CI. While all changes

<u>SPECIFICATION/TESTING REVIEW</u>

Configuration Item No. _____ Nomenclature _____

Specification No. _____

Test Procedures _____

Spec Ref TP Ref	Description	Test Result

Figure 11.2 Specification/testing review sheet.

should have been made prior to certification of the FCA, a corrective action from that audit might have included the processing of a formal change proposal or ECP. The developer will also prepare and distribute the audit meeting agenda for review and approval.

CM will manage the audit while the developer and customer software representatives will cochair it. When a combined hardware/software audit is conducted, the program managers of the buyer and seller will be the cochairs and the CM manager for the developer will be the manager.

FCA CERTIFICATION SHEET NO. 1
(For Equipment/Computer Software)

Contract: _____   Date: _____
Contractor: _____
Configuration Item No.: _____

Qualification Test Procedures and Results.   The qualification test/analysis results have been reviewed to ensure that testing is adequate, properly done, and certified. (All test procedures and interface documents shall be reviewed to assure that the documents have been approved by the Government. All test data sheets shall be reviewed to assure that the test was witnessed by a representative of the Government.)

Attached is a list of the documents reviewed.

Check One

          Procedures and results reviewed satisfy the requirements and are accepted.
          See Attachment ___ for comments.

          Attached is a list of deficiencies.

Signature(s) of FCA Team Member(s)

_____   _____
_____   _____
_____   _____
_____   _____
_____   _____

Sub-Team Chairperson

Figure 11.3   FCA certification sheet number 1 (for equipment/computer software).

CM will provide copies, to each participant, of the SPS, VDD, and software manuals prepared for the CI to be audited. In addition, copies of the CI's FCA minutes, completed corrective action items, and any findings made by software quality assurance and their status for the CI will be provided. In support of this data, the SRS, IRS, and approved changes, deviations, and waivers will be made available. Changes will include all of those made during a test and those that may not have been incorporated and tested.

The PCA checklist (see Figure 11.5) is more detailed than the FCA checklist. For the most part, CM is responsible for ensuring that all items have been satisfied. Those items that have been answered "NO" should be justified by the software project leader or the program manager. The primary purpose of the PCA is to make sure that all requirements have been met in the development and "building" of the product that sufficient material is validated to ensure that the software can be supported.

FCA DEFICIENCY SUMMARY LIST					

CONFIGURATION ITEM NO. _____ NOMENCLATURE_____

CONFIGURATION ITEM NUMBER	REPORT REFERENCE	DESCRIPTION	RESPONSIBILITY FOR CORRECTION	PLACE OF INSPECTION	INSPECTED BY

Figure 11.4   FCA deficiency summary list.

At the time an audit is to begin, the developer will brief the committee on any problems that are inherent with the CI, any solutions or recommended solutions to these problems, and the status of these problems and solutions. The briefing will also include any outstanding change problems, concurrent testing problems, or demonstration and simulation problems and their solutions.

At the conclusion of the briefing, the following audit tasks will be implemented (see the Tasks checklist in Figure 11.5):

- Perform a complete review of the software product Specification for format and completeness. If the SPS is comprised of several documents such as the SRS, IRS, and SDD, each document will also be reviewed to ensure completeness as well as compatibility.
- Review the FCA minutes for the corrective action items and the resulting solutions. If the committee does not agree with some of the resolutions, discussion will be held to resolve the concern and a possible new corrective action item may be created. Of course, the final certification of the PCA will be delayed until the committee's concerns are satisfied.
- Review all design descriptions for proper entries, symbols, labels, tags, references, and data descriptions. This is to ensure that the conventions and standards described in the software development manual have been followed by the coder, by the design

PCA CHECKLIST (SAMPLE)

The following hardware, computer software, documentation shall be available, and the following tasks shall be accomplished at the PCA.

Hardware:

Computer Software:

Documentation:

	YES	NO
(1) Approved final draft of the configuration item product specification.	___	___
(2) A list delineating both approved and outstanding changes against the configuration item.	___	___
(3) Complete shortage list.	___	___
(4) Acceptance test procedures and associated test data.	___	___
(5) Engineering Drawing Index.	___	___
(6) Operating, maintenance, and illustrated parts breakdown manuals.	___	___
(7) List of approved material review board actions on waivers.	___	___
(8) Proposed DD Form 250, "Material Inspection and Receiving Report."	___	___
(9) Approved nomenclature and nameplates.	___	___
(10) Manuscript copy of all software CI manuals.	___	___
(11) Computer Software Version Description Document.	___	___
(12) Current set of listings and updated design descriptions or other means of design portrayal for each software CI.	___	___
(13) FCA minutes for each configuration item.	___	___
(14) Program Parts Selection List (PPSL) (see MIL-STD-965).	___	___

Tasks:

	YES	NO
(1) Define Product Baseline.	___	___
(2) Specification Review and Validation.	___	___
(3) Drawing Review.	___	___
(4) Review acceptance test procedures and results.	___	___
(5) Review shortages and unincorporated design changes.	___	___
(6) Review deviations/waivers.	___	___
(7) Examine proposed DD 250.	___	___
(8) Review contractor's Engineering Release and Change Control System.	___	___
(9) Review system allocation document.	___	___
(10) Review Software User's Manuals, Software Programmer's Manuals, Computer System Operator's Manual, and Firmware Support Manual.	___	___
(11) Review software CIs for the following: (a) Preliminary and detail Software Component design descriptions. (b) Preliminary and detail Software interface requirements. (c) Data base characteristics, storage allocation charts and timing and sequencing characteristics.	___	___
(12) Review packaging plan and requirements.	___	___
(13) Review status of Rights in Data.	___	___
(14) Ensure that all appropriate items installed in the deliverable hardware, that should have been processed through the PCP, are identified on the PPSL or that the necessary approval documentation is avalilable and that the hardware does not contain items that should have been processed through the PCP but were not (see MIL-STD-965).	___	___

Figure 11.5 Sample certification attachment—sample PCA, checklist.

and code walkthrough teams, and by normal software quality assurance monitoring and inspection and that the descriptions are traceable to the software manuals and code that will go with the software for maintenance and support.

- Compare the top-level component design descriptions with the lower-level unit design descriptions for continuity and flow of information.
- Compare the unit descriptions with the related source code listings for accuracy and completeness.
- Review the software manuals for format, completeness, and conformance with applicable data item descriptions or similar format instructions. If the manuals have been prepared in the developer's format, evaluate whether the format and content are consistent with similar documents in the industry, are easy to understand, and can be adapted to any environment.
- Inspect the software medium. Today almost all software is on 3.5- or 5-inch floppy disks, however, many software applications may also be delivered in hard disk, magnetic tape, and even punched mylar. The team will review and inspect to ensure that the medium meets the intended purpose and the contract requirements.
- Review the source code listings for compliance with approved coding standards as specified in the SDP, the agreement with the customer, or as is consistent with industry practices.
- Review compliance with rights in data, proprietary information, adequate statements in the documentation, and markings on the medium and header sections of the software to ensure protection of the developer's intellectual property.
- Ensure that the source code as presented produces the accepted executable code for the FCA. This may require recompilation and building of the CI and a comparison of results.

These tasks provide the first evidence that there is a formal review of the software manuals. It is important for the software support function to know that the manuals received with the software agree with the software. It is even more important for the average customer to understand the manual and to perform the tasks necessary to operate the software application as intended. Support documentation should be considered as important as the requirements and design documents in order to maintain the software. If this is not determined until a review at the PCA, it may be very expensive to bring the manuals into line with the software.

In addition, the entire software project team must be aware of the law and the rules governing proprietary rights. Provisions should be made to mark, declare, and determine the rights desired for the software and its documentation while protecting the rights of third party software (that procured for use on this development project). Such software should be treated by CM in the same manner as software generated by the project.

There are a number of PCA certification forms available, including the overall audit certification (see Figure 11.6), the review of the specifications and documents (Figure 11.7), review of the engineering release system, (see Figure 11.8), and review of the status of deviations and waivers (see Figure 11.9). When conducting an equipment and software PCA, it is important to ensure that the *system* has received certification—not just the software and not just the hardware, but the system as a whole.

Next the product baseline is formalized. Figure 11.10 provides the form that will declare this baseline established. The certificate lists those specifications and documents that com-

PCA CERTIFICATION PACKAGE (SAMPLE)

FOR

CONFIGURATION ITEM NO.(s) ————————————————

CONTRACT NO———————————————————————

PRIME CONTRACTOR: EQUIPMENT MANUFACTURERS:

——————————————————   ——————————————————

——————————————————   ——————————————————

——————————————————   ——————————————————

APPROVED BY ___(DESIGNEE)___   APPROVED BY ___(DESIGNEE)___
          CONTRACTOR   GOVERNMENT

DATE _____   DATE _____

SCOPE/PURPOSE

A Physical Configuration Audit (PCA) was conducted on the following end items of equipment/computer software:

CONFIGURATION ITEM   NOMENCLATURE   PART NUMBER   SERIAL NO.   NSN

The purpose of the PCA was to ensure accuracy of the identifying documentation and to establish a product baseline.

The establishment of a product baseline for equipment/computer software is not to be construed as meeting Government requirements for delivery by the contractor of an operational system meeting approved acceptance criteria.

DEFINITION OF TERMS

COMMENT - A note explaining, illustrating, or criticizing the meaning of a writing. Items of this nature should be explored by the contractor and/or the Government, but corrective action is NOT necessary to successfully accomplish a PCA.

DISCREPANCY - A note explaining, illustrating, or criticizing the difference between writings. A note showing the variance between what exists and what is acceptable. Items of this nature shall be rectified by the contractor prior to successful accomplishments of a PCA.

Figure 11.6 PCA certification package.

PCA CERTIFICATION SHEET NO. 2
(For Equipment/Computer Software)

Contract: _____ Date: _____

Contractor: _____

_____

_____

Specification Review and Validation. Specifications have been reviewed and validated to assure that they adequately define the configuration item and the necessary testing, mobility/transportability and packaging requirements.

Check One

☐ The Type C Specifications are complete and adequately define the configuration item. They shall, therefore, constitute the product baseline. See Attachment ___ for comments

☐ The Type C Specifications are unacceptable. Attached is a list of discrepancies.

Signature(s) of PCA Team Member(s)

** _____   _____

* _____   _____

_____   _____

_____   _____

_____   _____

** Team Chairperson
* Sub-Team Chairperson

A. Specification Review and Validation Instructions. The detailed specifications listed in paragraph B. below shall be reviewed for compliance with the applicable requirements. Each specification shall serve as the basic document for configuration control of the subject configuration items. The information contained within the specifications shall be audited at the PCA.

B. Review and Validation Results:

1. Specifications reviewed and validated:

SPEC NO.	PART NO.	DATE	EQPT./COMP. SOFTWARE NOMENCLATURE	CONFIGURATION ITEM NO.

2. Specifications Reviewed and Disapproved:
   (Provide attachment for causes.)

Figure 11.7 Physical configuration audit certification sheet—review of specifications and documents.

<u>PCA CERTIFICATION SHEET NO. 8</u>
(For Equipment/Computer Software)

Contract: _____   Date: _____

Contractor: _____

_____

_____

<u>Review of Contractor's Engineering Release and Change Control System</u>. The contractor's engineering release system and change control procedures have been reviewed to ensure that they are adequate to properly control the processing and formal release of engineering changes.

<u>Check One</u>

☐ The contractor's engineering release system and change control procedures are adequate for the processing and formal release of engineering changes. See Attachment ___ for comments.

☐ Attachment ___ is a list of dificiencies.

Signature(s) of PCA Team Member(s)

* _____   _____

_____   _____

_____   _____

_____   _____

_____   _____

_____   _____

* Sub-Team Chairperson

Figure 11.8 Physical configuration audit certification sheet—review of engineering release.

prise this point of departure. Several of these forms may be needed if the baseline is being established on an iterative basis as each CI is audited.

ROLE OF CONFIGURATION MANAGEMENT IN AUDITS

The following tasks are performed by CM for any one of the audits discussed to this point.

- Review the customer's audit requirements.
- Advise the project team on what data and participation is required and when (what date).
- Arrange for location, facility, meeting rooms, and logistics for customer and developer participants (hotel rooms, breaks, and meals) and the data to be reviewed at each given audit.

<u>PCA CERTIFICATION SHEET NO. 6</u>
(For Equipment/Computer Software)

Contract: _____   Date: _____

Contractor: _____

_____

_____

<u>Review Deviations/Waivers</u>. A review of all deviations/waivers to military specifications and standards that have been approved. The purpose is to determine the extent to which the equipment(s)/computer software undergoing PCA vary from applicable specifications and standards and to form a basis for satisfactory compliance with these specifications and standards.

In accordance with this paragraph, all applicable deviations/waivers have been reviewed with the following results:

<u>Check One</u>

☐   The equipment(s)/computer software listed on Certification Sheet No. 1 of this report complies with all applicable specifications and standards. See Attachment ___ for comments.

☐   Attachment ___ is a list of discrepancies and/or comments.

Signature(s) of PCA Team Member(s)

* _____   _____

_____   _____

_____   _____

_____   _____

_____   _____

* Sub-Team Chairperson

<u>Deviation/Waiver Review Team Instructions</u>. All approved waivers and deviations to military specifications and standards shall be reviewed and recorded. Also, record any part of the PCA which fails to meet specifications or standards <u>but</u> is not an approved waiver/deviation.

<u>Results of Team Review</u>. List the deviations/waivers against the equipment/computer software being PCA'd that were reviewed

Figure 11.9   Physical configuration audit—review of deviations and waivers.

PCA CERTIFICATION SHEET NO. 1

(For Equipment/Computer Software)

Contract: _____   Date: _____

Contractor: _____

_____

_____

Product baseline. The following documents of the issue and date shown comprise the product baseline for the listed equipments(s)/computer software:

SPEC NO.	ASSEMBLY TOP DRAWING NO.	ISSUE	EQUPT./COMP. SOFTWARE NOMENCLATURE	CONFIGURATION ITEM NO.

Signature(s) of PCA Team Member(s)

**

•

** Team Chairperson
* Sub-Team Chairperson

Figure 11.10 Sample certification attachment—product baseline.

- Assemble in an audit binder all the necessary information including logistics, checklists, forms, reference data, specifications, and documents (SRS, IRS).
- Prepare the agenda for audit leader's review and approval.
- Submit a final draft of the software product specification, version description document to the customer for review prior to the audits (as specified in the requirements for audits).
- Ensure that all pertinent data are in place or are available on the date of the audit (this may include using terminals, PCs, wide screen view of monitor screens, etc.).
- Take minutes of the audit proceedings and corrective action items and distribute these minutes to the audit team at the conclusion of the audits.
- Provide follow up on corrective action items and submit to the audit team cochairs for final approvals.

CM should know how many audits will be conducted and when these sessions will take place so that the costs of this time and resources effort can be determined at the time of the proposal.

EXERCISES

1. Prepare a memo to the software project team informing them of a planned functional configuration audit. Describe what they will be required to do, to know, and to decide on.
2. Develop an overall company policy governing the FCA/PCA audit requirements.
3. Develop a checklist for an FCA and a PCA that fits the environment you are most familiar with.

CHAPTER 12

Performing Interface Control

The interface control activity should be a permanent part of the CM definition. Unfortunately, it is most often thought of as a function of system engineering, which ultimately becomes responsible for the definition, design, and control of interface control.

Interface is the functional and physical characteristics required for a common boundary to exist between two or more software products and computer systems that are provided by different organizations or sources. An interface control document defines the interfaces which may affect the operation of cofunctioning CIs, and is used for control as well as delineating the interface criteria and technical detail necessary to effect an economical and viable interface [32].

While the interface definition and the interface requirements are an activity of system engineering, the responsibility for identifying the defined interfaces, the control, and the status, and for performing configuration audits rests with CM.

A NASA Standard [33] which provides for an interface control plan (ICP) states in simple terms that the purpose of the plan is to define the process by which the developer defines and manages all external interfaces between the developer's information system or component and all users, including human or other information systems or components. In turn, the ICP produces a requirements specification, a design, and detailed design interface documents.

Another standard [23] states that interface control is the coordinated activity required to ensure that the functional and physical characteristics of systems and equipments are compatible. The interface control activity is responsible for ensuring that the configuration identification conforms to the functional interfaces established by system engineering and that the affected CIs are logically compatible and can be operated and supported as intended. The interface activity is also responsible for the control of the documentation, including an assessment of the impact of changes to control documentation or changes emanating from other document changes that could affect the interfaces.

Most of the software specifications and documents define or explain the interfaces between the CI being identified and another CI or computer system. All of these interfaces must be mapped so that everyone on the project will understand what has been defined and will be able to carry out their specified tasks. CM treats the interface design documents and drawings in the same manner as other documentation, except CM also provides for assessment of impacts to interfacing entities.

An example of the content of an interface control document (ICD) might be written from the sample top-level functional block diagram shown in Figure 12.1 [34]. This document might include:

Software.

Data: inputs, outputs, rates, accuracies.

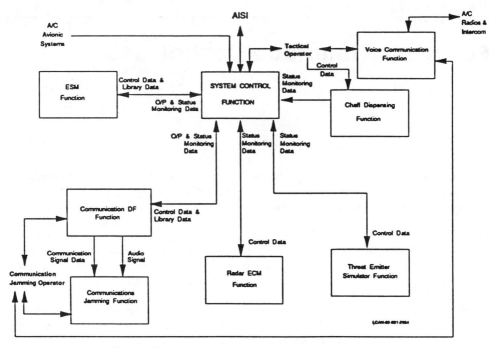

Figure 12.1   Sample top-level functional block diagram.

Messages: format, content, storage.

Protocols: enable, processing, validation error detection, and recovery.

Hardware and software.

Interface: diagrams, standards, and conventions.

Timing and Sequencing: control and logic, relationships, data transfers, input sensing.

In many cases, such as a multinational or international consortium of participating companies, an interface control working group (ICWG) is established by the designated interface control activity. This may be necessary because the large number of developers and organizations that may be participating in the design effort make it imperative to ensure compatibility of all interfacing entities. On the other hand, a developer and its major subcontractors may well decide to form a ICWG in order to establish better communication. In addition, the multinational consortium will normally designate, by vote, the interface control activity/developer.

The ICWG may have the task of preparing the interface documentation (the plan, the requirements specification, design, and detail design documentation). The group may also designate a CM activity to perform the identification, control, status monitoring, and configuration audit management during the FCA/PCA preparation (see Chapter 11). The CM activity will be responsible to the chairperson of the ICWG, just as that activity is responsible to its program manager. Design reviews of the interfaces will most likely take place during normal SSR, SDR, and PDR; however, the ICWG may choose to conduct its own review subsequent to a formal design review. In any case, as the interface documentation is

INTERFACE CONTROL DRAWINGS (ICD)

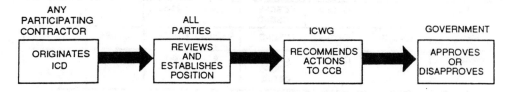

1. Any participating contractor originates ICD.

2. All affected parties review ICD and submit recommendations to ICWG Chairman.

3. ICWG Chairman evaluates proposed ICD.

4. ICWG approves/disapproves ICD.

    a. If ICWG decision is unanimous, the ICD is forwarded to the Government for review.

    b. If disagreement exists within ICWG, then ICWG Chairman forwards ICD to Government for resolution together with his recommendations.

5. When the ICD is incomplete and release must be made at that time, the ICD shall be appropriately identified and followup action assigned by ICWG Chairman for completion of ICD.

ENGINEERING CHANGE PROPOSALS (ECPs)

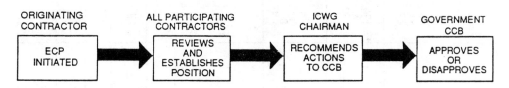

1. ECP prepared by initiator

2. All participating contractors review ECP for interface implications on their system/segment and submit recommendations to ICWG.

3. ICWG conducts evaluation of ECP and participating contractor's reccomendations.

4. ICWG Chairman recommends to CCB through Government approval/disapproval of ECP from interface point of view.

5. Government CCB evaluates and approves/disapproves ECP.

Figure 12.2 Flowchart of ICWG procedures for ICDs.

IDENTIFIER	DESCRIPTION	SOURCE CSCI	DESTINATION CSCI(s)	UNIT OF MEASURE	LIMIT/ RANGE	ACCURACY	PRECISION/ RESOLUTION
IFA001	VELOCITY	CSCI-A	CSCI-B CSCI-C	ft/sec	20-1000	+20	10^{-3}
IFA002	AZIMUTH	CSCI-A	CSCI-D	RADIANS	$0 - \pi/2$	+0.05	10^{-3}
IFA003	ALTITUDE	CSCI-C	CSCI-A CSCI-B CSCI-D	ft	0-1500	+10	10^{-2}

Figure 12.3   Flowchart of ICWG procedures for ECPs.

drafted and approved, CM will place it under formal control and process changes for formal ICWG review and approval.

Figure 12.2 illustrates the flow of the control process for an ICWG document and a change proposal. Note that the procedure is almost the same as that for a normal project change except that the CCB is the ICWG, unless the chair may have delegated that responsibility to a given developer's CCB. In processing the change request, however, CM must know what to look for. Most of the interface process is message handling, switching and processing at each end of the interface. Figure 12.3 provides a typical example. A change to any one of the factors could affect other interfaces as well as the one for velocity from CI-A to CI-B. In addition, changes should be expected for initiation criteria, expected responses, item usage

BRIEF DESCRIPTION OF FUNCTIONAL PHYSICAL INTERFACE	AGENCY AFFECTED CONT/GOVT	INTERFACE CONTROL DRAWING			TOOLING GAGE DOCUMENTS, IF AFFECTED	ICWG REVIEWS			ICWG ACTION ITEM NO.	ICD APP. DATE	ECP APPROVAL		
		NO.	TITLE	REV		PARTICIPATING AGENCIES	DATE	DATE MINS. DISTR.			CONTR	NO	DATE

Figure 12.4   Example of ICWG control sheet.

(such as control, data, and message handling), and switching, data attributes, and format conventions. What happens if there is a power failure? What happens if data overflows a given disk file and there is no more room for a larger disk? What if the message rate is too slow or too fast? Finally, there must be a verification of interface compatibility including testing, operations, safety, and reliability. Figure 12.4 illustrates a control sheet that may be used for documenting the current status of the interfaces and for keeping a historical and analytical record. Although most of this work is done by the correcting analyst, CM must be aware of where the analyst is looking so that these documents can be retrieved and set up for the expected changes.

Traceability is an important element of interface control. Some standards require that a mechanism for requirements traceability be maintained for purposes of determining the impact of change on the defined interfaces. This is not always easy to portray in a hierarchial chart since interfaces are horizontal as well as vertical. A data flow diagram is better for describing the horizontal flow (see Figure 12.5). Another method, which is very similar to system analysis flowcharts for movement of paper between functions and activities, portrays a horizontal flow using interface V's to denote the interfaces between data elements (see Figure 12.6).

There are several software tools that provide for requirements traceability; however, the tools must fit the need rather than the need fitting the tool.

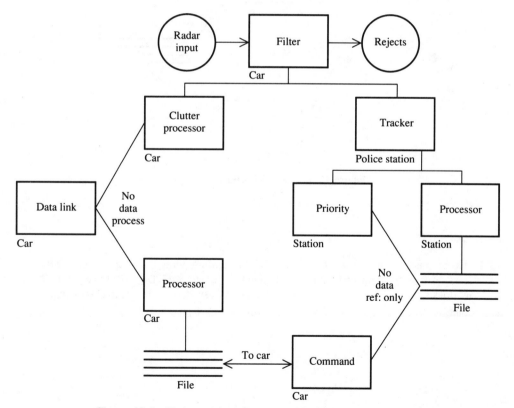

Figure 12.5   Horizontal interface control flow with reference point.

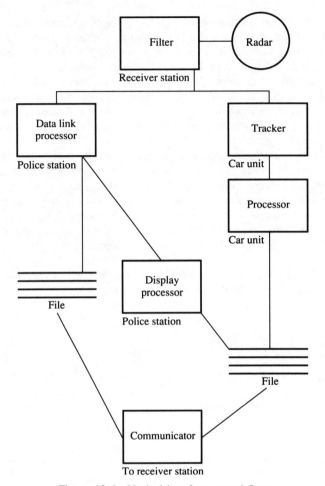

Figure 12.6   Vertical interface control flow.

EXERCISES

1. Think of possible interfaces that you may be dealing with on your current software project. Are they identified, controlled, and accounted for? Do you have an ICWG? How does it work in your environment? Discuss these items with your classmates.

2. Prepare an interface control section for a software CM plan.

CHAPTER 13

Performing Subcontractor Control

Subcontractor control is also an important part of the CM activity; however, many times it is not addressed at the time that subcontracts are being solicited. Too many times a well-meaning subcontract administrator will not provide the proper clauses and requirements to ensure that the requirements for CM are communicated to a subcontractor and are tailored to meet the scope and magnitude of the work to be performed. Therefore, it is important that the CM activity on a given project interface and work with those who will be soliciting and reviewing subcontractor responses.

There are three primary categories and three secondary categories of subcontracting in which CM has a vital role. The secondary categories include associate contractors, joint venture team members and interfacing organizations not bound by formal contract to prime contractor.

These categories include agreements and contracts of understanding for which no product or service is provided directly as a result of a purchase order. Associate contractor agreements are between organizations that are building related systems or equipment that when complete will constrain their own software product (such as the software for an auto-landing system sold by a third party to multiple airline companies). In order to provide the software package as specified, it is necessary to have access to the associate contractor's designs and specifications as well as to have the testing rights for the software package. To provide continuity in the development and building of the whole system associate contractors usually are part of an ICWG. The CM activity will be required to protect any technical data received from an associate and to place it under formal configuration control. In addition, technical data that may be provided by the prime contractor must be accounted for by CM and formally released to the associate. CM then ensures that subsequent changes are distributed to those associates receiving and using released documents.

The joint venture team (JVT/JV) is an agreement among coproducers who share design and development responsibility to produce the full-scale development models of equipment and software. At production time, the teams become competitive producers of the product they jointly designed, developed, built, and tested. One of the team members, by consensus, is one step ahead as the leader. The CM of that team is also the CM for the joint venture. The other team's CM "reports" to the JVT CM for matters pertaining to JVT business only.

The final secondary category is the interfacing organization that is not bound by formal contract but is still affected by the activity of the primary contractor's product. For example, a designer of car radios must know the size of the apertures for each 1990 model car—thus the need for interface and communication. CM's role in this category is much the same as that for an associated contractor, except in this case technical data are usually not released to the interfacing organization.

The three primary categories are determined by the degrees of responsibility given to the subcontractor: (1) in the first category full authority is given to design, develop, build, test, and deliver a specified CI or multiple CIs; (2) in the second category organization limited design responsibility is given, such as when modifying existing software or performing coding and unit testing only; (3) in the third category no design responsibility is given and the software to be delivered is termed a nondeveloped item (NDI) or computer off-the-shelf software (COTS).

The first primary category of subcontracting will provide the most activity for CM. For instance, if an organization is involved in the production of a command, control, and communication system and the command system CI is subcontracted, then that contractor is an extension of the prime contractor who did not have the capability or resources to produce the command system's software.

In order for the subcontractor to understand what is required, CM must prepare a specific section in the subcontract statement of work describing the requirements. Appendix 4 details what is required from the several categories of subcontractors. Note that in the first column every item required at the prime level is also required from the subcontractor. Tailoring these requirements, however, is an important consideration. CM must determine to what degree these items are required. If required, can they be input to the data the primary contractor is preparing or are they stand-alone? In addition, CM must also be aware that there may be lower-tier subcontractors. While it is the responsibility of the top-level subcontractor to communicate the job requirements, CM must also be assured of the lower-tier organizations' abilities to perform.

A typical subcontractor statement of work, written by CM, follows:

> The supplier shall establish and maintain an internal CM system to ensure control of the product baseline documentation and/or the product media, change data, inspection and test data, etc., and to provide a chronological history for each delivered CI. Completed document masters and media shall be protected from unauthorized changes. Authorized changes made to completed documents and media shall be subject to audit by the buyer. Changes proposed to the buyer shall have traceability starting with the buyer-approved change proposal to the supplier's design documentation or media and ending with the product and data change incorporation. The CM system shall prevent the use of obsolete and unauthorized documents or code and shall include a method for maintaining a complete record of all engineering documentation or code status created and/or used on the buyer's purchase order. The supplier shall submit for the buyer's approval a configuration management plan in accordance with the supplier data requirements list (SDRL) attached to this statement of work. The supplier shall also provide a proposed format for use in audits as specified in the SDRL. The buyer reserves the right to audit, with due notification, throughout the life of the contract or purchase order.

There are many adaptations of this statement; however, precision in language is important since this is a legal document. Remember that the only way to order an item is via the formal line item on the purchase order or contract and that data should be ordered only via the SDRL. The primary contractor cannot order anything through the statement of work.

CM also must evaluate the subcontractors' abilities to perform the CM activity in accordance with the statement of work. The evaluation may be satisfied by prior experience with the supplier or by the recommendations of others who have dealt with the subcontracting organization. If the supplier is unknown, the evaluation questionnaire contained in Appendix 4 might be used as is or modified to ensure that those bidding are all able to meet the CM requirement for this project. The proposal CM plans submitted are another indicator of a subcontractor's ability. In most cases, one plan stands above the others; however, the author of that plan may not be the winner of the subcontract because of other considerations.

If the winner did not have the best CM plan, the deficiences in the plan should be accounted for and corrected prior to signing a contract. This could mean placing a CM activity from the buyer's organization with the subcontractor in order to train and recommend corrective action. If this is not possible, all of the supplier's submissions should be carefully reviewed. They should not be accepted until they have been corrected to CM's satisfaction. Of course, this may be a costly scheme, but is is better to pay now than to pay later.

CM should ensure that the subcontractor's performance of CM is the same as the primary CM's performance. The buyer's CM should constantly monitor the supplier's CM performance against prescribed standards for establishing the baselines, processing changes, providing status, and performing well in the audits and design reviews.

CM can gauge the performance of the supplier in terms of on-time delivery of data, especially the software specifications and documents. If the submissions require little or no revision or modification, then the supplier's performance is outstanding. Likewise, if the supplier is submitting few changes and on-site reviews indicate few internal changes, the design criteria is being adhered to and performance is exceptional. Also, if the reports that are submitted are on time with minimal change data and provide full coverage of the specification and documentation status, the supplier is performing well. If the supplier passes the functional and physical configuration audits with few, if any, corrective action items, then CM has recommended an excellent supplier.

Such performance is the best case scenario. In many cases, the subcontract is terminated midway through the development cycle through no fault of CM's efforts. The cause might be poor specifications and/or an inadequate statement of work. Poor communication and gross misunderstandings between buyer and seller might be another reason for contract termination. On the seller side, management may have disregarded many of the buyer's requirements as unnecessary and costly. To save money to be applied to inevitable overruns, many required activities such as CM, reliability, and quality assurance will not be performed, which in turn will result in a poor product. To eliminate this problem, a subcontractor should not be chosen on price considerations alone.

On-site inspection of a supplier's facility and resources by the primary contractor's CM is vital, especially if there are many lines of code to be designed and produced. It gives the CM an opportunity to view their resources, to discuss their policy and procedure, and to arrive at agreements on a one-to-one basis. However, the CM must realize that discussion is limited to *what* is to be done. *How* to do it is up to the seller, although through discussion and demonstration the buyer's CM will be briefed on how the seller will perform the CM activity.

Lead time is very important when requesting data from a subcontractor. If the buyer is required to submit the primary CM plan in 90 days after contract award, then CM will have to have a subcontractor's plan in 60 days. when receiving changes from a seller, the buyer should process them expeditiously so as not to hold up the development effort, especially if the proposed change is to be passed up to the primary contractor for approval prior to incorporation. The same sense of urgency must prevail at the prime's customer level in order to be able to maintain schedules and not incur additional cost for developmental downtime.

Any acquiring activity must be organized to handle receipt of data from a seller, no matter if primary contractor or subcontractor, to process the data without delay, and to notify the sender of the disposition so that work can continue. Failure of CM to have a CCB established at the buyer's location can cause undue delay in approving and incorporating changes to the subcontractor's product.

The requirements placed on sellers in the second primary category—performing a modification process or partial design and development of new or existing software and its documentation—may be at the same level as those imposed for full development responsibility if the the CI is complex or critical in nature. A review of the applications table shows that most of the requirements for full development also may pertain to partial. Thus, it is important for the CM to assess the nature of the CIs that are to be subcontracted and make appropriate adjustment in the statements of work.

The third primary category is the procurement of COTS or NDIs. This type of procurement is becoming prevalent as an economical way of obtaining software from established vendors who have proven that their products meet specified requirements. The concern to CM is twofold: (1) obtaining sufficient documentation to incorporate the NDI into the baseline process, and (2) maintaining status of changes or enhancements to the software procured. These tasks require close cooperation with the CM's procurement activity to be able to obtain the necessary data. (A good example of this is the software requirements for the NASA Space Shuttle software environment. The majority of the software will be COTS.)

Most vendors will supply a user's manual with the purchase of their product; however, they will not supply a product specification as a developing subcontractor would. To stay competitive the COTS vendor must protect the intellectual property that is embodied in the product. If a product specification, version description documents, or diagnostics manual is required, then negotiations for rights in data, licensing agreements, and other legal matters must be undertaken at the time of request for procurement. The negotiations may be simple, but the price tag will be high. Even if the vendor assigns certain rights and licenses some aspect of the software, there is no guarantee that the buyer might not make modifications or turn the software over to a larger developer for reverse engineering and a redo—at lesser cost—of the vendor's product. It is important for CM to obtain as much descriptive data as possible and incorporate the data into the product baseline, and it is important for CM to maintain a status accounting of the software, test reports, and demonstration descriptions that are included in the SDF for each procured item.

When it is necessary to change or modify third party software, CM's task will be very difficult if there are not agreements for change. In many cases, the vendor will have little or no developmental documentation other than what may be described in the user's manual. If the software was acquired from a computer store, the developer has no idea what software modifications for adaptability would be required. In addition, the vendor may not have the resources or funding available to make the changes/modifications required. CM will have to work closely with the software person requesting the change in order to communicate the need to the SRB and the CCB in a manner that will detail the constraints on changing the software. This is the time to bring legal personnel into the CCB meeting to help arrive at the proper decision. There may be another product available that will meet the change requirement, and the cost of obtaining the replacement item may be less than the effort it would take to negotiate a change with the current vendor.

CM should include provisions for COTS in the CM plan as well as the software development plan to ensure that there is a procedure to follow when dealing with the COTS/NDI items. The procedure should provide for

- Documentation of the functional and physical characteristics of the software, its purpose, its interfaces, and other factors that can identify it as a CI, SCC, or SU. In addition, a configuration control number should be assigned, and the item should be entered on the software hierarchy.
- Creation of an SDF that will contain the documented identification, any and all technical documentation that has been provided by the vendor (including the user's manual), and all other data prescribed for developed items.
- Description of how the item was tested or demonstrated and reports recording the tests and compliance to the vendor's technical documentation and the SRS.
- Object listing of the software.

There may be additional requirements depending on the nature of the COTS being ordered. These decisions are made by project management, QA, and CM, if the CM feels that some aspect of identification may be missing under a firm's current regulations. From a data management point of view, the provisions of rights in data are very important and can affect CM if a change is requested or required. Be careful!

EXERCISES

1. Describe briefly your ideas for the control of subcontractors and their software products. Discuss your views in class.
2. Draw the flow of events for subcontractor control.
3. Write a short audit procedure for ensuring subcontractor compliance to CM requirements.
4. Explain rights in data or proprietary rights as it pertains to CM.

CHAPTER 14

Establishing and Maintaining the Software Library

The software library is an important asset to the performance of the CM process, especially in carrying out the control and status accounting activities.

A software library is defined [10] as a controlled collection of software and related documentation designed to aid in software development, use, or maintenance. Types include the *master library, production library, software development library, software repository, and system library.* This chapter will discuss the CM's use of the production libraries, the master library and the software repository.

The production library can be considered a single entity for the development of software code and an interim retention spot for such code during unit, component, and configuration item (CI) testing. Experience has proven that dividing the library into a working (developmental) segment and an interim, or programming support library segment, gives one a better means of control and accountability of the software being "produced." Figure 14.1 illustrates this concept. The production library is described as the working library for the production of the source code and the programming support library (PSL) for the retention of code deemed ready for component and CI testing.

The master library is described as the entity for retention of approved or released code as well as for the retention of approved and released software documents that will be delivered to a customer or distributed to the marketplace.

The software repository is the entity that archives software and related documentation at the close of the project. A segment of the repository may be established to temporarily retain a duplicate of current software, at the time it is copied, for use in case disaster hits the production or master libraries. Another segment may be established for the retention of software designated and designed for reuse or for other projects in parallel with the current project. All released documentation and software in the master library should be in the software repository (archive).

The status accounting activity may account for all of the software documentation and code in the various library segments and report their status at any given time, including the changes underway, approved or incorporated. The means for performing this activity is known as the software development file (SDF). The SDF may be hard-copy folders or notebooks as well as a CASE tool programmed to receive the status accounting data elements as the software code or documents are entered into the library.

THE PRODUCTION LIBRARY FUNCTIONS

Working Library

The working library, part of the production library, is known as the developmental file or programmer working area and is established at the start of the project to enable the programmers to set up their assigned areas for developing source code as assigned by the project leader. The programmer will perform the coding function, defect correction, and pre-

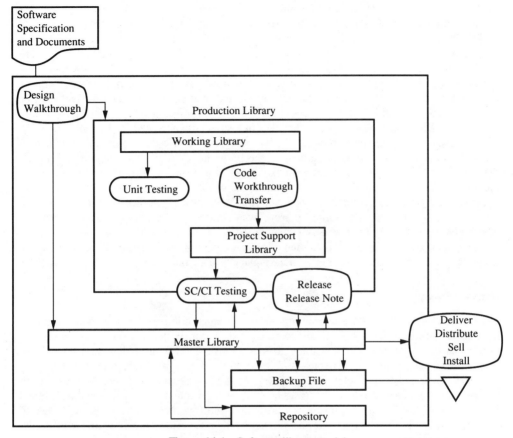

Figure 14.1 Software library model.

scribed unit tests in the assigned area. Once the programmer is satisfied that the testing has been successfully completed and that the code has been reviewed and accepted in a walk-through, the CM may initiate the transfer of the code from the working library to the project support library for further testing. The programmer, however, may be allowed to retain the code produced for further enhancement. In this event a notation is made in the PSL. Because the copy of the version retained is not under control in the working area, the code will not be allowed into the system unless a change is requested and is approved. The new version then replaces the earlier version of code in the PSL. All copies are obtained from the PSL only and should be so noted in the header.

Project Support Library

The project support library (PSL) is the storage place for those software units transferred from the working library along with the detailed design documentation used to produce the code. At the time of transfer, the code and documentation is considered under internal configuration control and any requested or desired changes are processed by procedures established by CM. The rule should be that changes cannot arbitrarily be made to the software elements in the PSL. The reason for this is that many times a unit transferred late in the day is picked up early the next morning by the test team for integration with another unit. If changes were made after this had occurred and the change were not made known to the test team, the test results could be invalid and cause other problems during the testing sequence.

The PSL may also be used as a "staging" area for the integration of a number of units into modules or components and subsequently components into configuration items before being released to the master file for final integration, test, and delivery. This procedure was practiced by a highly regarded test engineer who stated that he would not accept a unit or module until that element had been successfully tested with all other elements affected by or related to its performance. The CM process must therefore compensate for this by knowing that the module cannot be released to the next levels of testing until accepted by the testing activity.

The CM process must also provide for the possibility that a unit or module retained in the PSL could be removed and returned to the programmer for further work (back to the drawing board) and, in a sense, transferred back to the working file. This status must be recorded, because, as may have been noted in the chapter on control, the librarian has to know where a given element is in order to determine whether it is to receive full CCB review.

An advantage for having this interim or midway library point is that the master library can be maintained with only approved and accepted entities. In turn, CM is then able to ensure that only approved and released documentation and code will be issued to those who require it and that delivery to the customer or marketplace will be made with trust and confidence.

Master Library

The master library (ML) is the retention point for all units, components, CIs, and associated documents that have been tested, reviewed by a duly constituted review board, and have been released to the ML under a more formal configuration control than was maintained for the PSL, as explained in Chapter 9. Entry into the ML is normally accomplished with the approval of a software release notice, as described in Chapter 8, which describes each component of the baseline element, its nomenclature and version identifier. When distributed to the software project, the software release notice informs the members that the released elements are ready to be integrated into the hardware side of the system or delivered to the customer or marketplace as a quality product.

Access control is very tight for the ML. Normally, only the librarian function has access for read and write. The project engineer or lead software engineer can serve as backup. There should be no restriction on read-only, unless the element is competition-sensitive or has a government security classification. There may also be instances where the ML is a stand-alone PC or other type of computer located in a special access required (SAR) area. In these cases, even the CM, unless cleared, will not be able to fully perform the control and status accounting activities.

When security is very tight, CM should have appropriate security clearance and have procedures for others in the SAR areas to follow in controlling changes and maintaining status. In other instances, the creation of "dummy" numbers and nomenclature has been sufficient to enable the performance of control and accounting by the project's CM activity without violating the security of the software. Security has become a critical process and although it can hinder CM's performance, it also protects the success of the products' acceptance by customers, especially if it scoops the competition.

Software Repository

The dictionary defines repository as a place to store things—this could be a tomb, implying a quiet, safe place to store software that is unneeded but still worthy of safekeeping. The term *archive* also frequently represents storing software and the associated documentation.

The requirement for archiving in a repository should provide for sufficient record of the contents of the repository and provision whereby it can be queried and pulled for use if required. Thus CM is concerned that what is stored is properly identified and statused. It is also concerned that if some element of active software has been changed, having an impact on archived software or documents, that a fix can be made with relative ease.

There is one case that comes to mind, of a software project that was never under configuration management, with control in the hands of some very bright and well-meaning software engineers who, at the conclusion of the project, put the magnetic tapes in a file drawer and went off to do many other things. Seven years later the customer requested that the software be updated and delivered to a designated software support facility. With no identification or documentation, the company was very lucky that all of the seven programmers were still employed and could remember many things about the software package. In addition, the condition of the tape was perfect. The lesson to be learned here is that if one thinks that everyone will still be with the firm for five or more years, then trust their judgment. Otherwise, identify and control with great care!

Archiving software in a repository should be planned carefully so that the firm's CM activity is able to retrieve software needed on other projects. Another case of necessary retrieval is when software for an ongoing project is archived to get it out of the way, such as executive routines developed in the early stages of the project. Here such software may be needed almost as soon as it is placed in the repository. Since the repository is designed for long-term storage, one will get upset at the slowness of retrieval of the requested entities. Therefore the procedure should include leadership review to ensure that the elements will not be needed right away—such as, not needed within six months to a year.

There is another problem with long-term retention and it occurs when the platforms on which the software was created are replaced or break down. One then may be faced with the dilemma of not being able to replicate the software from tape to disk, no matter how well identified and controlled prior to the loss of the original computers. For one who may have the CM responsibility, this could create some serious problems, especially if documentation was needed in support of another project. The simple solution would be to keep one of the computers. This would be fine if it were a small PC, with nominal book value. If it were a mainframe computer, then all might have been lost. However, the capability of the new and larger units may provide emulation techniques that could get one back in business. As a minimum, the software baseline documentation must contain a description of the software support and development environment so that such an environment may be restored or suitably replicated.

Backup Library

Backup libraries contain duplicates of the versions of software and associated documentation at the time copies were made—also known as downloaded—from the active libraries. This action may take place nightly, weekly, or monthly depending on the criticality and level of change of the active libraries' contents and on the degree of system reliability not to fail, causing the loss of vital software files. Many, in the course of working with software, have suffered the loss of a software file caused by equipment failure, a sudden power outage, or hitting the EXIT key at the wrong time. The backup of that particular file, can many times be retrieved and thus "save the day."

Backup library tapes/disks are also stored in another location as protection against loss at a given area from flood, fire, and the like. Thus the term *disaster files* is often heard. Some of these files may be sent many miles away to backup library repositories or just to another building. Most major computer companies offer, for nominal fees, archive and backup protective services to their customers, which for developers with limited facilities or space can be very useful. Procedures for the backup library are very important in today's ongoing workstation environments where the engineers are not supported by an operations staff that will perform the backup functions on a scheduled basis. CM can assist in this vital effort by providing for the backup/archive facility for the engineer to use.

The CM process should include provisions for ensuring that proper rules for identification are followed. Looking for missing software that has not been properly documented and identified has caused much time and money to be wasted trying to locate the missing element. In many cases unidentified elements are not found, and many custodians of the backup library media will refuse to spend the time tracking down the element by use of mnemonical nomenclature.

ESTABLISHING THE LIBRARIES

The framework for a project's libraries should be planned at the start, if not during the planning stages prior to the start of the project. In some instances, the customer may ask for a description of the software development library: " . . . to be used for controlling the software and associated documentation . . . including the procedures and methods for establishing and implementing the library and the access and control procedures for data stored in the library . . . " ([26]). In other instances, a developer may well find that advertising a well-established and well-controlled library will convince a prospective client to contract for its services.

The master library is the first to be established and should be an integral segment of the host computer's data base so that there is an ease of entry of released software or software documentation as it becomes ready and is placed under configuration control.

Documentation is normally the first entry into the master library. Experience has proven that the software requirements specifications, interface requirements specification, design documents, test plan, and the like for each CI should be placed in the master library. The magnetic media for each of these documents is the "master copy" and not the hard copy output. The system/segment specification, if applicable, should also be entered. Many times the "top document" is provided on disk, thus making entry most efficient.

While the ML during this period will receive mostly documents, there may be customer-furnished software, existing software used for design and development, or software procured for development or testing of the code. This software will most likely be copyrighted and will require protection under the prevailing copyright laws or other agreements for the protection of software developed outside of one's own domain. The CM activity should have appropriate procedures for the identification and statusing of this type of software and should request changes if necessary during the course of development.

The production library's working library segment may also be established early in the program. Although the scheduling may indicate that full coding does not get underway until required documentation and the like are released, there are many instances in which the software developers will begin writing executive routines for editing, debugging, and controlling the software as it is developed. Some of the procured or provided software in the master library may be used to "set up" the host or development computer. This activity will require programmer working areas to be created as assigned.

The project support segment of the production library will become active when coding and unit testing of the CIs commence, which is usually on completion of a critical design review that freezes the design and signifies that the design detail is sufficient to start

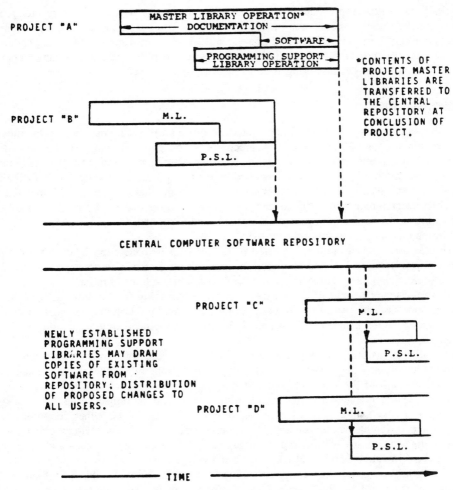

Figure 14.2   Software library relationships

coding and theoretically no additional design will be created. The PSL, then, is ready to accept transferred software for further testing and lower-level integration—units integrated into components and components into CIs. Figure 14.2 [35] depicts the interrelationships between libraries for retention of the documentation and code.

The archive segment can be established at any time. Normally there is no requirement until almost the end of the project, but there have been a number of occasions when many small software units and components were overflowing the disks and had to be archived. The one thing to remember, as was experienced on a project some years ago, is that an archive library is not designed to be speedy and provide instantaneous data the way development libraries will. In this case programmers archived the overflowing units, but soon found that they needed them almost as fast as they were archived. They discovered that it unfortunately took at least twenty-four hours to retrieve the data from high-density mag tapes, thus causing ill will among the programmers. The solution was to create an interim archive file that could produce the required data within a couple of hours of request.

The backup library procedures should be ready to use as soon as software production starts. Backup media should not be considered for use as an archive. Although there is access control, there is no CM. Thus what is on the backup may not be the latest version of the software desired. The single main purpose of backup is insurance that one can recuperate lost data from a disaster and bring it up to the lost version.

RESPONSIBILITIES

The librarian activity is normally assigned to a software project team member. At the time of the structured program Yourdan, et al. [3] recommended a chief programmer team consisting of a chief programmer, now commonly known as a project team leader, a programmer, and a backup programmer/librarian. As envisioned by the CM process, the librarian also assumed the CM tasks associated with capturing, storing, and maintaining the code generated by the chief programmer team. The concept took in many tasks that up to that point had been neglected. Software was now stored, controlled, and accounted for within each build cycle and in the end would represent the software system.

The librarian activity duties are listed in Figure 14.3 with notation as to which library segment is affected and treated by these functions. Using the Yourdan concepts any member of the project team, no matter how large, can assume the role of librarian.

There are many people who are experienced in performing the librarian activity. Some titles include librarian, software support specialist, or configuration management specialist. The responsibilities listed in Figure 14.3 [35] still prevail, no matter what title the job is given.

Overall responsibility for the library should rest with the software project leader. This becomes important when access controls are applied and one must determine who can have read/write access to the inner sanctums of the master library, much less the PSL. For the most part, experience indicates that the librarian activity and the project leader, as a backup, must have access authority to all files including the master library. Other conditions may prevail and different procedures apply. The important point to note here is that libraries contain the heart of any firm, company, organization, or group and the data and code must be protected by authoritative and responsible individuals.

Many company procedures designate CM as responsible for the establishment and maintenance of the libraries. Because of this, it is important that persons performing the CM process be knowledgeable, if not expert, in computer operations and data base administration. It is not hard to tell if people are experienced because if not, they tend to be very restrictive in how they receive, process, and report data to ensure that mistakes are not discovered. Those who are experienced tend to portray greater self-assurance, but at the same time will insist that the established procedures for operation and maintenance of the library be followed. To repeat, the library activity is responsible for protecting a developer's most important assets—its software.

LIBRARY PROCEDURES

Procedures for the establishment, operation, protection, and control of the library system should be developed and be part of the software development plan following the definition cited above. The initial procedure should describe the library segments to be established, such as the project support and master libraries. The operational procedures should describe how the library will receive the selected programming language such as FORTRAN, Pascal, C++, or Ada, and how they will be processed. And they should describe how documents will be entered and identified and how the content of the library will be protected

LIBRARIAN JOB DESCRIPTIONS

RESPONSIBILITY	APPLIES TO (LIBRARY TYPE)
1. Establish and maintain files of project documentation (specifications, drawings, plans, computer listings, etc.) in accordance with specified procedures.	All
2. Establish and maintain computer files of software and related information (operate computer) in accordance with specified procedures, using inputs provided by programmers. and keypunch machine or terminal.	PSL, ML (if on disc)
3. Identify and obtain supplies and facilities necessary for file maintenance (includes blank tapes, etc. when applied to PSL).	All
4. Inform users of procedures for submitting changes to files.	All
5. Carry out change requests in an orderly and timely fashion.	PSL, ML
6. Assign or record identification for files, documents, problem reports, change orders.	All
7. Distribute problem reports and change orders.	ML
8. Prepare and issue reports on change status and other activities in which library is involved.	PSL, ML
9. Maintain and distribute index of computer software modules (with abstracts) available for multi-project use.	SR
10. Maintain logs and retention schedules for project files.	All
11. Obtain additional clerical assistance (e.g., keypunch support) as required.	All
12. Issue copies of requested software and documentation in accordance with specified procedures.	All
13. Perform other support duties as assigned (e.g., secretarial tasks).	All

Figure 14.3 Software librarian job prescription

via access control and security measures devised by the software team. Control of the content is discussed below, but as a minimum, software elements under configuration control should be addressed in the *library operational procedure*.

The *procedure* should provide for the software elements listed:

- Source code for primary and support software
- Object code as applicable
- Load modules, build instruction, etc.
- Source listings and/or object listings
- Test plans, descriptions, reports, test cases, and data

- Selected sections of the software development plan, such as standards and conventions
- User manual segments as selected or required
- Specifications and documents such as software requirement, design documents, product specification, and version description document for each CI and other specified information described in Chapter 10.

Many other software elements can also be included and there are a number of software tools available to help one establish and develop a sufficient system. A very popular tool is CCC, Configuration Change Control by Softool and Aide-de-Camp, as well as those provided by the major computer companies such as Code Management System, Module Management System by Digital Equipment Corp. and Software Control System Segment for UNIX by AT&T.

PROCEDURES FOR CONTROL OF THE LIBRARY

The control imposed on entering, storing, updating, and retrieving the content of the libraries is of course most important.

The initial input to the PSL, for instance, is described in Figure 14.4. Once code and unit testing is completed by the programmer in the working library area, the software team leader is notified and a code walkthrough session is convened by the leader. When accepted, the CM activity will prepare a transfer notice for entry into the PSL. The transfer notice will then be distributed to the project members for their awareness—especially if one or more may have interfaces with the released software.

If the software and/or associated documentation has passed prescribed testing, the project software engineer/manager will convene a review board to review and determine if the software should be released to the master file, as illustrated in Figure 14.5. A review will require all of the software's listings; test descriptions and reports; history of changes; associated documentation, including the requirements specification section pertaining to the software; the design specification; and possibly, drafts of the product specification and version description document.

The library procedures should also provide for the review of data retained by the library, such as query and review of certain sections or elements and the printout of listings for a unit, component, or CI, as well as transfer of copies to programmers wishing (or assigned via a change order) to correct a given software element. As stated above, no software elements are changed without an approved change order.

When the time comes to deliver software from the master file, procedures should be in place to ensure that the right software (empty item index) is identified with its related documentation and is being delivered with the right documentation, as described in Figure 14.6. The minutes of the PCA should also indicate that there is a proper match of software to related documents and if not, discrepancies should be noted. There should be not even a shadow of a doubt in the developer's mind that the software derived is the latest or requested version and can be trusted and accepted without fear of failure.

CONTROL OF THE LIBRARY CONTENTS

One of the greater fears a software developer can have is that in some way or other the library's contents will be violated by unauthorized means. Oddly enough, however, some recent audits have come up with the alarming finding that some libraries had no protection or procedures for control of the data entered. When asked about this, the usual statement

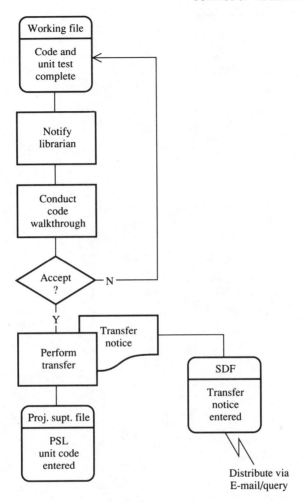

Figure 14.4 Initial input to library files

would be that the software was not so important or that everyone was trusted to do the right thing. Both statements may be true, but the reader, as a customer, must ask if that is the way he or she would want the software to be handled as it is developed.

A general overview of library and file control is illustrated in Figure 14.7 [68]. It is also a good framework for the development of procedures that will provide the instructions and guidance for entry, retrieval, and protection of the contents.

A procedure such as illustrated in Figures 14.8 and 14.9 has also proven to work quite well in ensuring that changes to data residing in a given library has been reviewed by a software review board (SRB) or a configuration control board (CCB). The SRB, which as noted in Chapter 8 is a section of the CCB, should normally review and approve changes to PSL software/documents and the CCB to software/documents retained in the ML. The same controls should also apply to software elements in the archive and reuse libraries.

As important as the initial control procedures may be, the incorporation of approved changes is also important and must be covered by an appropriate directive or procedure.

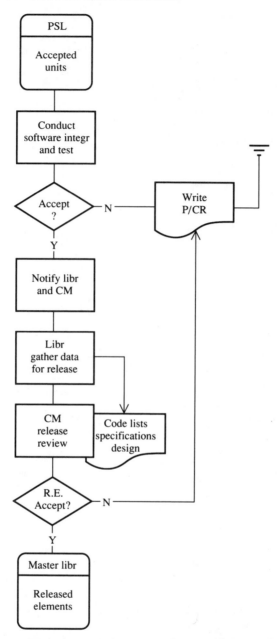

Figure 14.5 Software release to master library

The concern is that many programmers will trust only themselves to make a change to their original software. They may live in fear of a peer being assigned to make a change and of the peer being assigned to incorporate that change into the concerned programmers' software units. And even worse, many will refuse to let persons acting as the librarian, no matter how experienced, make the change.

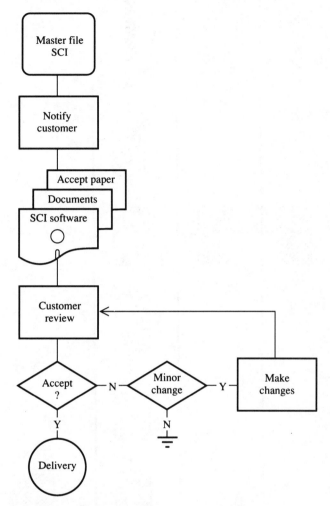

Figure 14.6 Delivery from ML

To ensure that those normally assigned incorporation tasks know who the originating programmer is and whether the programmer has waived his or her rights to make a change, provisions should be made that at the time of approval, the programmer be given a chance to waive incorporation rights. If this is refused, then that individual will have to make time to carry out the necessary action.

Control of content is also most important during a configuration audit, such as the functional and physical configuration audits. Most data audited will be from the master files. All, of course, will be copies of the masters, but changes may well be recommended as a result of demonstrations or conflicts between documents and code or between test reports and software performance and design requirements. The librarian and the CM activity will have to be watching for these occurrences and ensure that formal changes are requested, reviewed, approved, and incorporated. During an audit, one will be amazed how fast this can happen.

Most library systems have provisions for the recording of changes made to retained software and documentation. This data is stored in a sub-library that can be queried by the

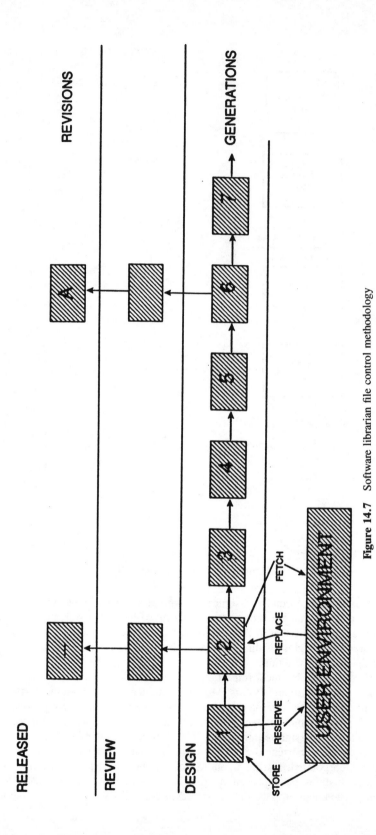

Figure 14.7 Software librarian file control methodology

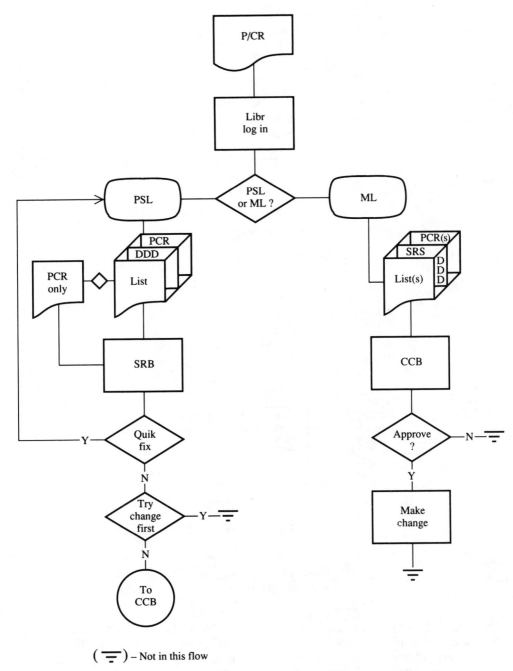

$(\overline{\overline{}})$ – Not in this flow

Figure 14.8   Change control activity

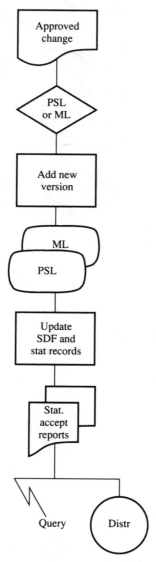

Figure 14.9 Incorporation of
approved changes

librarian activity or project members. Tools such as CCC, CMS, and SCCS are designed to
do this at the moment someone begins to add, delete, or modify source code instructions.
The assigned librarian or CM can thus find out at any time if read/write protection has
been violated. Likewise, the history is an invaluable record showing that an authorized
incorporation was made, also showing when, by whom, and what was done.

The master and project support libraries provide all of the data elements described in
Chapter 9 to support the establishment of the software development file—online. As previously noted, the SDF for each unit, component, and CI provides the developer with the

essential data necessary to complete the build of a given software element, repair it, enhance it, and if nothing else, maintain the history of the element as it evolves into a final product. The best use of SDF is evident when a change to a complex software element is required and the analyzer/corrector can go to the SDF to determine what has happened before, what the requirements were, how the element was designed and tested, and what the success rate of those tests were—especially in interfacing with other elements.

EXERCISES

1. Describe the types of libraries and their uses.
2. Write a plan for establishing a production and master library and how it will be controlled.

CHAPTER 15

Software Tools

Software tools have been viewed by many as the savior of the beleaguered programmer and of the software engineer who had to write the detailed specifications to guide the programmer's coding. Tools have also been condemned for having been conceived by developers—by those who procured the wrong tool and spent much time and money trying to satisfy the need for a tool.

Thus we have the axiom: good tools are those that were procured or developed to fit a specific need, and bad tools are those implemented that did not fit a set of given requirements, even though they appeared to fit or because the price was right.

SELECTING TOOLS

The discussion of tools is indeed a method of selecting the right tool to fit the job required. There are a number of guides that can be used for selection. On the other hand, it is easy to make up a selection list using a basic management systems-analysis approach of describing a problem, identifying the characteristics, and developing recommended solutions, one of which would be a selection list or matrix used in recommending the best course of action to take. For example, if the characteristics of the problem include processing an accounts payable authorization that requires eight people to review and approve a transaction containing eight justifications and description forms, such as the original request for purchase, the purchase order, the vendor shipping document, the receiving document, and if some of these are reviewed in eight different locations taking four weeks to get to the point of writing a check, then an analyst is going to look for a software tool to make this all more efficient. The analyst will develop a list of criteria needed to reduce the process of the payable authorization to one or two documents, two or four collocated approval reviews, and only one week to finally write the check.

The primary systematic approach to tool selection and implementation in a selected software engineering environment in this decade is called computer-aided software engineering—CASE. The term has been defined as the "application of automated technologies to the software engineering procedures." [36] CASE is needed, it is argued, "to improve the quality of our work" " . . . when we can reduce a task to a routine procedure and mechanize it, we both save labor and eliminate a human source of error" [37]. By following this very valid proposition, one begins to improve productivity and speed up the process of development with fewer mistakes, and doing so in turn reduces the time to test and analyze failures and may give a higher-quality product.

In order for CASE to be fully implemented in its most efficient manner, the process of selection becomes most important. Otherwise, one may have to pay the price for poor selection, which may well taint an already efficient environment. It is a necessity for the selection criteria to fit the complexity of the environment requiring the automated support.

The point here is that the software development environment must be characterized first and that people/process issues be identified and resolved, before a tool is considered. The tool selected should perform within the environment, supplement that environment, and not change it. CASE tools fail because of ineffective usage and not because they are good or bad. Again the tool must fit the job at hand. The job cannot be revised to fit a tool if one expects to meet stated objectives.

TOOL SELECTION LISTS

There are several examples of selection lists. M. L. Gibson's list [38] includes such simple questions as "Is the tool a DBMS or dictionary software system?" to "Does the tool have an effective interface to other CASE tools already purchased or under evaluation?" to the more complex "Will the tool soon be able to generate, automatically, first-cut physical design specifications from logical design specifications?"

Patricia K. Lawless has developed a detailed menu [39] that starts with correctness, extends to *interoperability,* on to transportability, and ends with verifiability. Each category is further broken down: completeness, consistency, and traceability for correctness and communicativeness, simplicity, and test availability for verifiability. Lawless's definition for evaluation is " . . . the process which assesses the characteristics of some software product and then reports the results of that assessment." Lawless also isolates the selection process as similar yet unique enough to be separate and includes the "determining features' criteria of interest, collecting reported evaluation data (results), weighing the chosen features and criteria, and applying decision analysis."

In a briefing to the IEEE Working Group P 1029 for Software Tool Evaluation, James K. Van Buren [40] presents a simple but effective matrix with criteria up and down and functional activities across. The criteria include "common user interfaces, on-line help, metrics data gathering, cost effectiveness, multi-user and vendor support." The functions include "program management, CM, engineering management . . . " [followed by] prototype, modeling and requirements definition. The matrix serves as a management overview and does not scale to detailed evaluations," as noted in the briefing paper.

CRITERIA AND THE SELECTION PROCESS

The bottom line for evaluation and selection, Watts [37] admonishes, is "that one's system must be placed under control before any activity takes place, but the activity must be a well planned process before proceeding. In addition the people factor relating to a conversion and the use of the chosen product(s) will be never ending." Thus the warning "Don't forget to *think!*"

As an aid to the selection process, the National Institute of Science and Technology— NIST—developed a classification scheme in its publication on a taxonomy data base [41], which breaks down the selection process to input, function, output, and special features, as noted in Figure 15.1. A schematic of this selection process is illustrated in Figure 15.2, showing the position of the attributes one is concerned with. This diagram is used to illustrate the quest for a software development file tool and the attributes most desired for that application.

The schematic is like a top-down breakdown and may be increased or decreased to fit the number of desired attributes. Likewise, functions may be added if the desired end result warrants it. Like the matrix, it is a good management tool to explain one's reasoning behind a recommended tool selection.

SELECTION — CLASSIFICATION SCHEME

- NIST* Taxonomy, Data Base
  NBSIR-80-2159

INPUT

Subject   i.e. Text, Code
Control   i.e. Commands, Parameters

FUNCTION

Transformation   Editing, formatting, etc.
Static Analysis Auditing, management, tracking
Dynamic Analysis Tracing, tuning

OUTPUT

Machine output   Graphics, listings, text
User output   Text

SPECIAL FEATURES → Unique to SCM

*U.S. National Institute of Science and Technology

Figure 15.1   Tool selection matrix.

220

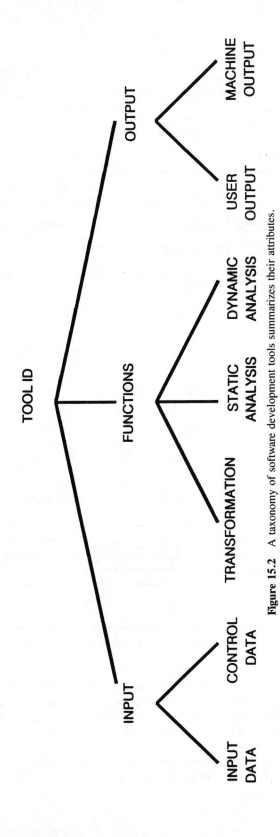

Figure 15.2 A taxonomy of software development tools summarizes their attributes.

1. TOOL TITLE:		2. ACRONYM:	3. CURRENT DATE:

4. STAGE OF DEVELOPMENT: ( ) Concept ( ) Design ( ) Implemented	5. CLASSIFICATION: ( ) MCM ( ) SMS ( ) RDA ( ) PAT ( ) GEN ( ) ENV		6. PURPOSE OF DEVELOPMENT: ( ) Research ( ) Experimental ( ) Production
7. HOST COMPUTER:	8. IMPLEMENTATION LANGUAGE(s):		9. DATE OF DEVELOPMENT:
10. TARGET COMPUTER(S)/(WORD SIZE(S)):		11. TOOL PRICE:	12. TOOL PORTABLE: ( ) Yes ( ) No

13. TOOL SIZE:			
Source Code (bytes):	Object Code (bytes):	Source Lines of Code:	Memory Requirements:

14. OPERATING SYSTEM:	15. OTHER SOFTWARE/UTILITIES REQUIRED:	16. TOOL AVAILABLE: ( ) Yes ( ) No
17. RESTRICTIONS (COPY RIGHTS, LICENSES, GOVERNMENT APPROVAL, ETC.):		18. PUBLIC DOMAIN: ( ) Yes ( ) No

19. TOOL SUPPORTED: ( ) Yes ( ) No	20. TOOL SUPPORT:

21. TOOL SUMMARY: Maximum 200 words

22. CONTACTS:	For More Information:	Tool Developer:	Tool Distributor:	Sponsoring Agency:
Name:				
Organization:				
Address:				
Phone:				

23. REFERENCE(s):	24. DOCUMENTATION:

Figure 15.3   Software development file.

The Data and Analysis Center for Software maintains a data base of software tools arranged according to the NIST data base [42]. The forms used for entry into the data base are quite specific. The General Characterization Form, Figure 15.3, and the Tool Features Taxonomy Form, Figure 15.4, provide the detail for one to select a form that fits a given needs-analysis recommendation.

There should be little doubt in anyone's mind that more and more of the functions performed within the CM process for a given activity, such as identification or control, will

1. SUBJECT:

( ) VHLL Very High Level Language
- ▢ design spec lang
- ▢ requirements spec lang
- ▢ program spec lang
- ▢ system spec lang
- ▢ algebraic spec lang
- ▢ model spec lang

( ) Code - list language(s):
- ▢ description lang
- ▢ structured lang
- ▢ requirements lang
- ▢ design lang
- ▢ specification lang

- ( ) Data
- ( ) Text
- ( ) Other_____

2. CONTROL INPUT:

- ( ) Commands
- ( ) Parameters
- ( ) Other_____

_____
_____

3. TRANSFORMATION:

- ( ) Formatting
- ( ) Translation

_____
_____

- ( ) Instrumentation
- ( ) Editing
- ( ) Synthesis
- ( ) Restructuring
- ( ) Optimization
- ( ) Other_____

_____

4. STATIC ANALYSIS:

- ( ) Management

_____
_____

- ( ) Cross Reference
- ( ) Scanning
- ( ) Auditing
- ( ) Data Flow Analysis
- ( ) Consistency Checking
- ( ) Statistical Analysis
- ( ) Error Checking
- ( ) Structure Checking

- ( ) Comparison
- ( ) Completeness Checking
- ( ) Complexity Measurement
- ( ) Tracking
- ( ) Interface Analysis
- ( ) I/O Specification Analysis
- ( ) Type Analysis
- ( ) Cost Estimation
- ( ) Units Analysis
- ( ) Scheduling
- ( ) Other_____

5. DYNAMIC ANALYSIS:

- ( ) Coverage Analysis
- ( ) Tracing_____

- ( ) Tuning ( ) Timing
- ( ) Simulation
- ( ) Resource Utilization
- ( ) Symbolic Execution
- ( ) Assertion Checking
- ( ) Regression Testing
- ( ) Constraint Evaluation
- ( ) Other_____

_____

6. USER OUTPUT:

- ( ) Listings
- ( ) Tables
- ( ) Diagnostics
- ( ) User-Oriented Text
  - ▢ documentation
  - ▢ reports

- ( ) Graphics

_____
_____

- ( ) Other_____

7. MACHINE OUTPUT:

( ) Source Code - list language(s):

_____

- ( ) Data
- ( ) Intermediate Code
- ( ) VHLL
- ( ) Prompts

- ( ) Object Code
- ( ) Other_____

I N P U T

F U N C T I O N

O U T P U T

Figure 15.4 Autocode with CASE tool.

223

be performed within the computer resources software engineering environment. Many tools for the CM process will come built in for a given software development environment. As an example, Figure 15.5 illustrates the flow of a development tool that provides for the input of a major algorithm for the development of a software unit. When the algorithm is entered, the programmer will perform the required functions to produce the code, but before proceeding, certain information must be entered, such as name, location, name of unit, work authorization number/code, and next higher–identified software element. Once entered, a software identification number, mnemonic, or code will be entered in a software development file with the entered data. This entry completes the first on-line entry of identifying the unit's document and code.

When the programmer's coding chores are completed and the unit tested, the code will be compiled, and with that compilation will be produced the documented description of that code as a product specification or, in some tools, a *design document*. This document will have been entered in the SDF with the code as well as in a master document file, which will compile all of the unit descriptions into a final reviewable document in hard copy or by query.

The description just given will fit the taxonomy chart in Figure 15.2 and will look like that portrayed in Figure 15.6 and will be titled the Taxonomy of autocode with CASE tool (Figure 15.7).

This illustrates the type of tools CM should be reviewing and working with. Many are not cheap and one will find that a great deal of cost/benefit analysis is required. In performing this analysis one will do best to work with the potential users of the tools. They will be able to describe, in detail, what they want the tool to do for them and then, after appropriate demonstration, indicate how close a given tool meets their objectives. If very close, one may have a "winner."

MAKING THE FINAL DECISIONS

Once a selection criteria list has been agreed on, the task of locating software tool vendors begins. One of the best ways to perform this task is to go to tools fairs or to software engineering conferences that have a tools exhibit area. However, it is wise to check first with the conference organizers to find out how many vendors will be exhibiting and who they are. At one very recent conference there was a very large hall filled with only a half-dozen vendors.

Another avenue is to review various tools directories such as DATAPRO's or the one published by the Data Analysis Center for Software (DACS) at the Rome Air Development Center, Rome, New York. There are also a number of consultants, some of whom advertise, who keep up with the ever-changing tools market and who can provide valuable advice on tool selection. Riefer Associates of Torrance, California, has provided this service for many years.

The important point is to find vendors who appear to have what is wanted and to provide them with a statement of work from one's selection list so that the vendor can supply the best possible suggestions and products to fit one's criteria. Major vendors include Softool Configuration Change Control, Goleta, California, which can be adapted to meet many different criteria; ADR, Princeton, New Jersey; and Aide-de-Camp, Waltham, Massachusetts.

When possible, a 30-, 60-, or 90-day trial of one or two products should be conducted at no cost to one's firm. If the product is very new, then one may be able to become a "beta" test site for a given period of time. If the tool fits the need, then cost is the only remaining

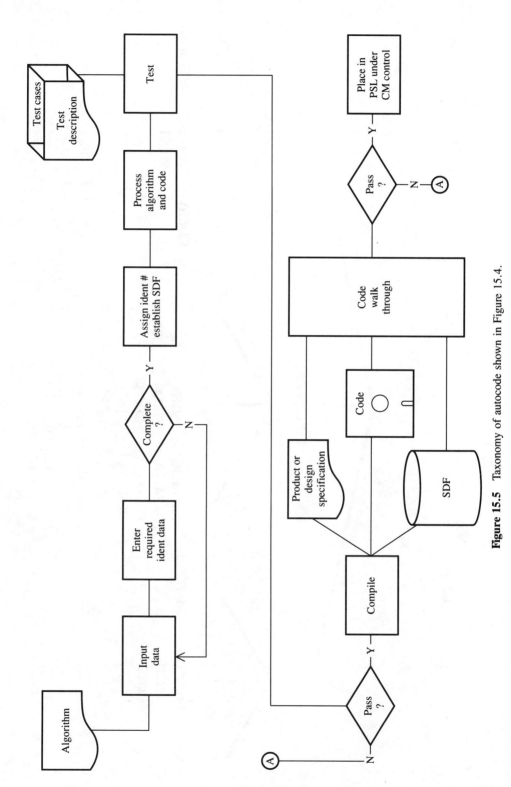

Figure 15.5 Taxonomy of autocode shown in Figure 15.4.

225

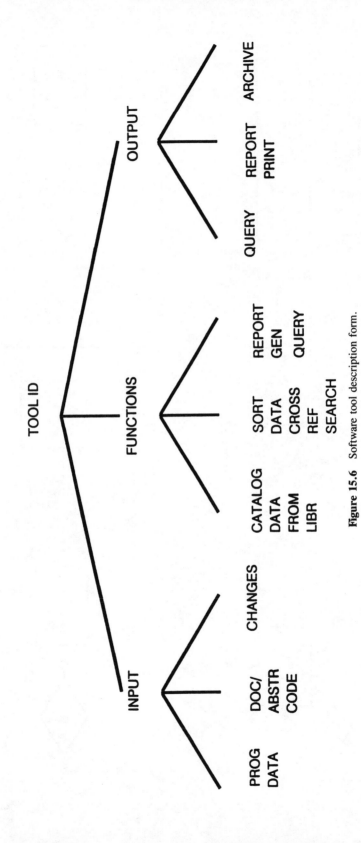

Figure 15.6 Software tool description form.

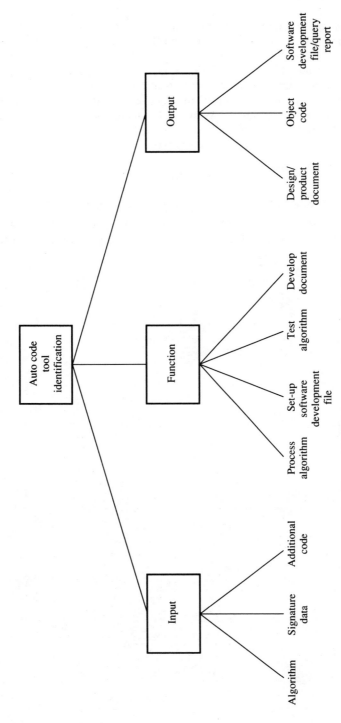

Figure 15.7 Taxonomy of autocode with CASE tool.

factor. If a competitor's tool is very close and is less costly, then one should assess the pros and cons, when cost is a serious consideration. If not, then go with the vendor that had the highest score. Do not, however, be lulled into the "we don't have everything you ask for now, but are working on it" story. If it's not there, don't expect it to be! However, if time is not of the essence, then one may wish to wait for the final attribute.

Tools are becoming more and more important and must be considered, as software requirements become more complex. As available funding becomes smaller, but demand for highly effective, well-identified, and controlled software persists, the tools that can meet the demand within one's funding constraints will prove to be a valuable investment.

EXERCISES

1. Develop a list of evaluation criteria for a given tool application.
2. Draw a data flow of a desired application as it is now and as you desire it to be.
3. Fit the attributes developed in Exercise 2 to a taxonomy diagram similar to Figure 15.2.

CHAPTER 16

Configuration Management with Ada

This chapter is not intended to be a tutorial of the mechanisms of Ada. It is important, however, to understand how CM is employed using Ada because of the many built-in controls Ada invokes as one creates instructions and those in effect when one has to make changes in the instruction sets.

If one is working with Ada, then there is a "configuration manager" in the Ada environment. This may sound wonderful and one will envision hours of unfettered worries, but that is not to be. As one program manager mused to his management staff: "we found, very quickly, that CM had to be on hand and in business from day 1, because of the way CM is applied in the Ada language structure."

> "Ada takes care of some aspects of configuration management. She knows what units need to be linked to create a main program. She knows if any of the units are obsolete. This could lead you to believe there is no need for configuration management if you use Ada. Unfortunately, that's not true."
>
> "Ada doesn't relieve you of the responsibility of configuration management . . . even if you use Ada, you still have to use some discipline and/or a configuration management tool to keep things straight."

So saith Do-While Jones in his book *Ada in Action* [43]. He is so right!

In the past, a developer's configuration control, scheduling, change-tracking, and other systems were hidden from or inaccessible to the customer's program manager. Information captured by these systems tended to reach the program manager via status accounting reports created by the developer, which may or may not have been slanted in favor of the developer. With Ada, however, the Ada Programming Support Environment (APSE), provides the capability of creating status accounting data [49] for the program manager to inspect; such as, code management data, source and documentation text, test results, and corrective action status, thus providing far greater visibility than has been possible in the past [44].

What is now available to the program manager should also be available to the configuration manager for both the customer and the developer. However, both have to be trained in the fundamentals of computer programming concepts and in the Ada Programming Support Environment (APSE) and Minimal Ada Programming Support Environment (MAPSE). With the MAPSE, one can create/utilize the tools necessary to form a configuration management system. The software configuration management plan should describe the APSE and the tools supported in the MAPSE in a manner that ensures that data from the MAPSE can be trusted and used in the manner for which it was intended, which is to control the software created in Ada.

THE CM PROCESS

In Software Engineering Institute's *Technical Report on Evaluation of Ada Environments* [45], for three Ada compilers, Chapter 3 (Configuration Management) identifies and classifies the major activities of CM in Ada as: version control, configuration control, and product release control.

Under version control the primary elements are

Create/delete element

Create new version of existing element

Merge variants of an element

Retrieve specific version of an element

Under configuration control the primary elements are

Define system model—including specifying source dependencies, transition rules and options and tools necessary for translation

Build system

For product release and control, the primary elements are

Baseline system, such as a product release

Maintain/display product release information, including number of distributed versions, differences among versions, locations of each version, required hardware for each version, correlation between versions and error reports, correlation between versions and components, and errors reported/fixed by version

Maintain/Display system release history to include what was built, when, why, and by whom

The process as described will enable one to track the relationships among the program units and identify the dependencies among the units, such as when a subprogram should be recompiled because a parent program was changed.

CRITERIA FOR A CM PROCESS IN ADA

According to the report, the system that provided the most support for CM activities involved common version control activities such as creating and deleting data base objects, fetching data base objects, reserving and replacing data base objects, creating successive and variant versions, and baselining. The system was able to support typical configuration control activities such as system modeling, automatic software system construction, and maintenance of historical information.

The system was user-friendly in that one could create, manipulate, and control the CM objects corresponding to a project's software and documentation. The CM objects were maintained within a library as file elements, composed of various successive and variant versions.

The typical approach was a project master library used to share and maintain the stable components of the system while allowing the programmer to maintain a working library during development. The system allowed sharing among the project members, allowing them access to modules/units so designated for sharing, thus preserving the right of a programmer to protect specified units until release is required.

The report's summary stated that the top system "provides a well integrated, comprehensive set of utilities capable of supporting the development, integration and configuration management of a large Ada software program . . . the system promotes and supports information sharing and . . . all typical version control functions . . . and the most common configuration control activities . . . for various project scenarios."

What has been described here is indeed a very efficient CM process internal to a software environment. In order to fully appreciate its capabilities or others like it, CM should have a good fundamental knowledge of the Ada language and the popular development method used with it: object-oriented development. This is not to say one must be able to program, but must understand the concepts such as program units, packages, library functions, information hiding, and objects. There are now a number of books, seminars, and courses one can take advantage of and be up to speed in a minimum amount of time. The references quoted in this chapter [43–50] are all recommended.

ADDITIONAL EXAMPLES OF CM

Wayne A. Babich's book, *Software Configuration Management, Coordination for Team Productivity* [46], specifically addresses CM with Ada in Chapter 8. Babich was chief designer for the Ada Language System (ALS) at SofTech Inc. The Ada Language System was intended to be the one compiler for Ada, transportable across all computer environments. It was soon discovered, however, that computer system architectures were too diverse, and thus there are many compilers today.

Babich notes that "the ALS does not provide a large set of automatic tools: instead it provides the building blocks necessary to support sophisticated configuration management tools for the upcoming decades." This is important for one to note when selecting Ada systems: one wants a system that can be tailored to the needs of a given software project and be able to incorporate a CM tool to meet the needs of the project.

Dr. Lawrence Wiseman, also of SofTech, has pointed out that every program manager has a personal view of how configuration control ought to be done [47]. Since there are many different ways, he stated, ALS provides basic primitives that can be used to build and model different procedures for configuration management, tailored to a particular project. The basic capabilities he described as the following.

Absolute identification of a version of an object (lowest manageable unit in Ada) including revisions and derivations

Enforcement of change — not allowing anyone to change anything randomly — access control

Families of programs and a method of sharing to reduce duplication of entities of the data

Figure 16.1 outlines the control enforcement principle showing that only the latest revision may be altered and that previous revisions are in a sense obsolete, but, Wiseman also noted, the change can be reviewed and if necessary made part of a new revision while still retaining sanctity of the latest revision as the only one deliverable/useable. Figure 16.2 illustrates the access control restriction. This control, though appearing to be simple, can be a disaster if the access command also excludes the programmer, which has happened [47]. In other words, one must determine who has a need to know or who will be authorized read/write privilege and, once determined, then set the control accordingly.

The overall support for CM, listed in Figure 16.3; requires absolute identification; enforcement of change control; provisions for families of programs and subsequent variations; and sharing or multi-use of programs, lessening the need for additional identification and control of multi-use programs [47].

All of this comes about through a progression of events that were originally spelled out by Professor John M. Buxton's *Stoneman* [49] (see Figure 16.4) and then adjusted and amended to suit the development of various compilers, such as ALS. Figure 16.5 gives three avenues of approach. Column 1 is that described by the Stoneman and Roy Freedman [48]; McDermid and Ripkin [49] have a slightly different means of obtaining the end result,

REVISIONS

- PROVIDE IMMUTABILITY AND IDENTIFICATION

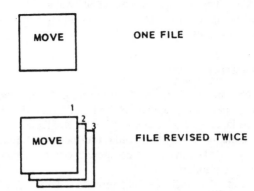

ONE FILE

FILE REVISED TWICE

- ONLY THE LATEST REVISION MAY BE ALTERED

- MAY-BE EXPLICITLY FROZEN

- FROZEN BY USE

REVISIONS

- ONCE FROZEN, EVEN OWNER MAY NOT ALTER IN-PLACE

- FREEZE IS IRREVOCABLE

- EXAMPLES

MOVE	--	REFERS TO THE LATEST, GO_UP(3)
MOVE(2)	--	SPECIFIC REVISION
MOVE(F)	--	THE LATEST FROZEN REVISION

- IN SOURCE CODE, REVISIONS ARE USED FOR BUG
CORRECTION, I.E., THE NEW REVISION MAKES ALL
OLDER REVISIONS OBSOLETE

Figure 16.1 Ada revision control enforcement.

LOCKS

KEYS

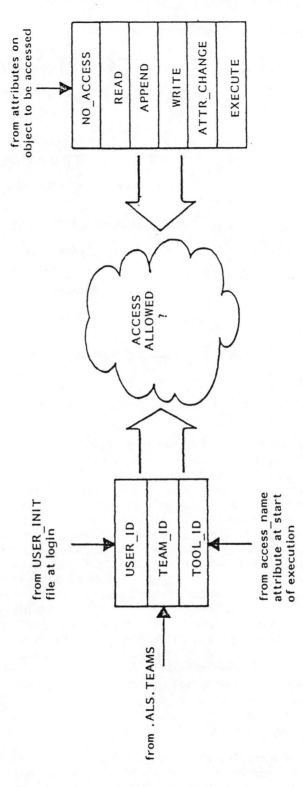

Figure 16.2 ALS revision control flow.

SUPPORTING CONFIGURATION MANAGEMENT

- ### ABSOLUTE IDENTIFICATION
  ### REVISIONS AND DERIVATIONS

- ### ENFORCEMENT OF CHANGE CONTROL
  ### ACCESS CONTROL

- ### FAMILIES OF PROGRAMS
  ### VARIATIONS

- ### REDUCED DUPLICATION
  ### SHARING

Figure 16.3 Supporting configuration management in ALS Ada.

and ALS as described by Babich presents a third view. Figure 16.6 is a summary overview of the CM process as described by Freedman with annotations to the right indicating the CM activities that are performed.

John Cupak of Lockheed Sanders, in commenting on this chapter, also points out that the relationship among Ada components is significantly different from other languages and thus affects the operations of the APSE and the performance of CM. In addition, he states, Ada can result in a proliferation of files making CM even more challenging in terms of being able to identify these files, control them, and account for their status. For example, there are package specifications, package bodies, library units, and subunits. These files often overburden the CM process. Finally, he continues, the ability to specify interfaces among components early in the life cycle means that package specs have to be identified, released, and placed under configuration control very early in the Ada life cycle.

Cupak continued by noting that the APSE can track the relationships among program units, but is not really performing a CM process. The APSE is only identifying dependencies among program units. It can tell, for instance, when a subprogram should be recompiled because a parent program changed, but does not maintain versions of source or identify builds, a task which should be and usually is performed by a CM system such as described above.

IMPLEMENTING CM IN ADA

The means of implementation according to Freedman is via path names. These constitute a network that starts with the assignment of an attribute/function name to a desired object. There can, in turn, be several versions of the object and subsequent revisions as changes oc-

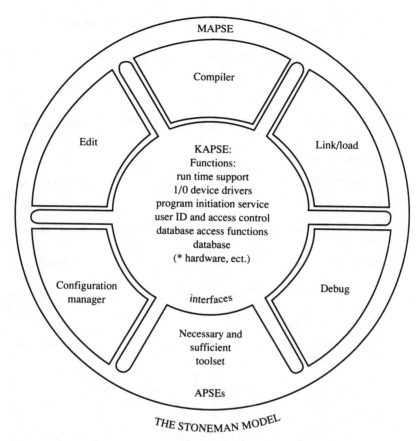

Figure 16.4 The Stoneman model for the Ada process.

cur. There may also be variations to these revisions, which leads to a configuration of the desired objects placed in partitions for entry into the libraries that house the finally compiled objects.

McDermid and Ripkin also use objects, but describe the path to the library as an assembly line. Once objects are named, there can be iterations and subsequent editions and then versions on these editions, which will then form a product to be incarcerated in the library.

Babich describes the ALS progression as interfaces with packages being the lowest elements — vice-objects — which in turn can have versions, revisions, and variations contained in directories within the library.

As Wiseman noted, access control is a key factor to the sanctity of the library, while still allowing the necessary visibility to produce status accounting data as required. Also as noted above, the ability of the selected configuration management tools will determine the creditability of the software product once produced.

In order for a CM to gain a better understanding of what will be happening within the APSE, Figure 16.6 spells out Freedman's description of the Stoneman path names with the author's annotations across from each element representing the CM equivalent. This illustration should emphasize the need for early configuration management activity and a well-defined plan that will detail the progression of events within the APSE and MAPSE that the project has chosen to use in producing the software product.

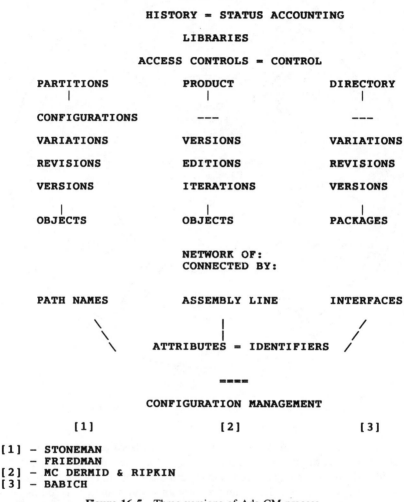

Figure 16.5   Three versions of Ada CM process.

ADA STANDARDS

One should be aware that there is no software development standard at the present time that has been totally accepted by the Ada software development community. Although the government's standard, 2167A, attempted to address Ada development issues, key issues still remain. One well-known issue is the interpretation and handling of 2167A's Computer Software Units (CSUs) and Computer Software Components (CSCs). The standard refers to a CSU as a separately testable element of the design of a CSC. It calls a CSC a distinct part of a CSCI that may be decomposed into other CSCs and CSUs.

Lewis Gray [50] notes that on one military software program "satisfying functional requirements with object-oriented CSCs led to uninformative requirements traceability matrixes in the software design documents." Since the standard allows CSCs to be collections of CSUs, it is possible to create either procedural or object-oriented CSCs by the

Ada   CONFIGURATION MANAGEMENT

LIBRARIES

    HISTORY.............STATUS ACCOUNTING/AUDIT

    ACCESS CONTROL......CONFIGURATION CONTROL

        PARTITIONS............IE: CSCI

        CONFIGURATIONS........IE: CSCs

        VARIATIONS...........OF THE REVISIONS

        REVISIONS............OF THE VERSIONS

        VERSIONS..............OF THE OBJECTS

        OBJECTS..............LOWEST - UNITS

        ATTRIBUTES...........IDENTIFY OBJECTS

    IDENTIFIED OBJECTS ARE CONNECTED BY PATH NAMES

        CONFIGURATION MANAGEMENT

REF: PROGRAMING WITH APSE SOFTWARE TOOLS, FRIEDMAN, ROY S.

Figure 16.6   Summary of Ada configuration management process.

proper choice of CSUs regardless of how the CSUs were designed. His example shows that the choice between procedural and object-oriented CSCs should be made with care if effective requirements traceability is to be maintained.

Gray also notes that the standard allows a CSU to be an Ada program unit nested within an Ada program library unit such as an Ada subprogram nested within an Ada package. A CSC in such a case may be the Ada program library unit—together with its secondary units. Referring to Configuration Management issues, Gray has argued, in essense, that in such cases, using common Ada coding practices, changes to CSUs will not be tracked by standard CM systems. The systems will only record that files have changed—not which CSUs have changed! In addition, CSCs will not correspond naturally to file directories because CSCs that are Ada program library units will be files within directories. It will require manual effort, or compiler technology, to locate the CSUs nested in these files. One technique that can be helpful to CM is to choose CSUs that correspond to files on the development (host) processor. Then CSCs would correspond naturally to file directories.

The bottom line, according to Gray, for presentation at formal design reviews, is not to confuse software organization (which the standard describes) and software architecture— they are not the same. If this confusion is avoided, several risks of creating CSCs and CSUs, such as excess design documentation, are easier to avoid. As a general rule for working with CSCs and CSUs, he says that programs should just decide what design information they want to present at formal design reviews, PDR, and CDR, and then choose CSCs and CSUs that provide that information (meanwhile being careful to comply with requirements in the standard and it DIDs as tailored by the program, of course).

There is work going on to resolve the issues described here. The IEEE is developing a standard for the software life cycle development process [P1074], as well as a guide [P1074.1]. These documents will not invoke mandatory requirements. They are left to be discussed and negotiated between customer and developer. The Ada developer can select those activities most beneficial to Ada development and modify or improvise on those such as unit designation. Likewise the ISO/IEC is developing a software development process standard that will provide a platform for development complementing the Ada technology. The Ada community has not yet had the opportunity to review the ISO Standard; however, it should provide the same latitude as the IEEE's national standard.

As noted in the beginning of this chapter, Ada provides the hooks and hangers for optimal and efficient CM tools for the primary activities of identification, control, and status accounting that in turn will provide the input for the CM audits, interface control, and subcontractor control. Ada will become more and more prominent in this decade and the CM Manager must be prepared for it. Hopefully a little insight has been provided here.

EXERCISE

1. Over the next several months select one or two books on Ada. Read and if possible attend an introductory seminar or course on Ada. In addition, begin to acquire a knowledge of CM tools that can be employed with Ada so that at some point in time you will be able to perform CM in an Ada environment.

CHAPTER 17

Performing the Software Support Process

Everyone has heard the old adages: "It isn't over till it's over" or "it ain't over until the fat lady sings." The software life cycle is in the same vein in that just because the development phase has been completed with a delivery subsequent to successful FCA/PCA doesn't mean that support of the software product ceases. The truth is that what was carried out in development to produce a successful product must now be carried on into the support phase and continue until the product is laid to rest.

THE SUPPORT ACTIVITY

A formal definition [51] for the support activity is the following.

> the performance of those activities required to keep a software system operational and responsive after it is accepted and placed into "production."

One might wish to change "production" to "assigned environment." Beyond that, the primary purpose of support is to provide the activity that can perform [51]:

- perfective maintenance or modifications and enhancements that will make the system better or bring it up to date.
- adaptive maintenance: adapting the software to its assigned environment or keeping it competitive in the marketplace.
- corrective maintenance or the handling of changes due to errors detected. In some cases such errors cause a total stopping of the software product, making this a must-fix situation.

An illustration of a general process model [52] is shown in Figure 17.1. Note that the process depicted is almost identical to the development process. What this really says is that the software engineering processes performed during development are carried over to the support phase. This is discussed in the next paragraph.

Although carrying over processes and activities may appear simple, one must remember that if the responsibility for support is assigned outside of the developer's facilities, then much of the development resources will not be available. Consider the host developing computer to be a large mainframe, but the resources available to support the delivered software consist of only the computer that the product is loaded on (it could be a PC or mid-size computer). What happens is that it may well be twice as hard to implement a change on lesser resources. If this is the case, then maintenance planning was done poorly or mutual agreements were obtained up front such that, for whatever reasons, this is how "we" will perform the maintenance.

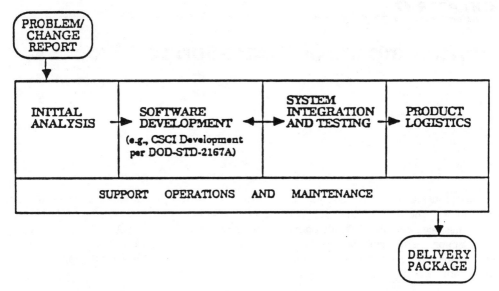

Figure 17.1 The general PDSS process.

This plus many other factors require some serious planning for support, which many have recommended start early in the development phase, when such aspects become apparent as the decomposition of the product, the number of CIs, the scope and magnitude of the selected CIs, components, and units, as well as the environment that the product will reside in.

SUPPORT ACTIVITY TASKS

Whether support is performed by the developer, customer, or independent, the plan should define the following:
define the system to

- describe the software product/system.
- describe the product's mission, intent, function, and/or purpose.
- identify the interoperability requirements.
- describe the primary system's functions.
- provide detail plans for growth, modifications, enhancements, as well as planned changes.
- describe the support that will be necessary including the human and physical resources that will be required.
- describe the computer architecture and computer resources, plus any other ancillary hardware and any constraints current or anticipated.
- identify the users, audience, locations, and other environmental issues including country customs and mores.
- describe the security required—human and physical.
- identify any major milestones for the support phase.

define initial software development and software support by

- identifying the requirements documents and specifications of description of what is to be developed.
- describe how one will support the software product once delivered.
- illustrate the organization that will perform the support activity and relate this organization to the developing organization's activity.
- identify the review board's function during development and then during support.
- describe the financing and budgets for transition to support and during the support cycle.
- describe how the software product will be transitioned from development to the support activity.
- describe the testing or validation and verification to be conducted on the product once received into the support activity.
- describe how the configuration management process will be performed by the support activity to include
  - how the development status accounting file will be utilized.
  - how the identification activity will be performed for new, modified, changed, or enhanced software/documentation.
  - how the change activity will be handled for software changed within the support activity's domain and those changes that emanate from foreign sites.
  - how the CCB will be conducted for review and approval of changes.
  - how configuration audits will be performed.
- describe how the data management process will be performed, especially for user manuals; and how diagnostic, firmware, and operator documentation will be maintained, distributed, and updated.
- describe, if applicable, how the software product will be sold, distributed, users identified, warranty provisions and customer service performed, including provisions for HELP/HOTLINE services.

The extent of the support plan depends on many factors. The topics above are suggestive and should be tailored to fit the normal magnitude of the product, the human and physical resources available, and of course the mission of the product. If the product is a relatively simple tool, little or no support may be required. In other instances, support may simply be an on-call situation, where if there is a problem, one member of the developing team will come to the problem site and fix the software. For large, complex software systems, such as an air traffic control system; a police command, control, and communication system; or a space tracking system; a support activity is co-located with the system, with the developer, or with a support activity contractor.

ORGANIZATION

Central Functional Entity

The functional organization for a centrally located support activity is illustrated in Figure 17.2. Almost all of the tasks performed during development are portrayed here with the

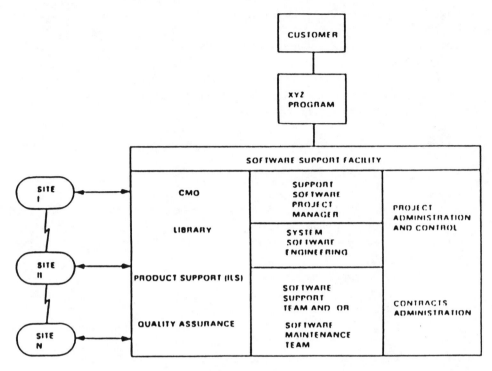

Figure 17.2 Functional organization for a software support activity.

normal management and supporting activities accounted for. The two most important tasks to be performed are the system/software engineering and the software support team or maintenance teams. The system/software engineering task is concerned with implementing the support activity plan and the determination of the extent of impact that a given change, modification, or enhancement might have on the overall system. Another part of the task may be to develop an additional set of software requirement specifications and documents if a new CI is needed for a major modification effort.

If the marketplace is involved, then part of the system/software engineering task will be to address the marketing and competition impact that could occur with a given change request. In addition, it may well be necessary to provide a detailed cost estimate for a major change, which would include the cost of marketing and distribution of the modified version. One has read many times of software firms incurring financial problems due to unexpected costs in modifying current versions of their product to meet the competition or to maintain a lead in this very competitive market.

A second task is determining the nature of a change request when the cause and effect are not known, such as making the error occur again via simulation or other means. Once a solution is found then the making and testing of the change, and the incorporation, are all part of this task. In some cases, incorporation at the site by the central support team may be required depending on the complexity of the revision. Depending on the available resources and availability of funding, the team travels to the site to install and test the changed version or add a new version to the system and could tie up the support activity's

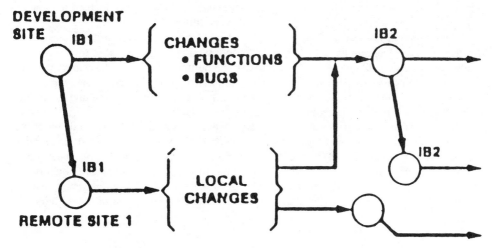

Figure 17.3   Comparison and flow of changes mode off-site.

resources for several weeks. The planning of this task is therefore very important if one is dealing with many sites around a country or around the world.

For CM, all of the procedures followed during development must also be carried out during the support phase, including the update of the SDF and status accounting records and subsequent reports. This is normally possible in a central location especially if the developer is designated as the support activity by the customer/user. If the activity is assumed by the customer, user, or one contracted to perform the support tasks, it is important to ensure that adequate CM can be performed.

The rule, that no changes will be made off-site or in the field, was issued after a good bit of experience with changes being made without communication throughout a software system, causing many other system failures. By having all changes come into one area for review and disposition much effort and money was saved. There will, of course, be situations when changes will have to be made off-site to keep the system up or fix a serious flaw that may have suddenly surfaced, such as not being able to detect a certain prescribed object. Figure 17.3 depicts the need for ensuring that local changes are made known to the support activity. A procedure for notification of such changes to the central CM function is necessary to communicate such an event and aid in determining whether the change may have other impacts or is just local to the site.

Off-Site Organization

Off-site support activities may be of two types. One is that it is the sole support activity and is located at the site of the operational software. The second type is the off-site activity, which is a branch of a central entity. The branch has been located there because of the critical nature of a given operation or because of the large volume of data processed giving a greater chance for errors to occur.

The personnel and computer resources provided to either type of site depends on the funds budgeted for the activity. Experience has proven that funding is less than required to maintain a first-class activity. However, many off-site managers have learned to cope and have been able to achieve optimum results with very little.

All things being normal, a singular off-site activity should perform in the same manner as a central one. One may expect, however, that physical resources equal to those employed during development will not be available and that the number of personnel assigned will have to double up on tasks to perform CM, quality assurance, testing, validation, verification, and so on. In addition, the software engineer(s) will be writing and coding and most likely testing their work prior to installation of the new version.

A branch off-site activity may possibly fare better than that just described; because if communication hookup is possible, work may be performed with the original development resources and transmitted back to the site team for final test and installation. The human-resource side may fare better because of being able to utilize the central CM, quality, and testing resources. It is easy to understand why planning for software support starts early in the development cycle in order to plan ahead for the final organization of the activity.

PROCEDURES

There are several different procedures one must follow in the support process. These are the procedures for corrective, adaptive, and perfective. *Corrective* action is one of the most important. Errors are prioritized from 1—the system is down, to 5—it's bothersome but it still works; 2—the system is down, but the operators are using a bypass of the problem; 3—the system is down, but a temporary fix has been made; and 4—there are problems identified that should be fixed as soon as possible. Naturally, priorities 1, 2, and 3 require the support activity's immediate attention.

The correction process is pretty straightforward, as illustrated in Figure 17.4. A problem is identified and a problem/change request (P/CR) is sent to the support activity. The activity will attempt to re-create the problem and come up with a solution for a fix. The impact of the change will be analyzed in terms of effect on the system as well as the marketplace, the assigned environment, or other existing sites the system operates in. A formal change document will then be prepared in the same manner that a change during development was handled. This will include the review by the CCB and if approved the change is designed, developed, tested, and incorporated in the appropriate software element. A verification and validation test will take place and once accepted a change kit or new media produced. At the same time all affected documents will also be updated and the entire package sent/released to the field, market, specific sites, or all sites.

As noted here and in Figure 17.3, impact on the using organizations is most important. As an example, when developing a standard [54] for control of software for commercial avionics, it became apparent that the larger airline companies had their own software engineering cadres. They could, with little effort, make corrective changes in the software procured for their planes. The smaller airline companies did not have this capability. Thus the latter had to call on the developer(s) to provide the corrective action. The situation created was that unless the developer knew what type of errors were being corrected at the larger airlines, one could not assess impact and determine whether new and revised software for all users was necessary. To cover this situation, a clause in the standard required the larger airlines to submit a notice of revision to the developer(s) so that impact and patterns could be established and corrective action implementation taken for the good of the industry.

If modification (*perfective* changes) on existing software is to take place, there are two scenarios. The first exists when the modification was planned, either at the time that the

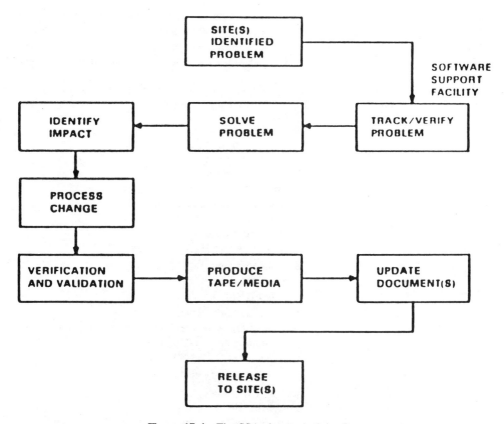

Figure 17.4   The SSA change Activity flow.

software was originally delivered or at the time such modification became apparent with changes in the assigned environment.

When the P/CR with the modification request is received, the support activity will in most cases treat the request as an RFQ and come up with a software development (modification) plan, budgets, resource requirements, schedules, and requests for necessary development hardware. Once this is all accomplished, the modification proceeds in the same fashion as it did during development. If the modification is to an existing SCI, then the related documentation is changed accordingly. If a new SCI has been added, then new documentation is created, reviewed, placed in the master file, and delivered with the software.

Adaptive change is for the most part handled in the same manner as described above; in many instances, however, such changes will occur on-site as the software is "tuned" to its assigned environment. Provisions for any additions/changes made during this period are included in the software development plan and require that detailed records be maintained by the software engineering team. Such records should be submitted once a week, if possible, and distributed by CM to the home development team. No formal change activity is required for these additions until after the specified performance and design criteria have been achieved and accepted, but all must have been recorded. This type of activity is predominant when interim software packages are delivered, and the software changes are made while undergoing test and evaluation. In the commercial environment such activity is commonly known as initial debugging, or alpha testing, with developer personnel on-site to make necessary corrections. Another term is initial operational testing. The final testing period, in which the users are on their own, is known as beta testing and final operational testing.

The activity's procedures should be structured to ensure that the following maintenance/support problems as described by NIST [51] are avoided:

SOFTWARE	poor program quality:
	software design
	software coding
	software documentation
	programming language used
	lack of common data definitions
	increasing inventory
	propagated variants
	excessive resource requirements
ENVIRONMENT	unplanned growth
	unanticipated changes
	new hardware
MANAGEMENT	poor maintenance controls
	lack of maintenance techniques and procedures
	poor maintenance-tool usage
	no standard enforcement of procedures
USERS	demanding more capabilities
PERSONNEL	lack of experience
	image/morale problems
	poor view of maintenance as unchallenging and unrewarding

RESOLVING THE PROBLEMS IN THE SSA

In order to meet these problems, the ideal maintainer or support activity, according to NIST [51], involves the following:

- flexible or adaptable to any given situation.
- self-motivated or able to keep a good system going without orders to do so.
- responsible—performs assigned tasks well.
- creative—applies innovative ideas when all else fails.
- disciplined—follows the procedures and the plan.
- analytic—analyzes tough problems as received.
- thorough—does a complete job in a high-quality manner.
- experienced—there is no substitute.
- copes with the difficulties to achieve the impossible.

The CM assigned to the maintenance or support activity should also meet these criteria, because in many instances, the CM will not have the physical resources, such as an adequate data base for status accounting. One must then conceive of methods to produce reports

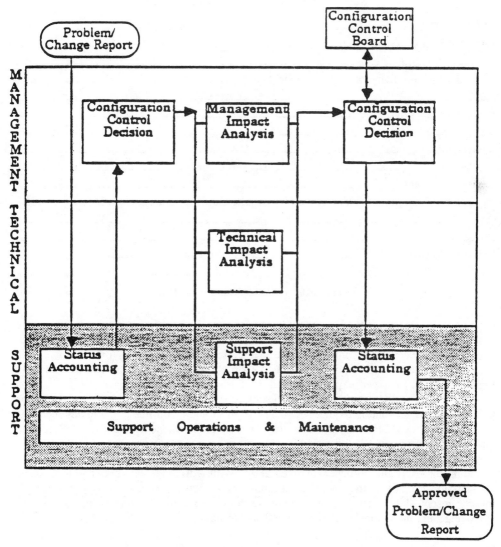

Figure 17.5   Detailed PDSS process model: initial analysis.

from less-automated means of capturing the required data. In some instances CCBs may be virtually impossible owing to one's environment, thus requiring innovative ways of review and disposition of changes. In many instances the CM activity may have to be performed by the support activity team, thus requiring adequate and understandable procedures for the team to perform the essential CM activities.

A major problem for the CM activity will be the handling of changes. One will find that without a CM presence, many are made without any written description of what the problem was or how it was corrected. In many instances one will never know that changes were made until some unrelated disaster takes place and the unknown change was part

Software Support Problem/Change Report

REQUESTOR _____ DATE _____

Address/location/system, platform, location, etc. _____

Description of problem/code and documents affected _____

Recommended solutions _____

Reviewed by _____ Disposition _____

Assigned to _____ Date to complete _____

Review-board approval _____

Disposition/instructions for implementation _____

Date Incorporated _____ Time to Correct _____

CM Close-out _____ By _____

Figure 17.6   Problem/change report form.

of the root cause. Even though the support plan may be very specific on procedures for change, approvals, and incorporation, there are bound to be exceptions. On the other hand, the financial success of a company in the marketplace depends heavily on its support and customer service staff. The procedure must be simple (as the detailed process illustrated in Figure 17.5) [S2] and self-explanatory and the form very simple and open.

As a minimum, the data in Figure 17.6 should provide the necessary information for the CCB and status accounting requirements. The form should be on-line to the maintainer. The data entered should also be entered in the given software element's SDF and be reported out by status accounting. With worldwide communication quickly improving and with systems such as CALS and others, one can envision a completely automated control process including the CCB and no paper involved at all. With worldwide networks and high-speed transmission capability, the maintenance and support activity should be able to meet its mission responsibilities in passing data among those responsible for processing, reviewing, approving, and incorporating changes or release of data.

EXERCISES

Select one of the three exercises.

1. Write an executive summary for a software support plan for a project you are now assigned to. Discuss with your peers at work and those in your class. Do you meet the criteria for a good support activity?

2. Develop a procedure/agreement for a support activity at a remote site. Have only two people responsible for maintaining the software system and making changes. Review, record, and submit the change records to the developing activity.

3. Write a short proposal for a support activity for a very popular business system as you would do if you were hired as a consultant.

CHAPTER 18

Training Guidelines

There are several approaches one can take in training people to be proficient in Config-uration Management. To begin with, one should understand a major distinction between hardware CM and software CM. One will find that the training curriculum for hardware will focus on development and use of engineering drawings, associated lists, and equipment and part specifications. For software one will concentrate on understanding the development of the software product's documented identification, the language used, and the computer architectures of the developing and using computers, host and target, respectively.

TRAINING-PROGRAM ISSUES

The methods for training span from one-, two-, or three-day seminars, the most predominant; to 13-week college-level courses, very rare. The majority of training is provided on the job by one already experienced in CM or, too many times, through reading the literature, standards, and statement of work instructions related to the software project.

There have been to date few texts on the subject. *Software Configuration Management* by Bersoff et al., published in 1980 [54], has been the most widely used. The need for additional texts such as this book has become apparent, and one may enjoy a larger selection in the near future.

The need to perform the CM process is driven primarily by a buyer/user/customer re-quirement. Few firms have developed procedures for a CM process as a matter of good business practice like those in the profession would wish. As a result, the seminar training approach has been the most predominant primarily because once a request for proposal or contract is received, time is critical When pressed, a manager will select a member of the project to be responsible for CM and tell that person to get trained fast! Thus the one-, two-, or three-day seminars have, for the most part, launched several thousand people into the world of CM with the ability and know how to start up and to look for detailed instruction.

There are some interesting statistics to support the statements above. A survey on software configuration management training [57] taken by the EIA's Computer Resource Committee and published in June of 1988 indicated that out of 96 respondents 70 percent received on-the-job training and some 42 percent attended seminars from 6 to 200 hours in length. Some 20 percent were trained in-house.

In addition, the survey notes that 50 percent of the 96 respondents had bachelors degrees with 22 percent holding masters. The majority of majors were in business, 38 percent, and engineering, 26 percent. The preference for type of course was 55 percent for 3–5-day seminars and 36 percent for 1- to 2-day sessions. More people preferred the advanced courses over the basic, which seemed to indicate some prior training or one to two years OJT. This author has found that a good majority are brand new to the subject, which might suggest that a survey outside a professional or industry association activity, such as readers of *Datamation* magazine, might number far into the majority for a basic course.

TYPES OF TRAINING PROGRAMS

One or two training firms have presented a one-week CM course that provides more detailed instruction (especially in the development of the CM plan), procedures for change control, conduct of the CCB, and developing a status accounting system. These courses have also proved very worthwhile.

The DOD service's schools normally provide two-week courses that include detailed analysis of the service's own doctrine, standards, and instruction. Many who have graduated from these courses also attend public seminars to get a more global perspective of the process.

The two- and three-day seminar has been very popular and has been given since the late 1970s by this author and a number of others. The Data Processing Management Association's Educational Foundation and the Technical Marketing Management Society have sponsored a series of popular seminars in the United States, Europe, and Asia. The IEEE Standard Seminars also sponsor sessions based on the IEEE Software Standards such as ANSI/IEEE Standard 828-1990, Standard for Software Configuration Management Plans. In addition, several firms and individuals also present seminars in greater detail lasting 3 to 5 days, such as the Software Configuration Management seminars for NASA and their contractors conducted by the System Technology Institute (STI) [56].

A typical outline, illustrated in Figure 18.1, is one for a course presented by the author and George Tice for STI. This type of outline is aimed at providing the most requisite information in a three-day period, but it also allows for class exercises including participating in a CCB and writing sections of a CM plan outline requirement. The seminar may also be tailored down to 1 day or even less depending on the requirement such as a executive overview in a half-day—with no exercise. The two- and three-day seminar, tailored to the company's needs, has worked well for the author, for in-house sessions, or at other companies.

James E. Tomayko of the Software Engineering Institute [69] published a curriculum model for CM in 1986. In the introduction Tomayko stated, "The module presented here is intended to be an in-depth consideration of configuration management, including configuration item identification, change reporting, and evaluation, change execution, and evaluation, and use, version control and management principles related to configuration control." He did not state the length of the course. The outline was based on a workshop that was held at SEI in 1986. Findings, as reported by Katherine E. Harvey [70], stated in the conclusion that

> "Education seems to be the place to start [developing good CM practice], but there seems to be much more involved than classroom development alone. It seemed that what the [workshop] group was trying to do was begin a program that would teach software engineers that they need to learn the concepts of Software Configuration Management wherever that education may be available (whether learning in the classroom or gaining experience in the field). I would conclude that what seems to be wrong in Software Configuration Management today is that too many software engineers don't seem to think they are missing much without a solid knowledge of SCM. If they can be shown the importance of SCM, then perhaps they will be more eager to learn its concepts and to use it more often and more effectively in the software development field today."

PLANNING AND INITIATING A TRAINING PROGRAM

What has just been stated is a major challenge to the training community and senior CM community. The big question is where one starts. The "start" begins with an expert in CM—who likes to teach—developing an outline for in-house use that will fit the customs and mores of the trainer's environment.

This three day course will provide participants with practical guidance for implementing software configuration management to improve the quality and productivity of their software acquisition and development.
In-class exercises based upon lessons-learned from real-life projects will reinforce the learning process.

Course Objectives:

Attendees Will Learn How To:
- Implement Configuration Management Procedures.
- Establish Configuration Identification Functions.
- Accomplish Configuration Status Accounting.
- Implement Software Library Functions.
- Accomplish Configuration Audits.
- Implement Configuration Control Procedures.

Who Will Benefit:
- Project Managers
- Individuals with Software Configuration Management Responsibilities
- Individuals who are affected by or interface with Software Configuration Management (QA, Supportability, Test, Security, etc.)

Course Content:

1. Introduction
- Scope of Course
- Course Objectives
- Definitions

2. Software Development Process
- Software Development Life Cycle (SDLC)
- Purpose of SDLC
- Relationships of CM to SDLC Phases
- When CM is Applied

3. CM Successes and Failures

4. Basic Concepts of Configuration Management
- CM and SW Acquisition Management
- CM Standards (IEEE, DoD, Industry, NASA)
- Overview of CM Functions
- Specifying Deliverables
- Concept of Baselines
- Software Configuration Item (SCI)
- Configuration Identification Functions
  - Objectives of Identification Scheme
  - SCI Level Identification
  - System Level Identification
- Configuration Control Functions
  - Change Request Processing
  - Change Control Board Functions
  - Multi-level Control

- Interface Control
- Configuration Status Accounting
- Functional and Physical Configuration Audits
- Comparison of SW and HW CM
- CM Plans
- What RFP's and Contracts Should Say about CM
- Evaluating Contractor Policies and Practices

5. Configuration Management Responsibilities
- Developer Responsibilities
- Staffing Requirements
- Cost of Configuration Management

6. Specific Configuration Identification Guidance
- Rules for Specifying Identification Schemes
- System Hierarchy Description
- Specifying System Identification Scheme
- Specifying SCI Identification Scheme
- Importance of SCI's
- How to Identify and Handle Items Below the SCI
- Defining Design Document Trees
- Configuration Identification Documents
- Recommended Identification Schemes
- Examples of Existing Schemes
- Identification Procedures

7. Specific Configuration Control Guidance
- Description and Purpose of Each SDLC Baseline
- Different Types of Changes
- Change Request Initiation
  - Change Request Form/Template
  - Change Request Submission and Review
  - Change Request Logging
- Change Request (CR) Coordination
  - Distribution
  - Change Request Coordination Procedure
  - Review and Technical Coordination/Trade Offs
  - Impact Analysis - General
  - Impact Form/Template
  - Impact Analysis Rules of Thumb
  - Preparation for Configuration Control Board (CCB)

- Maximum Time for Change Request Coordination
- Who Should Do It and How
- How to Handle Difficult-To-Coordinate Changes
- Using Electronic Mail to Coordinate
- Configuration Control Board Action
  - Concept of Two CCBs
  - Frequency of CCB Meetings/Actions
  - How CCB Should Handle CR Actions
  - Who Should Present CR to CCB
  - How CCB Operates
  - Recording CCB Actions
  - Dissemination of CCB Actions
  - Using Phone/Electronic Mail for CCB Actions
  - Responsibilities of CCB Chairman
  - Important Items to Discuss/Consider
  - Decisions/Recommendations from CCB
  - Criteria for Sending CR to Higher Level CCB

8. Interface Controls

9. Subcontractors

10. Specific Configuration Status Accounting Guidance
- Purpose and Functions
- Change Request Status and Reporting
- CCB Action Reporting
- Baseline Configuration Status Accounting
- Product Library Definition and Reporting
- Interface to CCB

11. Configuration Audits
- Functional Audits
- Physical Audits

12. Library Functions
- Software Library Role and Purpose
- Interface to Status Accounting
- Receiving Deliverables
- Criteria for Delivery
- Security Storage
- Archiving and Reuse
- Disbursement
- Support of System Releases
- Interface to CCB
- Staffing
- Facilities
- Costs
- RFP/Contract Specifications
- Evaluation of Contractor Practices
- Taking Delivery From Contractor
- Acceptance of the Products

13. Summary
- Key Points
- Lessons Learned
- Guidelines and References

- Automation of the Function
  - Standard Reports
  - Data Base Contents
  - READ-ONLY Access/Electronic Interfaces

COURSE AUTHOR

Ron Berlack is Manager of Configuration Management for Lockheed Sanders. His responsibilities include the implementation of hardware and software configuration management practices and information systems, as well as providing the necessary training and guidance to ensure cost-effective implementation of CM and SCM throughout the Company.

Mr. Berlack has lectured at numerous symposia on Software Configuration Management for EF/DPMA, IEEE, ACM, ADPA, EIA, NSIA and other organizations. He is a past Chairperson of the Electronic Industries Association (EIA), Data & Configuration Management Committee and the Computer Resources Committee. He is a developer of ANSI/IEEE Std. 828, "Software Configuration Management Plans," and a reviewer of ANSI/IEEE Std 1042 "Guide to Software Configuration Management," as well as a referee for Computer magazine. He is currently working with the ISO/IEC to develop an international standard for Software Configuration Management.

For further information contact System Technology Institute at (213) 457-0851

Figure 18.1 Software configuration management

To do this best is to choose a "white hat," who may be anxious (we like to think) to be trained in CM, one who recognizes the need, or one who has just been directed by the customer to implement the CM process. The steps to take are similar to those illustrated in Figure 18.2 [71]. The Analysis block detail, Figure 18.3, is even more revealing in terms of what one should be concentrating on, and Figure 18.4 is a good illustration for course content. Finally, Figure 18.5 is an illustration of a module for change control including a matrix showing which organizational elements are most affected by the control topics.

The following steps are suggested in initiating a training plan and conducting a training program:

- Select the project and determine the need, the environment, the customer (and customer's past history with CM), and the time to train and instruct.

- Prepare an overall procedure for performing the CM process or adapt a current company procedure. Prepare subsets for identification, control, status accounting, audits, interface control, and subcontractor control.

- Meet frequently and regularly with key project personnel in reviewing and obtaining approval/acceptance of the procedures and then proceed to brief the rest of the project in how to implement and the role each project member must play for CM to be successful.

- Use a good reference to obtain material for the formal training. The progression of events explained in this text has been most helpful. The outline of Figure 18.1 is also a good progression. The EIA Bulletin 6-1B, CM and DM References, provides up-to-date information on standards, specifications, books, publications, and articles relating to CM. The National Technical Information Service at Springfield, Virginia, also provides an abstracts publication of CM publications, which is updated on a yearly basis. A just published EIA Bulletin, CMB 6-10, A Training Guide for Configuration and Data Management, is also most worthwhile, although one may find it oriented more to the hardware CM environment.

- Develop training aids, such as transparencies for overhead projectors, that are not too detailed but describe the intent of what one is saying. Use lessons learned and case histories plus illustrations. Develop exercises that meet real-world situations such as processing change forms, conducting a CCB, or formatting a status accounting report.

- Once these details are completed, the project manager should select those who will perform the CM tasks and activities to take the selected course(s). The training person should then be close at hand to help initiate the process.

- Once the process is underway, the one-to-three-day seminar should be provided to all in the company who will interface with the project and need to understand their role. For instance, what a logistics person does when receiving an approved change for implementation in the logistics area. Another example is how a software engineer initiates a change request and, more importantly, how that engineer prevents unauthorized changes from occurring.

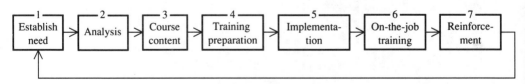

Figure 18.2   A training process flow.

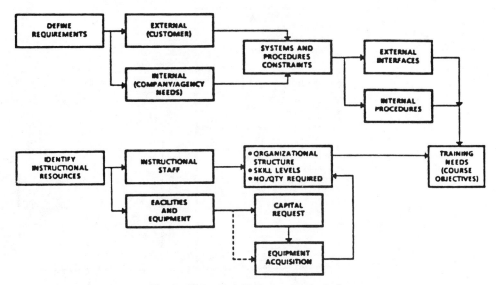

Figure 18.3 Training course analysis flow.

- As the project progresses, the training activity should be assessing performance of the trainees and evaluating the worth of the training provided. If there are problems or misunderstandings relative to certain procedural steps, they should be corrected immediately before the misconception(s) become practice, and corrections made in the course material if required.
- The on-the-job learning curve of the trainees should also be monitored closely to ensure that after a given period of time, a week or month, a task such as logging in a change should meet the minimum accepted time, such as five minutes.
- The training monitor(s) should also review completed release notices and change order forms for completeness, accuracy, and understandability. If there appear to be problems it may be that the form is not sufficient to meet the criteria set by the training and procedures group. The form may be too "busy" or cumbersome to understand and complete. These problems should be corrected at once to avoid discouragement on the part of the preparer or processor.
- Select an appropriate breakoff point and declare the training phase as complete.
- Conduct a lessons-learned postmortem and record the events of the training, adherence to the training plan, and corrective action required by the lessons learned.

New project participants should be solicited to sign up for CM training. If the last training effort was successful, others will normally follow. The basic problem is that most people do not want to be first and prefer to wait and see.

Finally, in-house training should be continuously offered at least once if not twice or three times a year depending on the size of the firm or company. If there is only a small group, then taking advantage of the public seminars for one/two people at a time over a one/two-year period might well be the way to go. The on-site presentations may also be advantageous, but one must be careful to try to limit the amount of time attendees spend running back to the office. At one seminar session that this author was giving, a note

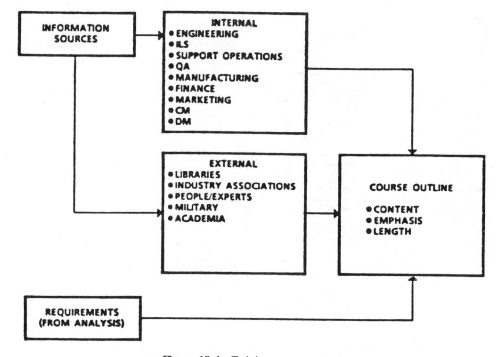

Figure 18.4   Training course content.

appeared on the door to the training room that read "Jack, forget the seminar, Ed wants to see you right away." This, of course, makes it difficult to maintain continuity, but must be expected.

BENEFITS FROM TRAINING

There are several benefits that come from training people in CM. The first is that it will get all those who have completed the session knowledgeable of the standards and procedures used in one's company/organization and that of the customer. It also conveys the company's customs and practices along with the customer's. This at least will enable one to start on common ground.

Another benefit is giving one the ability to know where to go for information and advice, and where to look for procedures and information to satisfy a given problem, providing enough knowledge to understand and even participate in meetings, discussions, CCBs, and so on without being totally lost. For example, the more that one may learn about the Ada language or C++ language, the less of a mystery the topic will be when attending a design review or other type of technical discussion.

A third benefit comes from growing one's own CM cadre and ensuring that talent is and will be available when needed for new projects, assistance on current projects, responding to requests for proposals, and so on. This availability can save quite a bit of money that would have to be spent hiring in the open market.

There are of course the benefits of increased productivity by now knowledgeable personnel who should in turn provide a better environment for control of the software product's

CONFIGURATION CONTROL

The goal of this module of instruction is to provide individuals with an in-depth awareness of what configuration control is and the importance of functional participation in the accomplishment of configuration management.

COURSE OUTLINE

1.   Baseline Management and Program Phasing.

2.   Engineering Drawing and Release System.

3.   Interface Control and Subcontracts.

4.   Change Control Plans and Process.

5.   Change Implementation Process.

6.   Specifications, Standards and Regulations.

ORGANIZATION/ELEMENTS MATRIX

	1	2	3	4	5	6
ENGINEERING	X	X	X	X	X	
ADMINISTRATION			X	X	X	
QUALITY		X	X	X	X	
MANUFACTURING		X		X	X	
INT LOGISTICS SUPT		X		X	X	
CONFIGURATION MGT	X	X	X	X	X	X
PROGRAM MANAGEMENT	X	X	X	X	X	
DATA MANAGEMENT	X	X	X	X	X	X

Figure 18.5   Module for change control.

evolution from beginning to end, and as the learning experience increases, the cost of performing CM should and will lessen.

EXERCISES

1. Develop an outline for a training course in software CM.
2. Develop a twenty-minute tutorial on CM.
3. Develop a course model for identification or status accounting similar to that in Figure 18.5.

Notes

1. Radio Technical Commission for Aeronautics (RTCA) 81—*Proceedings of Annual Assembly 18–20 Nov. 1981,* Washington, DC.
2. DOD, Joint Logistics Commanders Monterrey I Workshop, 1977.
3. E. Yourdon, and L. Constantine, *Structured Design* (Englewood Cliffs, NJ: Prentice-Hall, 1979).
4. *An Air Force Guide to Computer Program CM, ESD-TR-77,* (Santa Monica, CA: System Development Corp., 1977).
5. Brooks Act and Warner Amendment.
6. See Grady Booch, *Software Engineering with Ada,* (Menlo Park CA: Benjamin-Cummings Publishing, 1983) and Wayne H Babich, *Software Configuration Management,* (Reading, MA: Addison Wesley Publishing Co., 1986).
7. MIL STD 480, U.S. Department of Defense.
8. The American Heritage Dictionary, 2nd College Edition, Houghton Mifflin Co., Boston, MA, 1985.
9. DOD D 5010.19, U.S. Department of Defense.
10. IEEE STD 610.12-1990.
11. EIA Bulletin, CMB 6A, CM References.
12. L. Constantine, *Structured Design* (Englewood Cliffs, NJ: Prentice-Hall, 1979).
13. T. DeMarco, *Structured Analysis and System Specification,* (Englewood Cliffs, NJ: Prentice-Hall, 1979).
14. E. Yourdon and L. Constantine, *Structured Design* (Englewood Cliffs, NJ: Prentice-Hall, 1979).
15. Electronic Industries Association Bulletin SYSB-1 System Engineering, 1989, Washington, D.C. 20006.
16. G. Booch, *Software Engineering with Ada,* (Menlo Park, CA: Benjamin Commings Publishing, 1983).
17. Characteristics and functions of SEE. Electronic Industries Association.
18. NASA SMAP DID P100, *Concept Document,* 2 Feb 1989, NASA, Office of Safety, Reliability, Maintainability, and Quality Assurance, Software Management and Assurance Program (SMAP), Code QR, Washington, DC.
19. IEEE STD 828-1990, IEEE STD, *Software Configuration Management Plans,* IEEE Standards Dept., Box 1331, Piscataway, NJ 08855.
20. IEEE STD 1042-1986, *IEEE STD Guide to Software Configuration Management,* IEEE Standards Dept., Box 1331, Piscataway, NJ 08855.
21. MIL STD 1456A, U.S. Department of Defense, 11 Sep 1989, *Configuration Management Plan.*

22. NASA DID M 920, SCMP, Rel 4.3, 2Feb89, NASA, Office of Safety, Reliability, Maintainability, and Quality Assurance, Software Management and Assurance Program (SMAP), Code QR, Washington, DC.

23. MIL STD 483B, U.S. Department of Defense, 4 June 985, *CM Practices for Configuration Management Practices for Systems, Equipment, Munitions, and Computer Programs.*

24. EIA, Bulletin 4-2, Identification.

25. M. Naylor, *Interface Control Plan,* Lockheed Canada, Ottawa, Canada, 1990.

26. DOD STD 2167A, 29 Feb 1988, *Defense System Software Development.*

27. MIL STD 480B, U.S. Department of Defense, 15 Jul 1988, *Configuration Control, Engineering Changes, Deviations, and Waivers.*

28. ERBULEY—Selection of CSCI (DRAFT), Mitre Corp., Bedford, MA.

29. AFSC 375-1, 1964, *Configuration Management.*

30. IEEE STD 830-1984, *Guide to Software Requirement Specifications.*

31. EIA Bulletin 4.2, *Identification.*

32. MIL STD 483A App II, *Interface Control.*

33. NASA DID M242, *Management Plan.*

34. M. Naylor, Interface Control Plan, Lockheed, Canada, Ottawa, Canada, 1990.

35. EIA Bulletin 4-3, *Computer Software Libraries*

36. Albert F. Case, Jr., *Information Systems Development. Principles of CASE*, (Englewood Cliffs, NJ: Prentice-Hall, 1986).

37. Watts S. Humphry, *Case Planning and the Software Process.* Technical Report, CMU/SEI-89-TR-26, ESD TR-89-34-1989, NTIS AD-A219 066.

38. Michael L. Gibson, *A Guide to Selecting CASE Tools,* PP66-67, Datamation, July 1988, (location: Cahners Publishing Co., 1988).

39. Patricia K. Loveless, *A Supporting Framework for Software Evaluation and Selection—IEEE Standards Working Group P1029,* April 1990.

40. James K. Van Buren, *Case Tool Evaluation and Selection within the STSC* (SW Tool Sub Comm), STEM (SW Tool Eval Model) briefing to IEEE Standards Working Group P 1029, Feb 1990.

41. NIST, *Taxonomy Data Base.* Publication NSBIR-80-2159-1980.

42. Data and Analysis Center for Software, *Software Life Cycle Tools Directory—* STI185, 1985, RADC, Rome, NY.

43. Do-While Jones, *Ada in Action*, (New York: John Wiley & Sons, 1989).

44. *Preliminary Program Manager's Guide to Ada*, Sect 5.6, Project and Configuration Management, R. G. Howe, W. E. Bryne, E. C. Grund, R. F. Hilliard II, R. G. Munk, Mitre Corp. Bedford, MA, 1984.

45. *Technical Report on Evaluation of Ada Environments*, Chapter 3, Configuration Management, Software Engineering Institute, CMU, SEI-87-TR-1 [NTIS, Springfield VA AD A 180960]

46. Wayne A. Babich, *Software Configuration Management*, (Reading, MA: Addison-Wesley Publishing Co., 1986).

47. Dr. Lawrence Wiseman, *The Ada Language System—ALS—US Army,* Proceedings of Panel on Effect of Nebula ISA on Ada, EIA G-33 Computer Resources, Data and Configuration Management Workshop, 21–25 September 1981.

48. R. Freedman, *Programming with APSE Software Tools*, (Princeton, NJ: Petrocelli Books, 1985).

49. J. McDirmed and K. Ripkin, *Life Cycle Support in the Ada Environment*, (Cambridge, England: Cambridge University Press, 1984).

50. Lewis Gray, *Ada and DoD Std 2167A*, Ada Pros Inc. 2224 Grassy Hill Court, Fairfax, VA 2203-2819, 1989; and Lewis, "Decomposing an Ada CSCI of a Large Command and Control System into TLCSCs, LLCSCs, and Units: Guidelines, Reflections, and Suggestions for Using DOD-STD-2167A," in *Implementing the DOD-STD-2167 and DOD-STD-2167A Software Organizational Structure in Ada,* Report of the Association for Computing Machinery (ACM), Special Interest Group on Ada (SIGAda), Software Development Standards and Ada Working Group (SDSAWG), August 1990, page 2-41.

51. R. J. Martin and W. M.Osborne, *Guidance on Software Maintenance*, NBS[NIST] Special Publication, 500-106, NIST, Washington, DC 20234, 1983.

52. *Mil Handbook 347, Mission Critical Computer Resources Software Support*, U.S. Naval Publications Center, Philadelphia PA, May 1990.

53. Proceedings, Joint Logistic Commanders, 4th Biennial Software Workshop, Orlando II, Solving the Post Deployment Challenge, Commander, FCDSSA, Dam Neck, Virginia Beach, VA, 23461, 1987

54. Standard SC145, *Software Considerations in Airborne Systems and Equipment Certification*, November 1981, Radio Technical Commission for Aeronautics, Washington, DC 20006.

55. E. H. Bersoff, V. D. Henderson, and S. G. Siegel, *Software Configuration Management,* (Englewood Cliffs, NJ: Prentice-Hall, 1980).

56. The DPMEF and TMMS may be contacted through Technology Training Corp, 3420 Kashiwa Street, Suite 2000, Torrance, CA 90505-4025, USA. The IEEE may be contacted through Seminar Coordinator, IEEE Standards Department, PO Box 1331, Piscataway, NJ 08855-1331, USA. System Technology Institute is at 6994 Whitesand Place, Malibu, CA 90265, USA.

57. A Survey on Software Configuration Management Training, A. Sommers, 1317 Onstott Road, Lampoc CA 93436, Presented to the EIA, G-34 Committee, June 1988.

58. C. J. Bradshaw and C. E. Gardella, *AFSCM 375-1 in Retrospect, ESD-TR-67-230*, Technical Requirements and Standards Office, Electronic Systems Division, Air Force Systems Command, L.G. Hanscomb Field, Bedford MA, March 1967.

59. MIL STD 490, Specification Practices, Rev A, June 1985.

60. B. W. Boehm, *Software Engineering Economics,* (Englewood Cliffs, NJ: Prentice-Hall, 1981).

61. *Software Change Control*, EIA Bulletin, 4–3, Electronic Industries Association, 2001 Penn. Ave, NW, Washington DC, 20006, 1981.

62. MIL STD 481, *Short Form Engineering Change Proposal,* 1968.

63. *Data Item Description—DI-MCCR-80030, Software Development Plan,* DOD, 1988.

64. W. S. Humphrey and W. L. Sweet, *A Method for Assessing the Software Engineering Capability of Contractors*, CMU/SEI-87-TR-23, ESD-TR-87-186, Carnegie-Mellon University, Software Engineering Institute, Pittsburgh, PA 15213, USA, Sept 1987.

65. Stoneman—*Requirements for Ada Programming Support Environments*, Department of Defense, Professor John N. Buxton, February 1980.

66. Robert Loech, *Introduction to Software Engineering—Section—Object Based Computing and Ada,* System Technology Institute, Malibu, CA, 90265, 1988.

67. EIA Bulletin CMB6-5, *Textbook for Status Accounting,* EIA, 2001 Pennsylvania Ave NW, Washington DC 20006, 1988.

68. K. Sawyer, Lockheed Sanders, Nashua, NH, 1989. *File Control Methodology.*

69. James E. Tomayko, *Software Configuration Management, SEI* curriculum module SEI-CM4-1.1 (preliminary), Software Engineering Institute, CMU, Pittsburgh, PA, November 1986.

70. Katherine E. Harvey, *Summary of the SEI Workshop on Software Configuration Management,* CMU/SEI-86-TR-5, Software Engineering Institute, CMU, Pittsburgh, PA, December 1986.

71. J. Poore and D. Snowden, EIA Bulletin CMB 6-2, Configuration and Data Management In-House Training Plan, January, 1988.

72. EIA Bulletin CMB-5A, Configuration Management Requirements for Subcontractors/Vendors.

Abbreviations and Definitions

Although the following definitions are abstracted from MILSTD 973B, they very closely approximate those in IEEE STD 610.12–1990, Glossary of Software Engineering Terminology.

ABBREVIATIONS

ABL	ALLOCATED BASELINE
ACI	ALLOCATED CONFIGURATION IDENTIFICATION
ADP	AUTOMATED DATA PROCESSING
CCB	CONFIGURATION CONTROL BOARD
CDR	CRITICAL DESIGN REVIEW
CMP	CONFIGURATION MANAGEMENT PLAN
CI	CONFIGURATION ITEM
CSCP	COMPUTER SOFTWARE CHANGE PROPOSAL
DBDD	DATA BASE DESIGN DOCUMENT
DID	DATA ITEM DESCRIPTION
DOD	DEPARTMENT OF DEFENSE
DPSR	DATA PROCESSING SYSTEM REQUIREMENT
DDR	DESIGN DOCUMENT REVIEW
ECP	ENGINEERING CHANGE PROPOSAL
FBL	FUNCTIONAL BASELINE
FCA	FUNCTIONAL CONFIGURATION AUDIT
FCI	FUNCTIONAL CONFIGURATION IDENTIFICATION
IDS	INTERFACE DESIGN DOCUMENT
IRS	INTERFACE REQUIREMENT SPECIFICATION
ML	MASTER LIBRARY
O/M	OPERATIONAL AND MAINTENANCE
O/S	OPERATIONAL SYSTEM
PDS	PROGRAM DESIGN DOCUMENT
PCI	PRODUCT CONFIGURATION IDENTIFICATION
PBL	PRODUCT BASELINE

PDR	PRELIMINARY DESIGN REVIEW
PMP	PROGRAM MANAGEMENT PLAN
PROM	PROGRAMMABLE READ ONLY MEMORY
PSL	PROGRAM SUPPORT LIBRARY
PCA	PHYSICAL CONFIGURATION AUDIT
ROM	READ ONLY MEMORY
SCCB	SOFTWARE CONFIGURATION CONTROL BOARD
SCM	SOFTWARE CONFIGURATION MANAGEMENT
SCMP	SOFTWARE CONFIGURATION MANAGEMENT PLAN
SCN	SPECIFICATION CHANGE NOTICE
SDF	SOFTWARE DEVELOPMENT FILE
SDL	SOFTWARE DEVELOPMENT LIBRARY
SDP	SOFTWARE DEVELOPMENT PLAN
SDR	SYSTEMS DESIGN REVIEW
SPS	SOFTWARE PRODUCT SPECIFICATION
SRR	SYSTEMS REQUIREMENTS REVIEW
SRS	SOFTWARE REQUIREMENTS SPECIFICATION
SSF	SOFTWARE SUPPORT FACILITY
SSR	SOFTWARE SPECIFICATION REVIEW
SUM	SOFTWARE USERS MANUAL
TP	TEST PLAN
TPR	TEST PROCEDURE
TR	TEST REPORT
TRR	TEST READINESS REVIEW
TS	TEST SPECIFICATIONS
V&V	VALIDATION AND VERIFICATION
VDD	VERSION DESCRIPTION DOCUMENT
WBS	WORK BREAKDOWN STRUCTURE
WL	WORKING LIBRARY

DEFINITIONS

1. <u>Definitions used</u>.   For the purpose of this book the following definitions have been chosen.

1.1   <u>Allocated Configuration Identification (ACI)</u>.   Performance-oriented specifications governing the development of CIs, in which each specification:

    . a.   defines the functional characteristics that are allocated from those of the system or higher level CI;

    b.   establishes the verification required to demonstrate achievement of its allocated functional characteristics;

    c.   delineates necessary interface requirements with other associated CIs; and

    d.   establishes design constraints, if any, such as component standardization, use of inventory items, and integrated logistic support requirements.

1.3   <u>Baseline</u>.   A configuration identification document or a set of such documents formally designated by the Government at a specific time during a CI's life cycle. Baselines, plus approved changes from those baselines, constitute the current approved configuration identification. For configuration management purposes there are three baselines, which are established sequentially, as follows:

1.3.1   <u>Functional Baseline (FBL)</u>.   The initially approved documentation describing a system's or item's functional characteristics and the verification required to demonstrate the achievement of those specified functional characteristics.

1.3.2   <u>Allocated Baseline (ABL)</u>.   The initially approved documentation describing an item's functional and interface characteristics that are allocated from those of a higher level CI, interface requirements with interfacing configuration items, additional design constraints and the verification required to demonstrate the achievement of those specified functional and interface characteristics.

1.3.3   <u>Product Baseline (PBL)</u>.   The initially approved documentation describing all of the necessary functional and physical characteristics of the CI, any required joint and combined operations interoperability characteristics of a CI (including a comprehensive summary of the other service(s) and allied interfacing CIs or systems and equipments), and the selected functional and physical characteristics designated for production acceptance testing and tests necessary for support of the CI.

1.5   <u>Computer data base</u>.   A collection of data in a form capable of being processed by a computer.

1.6   <u>Computer program</u>.   A series of instructions or statements in a form acceptable to a computer, designed to cause the computer to execute an operation(s).

1.7   <u>Computer software (or software)</u>.   A combination of associated computer instructions and computer data definitions required to enable the computer hardware to perform computational or control functions.

1.8   <u>Computer Software Configuration Item (CSCI)</u>.   A configuration item for computer software.

1.9 <u>Computer software documentation</u>. Technical data or information, including computer listings and printouts, which documents the requirements, design, or details of computer software; explains the capabilities and limitations of the software; or provides operating instructions for using or supporting computer software during the software's operational life.

1.10 <u>Configuration</u>. The functional and physical characteristics of hardware, firmware, software or a combination thereof as set forth in technical documentation and achieved in a product.

1.11 <u>Configuration audit</u>. The verification of a CI's conformance to specifications, drawings and other contract requirements.

1.11.1 <u>Functional Configuration Audit (FCA)</u>. The formal examination of functional characteristics of a CI, prior to acceptance, to verify that the item has achieved the performance specified in its functional or allocated configuration identification.

1.11.2 <u>Physical Configuration Audit (PCA)</u>. The formal examination of the "as-built" configuration of a CI against its technical documentation to establish the CI's initial product configuration identification (PCI).

1.12 <u>Configuration control</u>. The systematic proposal, justification, evaluation, coordination, approval or disapproval of proposed changes, and the implementation of all approved changes in the configuration of a CI after formal establishment of its baseline.

1.13 <u>Configuration Control Board (CCB)</u>. A board composed of technical and administrative representatives who approve or disapprove proposed engineering changes to an approved baseline.

1.14 <u>Configuration identification</u>. The selection of the documents to comprise the baseline for the systems and CIs involved, and the numbers and other identifiers affixed to the items and documents. The approved documents that identify and define the item's functional and physical characteristics in the form of specifications, drawings, associated lists, interface control documents, and documents referenced therein. The configuration identification is developed and maintained through three distinct evolutionary increasing levels of detail, each used for establishing a specific baseline. The three levels of configuration identification are as follows:

1.14.1 <u>Functional Configuration Identification (FCI)</u>. The approved functional baseline plus approved changes. (See 3.1.41.)

1.14.2 <u>Allocated Configuration Identification (ACI)</u>. The approved allocated baseline plus approved changes. (See 3.1.1.)

1.14.3 <u>Product Configuration Identification (PCI)</u>. The approved product baseline plus approved changes. (See 3.1.56.)

1.15 <u>Configuration Item (CI)</u>. An aggregation of hardware, firmware, software, or any of its discrete portions, which satisfies an end use function and is designated for configuration management. CIs may vary widely in complexity, size and type, from an aircraft, ship or electronic system to a test meter or round of ammunition. During development and manufacture of the initial (prototype) production configuration, CIs are those items whose performance parameters and physical characteristics must be separately defined (specified) and controlled to provide management insight needed to achieve the overall end use function and performance. Any item required for logistic support and is designated for separate procurement is a CI.

1.16 <u>Configuration Management (CM)</u>. A discipline applying technical and administrative direction and surveillance to:

    a.   identify and document the functional and physical characteristics of CIs;

    b.   audit the CIs to verify conformance to specifications, interface control documents and other contract requirements;

    c.   control changes to CIs and their related documentation; and

    d.   record and report information needed to manage CIs effectively, including the status of proposed changes and the implementation status of approved changes.

1.17 <u>Configuration Status Accounting (CSA)</u>. The recording and reporting of information needed to manage configuration effectively, including:

    a.   a listing of the approved configuration identification;

    b.   the status of proposed changes, deviations, and waivers to the configuration;

    c.   the implementation status of approved changes; and

    d.   the configuration of all units of the CI in the operational inventory.

1.18 <u>Contract.</u> A legal agreement between buyer and seller or a similar internal agreement wholly within a company, for the development, production, maintenance or modificaation of an item.

1.20 <u>Contractor</u>. An individual, partnership, company, corporation, association or other service having a contract with the procuring activity for the design, development, manufacture, maintenance, modification or supply of items under the terms of a contract. An   activity performing any or all of the above functions is considered to be a contractor for configuration control purposes.

1.21.1 <u>Non-recurring costs</u>. One time costs which will be incurred if an   change is ordered and which are independent of the quantity of items changed, such as cost of redesign,   or qualification.

1.21.2 <u>Recurring costs</u>. Costs which are incurred for each item changed or for each service or document ordered.

1.22 <u>Critical item</u>. An item which, because of special engineering, procurement or logistic considerations, requires an approved specification to establish technical or inventory control.

1.23 <u>Data.</u> Recorded information, regardless of form or characteristics, including administrative, managerial, financial, scientific, technical, engineering, and logistics data, whether required to be delivered or retained by the contractor, as well as data developed by the buyer.

1.24 <u>Data Item Description (DID), DD Form 1664</u>. A completed form that defines the data required of a contractor. The form specifically defines the data content, preparation instructions, format and intended use.

1.25 <u>Defect</u>. Any nonconformance from specified requirements.

1.25.1 <u>Classification of defects</u>. The enumeration of possible defects of a unit or product, classified according to their seriousness. Defects will normally be grouped into classes of critical, major or minor; however, they may be grouped into other classes, or into subclasses within these classes.

1.26 <u>Deficiencies</u>. Deficiencies consist of two types:

a. conditions or characteristics in any hardware or software which are not in compliance with the specified configuration identification; or

b. inadequate (or erroneous) configuration identification which has resulted, or may result, in CIs that do not fulfill approved operational requirements.

1.27 <u>Design Change</u>. An   approved   change which modifies, adds to, deletes from or supersedes parts in a CI.

1.29 <u>Deviation</u>. A specific written authorization, granted prior to the manufacture of an item, to depart from a particular performance or design requirement of a specification, drawing or other document for a specific number of units or a specified period of time. A deviation differs from an engineering change in that an approved engineering change requires corresponding revision of the documentation defining the affected item, whereas a deviation does not contemplate revision of the applicable specification or drawing.

1.30 <u>Engineering change</u>. An alteration in the approved configuration identification of a CI under development, delivered or to be delivered.

1.32 <u>Engineering change priorities</u>. The priority assigned to a   change, which determines the methods and resources to be used in review, approval and implementation. The priority will determine the relative speed at which the ECP is to be reviewed, evaluated, ordered and implemented, if approved.

1.32.1 <u>Emergency priority</u>.   within 10 days–approval

1.32.2 <u>Urgent priority</u>.   within 20 days–approval

1.32.3 <u>Routine priority</u>.   within 30 days–approval

1.33 <u>Engineering Change Proposal (ECP)</u>. A proposed   change and the documentation by which the change is described, justified, and submitted to the procuring activity for approval or disapproval.

1.34 <u>ECP types</u>. A term covering the subdivision of ECPs on the basis of the completeness of the available information delineating and defining the engineering change. They will be identified as preliminary or formal.

1.35 <u>Firmware</u>. The combination of a hardware device and computer instructions or computer data that reside as read-only software on the hardware device. The software cannot be readily modified under program control.

1.36 <u>Fit</u>. The ability of an item to physically interface or interconnect with or become an integral part of another item.

1.37 <u>Form</u>. The defined configuration of an item including the geometrically measured configuration, density, and weight or other visual parameters which uniquely characterize an item, component or assembly. For software, form denotes the language, language level and media.

1.38 Function. The action or actions which an item is designed to perform.

1.39 Functional area. A distinct group of system performance requirements which, together with all other such groupings, forms the next lower level breakdown of the system on the basis of function.

1.40 Functional characteristics. Quantitative performance parameters and constraints, including operational and logistic parameters and their respective tolerances. Functional characteristics include all performance parameters, such as range, speed, lethality, reliability, maintainability, and safety.

1.41 Functional Configuration Identification (FCI). The initial approved technical documentation for a CI which prescribes:

    a.   all necessary functional characteristics;

    b.   the verification required to demonstrate achievement of specified functional characteristics;

    c.   the necessary interface characteristics with associated CIs;

    d.   CI key functional characteristics and lower level CIs, if any; and

    e.   design constraints, such as envelope dimensions, component standardization, use of inventory items and integrated logistics support policies.

1.42 Hardware. Articles made of material, such as tools, fittings, machine parts, weapons, vehicles, but not including computer programs or technical documentation.

1.43 Interface control. The process of:

    a.   identifying all functional and physical characteristics relevant to the interfacing of two or more items provided by one or more organizations; and

    b.   ensuring that proposed changes to these characteristics are evaluated and approved prior to implementation.

1.43.1 Interface Control Working Group (ICWG). For programs which encompass a system/CI, design cycle, an ICWG normally is established to control interface activity between the procuring activity, contractors or other agencies, including resolution of interface problems and documentation of interface agreements. (See MIL-STD-483.)

1.44 Integrated Logistics Support (ILS). A disciplined, unified and iterative approach to management and technical activities necessary to:

    a.   integrate support considerations into system and equipment design;

    b.   develop support requirements that are related consistently to design, readiness objectives and to each other;

    c.   acquire required support; and

    d.   provide required support during the operational phase at minimum cost.

1.45.1 <u>Interchangeable item</u>. An item, which:

    a.   possesses functional and physical characteristics equivalent in performance, reliability, and maintainability to another item of similar or identical purposes; and

    b.   is capable of being exchanged for the other item without alteration of the item or of adjoining items, except for adjustment or calibration.

1.46 <u>Interoperability</u>. The ability of systems, units or forces to provide services to and accept services from other systems, units or forces and to use the services so exchanged to enable them to operate effectively together.

1.47 <u>Item</u>. A non-specific term used to denote any product, including systems, subsystems, assemblies, subassemblies, units, sets, accessories, computer programs, computer software or parts.

1.51 <u>Nonconformance</u>. The failure of a unit or product to conform to specified requirements.

1.52 <u>Non-Developmental Item (NDI)</u>. Non-developmental items are existing developed and available hardware or software that are capable of fulfilling DoD requirements, thereby minimizing or eliminating the need for costly, Government-sponsored research and development (R&D) programs. An NDI is usually an off-the-shelf or commercial-type product, but may also include hardware or software already developed by or for the DoD, or other military services or foreign military forces.

1.53 <u>Notice of Revision (NOR)</u>. A document (DD Form 1695) used to propose revisions to drawings, associated lists, or other referenced documents which require revision after ECP approval. (See 5.5.)

1.54 <u>Physical characteristics</u>. Quantitative and qualitative expressions of materiel features, such as composition, dimensions, finishes, form, fit, and their respective tolerances.

1.55 <u>Privately Developed Item (PDI)</u>. An item developed at private expense and offered to the Government, with Government control of the article's configuration normally limited to its form, fit and function.

1.56 <u>Product Configuration Identification (PCI)</u>. The current approved technical documentation which defines the configuration of a CI during the production phase of its life cycle, and which prescribes:

    a.   all necessary physical or form, fit and function characteristics of a CI;

    b.   the selected functional characteristics designated for production acceptance testing; and

    c.   the production acceptance test requirements.

1.63 <u>Specification</u>. A document intended primarily for use in procurement, which describes the essential technical requirements for items, materiels or services including the procedures for determining whether or not the requirements have been met.

1.64 <u>Specification Change Notice (SCN)</u>. A document used to propose, transmit and record changes to a specification. In proposed form, prior to approval of a   change, the SCN supplies proposed changes in the text of each page affected. In final approved form, the SCN summarizes the approved changes to the text of each page affected.   )

1.65 <u>Subcontractor</u>. A person or business that contracts to provide some service or materiel necessary for the performance of another's contract.

1.66 <u>Support equipment</u>. Equipment required to operate and maintain an item, system, or facility in its intended environment. This includes:

    a.   all equipment required to maintain, test and operate the item, system or facility; and

    b.   computer programs related thereto.

1.67 <u>Survivability</u>. The capability of a system to avoid or withstand a hostile environment without suffering an abortive impairment of its ability to accomplish its designated mission. Survivability includes nuclear survivability.

1.68 <u>System</u>. A composite of equipment, skills, and techniques capable of performing or supporting an operational role, or both. A complete system includes all equipment, related facilities, material, software, services and personnel required for its operation and support to the degree that it can be considered a self-sufficient item in its intended operational environment.

1.69 <u>Technical data</u>. Recorded information, regardless of form or characteristics, of a technical nature. It may, for example, document research, experimental, developmental, or engineering work or be used to define a design or process or to procure, produce, support, maintain, or operate materiel. The data may be graphic or pictorial delineations in media such as drawings or photographs, text in specifications or related performance or design type documents, or computer printouts. Examples of technical data include research and engineering data, engineering drawings and associated lists, specifications, standards, process sheets, manuals, technical reports, catalog item identifications and related information, and computer software documentation. Technical data does not include computer software or financial, administrative, cost and pricing, and management data, or other information incidental to contract administration.

1.70 <u>Technical reviews</u>. A series of system engineering activities by which the technical progress on a project is assessed relative to its technical or contractual requirements. The reviews are conducted at logical transition points in the development effort to identify and correct problems resulting from the work completed thus far before the problems can disrupt or delay the technical progress. The reviews provide a method for the contractor and procuring activity to determine that the development of a CI and its identification have met contract requirements.

1.71 <u>Training equipment</u>. All types of maintenance and operator training hardware, devices, audio-visual training aids and related software which are:

    a.   used to train maintenance and operator personnel by depicting, simulating or portraying the operational or maintenance characteristics of an item, system or facility; and

b. must, by their nature, be kept consistent in design, construction and configuration with such items in order to provide required training capability.

unit. (1) A separately testable element specified in the design of a computer software component.
(2) A logically separable part of a computer program.
(3) A software component that is not subdivided into other components.
(4) (ANSI/IEEE Std 1008-1987) <u>See</u>: **test unit.**

<u>Note</u>: The terms "module," "component," and "unit" are often used interchangeably or defined to be sub-elements of one another in different ways depending upon the context. The relationship of these terms is not yet standardized.

1.74 <u>Waiver</u>. A written authorization to accept an item which, during manufacture or after having been submitted for inspection, is found to depart from specified requirements, but nevertheless is considered suitable for use "as is" or after repair by an approved method.

1.75 <u>Work Breakdown Structure (WBS)</u>. A product-oriented listing, in family tree order, of the hardware, software, services and other work tasks which completely defines a product or program. The listing results from project engineering during the development and production of a𝓃 item. A WBS relates the elements of work to be accomplished to each other and to the end product.

Selected CM Plan Outlines

The CM plan outlines in this appendix are provided to give the CM activity an example of the selection available to fit the type and size of project in which CM will be performed.

(Source: IEEE STD 828–1990)

MIL-STD-1456A

5. DETAILED REQUIREMENTS

5.1 <u>Format</u>. The format of the plan shall conform to the following outline. Optionally, sections listed may be further subdivided.

a. Self-cover

b. Record of reviews and history

c. Contents page

d. Section 1.   Introduction
       1.1   Description of the Configuration Item (CI)
       1.2   Program Phasing and Milestones
       1.3   Special Features

e. Section 2.   Organization
       2.1   Structure
       2.1.1 Structure (CM)
       2.1.2 Configuration control boards
       2.2   Authority and responsibility
       2.3   Policy directives
       2.4   Reference documents

f. Section 3.   Baseline identification
       3.1   Functional baseline
       3.2   Allocated baseline
       3.2.1 Specifications
       3.2.2 Drawings
       3.3   Product baseline
       3.3.1 Specifications
       3.3.2 Drawings and associated lists

g. Section 4.   Configuration control
       4.1   Responsibilities
       4.2   Procedures

h. Section 5.   Interface management
       5.1   Documentation
       5.2   Interface control

i. Section 6.   Configuration traceability
       6.1   Nomenclature
       6.2   Documentation numbering
       6.3   Hardware identification
       6.3.1 Documentation/hardware correlation
       6.4   Software and firmware identification

j. Section 7.   Configuration status accounting
       7.1   Data bank description
       7.2   Data bank content
       7.3   Reporting

k. Section 8.   Configuration management audits

l. Section 9.   Subcontractor/vendor control

MANAGEMENT PLAN DOCUMENTATION STANDARD
CONFIGURATION MANAGEMENT PLAN DID: SMAP-DID-M920

SMAP-DID-M920

CONFIGURATION MANAGEMENT PLAN

DATA ITEM DESCRIPTION

TABLE OF CONTENTS

MANAGEMENT PLAN DOCUMENTATION STANDARD
CONFIGURATION MANAGEMENT PLAN DID: SMAP-DID-M920

EXPLANATORY NOTE

The purpose of the configuration management plan is to
define the process by which the acquirer or provider
configuration manages the information system or component
products.

1.0   INTRODUCTION

The structure and content description to be used when preparing
this section is described in detail in the Management Plan
Template DID (SMAP-DID-M999).

2.0   RELATED DOCUMENTATION

The structure and content description to be used when preparing
this section is described in detail in the Management Plan
Template DID (SMAP-DID-M999).

3.0   RESOURCES, BUDGETS, SCHEDULES, AND ORGANIZATION

The structure and content description to be used when preparing
this section is described in detail in the Management Plan
Template DID (SMAP-DID-M999).

4.0   CONFIGURATION MANAGEMENT PROCESS OVERVIEW

Provide an overview of the configuration management process.
Discuss the various activities and summarize the flow of
information and products developed within the configuration
management structure.   Include a description of the process of
incorporating products received into the baselines maintained by
the preparing organization.   Be sure to address any access
restrictions.

Describe the configuration management information flow in terms
of a flow chart or similar graphic.   Show each review and control
board in the context of the information flow.   Summarize change
control reports to be generated and how they are to be tracked.

If appropriate, describe special considerations for security that
are to be supported by configuration management, such as
analyzing proposed changes for adverse effects on security or
recording each access to secure data under configuration
control.

MANAGEMENT PLAN DOCUMENTATION STANDARD
CONFIGURATION MANAGEMENT PLAN DID: SMAP-DID-M920

5.0   CONFIGURATION CONTROL ACTIVITIES

The purpose of this section is to identify and describe the
activities to be performed by a configuration control staff and
associated organizations.   Address at least the following topics
and include others, such as document revision and technical
information center activities, as appropriate.

5.1   Configuration Identification

Describe the configuration identification process and standards
for all items in the information system configuration(s).
Include a description of each provider's developmental
configuration with respect to the methods used by the provider in
establishing the configuration and identifying its contents.

Methods for establishing a configuration shall include the manner
of identifying (e.g., naming, marking, numbering) the system and
its associated components.

5.2   Configuration Change Control

Describe configuration change control responsibilities and
activities to be used in maintaining and controlling changes to
baselined products, including those identified in the following
subsections.

5.2.1   Controlled Storage and Release Management

Describe the methods and activities to be used to formally
control the receipt, storage, handling, and release of
deliverable configuration items.   Specify needs and methods for
restricting access to controlled items.   Be sure to address any
special considerations such as measures taken to ensure security
and privacy: e.g., access restrictions, consisting of codes to
protect data and system integrity against unauthorized use.

5.2.2   Change Control Flow

Discuss the initiation, transmittal, review, disposition,
implementation, and tracking of discrepancy reports and change
requests.   Use a graphic representation of the change control
flow if this provides clarity.

MANAGEMENT PLAN DOCUMENTATION STANDARD
CONFIGURATION MANAGEMENT PLAN DID: SMAP-DID-M920

5.2.3   Change Documentation

Describe each report used in the configuration management process
and explain its purpose and use.   Include an example of each
report form or cite the location where the forms can be found
(e.g., in the appropriate standards and procedures repository).

For each report:

1) Describe the function of this report.

2) Identify who may initiate the report.

3) Describe subsequent handling and updating of the
   report.

All reports shall be accessible through the management control
and status reports document for this information system or
component.   Also describe any metric data to be collected and
analyzed.

5.2.4   Change Review Process

Describe the process by which each control and review board for
configuration management carries out its responsibilities and
functions.   Describe how each board will provide historical
traceability with respect to the configuration identification
scheme.

5.3   Configuration Status Accounting

Define the configuration status accounting system's records and
reports in terms of purpose, general content, and accessibility.

6.0   SUPPORT ENVIRONMENT REQUIREMENTS AND TOOLS

Describe the use for configuration management of the
capabilities, rules, and tools provided by the support
environment.   For example:

o Controlled storage facilities
o Discrepancy and change reporting facilities
o Records management capabilities
o Access control capabilities

MANAGEMENT PLAN DOCUMENTATION STANDARD
CONFIGURATION MANAGEMENT PLAN DID: SMAP-DID-M920

7.0   ABBREVIATIONS AND ACRONYMS

Refer to the Management Plan Template DID (SMAP-DID-M999) for the detailed description of content for this section.

8.0   GLOSSARY

Refer to the Management Plan Template DID (SMAP-DID-M999) for the detailed description of content for this section.

9.0   NOTES

Refer to the Management Plan Template DID (SMAP-DID-M999) for the detailed description of content for this section.

10.0   APPENDICES

Refer to the Management Plan Template DID (SMAP-DID-M999) for the detailed description of content for this section.

C-1

ANNEX C to
STANAG 4159
(Edition 2)

CONFIGURATION MANAGEMENT PLAN

GENERAL

1. This Annex provides criteria to be followed in the development of Configuration Management Plans (CMPs) for the implementation of configuration management requirements on multinational joint projects.

2. The scope, organization and procedures for configuration management are described in several CMPs:

a.   the Project Management Office CMP;

b.   the contractor(s), CMP(s); and

c.   the CMP for the In-Service Phase if required.

These plans must be compatible.

3. All CMPs will be initiated as early as possible in the project.

4. This Annex mainly describes the requirements for the Project Management Office CMP.

CONTENT

5. The CMP is intended primarily as an exchange of information between participating organizations on configuration management policy and procedures.

6. The CMP shall include but need not be limited to the following:

a.   Introduction

   (1) Purpose and Scope. This paragraph shall state the purpose, scope, and general applicability of the CMP.

   (2) Description of the CI. The CI or family of CIs will be described. Included in the description will be a short statement of the mission and a list of the prime items including training devices and simulators showing their relationship to the work breakdown structure of the complete project.

   (3) Definitions. This paragraph shall reference applicable directives or glossaries containing definitions of terms.

N A T O   U N C L A S S I F I E D

(2) formatting, processing, and submitting of ECPs to the
     configuration control board;

(3) formatting, processing, and submitting of Requests for Deviations
     and Requests for Waivers;

(4) promulgation of decisions concerning ECPs, Deviations and
     Waivers; and

(5) ensuring that the implementation of approved changes is reflected
     in all configuration documentation.

f. Configuration Status Accounting. This section shall present the
    procedures for collecting, recording, processing, and maintaining data
    necessary for producing configuration status accounting reports. It
    shall include:

(1) formats and data elements for all CM status accounting records;
     and

(2) content and format of all CM reports.

g. Configuration Audits. This section shall include:

(1) procedures for functional configuration audits and physical
     configuration audits;

(2) format for the reporting results of configuration audits; and

(3) schedules for the conduct of CM audits.

h. Technical Reviews. A schedule of the technical reviews applicable to
    CM shall be listed in this section.

j. Configuration Management Major Milestones. This section shall
    identify Major CM-related milestones for the life cycle phases of the
    project.

APPROVAL

7. CMPs shall be submitted to the JCMC for approval.

Forms and Formats

The forms and formats in this section are provided to enable Configuration Management to design a form suitable for internal use, such as the P/CR, and for external or formal change formats agreed on the buyer and seller or imposed on the seller by the buyer.

It is important, however, that the form provide for unambiguous identification of the problem and affected software and provide for action and disposition taken by the CCB in order to enable a quick, but accurate, solution to a problem.

ENGINEERING CHANGE PROPOSAL, PAGE 1 (See MIL-STD-480 for instructions)	DATE (YYMMDD)	Form Approved OMB No. 0704-0188

Public reporting burden for this collection of information is estimated to average 2 hours per response, including the time for reviewing instructions, searching existing data sources, gathering and maintaining the data needed, and completing and reviewing the collection of information. Send comments regarding this burden estimate or any other aspect of this collection of information, including suggestions for reducing this burden, to Washington Headquarters Services, Directorate for Information Operations and Reports, 1215 Jefferson Davis Highway, Suite 1204, Arlington, VA 22202-4302, and to the Office of Information and Regulatory Affairs, Office of Management and Budget, Washington, DC 20503

PROCURING ACTIVITY NO.

1. ORIGINATOR NAME AND ADDRESS

2. CLASS OF ECP

3. JUST. CODE

4. PRIORITY

5. ECP DESIGNATION

a. MODEL / TYPE	b. CAGE CODE	c SYSTEM DESIGNATION

6. BASELINE AFFECTED
- ☐ FUNCTIONAL   ☐ ALLOCATED
- ☐ PRODUCT

d. ECP NO.	e. TYPE	f. REV	g. AMEND

7. OTHER SYS. / CONFIG. ITEMS AFFECTED
☐ YES   ☐ NO

8. SPECIFICATIONS AFFECTED - TEST PLAN	CAGE CODE	SPEC./DOC. NO	REV	SCN	9. DRAWINGS AFFECTED CAGE CODE	NUMBER	REV	NOR
a. SYSTEM								
b. ITEM								
c. TEST PLAN								

10. TITLE OF CHANGE

10 a. WEAPON SYSTEM CODE OR DESIGNATION

11. CONTRACT NO. AND LINE ITEM

12. PROCURING CONTRACTING OFFICER

CODE | TEL

13. CONFIGURATION ITEM NOMENCLATURE

14. IN PRODUCTION
☐ YES   ☐ NO

15. LOWEST ASSEMBLY AFFECTED

NOMENCLATURE	PART NO.	NSN

16. DESCRIPTION OF CHANGE

17. NEED FOR CHANGE

18. PRODUCTION EFFECTIVITY BY SERIAL NUMBER	19. EFFECT ON PRODUCTION DELIVERY SCHEDULE

20. RETROFIT

a. RECOMMENDED ITEM EFFECTIVITY	c. SHIP / VEHICLE CLASS AFFECTED
b. ESTIMATED KIT DELIVERY SCHEDULE	d. LOCATIONS OR SHIP / VEHICLE NUMBERS AFFECTED

21. ESTIMATED COSTS / SAVINGS UNDER CONTRACT	22. ESTIMATED NET TOTAL COSTS / SAVINGS

23. SUBMITTING ACTIVITY AUTHORIZED SIGNATURE	23.a. TITLE

24. APPROVAL / DISAPPROVAL

a. CLASS I	b. CLASS II	c. CLASS II
☐ APPROVAL RECOMMENDED ☐ DISAPPROVAL RECOMMENDED	☐ APPROVED ☐ DISAPPROVED	☐ CONCUR IN CLASSIFICATION OF CHANGE ☐ DO NOT CONCUR IN CLASSIFICATION OF CHANGE

d. GOVERNMENT ACTIVITY	SIGNATURE	DATE (YYMMDD)

e. APPROVAL	f. GOVERNMENT ACTIVITY	SIGNATURE	DATE (YYMMDD)
☐ APPROVED ☐ DISAPPROVED			

ENGINEERING CHANGE PROPOSAL, PAGE 2 (See MIL-STD-480 for instructions)	Form Approved OMB No. 0704-0188

Public reporting burden for this collection of information is estimated to average 1 hour per response, including the time for reviewing instructions, searching existing data sources, gathering and maintaining the data needed, and completing and reviewing the collection of information. Send comments regarding this burden estimate or any other aspect of this collection of information, including suggestions for reducing this burden, to Washington Headquarters Services, Directorate for Information Operations and Reports, 1215 Jefferson Davis Highway, Suite 1204, Arlington, VA 22202-4302, and to the Office of Information and Regulatory Affairs, Office of Management and Budget, Washington, DC 20503.

ORIGINATOR NAME AND ADDRESS	PROCURING ACTIVITY NUMBER
	ECP NUMBER

EFFECTS ON FUNCTIONAL / ALLOCATED CONFIGURATION IDENTIFICATION

25. OTHER SYSTEMS AFFECTED	26. OTHER CONTRACTORS / ACTIVITIES AFFECTED

27. CONFIGURATION ITEMS AFFECTED

28. EFFECTS ON PERFORMANCE ALLOCATIONS AND INTERFACES IN SYSTEM SPECIFICATION

29. EFFECTS ON EMPLOYMENT, INTEGRATED LOGISTICS SUPPORT, TRAINING, OPERATIONAL EFFECTIVENESS OR SOFTWARE

30. EFFECTS ON CONFIGURATION ITEM SPECIFICATIONS

31. DEVELOPMENTAL REQUIREMENTS AND STATUS

32. TRADE-OFFS AND ALTERNATIVE SOLUTIONS

33. DATE BY WHICH CONTRACTUAL AUTHORITY IS NEEDED

ENGINEERING CHANGE PROPOSAL, PAGE 3	Form Approved
(See MIL-STD-480 for instructions)	OMB No. 0704-0188

ORIGINATOR NAME AND ADDRESS

PROCURING ACTIVITY NUMBER

ECP NUMBER

EFFECTS ON PRODUCT CONFIGURATION IDENTIFICATION, LOGISTICS AND OPERATIONS

(X)	FACTOR	ENCL.	PAR.	(X)	FACTOR	ENCL.	PAR.
	34. EFFECT ON PRODUCT CONFIGURATION IDENTIFICATION OR CONTRACT				**36. EFFECT ON OPERATIONAL EMPLOYMENT**		
	a. PERFORMANCE				a. SAFETY		
	b. WEIGHT-BALANCE-STABILITY (Aircraft)				b. SURVIVABILITY		
	c. WEIGHT-MOMENT (Other equipment)				c. RELIABILITY		
	d. CDRL, TECHNICAL DATA				d. MAINTAINABILITY		
	e. NOMENCLATURE				e. SERVICE LIFE		
					f. OPERATING PROCEDURES		
	35. EFFECT ON INTEGRATED LOGISTICS SUPPORT (ILS) ELEMENTS				g. ELECTROMAGNETIC INTERFERENCE		
	a. ILS PLANS				h. ACTIVATION SCHEDULE		
	b. MAINTENANCE CONCEPT, PLANS AND PROCEDURES				i. CRITICAL SINGLE POINT FAILURE ITEMS		
	c. LOGISTICS SUPPORT ANALYSES				j. INTEROPERABILITY		
	d. INTERIM SUPPORT PROGRAMS						
	e. SPARES AND REPAIR PARTS				**37. OTHER CONSIDERATIONS**		
	f. TECH MANUALS/PROGRAMMING TAPES				a. INTERFACE		
	g. FACILITIES				b. OTHER AFFECTED EQUIPMENT/GFE/GFP		
	h. SUPPORT EQUIPMENT				c. PHYSICAL CONSTRAINTS		
	i. OPERATOR TRAINING				d. COMPUTER PROGRAMS AND RESOURCES		
	j. OPERATOR TRAINING EQUIPMENT				e. REWORK OF OTHER EQUIPMENT		
	k. MAINTENANCE TRAINING				f. SYSTEM TEST PROCEDURES		
	l. MAINTENANCE TRAINING EQUIPMENT				g. WARRANTY/GUARANTEE		
	m. CONTRACT MAINTENANCE				h. PARTS CONTROL		
	n. PACKAGING, HANDLING, STORAGE, TRANSPORTABILITY						

38. ALTERNATE SOLUTIONS

39. DEVELOPMENTAL STATUS

40. RECOMMENDATIONS FOR RETROFIT

41. WORK-HOURS PER UNIT TO INSTALL RETROFIT KITS				**42. WORK-HOURS TO CONDUCT SYSTEM TESTS AFTER RETROFIT**
a. ORGANIZATION	b. INTERMEDIATE	c. DEPOT	d. OTHER	

43. THIS CHANGE MUST BE ACCOMPLISHED	**44. IS CONTRACTOR FIELD SERVICE ENGINEERING REQUIRED?**	**45. OUT OF SERVICE TIME**
☐ BEFORE ☐ WITH ☐ AFTER THE FOLLOWING CHANGES	☐ YES ☐ NO	

46. EFFECT OF THIS ECP AND PREVIOUSLY APPROVED ECP'S ON ITEM	**47. DATE CONTRACTUAL AUTHORITY NEEDED FOR**
	PRODUCTION _____
	RETROFIT _____

ENGINEERING CHANGE PROPOSAL, PAGE 4

(See MIL-STD-480 for instructions)

Form Approved
OMB No. 0704-0188

Public reporting burden for this collection of information is estimated to average 3 hours per response, including the time for reviewing instructions, searching existing data sources, gathering and maintaining the data needed, and completing and reviewing the collection of information. Send comments regarding this burden estimate or any other aspect of this collection of information, including suggestions for reducing this burden, to Washington Headquarters Services, Directorate for Information Operations and Reports, 1215 Jefferson Davis Highway, Suite 1204, Arlington, VA 22202-4302, and to the Office of Information and Regulatory Affairs, Office of Management and Budget, Washington, DC 20503.

ORIGINATOR NAME AND ADDRESS

PROCURING ACTIVITY NUMBER

ECP NUMBER

48. ESTIMATED NET TOTAL COST IMPACT *(Use parentheses for savings)*

FACTOR	NON-RECURRING (1)	COSTS / SAVINGS UNDER CONTRACT			TOTAL (5)	OTHER COSTS/ SAVINGS TO THE GOVERNMENT (6)
		RECURRING				
		UNIT (2)	QUANTITY (3)	TOTAL (Recurring) (4)		
a. PRODUCTION COSTS / SAVINGS						
CONFIGURATION ITEM / CSCI						
FACTORY TEST EQUIPMENT						
SPECIAL FACTORY TOOLING						
SCRAP						
ENGINEERING, ENGINEERING DATA REVISION						
REVISION OF TEST PROCEDURES						
QUALIFICATION OF NEW ITEMS						
SUBTOTAL OF PROD COSTS / SAVINGS						
b. RETROFIT COSTS						
ENGINEERING DATA REVISION						
PROTOTYPE TESTING						
KIT PROOF TESTING						
RETROFIT KITS FOR OPERATIONAL SYSTEMS						
PREP. OF MWO / TCTO / SC / ALT / TD						
SPECIAL TOOLING FOR RETROFIT						
CONTRACTOR FIELD SERVICE ENGINEERING						
GOV'T PERSONNEL INSTALLATION						
TESTING AFTER RETROFIT						
MODIFICATION OF GFE / GFP						
QUALIFICATION OF GFE / GFP						
SUBTOTAL OF RETROFIT COSTS / SAVINGS						
c. INTEGRATED LOGISTICS SUPPORT COSTS/ SAVINGS						
SPARES / REPAIR PARTS REWORK						
NEW SPARES AND REPAIR PARTS						
SUPPLY / PROVISIONING DATA						
SUPPORT EQUIPMENT						
RETROFIT KITS FOR SPARES						
OPERATOR TRAINING COURSES						
MAINTENANCE TRAINING COURSES						
REV. OF TECH MAN./PROGRAMMING TAPES						
NEW TECH MAN./PROGRAMMING TAPES						
TRAINING / TRAINERS						
INTERIM SUPPORT						
MAINTENANCE MANPOWER						
COMPUTER PROGRAMS / DOCUMENTATION						
SUBTOTAL OF ILS COSTS / SAVINGS						
d. OTHER COSTS / SAVINGS						
e. SUBTOTAL COSTS / SAVINGS						
SUBTOTAL UNDER CONTRACT						
f. COORDINATION OF CHANGES WITH OTHER CONTRACTORS						
g. COORDINATION CHANGES BY GOVERNMENT						
ESTIMATED NET TOTAL COSTS / SAVINGS						

ENGINEERING CHANGE PROPOSAL, PAGE 5
(See MIL-STD-480 for instructions)

Form Approved
OMB No. 0704-0188

Public reporting burden for this collection of information is estimated to average 1 hour per response, including the time for reviewing instructions, searching existing data sources, gathering and maintaining the data needed, and completing and reviewing the collection of information. Send comments regarding this burden estimate or any other aspect of this collection of information, including suggestions for reducing this burden, to Washington Headquarters Services, Directorate for Information Operations and Reports, 1215 Jefferson Davis Highway, Suite 1204, Arlington, VA 22202-4302, and to the Office of Information and Regulatory Affairs, Office of Management and Budget, Washington, DC 20503.

ORIGINATOR NAME AND ADDRESS

PROCURING ACTIVITY NUMBER

ECP NUMBER

49. **ESTIMATED COSTS/SAVINGS SUMMARY, RELATED ECP'S** (Use parentheses for savings)	CAGE CODE (1)	ECP NUMBER (2)	COSTS/SAVINGS UNDER CONTRACTS (3)	OTHER COSTS SAVINGS TO GOVERNMENT (4)
a. PRODUCTION COSTS/SAVINGS (Subtotal of Costs/Savings Elements from block 48a applicable to aircraft, ship, tank, vehicle, missile or its subsystem)				
SUBTOTAL PRODUCTION COSTS/SAVINGS				
b. RETROFIT COSTS (Applicable to aircraft, ship, tank, vehicle, missile or its subsystem)				
SUBTOTAL RETROFIT COSTS				
c. INTEGRATED LOGISTICS SUPPORT COSTS/SAVINGS				
REVISED REQUIREMENTS				
1. ITEM RETROFIT (If not covered under "b") (Applicable to aircraft, ship, tank, vehicle, missile or its subsystem)				
2. ILS SUBTOTAL (Applicable to aircraft, ship, tank, vehicle, missile or its subsystem)				
3. OPERATOR TRAINER (Net total cost/saving from each ECP covering operator trainer)				
4. MAINTENANCE TRAINER (Net total cost/saving from each ECP covering maintenance trainer)				
5. OTHER TRAINING EQUIPMENT				
6. SUPPORT EQUIPMENT (Net total cost/saving from each ECP on support equipment)				
7. ILS PLANS				
8. MAINTENANCE CONCEPT, PLANS, SYSTEM DOCUMENTS				
9. INTERIM SUPPORT PLAN				

NEW REQUIREMENTS	PROCURING ACTIVITY CODE	NON-RECURRING COSTS	RECURRING COSTS				
			UNIT	QTY	TOTAL		
10. PROVISIONING DOCUMENTATION							
11. OPER TRNR/TRNG DEVICES/EQUIP							
12. MANUALS/PROGRAMMING TAPES, SPARES, REPAIR PARTS (For 11)							
13. MAINTENANCE TRNR/TRNG DEVICES/EQUIPMENT							
14. MANUALS/PROGRAMMING TAPES, SPARES, REPAIR PARTS (For 13)							
15. SUPPORT EQUIPMENT							
16. MANUALS/PROGRAMMING TAPES (For 15)							
17. PROVISIONING DOCUMENTATION (For 15)							
18. REPAIR PARTS (For 15)							
SUBTOTAL ILS COSTS/SAVINGS (Sum of c.1 through c.18)							

d. OTHER COSTS/SAVINGS (Total from block 48d of related ECP's)	CAGE CODE	ECP NUMBER		
TOTAL OTHER COSTS/SAVINGS				
SUBTOTALS OF COLUMNS				
SUBTOTAL UNDER CONTRACT				
e. ESTIMATED NET TOTAL COSTS/SAVINGS (a + b + c + d)				

ENGINEERING CHANGE PROPOSAL, PAGE 6 (MILESTONE CHART)
(See MIL-STD-480 for instructions)

DATE (YYMMDD)

Form Approved
OMB No. 0704-0188

Public reporting burden for this collection of information is estimated to average 30 minutes per response, including the time for reviewing instructions, searching existing data sources, gathering and maintaining the data needed, and completing and reviewing the collection of information. Send comments regarding this burden estimate or any other aspect of this collection of information, including suggestions for reducing this burden, to Washington Headquarters Services, Directorate for Information Operations and Reports, 1215 Jefferson Davis Highway, Suite 1204, Arlington, VA 22202-4302, and to the Office of Information and Regulatory Affairs, Office of Management and Budget, Washington, DC 20503.

ORIGINATOR NAME AND ADDRESS

PROCURING ACTIVITY NUMBER

CAGE CODE

ECP NUMBER

CONFIGURATION ITEM NOMENCLATURE

TITLE OF CHANGE

DATE AUTHORIZATION TO PROCEED
RECEIVED BY CONTRACTOR

S — START DELIVERY   C — COMPLETE DELIVERY   ▼ PROGRESS POINT

	NO. OF MONTHS	1	2	3	4	5	6	7	8	9	10	11	12	13	14	15	16	17	18	19	20	21	22	23	24	25	26	27	28	29	30	31	32	33	34	35	36
C O N F I G U R A T I O N I T E M	PRODUCTION																																				
	TECH MANUALS																																				
	RETROFIT																																				
	MWO/TCTO/SC/ALT/TD																																				
	SPARES/REPAIR PARTS																																				
	SOFTWARE																																				
S U P P O R T E Q U I P M E N T	PRODUCTION																																				
	TECH MANUALS/PROG. TAPES																																				
	RETROFIT																																				
	MWO/TCTO/SC/ALT/TD																																				
	REPAIR PARTS																																				
T R A I N E R	OPERATOR																																				
	MAINTENANCE																																				
	NO. OF MONTHS	1	2	3	4	5	6	7	8	9	10	11	12	13	14	15	16	17	18	19	20	21	22	23	24	25	26	27	28	29	30	31	32	33	34	35	36

ORIGINATOR – AUTEUR

FILE NUMBER   NUMÉRO DE DOSSIER

PMRB NUMBER – NUMERO CPEM

CFTO – ITFC

$\begin{pmatrix}\text{for CF use only} \\ \text{Réservé aux FC}\end{pmatrix}$

AEROSPACE
ENGINEERING CHANGE PROPOSAL

PROJET DE MODIFICATION
DE MATÉRIEL AÉROSPATIAL

SECTION I

1. CONTRACTOR AECP NUMBER			Numéro PMMA du constructeur ou réparateur

REVISION Révision	DATE	CATEGORY Catégorie	CONTRACT CD NUMBER (if applicable) Numéro du contrat ou de la demande de contrat (s'il y a lieu)

2. NAME OF COMPLETE ASSEMBLY (aircraft, engine, etc) Nom de l'ensemble (aéronef, moteur, etc.)	MODEL/TYPE DESIGNATION Appellation du modèle ou du type	AECP TITLE – Titre du PMMA

3. PART OR SUB ASSEMBLY AFFECTED Pièce ou sous-ensemble touché	
	NATO STOCK NUMBER Numéro nomenclature OTAN
	PART NUMBER Numéro de pièce
	MODEL TYPE Modèle ou type

4. NATURE OF CHANGE – Nature de la modification

CF 695 (11/76)

5. CHECK ITEMS THAT ARE AFFECTED BY THE CHANGE AND EXPLAIN IN BLOCK 6 OR BY ATTACHMENT
Cocher les articles touchés par la modification et donner des explications à la case 6 ou sur feuillet annexé.

AIRWORTHINESS
Navigabilité ☐

COMBAT EFFECTIVENESS
Efficacité au combat ☐

PERFORMANCE
Rendement ☐

OPERATING PROCEDURES
Méthodes d'exploitation ☐

INTERCHANGEABILITY
Interchangeabilité ☐

OVERHAUL METHODS
Méthodes de révision ☐

ELECTRO MAGNETIC COMPATIBILITY & ELECTRICAL LOADING
Compatibilité électro-magnétique et charge électrique ☐

WEIGHT & BALANCE
Masse et centrage ☐

TOOLS & TEST EQUIPMENT
Outils et matériel d'essai ☐

MAINTENANCE PROCEDURES
Méthodes d'entretien ☐

SPARES
Pièces de rechange ☐

SIMULATORS & TRAINERS
Simulateurs et maquettes d'instructions ☐

AMSE
Matériel aéronautique de servitude ☐

OTHER
Divers ☐

6. REASON FOR CHANGE — Raison de la modification

7. CHANGE INITIATED BY CONTRACTOR FOR — Modification proposée par le constructeur ou le réparateur pour:

COMPLIANCE WITH NEW OR REVISED SPEC
Se conformer à une nouvelle norme ou à une norme révisée

(quote Spec number and CF authority — Citer le numéro de la norme et l'autorité FC)
FIX FOR UCR NUMBER
Donner suite au RENS N°

(quote UCR number and CF authority — Citer le numéro du RENS et l'autorité FC)
COMPLIANCE WITH CF INSTRUCTION NUMBER
Se conformer à l'instruction des FC n°

(quote CF Instruction Number and CF authority — Citer le numéro de l'instruction des FC et l'autorité FC)
OTHER
Autre raison

8. EFFECT ON WEIGHT AND BALANCE — Influence sur masse et centrage

WEIGHT CHANGE Changement de masse	LBS lb	AT STATION à la référence

VERIFIED AIRCRAFT PROJECT OFFICER — Vérifié Officier de projets (aérona fs)

SIGNATURE	DESIGNATION — Fonction	DATE

9. ELECTRO MAGNETIC COMPATIBILITY AND ELECTRICAL LOADING ASSESSMENT
Evaluation de la compatibilité électro-magnétique et de la charge électrique

SPECIAL OFFICER — Officier spécialiste

SIGNATURE	DESIGNATION — Fonction	DATE

10. NON RECURRING COSTS — Frais non répétés

	MAN HOURS Heures-hommes	COST MH Coût/ heures-hommes	TOTAL
ENGINEERING Technologie			
TOOLING Outillage			
PUBLICATIONS			
TRAINING Formation			
PROTOTYPE			
OTHER Divers			

11. COST OF KITS/REWORK ITEMS — Coût des lots de modifications ou des articles réusinés

	MAN HOURS heures-hommes	COST MH Coût/ heures-hommes	TOTAL
MATERIAL PER KIT — Matériel par lot			
FABRICATION/REWORK (per item or kit) Fabrication ou réusinage (par articles ou par lot)			
ASSEMBLY PER ITEM KIT Assemblage par article ou par lot			
OTHER Divers			

TOTAL COST PER KIT REWORK
COÛT TOTAL PAR LOT OU PAR ARTICLE RÉUSINÉ   a) _____

INSTALLATION COST (per kit)
FRAIS D'INSTALLATION (par lot)   b) _____

TOTAL KIT REWORK PLUS INSTALLATION PER KIT   = a + b =
TOTAL LOT OU RÉUSINAGE PLUS INSTALLATION PAR LOT   _____

12. NUMBER OF KITS (include spares training and trainers)
Nombre de lots (y compris rechange, formation et maquettes)   (c) _____

NUMBER OF INSTALLATIONS
Nombre d'installations   (d) _____

TOTAL KIT COST (a x c)
Coût total des lots (a x c)   (e) _____

TOTAL INSTALLATION COST (b x d)
Coût total des installations (b x d)   (f) _____

TOTAL COST KITS PLUS INSTALLATION (e + f)
Coût total: lots plus installations (e + f)   (g) _____

DUTY AND TAXES (if applicable)
Douane et taxes (s'il y a lieu)   (h) _____

GRAND TOTAL
(non recurring + total kits + installations cost + duty and taxes)
(para 10 total + g + h)
(Frais non répétés + coût des lots + coût des installations + douanes et taxes)
(total du par. 10 + g + h)   _____

13 CHECK ITEMS THAT ARE AFFECTED AND LIST CFTO OR PUBLICATION (Attach list if necessary)
Cocher les publications touchées et en indiquer le numéro (annexer un feuillet au besoin)

AIRCRAFT OPERATING INSTRUCTIONS Instructions d'exploitation de matériel aérien	☐	CFTO/PUB ITFC/Public.	_____
DESCRIPTION AND MAINTENANCE Description et instructions d'entretien	☐	CFTO/PUB ITFC/Public.	_____
REPAIR AND OVERHAUL/REPAIR SCHEMES Instructions de réparation et de révision	☐	CFTO/PUB ITFC/Public.	_____
PARTS LIST Nomenclature des pièces	☐	CFTO/PUB ITFC/Public.	_____
SIMULATORS AND TRAINERS Simulateurs et maquettes d'instruction	☐	CFTO/PUB ITFC/Public.	_____
OTHER Divers	☐	CFTO/PUB ITFC/Public.	_____

14. LIST DRAWINGS AFFECTED – Dessins touchés

---

15. **ASSEMBLY IN PRODUCTION?** Incorporation lors de la fabrication? YES ☐ NO ☐ Oui Non	IF YES – ESTIMATE EFFECTIVE DATE OR SERIAL NUMBERS Le cas échéant, date approximative de prise d'effet ou premier numéro de série modifié	IF YES – IS GOVERNMENT SUPPLIED MATERIAL AFFECTED? Le cas échéant, est-ce que le matériel fourni par l'État est touché? YES ☐ NO ☐ Oui Non DATE REQUIRED AT PLANT Les lots doivent arriver à l'usine le

---

16. DOES CONTRACTOR RECOMMEND THAT CHANGES BE MADE RETROACTIVE ON ITEMS ALREADY DELIVERED TO CF?
Est-ce que le constructeur ou le réparateur recommande que les modifications soient incorporées aux articles déjà livrés?

YES ☐ NO ☐ IF YES COMPLETE BLOCKS 17, 18, 19, 20 AND SECTION 2.
Oui Non Le cas échéant, remplir les cases 17, 18, 19 et 20, ainsi que la section 2.

REASONS FOR RECOMMENDATION – Raisons de la recommandation

---

17. SERIAL NUMBERS AFFECTED (aircraft, engine, components) Numéros de série touchés (aéronefs, moteur, organes)	WHEN MODIFICATION SHOULD BE EMBODIED? (ie next periodic, on overhaul) Quand la modification devrait-elle être incorporée? (ex. prochaine inspection périodique, révision)
18. BY WHOM WORK SHOULD BE PERFORMED (ie mobile repair party contractor) Par qui la modification devrait-elle être incorporée? (ex. équipe mobile de réparation, réparateur)	SOURCE OF KITS OR PARTS Source des lots ou des pièces DATE AVAILABLE Disponibles le

19. ASSOCIATED MODIFICATIONS (CFTO Number and Title if known)
    Modifications connexes (Citer le n° et le nom de l'ITFC, autant que possible)

20. SPECIAL INSTRUCTIONS RE SPARES IN STOCK
    Instructions spéciales sur les pièces de rechange en stock

21. CONTRACTORS CERTIFICATION — Attestation du constructeur ou du réparateur
    REMARKS — Remarques

| SIGNATURE |
| DESIGNATION/POSITION
Fonction |
| DATE |

22. AREA CANADIAN FORCES REPRESENTATIVE — REMARKS
    Remarques du représentant régional des CF

| SIGNATURE |
| RANK — Grade |
| DESIGNATION — Fonction |
| DATE |

SECTION 2

MODIFICATION DATA — LISTE DES PIECES

PARTS REQUIRED NATO STOCK NUMBER Pièces nécessaires Numéro nomenclature OTAN	PART NUMBER Numéro de pièces	DESCRIPTION	QUANTITY Quantité

24. CERTIFIED THAT — Je certifie que:

   (a) NATO stock numbers are correct
      les numéros de nomenclature OTAN sont exacts,

   (b) Items without NSN are accounted for by part number
      les articles sans NNO sont comptabilisés par numéro de pièce,

   (c) Cataloguing action initiated on items listed at para (b) above
      des mesures ont été prises pour cataloguer les articles énumérés en (b) et

   (d) Modification kit alloted NSN
      qu'on a donné au lot de modification le NNO

TECHNICAL AUTHORITY/EQUIPMENT SPECIALIST — Responsable technique/spécialiste du matériel
REMARKS — Remarques

SIGNATURE
RANK — Grade
DESIGNATION — Fonction
DATE

25. MODIFICATION DATA – LISTE DES PIÈCES

- PARTS REMOVED NATO STOCK NUMBER Pièces déposés Numéro nomenclature OTAN	PART NUMBER Numéro de pièce	DESCRIPTION	QUANTITY Quantité	DISPOSAL CLASS Catégorie d'affecta. (SEE PARA 26) (Voir par. 26)

26. STANDARD DISPOSAL CLASSES – CATÉGORIES RÉGULIÈRES D'AFFECTATION

(a) Items removed as a result of this modification, plus total stocks of these items, are of no further use to the CFSS.
Les articles déposés à la suite de la présente modification ainsi que tous les stocks de ces articles ne sont plus d'aucune utilité au SAFC.

(b) Items removed as a result of this modification, are of no further use to the CFSS. Serviceable items in stock are required.
Les articles déposés à la suite de la présente modification ne sont plus d'aucune utilité au SAFC. Les articles en stock et en état de service doivent être retenus.

(c) Items removed as a result of this modification, if serviceable, are to be returned to stock.
Les articles qui sont déposés à la suite de la présente modification et qui sont en état de service, doivent être remis en stock.

(d) Repairable items removed are to be actioned in accordance with CFP 189.
Les articles déposés et réparables doivent être traités conformément à la PFC 189.

(e) Items not listed in CFP 189 are to be reported to NDHQ/DPSUPS5 requesting allotment of repair authority.
Les articles qui ne figurent pas à la PFC 189 doivent être signalés au QGDN/DOMSA5 pour qu'il en autorise la réparation.

(f) Items removed as a result of this modification plus total stocks are to be retained for instructional purposes.
Les articles déposés à la suite de la présente modification ainsi que tous les stocks de ces articles doivent être retenus comme matériel didactique.

(g) Items removed as a result of this modification, plus total stock, are to be reworked and reused.
Les articles déposés à la suite de la présente modification ainsi que tous les stocks de ces articles doivent être réusinés et réutilisés.

27. APPROPRIATE DISPOSAL ACTION TAKEN FOR ITEMS LISTED AT PARA 25.
Les mesures appropriées ont été prises pour l'élimination des articles énumérés au par. 25.

TECHNICAL AUTHORITY/EQUIPMENT SPECIALIST – Responsable technique/spécialiste du matériel
REMARKS – Remarques

SIGNATURE	
RANK – Grade	
DESIGNATION – Fonction	
DATE	

National Defence	Défense nationale		CONTRACTOR'S SERIAL NO / N° D'ORDRE DE L'ENTREPRENEUR
			CONTRACT DEMAND NO / N° DE LA DEMANDE DE CONTRAT
DESIGN CHANGE/DEVIATION			DSS CONTRACT SERIAL NO / N° D'ORDRE DU CONTRAT DU MAS
MODIFICATION DU MODÈLE OU ÉCART AUTORISÉ			DSS FILE NO / N° DU DOSSIER DU MAS
Change Modification ☐ Deviation Écart ☐			DESIGN AUTHORITY SERIAL NO / N° D'ORDRE DU BUREAU TECHNIQUE RESPONSABLE

PART – PARTIE – I

1 ITEM AFFECTED – ARTICLE TOUCHÉ

2 MAIN EQUIPMENT(S) AFFECTED – MATÉRIEL TOUCHÉ.

3. DESCRIPTION OF DEPARTURE FROM ORIGINAL TECHNICAL DATA
DESCRIPTION DES POINTS QUI DIFFÈRENT DES DONNÉES TECHNIQUES

4. REASON FOR REQUEST – NOTIF DE LA DEMANDE

5. WILL INTERCHANGEABILITY BE AFFECTED? –
L'INTERCHANGEABILITÉ EST-ELLE RÉDUITE?   Component Parts – Yes ☐ No ☐   Assemblies – Yes ☐ No ☐
Organes – Oui   Non   Ensembles – Oui   Non

6 WILL SPARE PARTS SCHEDULE BE AFFECTED?
LE TABLEAU EN PIÈCES DE RECHANGE EST-IL MODIFIÉ?   Yes ☐ No ☐   (If "YES" state details)
Oui   Non   (Le cas échéant, donner des détails)

7 PRODUCTION DATA – RENSEIGNEMENTS SUR LA PRODUCTION

7 1 COST AND DELIVERY
COÛT ET LIVRAISON

  7 1 1 Estimated Effect on Delivery
    Effet prévu sur la livraison _____

  7 1 2 Estimated Added Tooling Cost $
    Coût supplémentaire prévu de l'usinage $ _____

  7 1 3 Estimated Surplus Material Value $
    Valeur prévue des matériaux supplémentaires $ _____

  7 1 4 Estimated Change in Contract Cost
    Including Sales Tax and 7 1 2 and
    7 1 3 above (indicate + or –) $
    variation prévue du coût stipulé dans le contrat
    (y compris la taxe de vente et les montants
    prévus en 7 1 2 et 7 1 3) (indiquer + ou –) $ _____

7 2 PRODUCTION CHANGE POINT
INTRODUCTION DE LA MODIFICATION

  7 2 1 Estimated Starting Date and Serial No
    Date d'introduction et
    N° de série prévue _____

  7 2 2 Total Number of Units Involved
    Nombre total d'unités touchées _____

7 3 RECOMMENDATIONS FOR PRIOR BUILT UNITS IN SERVICE
RECOMMANDATIONS QUANT AUX UNITÉS DÉJÀ EN SERVICE

  7 3.1 Should Prior-Built Units be modified?
    Les unités déjà en service devraient-elles   Yes ☐ No ☐
    être modifiées?   Oui   Non

  7.3.2 Estimated Cost Per Unit – Coût prévu par unité

    Cost of Kit
    Coût du lot $ _____

    Cost of Rework
    Coût de réusinage $ _____

  7.3.3 Government held Spare Parts –
    Pièces de rechange appartenant à l'État

    Use ☐   Rework ☐   Scrap ☐
    Utilisez   Réusinage   Mise au rebut

    Estimated Cost Each to Rework or Replace $
    Coût unitaire prévu du réusinage ou du remplacement $ _____

8 ORIGINATOR – AUTEUR DE LA DEMANDE

DATE	SIGNATURE (if other than Prime Contractor / autre que l'entrepreneur principal)	DATE	SIGNATURE (Prime Contractor / entrepreneur principal)

DND 672 (8-84) 7530-21-846-6621

PART – PARTIE II

9. RECOMMENDATIONS OR QUALITY ASSURANCE REPRESENTATIVE – RECOMMENDATIONS DU REPRÉSENTANT DE L'ASSURANCE DE LA QUALITÉ

DATE	DESIGNATION – DÉSIGNATION	SIGNATURE

10. RECOMMENDATIONS OF DESIGN AUTHORITY – RECOMMENDATIONS DU BUREAU TECHNIQUE RESPONSABLE

Approved:
Approuvé: Change
             Modification ☐   Deviation
                                 Écart ☐   Per Part I
                                                   Voir partie I ☐   or
                                                                     ou   See remarks
                                                                           Voir observations ☐   Not approved
                                                                                                    Royetée

DATE	DESIGNATION – DÉSIGNATION	SIGNATURE

11. APPROVAL OF PROCUREMENT AUTHORITY – APPROBATION DE L'INSTANCE D'ACQUISITION

DATE	DESIGNATION – DÉSIGNATION	SIGNATURE

12. REFERENCES – DOCUMENTS DE RÉFÉRENCE (Departmental file numbers etc. – numéros de dossier ministère etc.)

13. AUTHORIZED PRODUCTION ACTION ON THIS CONTRACT – MESURE DE PRODUCTION AUTORISÉE POUR LE PRÉSENT CONTRAT

a. Change
   Modification ☐

When to take effect:
Prise d'effet: _____

b. Deviation
   Écart ☐   TOTAL NUMBER OF UNITS INVOLVED
                NOMBRE D'UNITÉS TOUCHÉES _____

| | Complete Units
Unités entières | Assemblies
Ensembles | Component Parts
Organes |
|------------------------------|------|------|------|
| Existing Stock
Stock actuel | Use
Utilisez | ☐ | ☐ | ☐ |
| | Rework
Réusinage | ☐ | ☐ | ☐ |
| | Scrape
Mise au rebut | ☐ | ☐ | ☐ |

SERIAL NO. S
N° (S) DE SÉRIE _____

14. FORM DND 678 REQUIRED FROM MANUFACTURER
    DND 678 EXIGÉE DU FABRICANT MESURE À PRENDRE À L'ÉGARD DU MATÉRIEL EN STOCK ET EN SERVICE   Yes
Oui ☐   No
Non ☐

15. ACTION ON EQUIPMENT IN STOCK AND USE – MESURE À PRENDRE À L'ÉGARD DU MATÉRIEL EN STOCK ET EN SERVICE:

16. ACTION ON SPARES IN STOCK – MESURE À PRENDRE À L'ÉGARD DES PIÈCES DE RECHANGE EN STOCK:

| 17. DATE | SIGNATURE (for Department of National Defence
pour le ministère de la Défense Nationale) | 18. DATE | SIGNATURE (for Department of Supply and Services
pour le ministère des Approvisionnements et Services) |
|----------|--------|----------|--------|
| | | | |

| 19. DISTRIBUTION LIST – LISTE DE DIFFUSION | Copies
Exemplaires | DISTRIBUTION LIST – LISTE DE DIFFUSION | Copies
Exemplaires |
|--|----------|--|----------|
| | | | |

MINIMUM CONTENTS FOR DISCREPANCY (NRCA) REPORT

EXPLANATORY NOTE

The purpose of the report is to state a discrepancy to a product or product specification. The process of filing a report of this type may be referred to as nonconformance reporting and corrective action (NRCA). A nonconformance is defined as any deviation of a product or process from applicable requirements, standards, or procedures. The requirement for reports of this type and the process for analysis and disposition is specified in the management plan. The information listed below is considered to be the minimum content for a Discrepancy (NRCA) report.

Topics to be included in the Discrepancy (NRCA) report are:

o Report identification (Discrepancy Report or NRCA number)

o Originator identification including
   - name and organization
   - address and phone
   - unit or site of occurrence

o Product identification including
   - name
   - version number (plus release date if applicable)
   - if applicable, environment information (e.g., hardware and operating system for a software product)
   - life-cycle phase in which nonconformance detected

o Discrepancy Report (NRCA) information including
   - title
   - date
   - type of nonconformance
   - description
   - recommendation for proposed solution (if any), including code, data, or documentation where corrective action must be taken

o Approval authority including
   - criticality
   - disposition
   - resolution
   - implementation schedule
   - date/version of the item in which the corrective action will be included
   - authority signature
   - date tested
   - date of closure

CONFIGURATION CONTROL

GENERAL

1.   Configuration control serves to support the standardization of defence materiel, provides procedures for the uniform implementation of engineering changes, and avoids interoperability and supportability problems resulting from uncoordinated engineering changes caused by independent, individual actions of the participants in a multi-national joint project.

2.   Fundamental to configuration control is the concept of project management by baselines. This concept presupposes that there must be a recognized, documented and formally approved statement of requirements (i.e. a functional baseline), and that once stated, any change in requirements will be documented so that the current status of the project is known at any point in time.

3.   Baseline documentation also provides a basis for cost estimates and is essential to establish the effect of engineering changes on overall costs.

ENGINEERING CHANGE PROPOSALS

4.   Engineering Change Proposals (ECPs) affecting a configuration baseline of a JCI may originate from a nation, the Project Management Office, a contractor or an Interface Control Group.

5.   All ECPs should be prepared in an agreed format and submitted to the Project Management Office for review and processing.

6.   The Project Management Office will ensure that a file of all ECPs and their rationale for approval/disapproval are maintained. When an ECP is disapproved, the ECP and the rationale for disapproval shall be returned to the proposer.

7.   Supporting data required to be submitted with each ECP shall include, but not be limited to, the following:

      a.   Project name, JCIs affected, configuration identification documents, numbers and title, description of change to functional and physical characteristics, reason for change, and consequence of disapproval, alternatives.

    c.   <u>Routine</u>. Routine is to be assigned if "emergency" and "urgent" are not applicable; usually applies in the in-service phase when the change can be implemented in conjunction with routine maintenance.

9.   The JCMC will review the priority rating and ensure timely action. The JCMC may re-assign a priority rating when appropriate.

10.   The priority rating will determine the speed with which the ECP is reviewed, evaluated, ordered and implemented.

<u>AUTHORIZATION CRITERIA</u>

11.   The JCMC will normally consider favourable only those ECPs which are for purposes of:

    a.   Eliminating hazardous conditions to personnel or materiel safety.

    b.   Complying with the relevant (national) safety regulations and legal requirements.

    c.   Correcting excessive and recurrent malfunctions and frequently occuring unscheduled maintenance.

    d.   Achieving considerable savings in procurement and/or lifecycle costs.

    e.   Increasing significantly the effectiveness of mission operational capabilities.

12.   If none of the above criteria are pertinent, the ECP should not be submitted to the JCMC. The general process of engineering change authorization is illustrated in Figure 8 of Annex J.

<u>DEVIATIONS AND WAIVERS</u>

13.   Deviations and Waivers are also a means by which authorization of changes to configuration items may be achieved. Requests for Deviations or Requests for Waivers shall be referred to the Project Management Office in an agreed format for action as appropriate.

PROBLEM/CHANGE REPORT   PCR NO._____

SYSTEM/PROJ _____   PAGE _____ OF _____

PCR

TITLE/DESCRIPTION		SITE	CONTRACT NO.

PROBLEM DATE/TIME	FAILED OR SUSPECTED ELEMENT (NAME)	ELEMENT ID NO.	VER/REV	NEXT HIGHER LEVEL ID NO

TEST NAME	RELATED DOCUMENT (TITLE)	DOCUMENT NO	REV

SUBMITTED BY	DATE	ECP NO.	CLASS ☐ I ☐ II	CUSTOMER CONCURRENCE IN CLASSIFICATION DATE	EFFECTIVITY

PROBLEM DESCRIPTION:

SUMMARY OF CHANGE AND REASON:

—SOFTWARE ELEMENTS AND DOCUMENTS CHANGED

SOFTWARE ELEMENT NAME OR DOCUMENT TITLE	IDENTIFICATION NO.	NEXT HIGHER LEVEL ID NO	NEW VER/REV

ACTION REQUIRED TO CLOSE:

IMPACT ON:	Y	N		Y	N		Y	N		Y	N	
☐ PSL			SCHEDULE			TEST EQUIPMENT/SW			DELIVERABLE HDW			SW DOCUMENTATION
☐ ML			SUBCONTRACT			FIRMWARE			TRAINING			SUPPORT SW/SW TOOLS
			DATA ITEM			FACILITY/SITE			SW MANUALS			OTHER

SRB DISPOSITION   ☐ APPROVE   ☐ DISAPPROVE   ☐ DEFER UNTIL:

SRB CHAIRPERSON	DATE	SYSTEMS ENGR	DATE	SRB MEMBER	DATE	SRB MEMBER	DATE
PROBLEM/CHANGE TYPE		ASSIGNED TO	DATE	PRIORITY	SCHED DATE	ANALYSIS TIME DATE COMPLETE (HRS)	

SCCB DISPOSITION   ☐ APPROVE   ☐ DISAPPROVE   ☐ DEFER UNTIL:

SCCB CHAIRPERSON	DATE	SW PROJECT LEADER	DATE	SYSTEMS ENGR	DATE	PROGRAM MGMT	DATE
CONFIGURATION MGMT	DATE	QUALITY ASSURANCE	DATE	SOFTWARE TEST	DATE	ILS MGMT	DATE

CLOSURE ACTION

INCORPORATED BY	DATE	VERIFIED BY	DATE	INCORP. TIME (HRS)	VERIF. TIME (HRS)	CLOSED BY	DATE

PROBLEM/CHANGE REPORT

PCR NO. _____

CONTINUATION SHEET

PAGE _____ OF _____

SOFTWARE ELEMENT NAME OR DOCUMENT TITLE	IDENTIFICATION NO.	NEXT HIGHER LEVEL ID NO	NEW VER/REV

PCR

SOFTWARE TROUBLE REPORT   STR _____

TITLE/DESCRIPTION			CONTRACT	REPORT DATE
PROBLEM DATE/TIME	SITE	COMPUTER/TERMINAL	OPERATING SYSTEM	
TEST NAME	FAILED OR SUSPECTED MODULE/SPEC		VERSION	

PROBLEM DESCRIPTION

ACTION REQUESTED/RECOMMENDED

SUBMITTED BY/DATE	ASSIGNED TO/DATE	APPROVED BY/DATE
DATE RC'D/CMO	BY:	PRIORITY:

DISPOSITION

CLOSED BY:	DATE:

PROGRAM TROUBLE REPORT

PTR NO._____

PTR

TITLE: DESCRIPTION		PROJECT IDENTIFIER	CONTRACT NO.
PROBLEM DATE: TIME	SITE	COMPUTER/TERMINAL	OPERATING SYSTEM

TEST NAME	FAILED OR SUSPECTED ELEMENT (NAME)	ELEMENT ID NO.	VER/REV

RELATED S W DOCUMENT TITLE	S/W DOC. NO.	CURR REV

PROBLEM DESCRIPTION:

ACTION REQUESTED: RECOMMENDED

SUBMITTED BY: DATE	ASSIGNED TO/DATE	PRIORITY H M L	SCHED. COMPL. DATE

SOFTWARE REVIEW BOARD DISPOSITION ☐ APPROVE ☐ DISAPPROVE ☐ DEFER DATE: CODE:

SRB CHAIRPERSON	DATE	SRB MEMBER	DATE	SRB MEMBER	DATE	SRB MEMBER	DATE

DISPOSITION:

S W DOC(S) REQ CHANGE ☐ Y ☐ N	DCR OR SCN NO.(S)	ATTACH TO SCO NO.(S)	RELATED ECO NO.(S)

SOFTWARE CHANGE ORDER   SCO NO.＿＿＿＿＿

PAGE ＿＿＿   OF ＿＿＿

SCO

SOFTWARE ELEMENT NAME	VER/REV	IDENTIFICATION NO.	NEXT HIGHER LEVEL ID NO.	NEW VER/REV

REQUESTED BY	DATE	PROJECT IDENTIFIER	ECP/SCP/SEP NO. CLASS ☐ I ☐ II	CONTRACT NO.

TOP LEVEL S/W PROGRAM NAME	TOP LEVEL ID NO.	OTHER USING PROJECTS

PTR(S) ATTACHED:

1. SUMMARY OF CHANGE AND REASON PER ATTACHED PTRs: (ATTACH ADDITIONAL PAGES AS NECESSARY)

2. ACTION REQUIRED: (ATTACH DCR(S) IF AFFECTED)

  A. SOFTWARE ELEMENTS: ＿＿＿＿＿＿＿＿＿＿＿＿＿＿＿＿＿＿＿＿＿＿＿＿＿＿＿＿＿
  ＿＿＿
  ＿＿＿

  B. DOCUMENTATION: (ATTACH DCR(S) IF AFFECTED) ＿＿＿＿＿＿＿＿＿＿＿＿＿＿＿＿＿
  ＿＿＿
  ＿＿＿

  C. TESTS: ＿＿＿＿＿＿＿＿＿＿＿＿＿＿＿＿＿＿＿＿＿＿＿＿＿＿＿＿＿＿＿＿＿＿＿＿
  ＿＿＿

3. COST ESTIMATE OF CHANGE	☐ INCREASE ☐ DECREASE ☐ N/A	4. RELATIONSHIP TO OTHER CHANGES: (REF. RELATED H/W ECO)
HRS $		

5. SCHEDULE:	6. EFFECTIVITY

7. IMPACT ON:

	Y	N		Y	N		Y	N		Y	N	
			SCHEDULE			TEST SOFTWARE			DELIVERABLE HDW			HOST/TARGET COMPUTER
			CUSTOMER SPEC			SOFTWARE TOOLS			FACILITY/SITE			SW DOCUMENTATION
			SUBCONTRACT			FIRMWARE			TRAINING			DATA ITEM
			SUPPORT SOFTWARE			TEST EQUIP HDW			SW MANUALS			OTHER:

SOFTWARE REVIEW BOARD DISPOSITION   ☐ APPROVE   ☐ DISAPPROVE   ☐ DEFER   DATE:＿＿＿   CODE:＿＿＿

SRB CHAIRPERSON	DATE	SRB MEMBER	DATE	SRB MEMBER	DATE	SRB MEMBER	DATE

SOFTWARE CHANGE CONTROL BOARD DISPOSITION   ☐ APPROVE   ☐ DISAPPROVE   ☐ DEFER   DATE:＿＿＿   CODE:＿＿＿

SOFTWARE ENGR.	DATE	CONFIGURATION MGMT.	DATE	SOFTWARE TEST	DATE		DATE
S/W TEAM LEADER	DATE	PROGRAM MGMT.	DATE	SYSTEMS ENGR.	DATE		DATE
PROJECT S/W MGMT.	DATE	QUALITY ASSURANCE	DATE	PRODUCT SUPPORT	DATE		DATE

<u>CRITERIA FOR CCB DECISIONS</u>

1. Operational Impact

2. Contractual Requirements, Including Cost Schedule and Fee

3. Produceability

4. Feasibility

5. Impact on Performance

6. Impact on Standardization

7. Safety Factors

8. Human Engineering Factors

9. Impact on Rework

10. Retrofit Requirements

11. Impact on Support Equipment, Test Equipment, Support Software, Training Equipment/Simulator Programs

12. Impact on Documentation and Technical/Field Manuals

13. Testability Impact

14. Impact on Other Using Programs

15. Impact on Functions Performing Work Affected by the Change

16. Resources Availability

17. Parts Availability

18. Substitute/Exchangeable Parts Considerations

19. Cost of Incorporating Change

20. Total Impact of Incorporation

21. Serial Number(s) and Effectivity of Change

Subcontractor Control

Subcontractors should be considered an extension of the buyer organization in responding to the buyer's customer's requirements. CM should require that prospective subcontractors perform in the same way the buyer's CM activity will perform. The following matrix provides guidance on what should be required for several types of subcontracts. The questionnaire provides a means to determine if the prospective subcontractor meets the buyer's requirements [72].

SUBCONTRACTOR/VENDOR CM REQUIREMENTS MATRIX

	DEVELOP-MENT ITEMS	MODIFIED OFF-THE-SHELF ITEMS	OFF-THE-SHELF ITEMS	BUILD-TO-PRINT-ITEMS	PIECE PARTS
SPECIFIC CM REQUIREMENTS					
CM ORGANIZATION/ADMINISTRATION					
RESPONSIBILITY FOR CM	Y	Y	M	Y	N
MANAGEMENT INTEGRATION OF CM	Y	Y	M	Y	N
CM FOCAL POINT	Y	Y	Y	Y	Y
CM POLICIES/PROCEDURES	Y	Y	Y	Y	M
CONFIGURATION IDENTIFICATION					
BASELINE MANAGEMENT					
a. FUNCTIONAL	Y	M	M	N	N
b. ALLOCATED	Y	M	N	N	N
c. PRODUCT	Y	Y	M	N	M
SPECIFICATIONS (DESIGN REQUIREMENTS					
a. DEVELOPMENT (FUNCTIONAL/ DESIGN/PERF)	Y	Y	Y	N	N
b. INTERFACE	M	M	N	N	N
c. PRODUCT	Y	Y	Y	N	N
d. TEST	Y	Y	Y	N	N
ENGINEERING DRAWINGS	Y	Y	M	N	M
SOFTWARE DOCUMENTATION	Y	Y	M	N	N
a. SPECIFICATION NUMBERS	Y	Y	M	N	N
c. NUMBERS	Y	Y	Y	N	Y
d. MARKING	Y	Y	M	Y	M
e. REFERENCE DESIGNATORS	Y	Y	M	Y	N
f. SERIALIZATION (S/N, LOT NO., DATE CODE)	Y	Y	M	Y	M
g.					
h. SOFTWARE/FIRMWARE NUMBERS (LISTINGS/TAPES/DISCS/ CASSETTES)	Y	Y	Y	N	N
RELEASE SYSTEM					
a. AUTHORIZATION DOCUMENT NUMBER	Y	Y	Y	Y	Y
b. DOCUMENT NUMBER	Y	Y	Y	Y	Y
c. DOCUMENT REVISION LETTER/ ISSUE NUMBER	Y	Y	Y	Y	Y
d. INITIAL & CHANGE RELEASE DATES	Y	Y	Y	Y	Y
e. LATEST PART NUMBER/VERSION DESCRIPTION NUMBERS ASSIGNED	Y	Y	Y	Y	Y
f. CHANGE IDENTIFICATION NUMBER	Y	Y	M	M	M
g. PART/VERSION DESCRIPTION	Y	Y	M	M	N
CONFIGURATION CONTROL					
CHANGE CONTROL BOARD (CCB)	Y	M	M	M	M
PROCESSING OF CHANGES	Y	Y	Y	Y	Y
CLASSIFICATION OF CHANGES	Y	Y	Y	Y	Y
SUBMITTAL OF CHANGES					
a. FUNCTIONAL BASELINE	Y	Y	M	N	N
b. ALLOCATED BASELINE	Y	Y	M	N	N
c. PRE-PRODUCT BASELINE	M	N	N	N	N
d. POST-PRODUCT BASELINE	Y	Y	Y	M	Y
e. CHANGE PROPOSAL AND REQUEST FOR DEVIATION/WAIVER (RFD/RFW)	Y	Y	Y	Y	M
APPROVAL OF CHANGES					

a.	FUNCTIONAL BASELINE	Y	Y	N	N	N
b.	ALLOCATED BASELINE	Y	Y	N	N	N
c.	PRE-PRODUCT BASELINE	N	N	N	N	N
d.	POST-PRODUCT BASELINE	Y	Y	M	Y	Y
	INCORPORATION OF CHANGE INTO					
	ENGINEERING DOCUMENTATION	Y	Y	Y	M	Y
	CONFIGURATION					
	AUDIT					
	FUNCTIONAL CONFIG AUDIT	Y	Y	M	M	N
	PHYSICAL CONFIG AUDIT	Y	Y	N	M	N
	AS BUILT/AS SHIPPED					
	RECORDS/LISTS					
	RECORDS (MAINTAIN IN HOUSE)	Y	Y	Y	Y	M
	LISTS (DELIVERED W/EQUIPMENT)	Y	Y	M	M	N
	CONFIGURATION STATUS ACCOUNTING/					
	REPORTING (CSAR)					
	BASELINE LISTINGS/REPORTS	Y	Y	N	N	N
	CHANGE STATUS REPORTS					
	RFD/RFW SUBMITTAL/APPROVAL	Y	Y	N	Y	N
	INCORPORATION IN					
	DOCUMENTATION	Y	Y	N	Y	N
	MODIFIED/RETROFIT/					
	INCORPORATION STATUS RECORDS					
	IN-HOUSE RECORDS	Y	Y	N	N	N
	NOTIFICATION TO CUSTOMERS	Y	Y	Y	N	N
	SUBCONTRACT/VENDOR CM					
	FLOWDOWN REQUIREMENTS	Y	Y	N	M	N
	FACTFINDING/EVALUATION/					
	SURVEILLANCE	Y	Y	Y	Y	N

DELIVERABLE CM DATA ITEMS

LEGEND: Y = YES THIS CM REQUIREMENT SHOULD BE
              LEVIED ON THE SUBCONTRACTOR/VENDOR

          N = NO THIS CM REQUIREMENT SHOULD NOT BE
              LEVIED ON THE SUBCONTRACTOR/VENDOR

          M = MAYBE THIS CM REQUIREMENT SHOULD BE
              LEVIED ON THE SUBCONTRACTOR/VENDOR -
              IT WILL DEPEND ON THE COMPLEXITY/THE
              CONTRACTOR/CUSTOMER REQUIREMENTS/
              NATURE OF THE ITEM BEING PURCHASED

SUPPLIER CONFIGURATION MANAGEMENT QUESTIONNAIRE

3.1 **Baselines**

a. **Configuration Baselines** – Is your company experienced in the practice of working to customer imposed configuration baselines?   ☐ Yes   ☐ No

b. **Types of Baselines** – Which of the following types of baselines has your company had experience in working to?

☐ Functional   ☐ Allocated   ☐ Product

☐ Other (Describe)_____

3.2 **Specifications** – Which of the following describes how your company specifications practices/procedures are prepared?

a. **Preparation of specifications** – Specifications are prepared to meet:

b. **Types of Specifications** have been prepared.

Types: ☐ System   ☐ Software Requirement   ☐ Design

☐ Interface   ☐ Data Base   ☐ Test   ☐ Product

☐

c. **Specification Maintenance** – The following methods have been used to control and maintain specifications.

☐ Revision letters   ☐ Version numbers   ☐ Amendment

b. **Rights in Data** – Do you consider your design and drawings to be

☐ Proprietary   ☐ Limited   ☐ Unlimited rights?

If proprietary or limited rights, your proposal response should identify these drawings and provide stated rationale for your claim to rights in data.

3.4 Numbers. –

Number systems are vital to identification and control of documents,   and products to ensure proper   support of   /software. Provide explanation of your numbering system for the following items.

a.   Specifications – Numbers assigned to specifications are:

    Significant (prefix, suffix, dash) numbers or   Non-significant numbers and are assigned by

_____

d.   Serialization –   Serial numbers   Date codes

are assigned to: Assemblies   Units

    systems and are assigned by _____

3.5 Design Check – Identify who is responsible for the design check or verification of:

    Specifications: _____   _____

    Software/firmware _____

3.6 Release

a.   Release System. Do you have   informal   development   formal release system?

b.   Release Forms. Identify forms used to release:

    Specifications _____   _____

    Software/firmware _____

c.   Release Approval. Identify who is responsible for release approval of:

    Specifications _____   _____

    Software/firmware _____

d.   Release Records. Identify who is responsible to maintain release records. ___

_____

Which of the following information is recorded in your release records?

☐ Document number   ☐ Document title   ☐ Number of sheets

☐ Size   ☐ Date of Release   ☐ Project Name

☐ Documentation revision letter   ☐ Revision letter release date

☐ Authorized release document number   ☐ Latest assigned   number

    —   ☐ Version description document

☐ Security Classification   ☐ Proprietary status

☐ Release records are: ☐ manual   ☐ automated

e.   <u>Impound of Released Documents</u>.   Identify who is responsible to control released

documents: _____

Released documents are impounded in:

☐ Open accessible   ☐ Restricted closed area

☐ Withdrawal of released documents is authorized by: _____

_____

f.   <u>Software Development Library</u>.   Identify who is responsible to maintain the

Software Development Library: _____

_____

3.7 <u>Software Library Controls and Records</u> - Are the following controls and records
established and maintained in your system for software?

☐ Program/Project Support Library

☐ Program/Project Master Library

☐ Company Back Up and Archival Libraries

☐ Unit Development Folders/Files (UDF)

What function is responsible for:

Libraries _____   UDF _____

4.0 CONFIGURATION CONTROL

4.1 Configuration Control System (CCS) - Is your CCS   ☐ informal   ☐ formal?

Is your CCS   ☐ verbal   ☐ written   ☐ Other (Describe)? _____

_____

Does your CCS provide for: ☐ Review   ☐ Analysis   ☐ Customer approval?

4.2 Change Control Board (CCB)

a.   Is your CCB   ☐ informal   ☐ companywide   ☐ projectized?

b.   IS CM a member of CCB   ☐ Yes   ☐ No?   If yes, what capacity?

_____

c.   Does your CCB   meet on a   ☐ schedule   ☐ As needed basis?

d.

how do you classify your changes?   (Explain) _____

_____

_____

e. Which of the following functions participate to analyze/review a change before approval?

☐ CM   ☐ Project Manager   ☐ System Engr.

☐ Test Engr.   ☐ Support

☐ Computer/Software Engr.   ☐ Contracts   ☐ Q.A.

☐ Other (Identify) _____

_____

f. Identify who has the final authority for change approval _____

_____

4.3 Change Processing

a. Is your change processing system?   ☐ Formal   ☐ Informal?

b. Identify forms used to process changes to hardware/software _____

_____

c. Who is responsible to prepare:

_____   _____

Waivers _____   Deviations _____

Software Problem Reports _____

4.4 Change Numbering System

a. What numbering system do you use for identifying and tracking of:

_____   _____

Waivers _____   Deviations _____

Software Problem Reports _____

b. Who assigns and controls change numbers for:

_____   _____

Waivers _____   Deviations _____

Software Problem Reports _____

4.

4.6 Change Implementation

    a.   Identify and provide copies of change forms used to incorporate Engineering changes into drawings/software/firmware documentation.

_____

    b.   Identify who receives released changes and how distribution is maintained.

_____

_____

    c.   Identify QA/inspection paperwork which records the change documentation revision status.

_____

    d.   Identify and provide a sample of how your flowdown changes to your Supplier ___

_____

_____

5.3 Configuration Audits. In which of the following kinds of audits has your company been experienced.

☐ FCA   ☐ PCA

Preparation of audit: ☐ plans   ☐ agendas   ☐ minutes

5.4 Audit Responsibility/Participation.

Identify who is responsible for planning/conducting of audits?

_____

Identify who is responsible for preparation of audit plans, agendas, or minutes.

_____

Identify who is the chairman of your:

FCA _____ PCA _____

Identify who are typical participants in your audit teams.

_____

5.5 Documentation for Audits. Which of the following documentation/material do you provide at the audit:

☐ Specifications   ☐ Customer approved test specifications

☐ Manuals

☐ Test reports/records   ☐ QA inspection records

☐ Nonstandard parts approvals

Conduct of Audits

FCA/PCA is conducted on: ☐ first   ☐ specified item

Audits are conducted at: ☐ equipment   ☐ unit   ☐ assembly

☐ piece part level   ☐ software system

☐ CI level

PCA verifies: ☐ drawing package   ☐ release system   ☐ control system

☐ inspection records   ☐ manuals

PCA ensures the S W   and/or documentation represents and depicts:

☐ As-built = as designed   ☐ As coded = as designed

6.0   CONFIGURATION STATUS ACCOUNTING

6.1   Configuration Status Accounting/Reporting (CSAR) System. Which of the following best describes your CSAR system:

Company   ☐ Informal   ☐ Written practices/procedures

6.2   Responsibility for CSAR System - Identify who is responsible for the generation and maintenance of your CSAR system:

6.3   CSAR Report Information - Which of the following documents and their revision status are included in your CSAR reports:

☐   ./Documents   ☐ Specifications   ☐ Test Specifications   ☐

6.4   CSAR Reports - Identify the following reports which are used in your CSAR system.

☐ Configuration baseline reports   ☐ Internal change status reports

☐   Change   status reports   ☐ Modification/

☐ Retrofit incorporation status report   ☐ Change incorporation records

☐ As-built records   ☐ Software Change Reports

7.0   FLOWDOWN OF CM REQUIREMENTS TO SUBCONTRACTOR/SUPPLIERS

a.   Type of items that the flowdown of CM requirements is applied to:

☐ Piece parts   ☐ Off-The-Shelf   ☐ Modified Off-The-Shelf

☐ Build-to-print   ☐ Development   ☐ Software

b.   Method of imposing CM requirements:

☐ Standard CM statement of work (SOW)   ☐ Tailored CM

☐ Standard P.O. attachments   ☐ Others (described) _____

Name of Company: _____

Address: _____

_____

Name and position/title of company representative completing/approving this form (typed).

_____

Signature _____   Date Completed: _____

Configuration Management Procedure

This procedure is provided as an example and guide to those who are given the job of developing a procedure for a company, firm, or specific project.

This example should be tailored to the environment in which the software project will reside. For instance, there may be no subcontractors or no system-to-system interfaces.

The activities listed under the heading *responsibility* will have different titles and duties and should be tailored accordingly.

CONFIGURATION MANAGEMENT PROCEDURE

Subject:
Software Configuration Management

1.0 *PURPOSE*—This procedure provides the detailed guidance for implementing Configuration Management for deliverable software, firmware, media, and associated documentation that is under development, production, and deployment.

This procedure may be tailored—by agreement between the Program Manager, the Software Engineering Department Manager, and the Configuration Manager—to be compatible with needs of small, less complex programs as well as strengthened for larger, more complex or difficult programs.

2.0 *RESPONSIBILITY*

2.1 *Program Managers (PM)*—Ensure that the Software Configuration Management function, as specified in the Engineering Plan segment of the Program Plan, is established and implemented.

2.2 *Program Engineering Management (PEM)*—Ensure compliance with all contractual and company requirements for documenting the software configuration item including proprietary, patent, archiving, and security considerations.

2.3 *System Engineering Management*—Partition system requirements into hardware and computer software configuration items to allow development of requirement specifications and the software portion of the specification tree.

2.4 *Configuration Management (CM)*—Implement and maintain the software configuration management discipline on assigned programs in accordance with contract requirements, approved Configuration Management Plans, or configuration management section in the Software Development Plan.

2.5 *Software Design Team Leader*—Assure adherence, as specified in the Configuration Management Plan or the configuration management section of the Software Development Plan, are adhered to by members of the software team.

2.6 *Software Support*—Comply with established software configuration control procedures through close coordination and interface with Software Engineering, Configuration Management, and Software Quality Assurance personnel. Serve as the focal point for recording, maintaining, and retrieving controlled software and associated documentation.

2.7 *Software Quality Assurance*—Audit Configuration Management practices on a software program/project for compliance with this procedure.

2.8 *Company/Division Configuration Management*—Provide direction and guidance for the implementation of Configuration Management.

3.0 *DEFINITIONS*—Provide an appendix if extensive

4.0 *GENERAL*

4.1 It is company policy to apply the principles of Configuration Management (CM) to software, firmware, media, and associated documentation.

4.2 The principal elements of Configuration Management for software, firmware, media, and associated documentation are identification, configuration control, status accounting, and audits/reviews. This procedure provides for the application of these principles to software, firmware, media, and associated documentation during development, production, and deployment.

4.3 *Identification*—The Configuration Identification for software is the documentation that defines the Software Configuration Item (SCI), such as a Software Requirements Specification or a Software Design Document. Different types of software documents may be required the customer.

4.3.1 *Baselines*—Baselines comprise the software, firmware, media, and associated documentation that have been reviewed and agreed upon and thereafter serve as a basis for further development or a specific use (e.g., deployment). After software, associated documentation, or media is made part of a baseline, it can only be changed through the established change control process.

Baselines may be:

- Formal baselines or point of departure as specified by contract (Functional, Allocated, Developmental Configuration, and Product) or;

- As determined by the Program Manager, Software Design Team Leader, and Configuration Manager (which may include some or all of the formal baselines plus Developmental Configuration).

4.3.1.1 Media control drawings (hardware drawings) when used, are released and controlled.

4.3.1.2 CM assures that when software, firmware, media, and associated documentation is transferred or released it is committed to a software library for secured retention. Classified items are retained in accordance with the Corporate Security Manual.

4.3.2 *Specification Tree*—The software portion of the specification tree is developed by the program Systems Engineer to depict the hierarchy of the software Specifications. It is kept current by CM to reflect the latest changes, additions, and deletions as provided to CM by the Systems Engineer. It is released as a system-level document (combined HW&SW) and controlled by Configuration Management.

4.3.3 *Software Level Breakdown (SWLBD)*—The software-level breakdown is developed by the Software Design Team Leader to identify, in a hierarchical format, all the components of the software under development. The SWLBD is the focal point for identification down to the unit level. It is kept current by CM to reflect the latest changes, additions, and deletions as provided to CM by the Software Design Team Leader.

4.3.4 *Identification Numbers*

4.3.4.1 Software, firmware, media, and associated documentation is identified with an identification number. The identification numbers are obtained by the document preparer from the Software Support Specialist, who is allocated a block of numbers for this purpose by Configuration Management.

4.3.4.2 When documents/specifications are prepared on computer systems the document/specification identification number becomes part of the associated computer file and media identification.

4.3.4.3 Identification of software residing in memory devices (PROMS, EPROMS, etc.) is described in the "Engineering Drawing Requirements Manual" (EDRM)

4.3.4.4 A two-character alpha-prefix, listed in Appendix I, may be used with the identification number when it is determined that it will serve as a useful aid to the identification of an item. Program CM will inform division CM of program-unique prefixes.

4.3.5 *Naming Conventions*—Although software is assigned identification numbers, the names associated with software are also critical to the identification process. Naming conventions may be specified:

By contract- and when not

By project per the "Software Engineering Handbook"

4.3.6 *Marking*—Software media and software documentation shall be marked and labeled in accordance with Appendix I.

4.3.7 *Serial Numbers*—Serial numbers are sequential identifiers (composed of numbers or a combination of numbers and letters) used to differentiate between multiple copies of like items such as deliverable media. Unless the contract requires use of special serial numbers, the numbers shall be assigned by CM. The Configuration Management Plan or configuration management section of the Software Development Plan shall describe the criteria and methods for serial number assignment.

4.4 *Configuration Control*—Change control procedures are in effect at the start of the project, and control is normally implemented down to the unit level, as depicted in the software-level breakdown.

4.4.1 The two review and control boards for implementing software configuration controls are:

- *Software Review Board (SRB)*—composed of four primary CCB members to relieve that board of many mandated changes, is established at the start of a program to review Project Support Library [PSL]-controlled software, firmware, media, associated documentation, and proposed changes. The SRB consists of four people approved by the Program Manager. The SRB operates in accordance with FDP under the auspices of the configuration and Control Board.

- *Configuration Control Board (CCB)*—established at the start of a program by the Program Manager to review Master Library [ML]-controlled software, firmware, media, associated documentation, and proposed changes. The CCB operates in the same manner as a hardware CCB.

4.4.2 An approval matrix indicating the individuals authorized to sign engineering change documentation is prepared and maintained by CM.

4.4.3 *Interface Control Working Group (ICWG)*—An ICWG shall be established when required by contract or for multidivision programs, major subcontractors, and associate or joint venture contractors. Contractual requirements, when imposed, shall govern the scope of the interface control program (See Para 4.7)

4.5 *Audits and Reviews*

4.5.1 *Software Configuration Verification*—Configuration Management regularly reviews software, firmware, media, and associated documentation to ensure they are updated to reflect version/revision levels authorized by SRB/SCCB actions and to ensure the correct version/revision levels are accurately recorded in the library records and data contained in file headers, Software Development Files (SDFs), log books, and status accounting records.

4.5.2 *Configuration Audits and Design Reviews*—CM adheres to the configuration and design review milestones and requirements established by the customer; manages the customer designated audits (i.e., FCA, PCA); supports formal reviews (i.e., SRR, SDR, PDR, CDR) and program internal design reviews as specified in the program plan.

4.6 *Status Accounting*—Provisions for recording and reporting the current status and past history of software, firmware, media, and associated documentation are established by Configuration Management. Requirements for status accounting records and reports shall be specified in the Software Configuration Management Plan or configuration management section of the Software Development Plan as follows:

- *Software Development File*

The primary status accounting record is the Software Development File (SDF), which contains a complete history of design, development, and change data for software, firmware, media, and associated documentation. SDF's are established per SW Practice and may physically be a folder or a part of a computer-maintained file.

- *Software Library*

The Software Library shall retain essential status accounting information that is used to produce configuration status accounting reports. Report data shall be gathered and presented as required. CM ensures that the library will meet the needs of Configuration Management and necessary status reporting.

4.6.1 *Status Accounting Reports*—Report format, data elements, and frequency of reports may be dictated by contractual requirements for specified data. The format of internal reports shall be prescribed by Configuration Management. Data must be available upon request for review or audit.

4.6.2 *Revision Letters and Version Numbers*—Assignment of revision letters to approved/incorporated *document* changes and version numbers to approved/incorporated *software/firmware* changes shall be as specified in the Configuration Management Plan or configuration management section of the Software Development Plan.

4.7 *Interface Management*

4.7.1 CM ensures that all documentation related to interface control of computer systems, subcontractor system/subsystem, and divisions system/subsystem is identified, accounted for, and controlled. For subcontractors, CM ensures that this is accomplished in the same manner as for generated documents developed specifically for use on the applicable contract.

4.7.2 Changes to interface control documentation may require CM to request the convening of an Interface Control Working Group (ICWG) to review proposed changes. An ICWG, if required, is comprised of representatives from each activity or agency participating in the system/project development.

4.8 *Subcontractor/Vendor and Interface Control*—Configuration management is applied to subcontractors/suppliers to the degree they are designing products for delivery to the company.

1. *Subcontractors With Full Design Responsibility*—Where subcontractors are given full design responsibility for review and evaluation of the subcontractor's configuration management system to ensure it is compatible with the configuration management practices set forth in this Practice.

     CM assists in the preparation of the subcontractor's Statement of Work and Supplier Data Requirements List to ensure incorporation of applicable configuration management requirements.

2. *Subcontractors/Suppliers With Limited Design Responsibility*—Where subcontractors/suppliers are given only limited design responsibility (i.e., they supply commercial or modified commercial items to a company's provided specification. This does not require full configuration management. However, it does require them to internally control configuration changes to prevent changes that are not in compliance with requirements.

     If a commercial item is selected as a Controlled Configuration item, the subcontractor/supplier is required to apply the drawing number and serial numbers to the product and to maintain traceability records to a level designated by the company. These records must be made available upon request.

3. *Subcontractors/Suppliers Without Design Responsibilities*—Where subcontractors/suppliers are not given design responsibility, the company does not require configuration management. Instead, the company requires they provide the product to their own specific subcontractor/supplier product specifications, as quoted in our purchase documentation.

4.9 *Subcontractor/Vendor Control*

4.9.1 CM shall prepare a directive detailing identification and control of purchased software that is to be delivered with a developed product. Purchased software shall be placed in the ML under the control of the SCCB.

4.10 *Deliverable Government and Customer Furnished Software*—CM shall prepare a directive detailing identification and control of deliverable government- and customer-furnished software, firmware, media, and associated documentation. Deliverable customer-furnished software, firmware, media, and associated documentation shall be placed in the ML under the control of the SCCB.

4.11 *Nondeliverable Software/Firmware*—Nondeliverable software/firmware is controlled by the Software Design Team.

4.12 *On-Site/Field Installation CM Control*—When a contract requires control of software changes on-site at field installations, the CM establishes a procedure, approved by the Program Manager, which provides for:

A. Designation of a company (Program, Product Support, etc.) or customer individual to be directly responsible for on-site approval of changes.

B. Designation of person-to-process changes.

C. Transmittal of change documentation to the company Program Manager/CM for documentation update/maintenance and the processing of notice of change to the customer.

4.13 *Software Configuration Management Plan*—The following paragraphs contain the requirements to prepare a Software Configuration Management Plan or configuration management section in the Software Development Plan unless another outline is required.

4.13.1 An approved Software Configuration Management Plan (SCMP) or configuration management section in the Software Development Plan, is required for all programs/projects with contractual requirements for software configuration management or those with a significant software-development cycle.

4.13.2 The plan is prepared by Configuratin Management in accordance with contract requirements or as required by the Division Configuration Management to support program requirements.

4.13.3 The plan describes the principle elements of software configuration management applicable to the program, the ways in which these elements are to be accomplished, a phased (milestone) schedule for accomplishment, and the organizational/individual responsiblities associated with implementation.

4.13.4 The plan includes the scope and magnitude of configuration management application and implementation as determined by specific contract CM requirements or, in lieu thereof, by program/project requirements.

4.13.5 The plan shall be reviewed by CM management and approved by the Program Manager prior to implementation. In addition, the plan will also be reviewed by the Software Design Team Leader, Software Quality Assurance, and other functions as may be directed by the program manager.

5.0 *REFERENCES*

APPENDIX I

MARKING AND LABELING
OF SOFTWARE DOCUMENTATION AND MEDIA

Documentation

Unless otherwise specified by contract, documentation shall bear the assigned company document number and appropriate revision letter in the upper right-hand corner of the cover and shall appear on all pages comprising the document. This requirement applies to all software documents prepared in "book form" format.

Documentation prepared and submitted by software subcontractors/vendors shall be in accordance with the marking requirements stipulated in their subcontract.

Media

Unless otherwise specified by contract, media shall be labeled as follows:

A. *Media and Location of Label*

Paper/mylar punched tape—leading end of tape and containment box or reel

Magnetic tape—on reel and cover if applicable

Removable Disk—on disk pack cover

Cassettes—on cassette and case

Diskettes—on diskette

B. *Minimum Data to Appear on Label/Marking*

Identification Number and Design Activity Number

Revision Letter (Documents) or Version Number (Software/Firmware/Media)

Title or description

Date created or updated

Serial Number

Classified Media Marking (Per contract requirements as directed by Document Control)

   Classification level and Document Control Number

Limited Rights Marking

C. *Additional Data May Include*

Project Identifier

Contract Number

Customer reference

Customer assigned nomenclature or number

Media recording parameters

Filename(s)

Mnemonic(s)

APPENDIX II

REFERENCES

References

The following procedural documents are pertinent to the conduct of Configuration Management on software projects.

COMPANY PROCEDURE NUMBER	SUBJECT
D 11.7	Configuration Management For Hardware and Software
D 12.7	Software Design Team
D 21.53	Control of Government Property
D 24.7	Protecting Proprietary Information
P 1-2	Program Configuration Management
P 1-4	Transfer or Release of Software and Software Documentation
P 1-6	Engineering Change Orders
P 1-7	Configuration Control Board (CCB)
P 1-9	Software Changes
P 1-11	Release Review of Engineering Data
P 1-19	Designating Reviewers and Approvers of Engineering Data
CDMP 1-30	Identification of Items, Engineering Data, and Related Engineering Documents

OTHER DOCUMENTS	SUBJECT
—	Software Engineering Manual
	Engineering Drawing Requirements Manual
—	Corporate Security Manual

GOVERNMENT DOCUMENT NUMBER	SUBJECT
DOD-STD-2167A	Software Development

APPENDIX III

1.0 *BASELINES AND DEVELOPMENTAL CONFIGURATIONS*
Recognized external baselines are the following:

1.1 *Functional Baseline*—The functional baseline is established by the authenticated System/System Segment Specification. The functional baseline is normally established at the end of the conceptual phase as marked by a System Design Review (SDR).

1.2 *Allocated Baseline*—The allocated baseline is the initial approved allocated configuration identification established by the authenticated development specification(s). The establishment of the allocated baseline for a computer software configuration item (CSCI) normally signals the end of the requirements phase or the beginning of the preliminary design phase as marked by the Software Specification Review (SSR).

1.3 *Product Baseline*—The product baseline is established by the authenticated product specification or its equivalent. The product baseline is normally established by the customer at the end of the full-scale development phase, which is marked by completion of the functional and physical configuration audits, and if required, the formal qualification review.

1.4 *DEVELOPMENTAL CONFIGURATIONS*

1.4.1 During the development phase, internal development configurations are defined according to the state of the software development. *Developmental Configurations* are established for software, firmware, media, and associated documentation to define the evolving configuration of a CSCI during the development phase. The software and associated documentation is under internal (contractors) configuration control and describes the software configuration at any stage of the design, coding, and testing effort.

1.4.2 *Implementing Developmental Configurations*—The Software Configuration Management Plan or configuration management section in the Software Development Plan will specify the method for implementing developmental configurations.

RESPONSIBILITIES

PROGRAM CONFIGURATION MANAGER

Reports To:

"Division" Configuration Management and assigned to the Program Manager

Basic Objective:

Provide Effective Program Configuration Management (CM) for hardware and software.

Responsibilities:

1. Personally responsible for and accountable to the Program Manager to maintain an effective program for hardware and software configuration identification, control, status accounting, audit, interface management, and supplier control that meets contract and company requirements.
2. Responsible to "Division" Configuration Management for CM goals and objectives.
3. Provides leadership and direction for all program CM activities.
4. Is responsible for advising the program team of potential CM problems and providing solutions.
5. Accountable for timely CM inputs to proposals that ensure all CM requirements are met and are realistic.
6. Establishes and maintains an effective working relationship with customers and their representatives. Participates in reviews, and assures that company and customer CM needs and interests are satisfied.
7. Accountable for the Program CM Plan. As a member of the program team, reviews the contract, identifies the contractual CM requirement, and clarifies interpretations when required. Disseminates the CM requirements to the program team in order to ensure that the delivered product(s) meet the contractual requirements.
8. Flows down CM requirements to suppliers and coordinates with Procurement Management to ensure that CM is performed by our suppliers to meet company and customers' needs and requirements.
9. Responsible for review and concurrence of Functional Plans to assure integration of CM tasks.
10. Is accountable for the functional and physical configuration audits of configuration items. Records and monitors corrective action requests for nonconforming situations.
11. Program Configuration Manager is accountable for the as-designed and as-built configuration records and is responsible for establishing and maintaining an effective interface with Manufacturing Configuration Control.
12. Is accountable for negotiating budgets and meeting the CM schedule and budget commitments.